A Democratic Theory
of Judgment

A Democratic Theory of Judgment

LINDA M. G. ZERILLI

The University of Chicago Press   Chicago and London

The University of Chicago Press, Chicago 60637
The University of Chicago Press, Ltd., London
© 2016 by The University of Chicago
All rights reserved. Published 2016.
Printed in the United States of America

25 24 23 22 21 20 19 18 17 16   1 2 3 4 5

ISBN-13: 978-0-226-39784-9 (cloth)
ISBN-13: 978-0-226-39798-6 (paper)
ISBN-13: 978-0-226-39803-7 (e-book)
DOI: 10.7208/chicago/9780226398037.001.0001

Library of Congress Cataloging-in-Publication Data

Names: Zerilli, Linda M. G. (Linda Marie-Gelsomina), 1956– author.
Title: A democratic theory of judgment / Linda M. G. Zerilli.
Description: Chicago ; London : The University of Chicago Press,
    2016. | Includes bibliographical references and index.
Identifiers: LCCN 2016015888 | ISBN 9780226397849 (cloth :
    alk. paper) | ISBN 9780226397986 (pbk. : alk. paper) |
    ISBN 9780226398037 (e-book)
Subjects: LCSH: Judgment—Political aspects. | Judgment. |
    Democracy—Philosophy.
Classification: LCC JA71 .Z453 2016 | DDC 320.01/9—dc23 LC record
    available at https://lccn.loc.gov/2016015888

For Gregor

We want to *understand* something that is already in plain view. For *this* is what we seem in some sense not to understand.   LUDWIG WITTGENSTEIN

Contents

Preface

The third volume of Hannah Arendt's *The Life of the Mind* was never written. As Arendt's editor, Mary McCarthy, observed, "After her death, a sheet of paper was found in her typewriter, blank except for the heading 'Judging' and two epigraphs. Some time between the Saturday of finishing 'Willing' [the second volume of the aforementioned work] and the Thursday of her death, she must have sat down to confront the final section." Fond of quoting McCarthy, commentators have turned the missing volume on judging into an enigma of spectral proportions. What would Arendt have written had she lived long enough to finish her tripartite work? How would the volume on judging have fit with the rest of her oeuvre? What kinds of problems would that volume have addressed and perhaps solved?

Although we cannot know what Arendt would have written, we might reflect on the role that judging plays in her extant political theory and, more important for this book, what role it might play in contemporary democratic and feminist political theory. In her strikingly original view, the capacity to judge should be expected from each and every citizen. Although Arendt turned to Homeric impartiality, to Aristotelian *phronesis*, and to Kantian enlarged thinking, it is not Homer or Aristotle or for that matter Immanuel Kant to whom we can attribute her novel account of judgment. Rather, it is Hannah Arendt herself who first discovers judgment as a political capacity of ordinary democratic citizens, not elites with special knowledge or abilities. This discovery is at least equal to her conception of action, which is normally taken to be the central feature of her political thought.

Notwithstanding the high aspirations suggested by its title, this book does not pretend to produce a definitive democratic theory of judgment, let alone a "how-to-judge" manual based on an imagined application of Arendt's unwritten doctrine. My aim is to explore how Arendt might help us reframe the problem of judgment in contemporary democratic societies characterized by deep value pluralism. Wanting to affirm such pluralism as an achievement of such societies, yet understandably unwilling to declare all values to be of equal worth, an array of political thinkers has sought various means of adjudication based on a conception of validity (e.g., the "right" over the "good") that is consistent with the principles of a liberal democracy. Over the course of time, I have come to see this otherwise reasonable concern with adjudication—indeed, the whole question of validity itself—as a kind of theoretical obsession that might well lead us to misunderstand what is at stake in judging politically.

Critique of obsession with validity / adjudication imperative

What don't we see when validity (or what I call an "adjudication imperative") serves as the undisputed if often invisible frame of reference for a democratic theory and practice of judgment? The more I thought about this question, the more convinced I became that the answer was most likely right there in front of me, almost too ordinary to count as serious. One clue came in the form of Arendt's own stunning indifference to judging, understood as the problem of adjudicating incommensurable value differences in the absence of a transcendent conception of the good. Arendt seemed almost blissfully unaware of the eternal war of the "gods" of ultimate values that had captured the imagination of Max Weber long before her and that has continued to define the problem of judgment for neo-Kantians such as Jürgen Habermas and John Rawls long after. For many critics, Arendt has no credible way of addressing the value relativism to which her own account of a kind of unfettered human plurality seems to lead. Was she blind?

Arendt's "unawareness"

And yet we know that whatever Arendt was, surely she was not blind to the corrosive character of the radical subjectivism and world-alienation that has come to define modern mass society. This destruction of what she called "the common world" and not the deadly conflict of plural worldviews, I began to see, was the real problem that concerned her. It was what led Arendt to seek an account of judging that was less adjudicative and more creative and reflective, the kind of judging without the mediation of a concept that she found in the aesthetic theory of Kant. As controversial and idiosyncratic as her turn to

Kant may be, it perfectly captures Arendt's sense that judging must involve more than deciding questions of validity; it must be a democratic world-building practice that creates and sustains human freedom and the common space in which shared objects of judgment can appear in the first place.

This book extends my earlier arguments about the importance of political freedom to Arendt's account of judging, but it departs from certain aspects of my critique of critics who had accused her of failing to answer to the all-important problem of validity. That defense made it sound as if Arendt were right to dismiss the question of truth and objectivity as irrelevant to politics. And though I still think it is freedom, not validity, that stands at the heart of Arendt's account, I have come to see that judging cannot wholly evade the question of what counts as real or objective, perhaps as true, even if that question cannot be answered adequately in the manner of the validity thinkers.

Freedom > Validity. d.14 but real /objective/ true, matters

Political judgments are evaluative judgments, the kind of judgments we make when calling something "good" or "bad," "just" or "unjust," "beautiful" or "ugly." If we affirm with Arendt that they register more than merely subjective preferences, what kind of rationality and objectivity can evaluative judgments possibly have? And what would it mean to speak of better or worse evaluative judgments and ways of judging in democratic societies characterized by widespread value pluralism? These questions express concerns about the potential for interminable disagreement in such judgments that seem to present a genuine problem of value conflict and a democratic puzzle of fair adjudication.

David Hume, whose aesthetic theory I examine in chapter 2 of the present work, found scandalous those who "would assert an equality of genius and elegance between Ogilby and Milton, or Bunyan and Addison." Although Hume generally holds fast to the fact/value dichotomy for which "all sentiment is right," when faced with such "absurd and ridiculous comparisons," he quickly declares that the "the principle of the natural equality of tastes is then totally forgot." We are justly compelled to rank such value judgments—but how? What rational grounds can we have for defending a judgment that amounts in Hume's view to little more than the projection of a feeling onto an object utterly devoid of value? How can we possibly justify the universality of a subjective preference, make a legitimate claim to the agreement of all?

As Kant would later see, "Of the Standard of Taste" could not solve the problem it so astutely diagnosed; the projectivist metaphysic to which Hume subscribed foreclosed all talk about the validity of a judgment based on feeling. And yet Kant's famous account of the "subjective universality" or validity that characterizes aesthetic judgments in the third *Critique* would prove no less controversial than Hume's earlier view. Though it has served as the basis for my own previous defense of Arendt, Kantian judgments of taste too leave us wondering how the affective response of a judging subject can claim to speak to how things actually stand in the world. Being irreducibly affective and yet no mere avowal, such judgments seem stranded somewhere between the register of the objective and the merely subjective, virtually doomed to make a claim they can never properly defend—that is, defend without recourse to Kant's transcendental approach.

Notwithstanding these shortcomings, this in-between space (neither *objective* nor *subjective*, as philosophy has traditionally defined those terms) is where I shall continue to place the democratic world-building practice of judging politically as Arendt inspires me to describe it. How, then, might we defend the idea that to judge politically is to say how things stand not only with judging subjects (their affective response) but also with judged objects: how things actually stand in the world? To say, "This war is wrong," is not to claim it is wrong to *me* but that others too ought to find it wrong—because it *is* wrong. On what basis can we defend that further claim to how something *is* if we neither subscribe to a philosophical idea of objectivity, devoid of anything subjective, nor restrict ourselves to the limited Kantian idea of subjective universality? How can we defend it while also upholding the raison d'être of Arendt's approach to judgment—namely, human freedom and plurality?

Reflecting on these questions, I have become increasingly concerned about the reluctance of many democratic theorists to advance or to encourage citizens to advance publicly substantive (value-laden) views of the good without the significant constraints of adjudicative mechanisms such as public reason. And though I share the concern that such views have in the past been used—and indeed still are used—to enlist the power of the state to enforce normative ideals that do real damage to the many marginalized individuals and groups in modern democratic societies, I am not convinced that the alternative perspectives of the marginalized are better served by gestures of neutrality when it comes to matters of common concern. There is no singular idea of the good which all citizens ought to affirm, nor should there be. But there should be more public debate about what our competing visions are and what our shared visions might be. The tendency to seek ever more neutral grounds for public justification and judgment evades even as it claims to respect and safeguard plurality. It is as if plurality were not the source of judging politically, as it clearly was for Arendt, but rather that which judging must manage, contain, or transcend.

A democratic theory of judgment must be more than a theory of normative justification or the adjudication of different perspectives. It must be a world-building practice of freedom rooted in the plurality of perspectives that alone facilitates our capacity to count as real, as part of the common world, what is real. In this spirit I present the following reflections.

Acknowledgments

I have benefited from the support and advice of many people in the long process of writing this book. Thanks, first, to my current and former political theory colleagues in the Department of Political Science at the University of Chicago: Julie Cooper, Robert Gooding-Williams, Bernard Harcourt, Patchen Markell, John McCormick, Sankar Muthu, Jennifer Pitts, Nathan Tarcov, and most especially Lisa Wedeen. I am grateful for the patience and care with which they have engaged me over the years, challenging me to refine and deepen my arguments. Thanks to my political science colleagues Cathy Cohen and Michael Dawson, who have been immensely supportive of my work and helped me see more politically.

I owe special thanks to my very dear friends and former Northwestern colleagues Mary Dietz and Ann Orloff, who have provided essential intellectual and personal sustenance over the years and who have shared their joy for life and commitment to feminism in ways that inspire me daily. Thanks to James Farr for his sharp wit, keen intellect, and generosity. Likewise George Shulman, who has read many drafts of this book and whose trenchant and unique critical voice I cherish. Thanks to Chantal Mouffe for her vigorous writing on democratic and feminist politics and support of my work. Thanks to Ernesto Laclau, whose dear friendship and intellectual clarity have sustained me in ways that will survive his untimely death.

At the University of Chicago's Center for the Study of Gender and Sexuality, where I have the privilege of serving as faculty director, I have been fortunate to find a creative group of feminist and queer studies colleagues, who have pushed me to rethink my ideas in sometimes radical and unexpected ways. Special thanks to Leora Auslander, Mary Anne Case, Hillary Chute, Jennifer Cole, Jane Dailey, Daisy Delogu, Susan Gal, Agnes Lugo-Ortiz, Rochona Majumdar, Deborah Nelson, Martha Nussbaum, Lucy Pick, Jennifer Wild, and especially Lauren Berlant and Kristen Schilt. Special thanks as well to the center's associate director Gina Olson, program coordinator Tate Brazas, and student affairs administrator Sarah Tuohey for the verve and excellence with which they have advanced gender and sexuality studies at Chicago and provided me with all manner of institutional and personal support. Thanks to Geoffrey Stone, former provost Thomas Rosenbaum, provost Eric Isaacs, and deans John Boyer, David Nirenberg, and Martha Roth for their support of the center's initiatives and my own scholarship in feminist and political thought.

I am grateful to the many superb graduate students I have had over the years, at both Northwestern and Chicago, who have patiently worked through the central concepts of this book in various seminars. Very special thanks to Amanda Blair, Ashleigh Campi, Laura Ephraim, Ann Heffernan, Ainsley LeSure, Tanner McFadden, Claire McKinney, Daniel Nichanian, and Ian Storey. Thanks to the wider group of feminist and political theorists whose work has greatly inspired me over the years: Michaele Ferguson, Jill Locke, Angela Maione, Lori Marso, Ella Myers, Laurie Naranch, Aletta Norval, and Torrey Shanks.

My interests in Wittgenstein and ordinary-language philosophy have found engaging colleagues in John G. Gunnell and Tracy Strong, both of whom gave excellent comments on the entire manuscript and from whose own work I have benefited tremendously. Thanks to my Feminism and Ordinary Language Philosophy group, Nancy Bauer, Sarah Beckwith, Alice Crary, Sandra Laugier, and especially Toril Moi, whose deep knowledge of Wittgenstein, feminist commitment, and ongoing engagement with my work have been essential to my intellectual development. Thanks to Jason Stanley for his helpful comments on my critique of affect theory and to Joseph Tinguely for his thoughtful comments on Kant's aesthetics.

I have been very fortunate to have superb research assistants, whose precision and exacting scholarly standards have contributed to the quality of this book. Thanks to Laura Ephraim and Claire McKinney. Special thanks both to Sarah Johnson for her invaluable assistance over the years and to Ann Heffernan for the extraordinary care with which she edited the final manuscript.

Thanks again to my parents, Marie Antoinette Zerilli and Armand

Frank Zerilli, for their example of lives well lived, inspiration, and love. Finally, *mille grazie* to Gregor Gnädig, whose humor, brilliance, and love of life captivated me in Florence decades ago and energizes me daily.

This project was supported by generous research leaves and grants from the University of Chicago and a 2006–2007 Martha Sutton Weeks faculty fellowship at the Stanford Humanities Center. Additional financial support was provided by a 2010–2011 Mellon Foundation Sawyer Seminar grant on Women's International Rights.

Earlier versions of chapters 4, 5, 6, and 9 were published, respectively, as follows: "Truth and Politics," *Theory and Event* 9, no. 4 (2006); "Value Pluralism and the Problem of Judgment: Farewell to Public Reason," *Political Theory* 40, no. 1 (February 2012): 6–32; "Toward a Feminist Theory of Judgment," *Signs: Journal of Women in Culture and Society* 34, no. 2 (Winter 2009): 295–317; "The Turn to Affect and the Problem of Judgment," *New Literary History* 6, no. 2 (Summer 2015): 261–86.

ONE

Democracy and the Problem of Judgment

The loss of standards, which does indeed define the modern world in its facticity and cannot be reversed by any sort of return to the good old days or by
some arbitrary promulgation of new standards and values, is . . . a catastro-
phe in the moral world only if one assumes that people are actually incapable
of judging things per se, that their faculty of judgment is inadequate for making original judgments, and that the most we can demand of it is the correct
application of familiar rules derived from already established standards.
HANNAH ARENDT[1]

What would it mean to foreground the capacity to judge
critically and reflectively as a central feature of modern
democratic citizenship? This question, raised poignantly
albeit not systematically in the work of Hannah Arendt,
is of crucial importance for political theory today. In light
of the widespread value pluralism of multicultural democracies, we, democratic citizens, find ourselves increasingly
called upon to make judgments about practices not always
our own, judgments that require what Arendt called the
capacity for "representative thinking"—that is, an ability
and willingness to imagine how the world looks to people
whose standpoints one does not necessarily share. To engage in such thinking, she argued, is to resist the temptation, on the one hand, to employ our own concepts as
rules with which to subsume the particulars calling for
judgment and, on the other hand, to assume that in the
absence of rules, we cannot judge at all. The break in tradition and the unprecedented experience of totalitarianism

led to the modern problem of judgment, Arendt held, but the irrevocable loss of standards also opened up a space for the democratic world-building potential of judging anew.

However we may share Arendt's optimism, her valorization of opinion as the sole coinage of politics and refusal to regard political judgments as making cognitive validity claims that can be adjudicated according to shared truth criteria, critics charge, leaves her unable to answer what is arguably the most pressing question for a contemporary democratic theory of judgment; namely, how can we decide which judgment is correct?[2] In multicultural democracies the problem of how to adjudicate among competing points of view seems paramount. "A modern democratic society is characterized not simply by a pluralism of comprehensive religious, philosophical, and moral doctrines but by a pluralism of incompatible yet reasonable comprehensive doctrines," writes John Rawls.[3] Given equally reasonable yet incompatible worldviews, whose criteria shall decide? That would appear to be the real problem of judgment in a democracy.[4]

In the most widely read and cited texts in contemporary democratic theory—namely, those of neo-Kantians such as Rawls and Jürgen Habermas—judgment is defined almost wholly as a problem of adjudicating value conflicts in the absence of universal criteria and a transcendent or authoritative conception of the good. More precisely, it is a problem of finding the proper criteria according to which such conflicts could be fairly and rationally adjudicated given widespread value pluralism. It is not that these theorists mourn the loss of a common standard according to which such conflicts could be rationally settled, nor do they lament the empirical fact of value pluralism itself; on the contrary, they celebrate both as the achievement of liberal democratic societies. Nevertheless, this celebratory spirit is also deeply cautious and tempered by a persistent worry about widespread value differences run amok, as it were, with parochial perspectives and affects unchecked by reason and no way of deciding in favor of liberal democratic values, save by means of a groundless will. To forestall irreconcilable political conflict and decisionism, neo-Kantians advance (various versions of) "public reason,"[5] with which they seek ever more neutral grounds "to separate by argumentation generalizable interests from those that are and remain particular," as Habermas puts it.[6]

The ability of conceptual, discursive rationality to settle stark differences of opinion on public issues tends to presuppose the very shared sensibility that neo-Kantians minimize as having any real relevance to political life. As I argue in chapter 5, it is not difficult to see how I might reach agreement with someone who already shares my sense of what Rawls calls "reasonableness," itself rooted in basic values, cultural background, or worldview. In that case, the proper application of concepts to the particulars of political life may well strike me as having "the unforced force of the better argument," to speak with Habermas.[7] But are those the conflicts that really concern us today?

In the view of critics, the idea of public reason expresses the residual rationalism of the deliberative model. To purge such rationalism and the quest for public reason as the new standard of judgment, political theorists such as William Connolly, Leslie Paul Thiele, and John Protevi would have us focus not on political judgment but on political affect.[8] Rather than view political judgment as a conscious language game of giving and asking for reasons, they see it as the modulated expression of the already primed, preconscious dispositions that are formed through the complex interaction of the social and the somatic. Rooted in various theories of body/brain processes (e.g., cognitive neuroscience, the complexity theory of Gilles Deleuze, the somatic theory of Antonio Damasio, the basic emotions theory of Silvan Tomkins and Paul Ekman, or some combination of these), these accounts of political affect distance themselves not only from the strict cognitivism of the neo-Kantians but also from the more familiar accounts of feeling, emotion, or sentiment that play a role in many feminist strands of affect theory, in theories of political judgment from Aristotle through John Stuart Mill, and in more recent feminist critiques of the deliberative models.[9] Such accounts, it is argued, remain too tightly bound to the idea of a political subject as a rational cognitive subject. In new theories of political affect, affect is seen as a distinct layer of experience that is both prior to and beneath language and intentional consciousness, an irreducibly bodily and autonomic force that shapes, without the subject's awareness, conscious judgment. As Connolly puts it, "Affect is a wild card in the layered game of thinking [acting and judging]."[10]

Whereas deliberative approaches to intercultural value conflicts and the problem of judgment assume that disputes can be resolved by discursive argumentation once the ground rules for engaging in public debate are clear, many political affect thinkers regard public reason as a rationalist exercise in wishful thinking. The problem of judgment cannot be the presumably neutral adjudication of equally reasonable yet incommensurable worldviews, for these are little more than post hoc rationalizations of affective response. Rather, the problem of judgment is how to redirect affects through tactical work on dispositions installed below consciousness with the aim of promoting new modes

3

of affective responsiveness. For now, they argue, it is best to be deeply wary of any claims about our capacity for rational judgment if not to suspend judgment altogether.

What interests me in these two broadly construed contemporary ways of posing the democratic problem of judgment is less their easily discerned differences than how much they less obviously share. Theorists of political affect share with deliberative democrats a deep suspicion of our ordinary modes of judging and the pervasive sense that these are based on affective and parochial attachments that impair our ability to get the world in view. Whether figured in terms of the "lifeworld" (Habermas), a "comprehensive doctrine" (Rawls), or the subrational workings of affect, both approaches tend to see our ordinary modes of judging as intrinsically partial and distorting, especially when it comes to public matters of common concern. And though each puts forward a mechanism that would supposedly mitigate if not correct for that distortion, what remains is the basic sense that our ordinary criteria of judgment are not good enough and are in need of some sort of correcting supplement. Insofar as this supplement in multicultural democracies cannot take any substantive form of the good, it tends to be construed in increasingly neutral or minimal terms, be it public reason based on an empty rule of argumentation (Habermas) or an overlapping consensus about justice as fairness (Rawls), or the replacement of such reason with a vague conception of democratic ethos (political affect theory).

The distrust of ordinary modes of judging is rooted in a more general distrust of the intrinsic partiality and affective character of the perspectives with which each of us views the world. There is no doubt that our individual perspectives can and often do distort our view of any particular object or that our attachments, worldviews, and values can play a large role in such distortion, giving rise to false beliefs and ideological blind spots that deeply restrict our capacity to judge critically and reflectively—that is, without reliance on fixed rules that neglect the particulars of any given case. The issue, however, is not whether our perspectives sometimes or even many times distort our judgment but whether qua *human perspectives* they always distort, rooted as they are in our subjective and affective modes of apprehending the world.

The view of perspective as irremediably distorting, as James Conant argues, radically departs from the original historical understanding of perspective (in Renaissance painting), which lives on—albeit it in an often unacknowledged way—in our everyday understanding.[11] On this ordinary view, objects can appear different depending on the condi-

4

tions and the perspective in which they are viewed (e.g., the same coin can seem elliptical when viewed from the side or round when viewed straight on). Whatever distortions arise from viewing the object from one perspective can be corrected by viewing the same object from other perspectives. Judging rightly would involve correcting for distortions in this way. Furthermore, the irreducibly subjective (human) dimension to perspective, though it surely can distort, is also crucial to our sense of an object's shared reality and so to objectivity. "The concept of perspective," observes Conant, "from its very beginning, involves an internal relation between objective and subjective moments in a perceptual encounter between a perceiving subject and the object(s) of his [or her] perception."[12]

For a democratic theory of judgment, the problem with thinking about perspective as irremediably distorting is that it can never quite shake the nagging sense that a plurality of perspectives and "affective interpretations"—the term is Friedrich Nietzsche's—though clearly crucial to democracy, is also the greatest threat to democracy. What could the addition of more perspectives be other than more opportunities to distort? Suspicion toward our ordinary idea of perspective can lead us to think of its corrigibility in terms of something extraperspectival rather than the plurality of citizen perspectives themselves. Both the search to find ever more neutral rational grounds for democratic justification and the denial that any rational justification of a judgment can be achieved are symptomatic of a view of perspective and affective interpretations as intrinsically distorting and not corrigible by other perspectives. As I shall argue subsequently and develop in the following chapters, this suspicion is part of a larger problem of thinking about perspective as that which is "merely" subjective in our claims to what is objective or, put somewhat differently, thinking about our subjective endowments as limiting our access to how things stand in the world, as if we were confined in our current modes of subjectivity—absent, that is, a saving supplement.

The suspicion with which democratic theorists tend to view the particular affects and values that each of us brings to our encounters with the world takes the shape of an ongoing oscillation between celebrating the impossibility of ever affirming the objectivity of our judgments and recoiling into the ideal of objectivity that democratic citizens really can do without, one based on an ideal of reason that requires the elimination of "any admixture of subjectivity" that can only be hostile to plurality.[13] This oscillation leads to the curiously shared view of deliberative democrats and some affect theorists that the capacity to judge itself—insofar as it operates within "the space of reasons" (that is, the rational and normative structure that governs the use of concepts)—must involve the wholly conscious and rule-governed practice of subsuming particulars under concepts.[14] The problem of judgment, as defined and debated by both sides, remains in the grip of the intellectualist conception of knowledge, according to which judgments, to be rational, require that the judging subject disengage its affective propensities and exercise a fully cognitive grasp of concepts as if "operating a calculus according to definite rules," to cite Ludwig Wittgenstein.[15] Failing that, judgments are little more than the effects of already primed dispositions that lie beyond the reach of consciousness and meaning.

Worries concerning the place of our subjective endowments in anything we judge to be objective are visible in the opposition between reason and affect not only as this opposition maps onto the self-identified differences between deliberative democrats and political affect theorists but, more broadly, in debates about cognitive versus noncognitive modes of judging—that is, judgments (or states) with a truth-evaluable content and judgments (or states) without a truth-evaluable content. The political stakes of this opposition animate the now extensive critical literature on Hannah Arendt's turn to the aesthetic judgments of Kant's third *Critique*.

Arendt's Kantian Alternative

The chapters that follow take up Arendt's creative appropriation of Kant's *Critique of Judgment* in an attempt to rethink the problem of judgment in late modernity beyond the frame of the intellectualist conception, be it the cognitivism of many neo-Kantian deliberative approaches to judgment or the noncognitivism of many forms of political affect theory, and to resituate the problem within the register of the ordinary.[16] It may seem strange to present Arendt's reading of Kant as an alternative to noncognitivism, since it is precisely noncognitivism of which her reliance on the third *Critique* stands accused in neo-Kantian (and neo-Aristotelian) receptions of her work. This debate turns on Arendt's insistence that politics involves the exchange of opinions that seek to persuade others, not truths that compel their agreement. Like aesthetic judgments on Kant's account, political judgments cannot be treated as truth claims, for they are not based on concepts or the giving of proofs. Arendt's turn to the third *Critique*, argues Habermas, is symptomatic of her refusal to provide a "cognitive foundation" for politics and public debate ("ACCP," 225). As Ronald Beiner, editor of Arendt's Kant lectures, explains, "It is not clear how we could make sense of opinions that did not involve *any* cognitive claims (and therefore, by implication, truth-claims that are potentially corrigible) or why we should be expected to take seriously opinions that assert no claims to truth (or do not at least claim *more* truth than is claimed by available alternative opinions). It would seem that *all* human judgments, including aesthetic (and certainly political) judgments, incorporate a necessary cognitive dimension."[17]

In Beiner's influential extension of Habermas's critique, noncognitivism is just where the problems begin. Not only does Arendt reject cognition as relevant to political judgment, she also seems to reject the idea that there is a "distinct faculty that we might identify, characteristically, as *political* judgment; there is only the ordinary capacity of judgment, now addressing itself to political events (or as Arendt would say, political appearances)."[18] This shift from the specific faculty of political judgment to a "unitary and indivisible" (ordinary) faculty of judgment as such, argues Beiner, reveals the gap between Arendt's earlier account, where judgment was linked to "'representative thinking' and opinion . . . [and] exercised by actors in political deliberation and action," and what emerges as her "definitive formulation," in which judging withdraws from the *vita activa* into the *vita contemplativa*, the life of the mind.[19]

The claim that Arendt's later work on judgment represents a withdrawal from politics, then, is rooted in more than the charge of noncognitivism.[20] It is also rooted in the accusing observation that she is no longer interested in *political* judgment as a distinct species of judgment at all, but only in the ordinary faculty of judging as such. This observation turns on the idea that political judgment is political because it takes as its object political things. What could count as a political thing in Arendt's work is notoriously hard to pin down. Let's take as an ordinary example the election of political representatives. So a judgment about, say, who should be the next mayor of Chicago would be a political judgment because the office of mayor is a political matter.

But there is another way of thinking about what makes a judgment political, and that is when we say that "political" characterizes the means or process by which the judgment proceeds. (To see the contrast here, consider the phrase "diplomatic policy": "it can describe policies about diplomatic matters," writes Joseph Tinguely, that "need not themselves be arrived at by any diplomatic procedures"; or "it can

be understood to mean a policy which is arrived at diplomatically."[21])
Thus the notion of "political judgment" can be understood in two
quite distinct senses. In the first case, "political" is that about which a
judgment is made—that is, about an external and prior or given object
that is independent of the judgment itself (e.g., the office of mayor);
in the second case, the "political" arises as something internal to the
process of judging itself. Just as we can think of the first case in terms
of an existing political object (e.g., the office of mayor), we might think
of the second case as one in which something that was not already
considered political (e.g., housework, sexuality, and reproduction, as
feminists claim) can come to be seen and judged as such. The key interpretive question in reading Arendt and, more generally, in developing
a democratic theory of judgment is whether the term *political* refers to
a particular mode (form) of judgment or only to a particular kind of
object (referent) judgments can have. I shall argue that it is the former,
and I will be basing my case on a parallel argument in chapter 2 about
how to understand Kantian aesthetic judgments.

Political(e) mode of judging, not object.

Even to ask what Arendt means by "political judgment" is decep-
tive: Arendt rarely uses the term *political judgment*,[22] preferring rather
to speak of "the capacity to judge [as] a specifically political ability."[23]
For her, judging is an activity, and judgment is not political because it
is about political things that are prior, independent, and external to it;
it is political because it is a judgment that is arrived at politically—that
is to say, with Arendt's Kant, by "'think[ing] in the place of everybody
else.'"[24] This form of thinking from the perspectives of other people,
which Kant calls an "enlarged way of thinking" (*eine erweiterte Den-
kungsart*) and Arendt redescribes as "representative thinking,"[25] is a
crucial part of judging in the absence of known rules in her view.[26]
As I shall explain in this chapter, such thinking takes for granted that
perspectives are corrigible not by something that is extraperspectival
or neutral but by other perspectives themselves. The objects one considers from these perspectives are not external objects in the way that,
say, the office of mayor is. They emerge into view *as* "objects" in need
of our judgment, the judgment of citizens, only as part of the process
of judging and of a broader process of orienting oneself in what Arendt
calls "the common world." Arendt elaborates, "The capacity to judge
is a specifically political ability in exactly the sense denoted by Kant,
namely, the ability to see things not only from one's own point of
view but in the perspective of all those who happen to be present."[27]
Arendt's formulations waver somewhat on the scope of the people
whose perspectives need to be taken into account. But she never wa-

vers on speaking about judgment as political because of the means or process by which it proceeds, not because it judges political objects that are prior and external to it.

If one thinks, with Arendt's critics, that the proper meaning of political judgment is judgment of objects that are prior and external to the operation of judging itself, then it must indeed seem puzzling to exclude the cognitive dimension of judgment. What else would the faculty of judgment be judging if not the status of these objects? But if one thinks about what is political in judgment as a *mode* (form) of judging rather than as a particular kind of *object* (referent) judgment can have, as Arendt does, then cognition is only one way in which judgment might proceed. Arendt's point was never to exclude cognition from judgments about the common world; it was to question the reduction of judging politically to the adjudication of validity claims. On this view, the objects of judgment are already given to us, and judging itself is a cognitive practice of subsuming an object under a concept. As we have seen, this is the position advanced by neo-Kantians such as Habermas and Rawls, for whom the whole problem of judgment in multicultural democracies is how to decide among competing claims about *existing* objects of judgment in the absence of universally shared standards. For Arendt, by contrast, the problem is rather how it is that citizens *get certain objects into view as objects of judgment at all*. That is the problem of what she calls "the common world," as we shall see. Rather than embrace a politically naive noncognitivism, as her critics claim, Arendt's turn to the third *Critique* advances a form of interpretive understanding focused on the creation and maintenance of the common world and how it is that new "objects" of judgment—or, more precisely, matters of common concern—can come into view for us.[28]

We can now better grasp why Arendt's turn to Kantian aesthetics to talk about her ostensible topic of political judgment would strike critics as deeply puzzling, for they have a different understanding of the judging faculty. This difference concerns more than the mode versus referent models of judging just described. The critique of Arendt's noncognitivism also turns on her critics' fairly strict division between aesthetic and empirical judging, between the reflective judgments of taste, discussed in the third *Critique*, and the determinative judgments of objects discussed in the first, the *Critique of Pure Reason*. But this strict division does not hold in Arendt's interpretation of Kant any more than it holds in Kant's own work. As I argue in chapter 2, the point is not to exclude the relevance of cognition to politics; it is to emphasize the reflective and affective character of all judging, aesthetic and empirical.

Recap.
of
new
argument

I have suggested that judging is political, not because it is about political objects that are prior and external to it, but because it proceeds by taking into account the perspectives of others and does not rely on an algorithmic decision procedure or the mechanical subsumption of particulars under known rules. It is, however, not only a matter of discovering new "objects" for judgment but also one of judging politically those that are already in our view. It is possible to imagine cases in which objects already counted as political are nonetheless not judged in the political manner or mode so described. In these cases, judgments are treated as validity claims subject to a decision procedure based on the giving of proofs. Whether discovering new objects or judging politically objects already within view, what we count as "political" in the sense described here arises within the process of democratic judging itself. Understood in this way, judging is constitutive of the space in which the common objects of democratic judgment can appear, including those that are already known to us as political (e.g., the office of mayor) and those that have yet to be constituted or acknowledged as such.

Rather than think of the problem of judgment as the quest for the proper criteria to adjudicate value conflicts in the absence of a universal idea of the good, we need to focus our attention on what I shall call the prior question of what it means to have a world in common, a world in which so-called value differences present themselves, and are taken up, not as mere preferences but as politically relevant "objects" for judgment, matters of common concern. The problem of preferences is the problem of what Habermas calls the otherwise "impenetrable pluralism of apparently ultimate value orientations" that the deliberative approach would bring into a public language game of giving and asking for reasons.[29] That is another way of saying—quite rightly, in my view—that so-called value judgments, if they are to have any democratic political resonance at all, cannot be mere preferences but must make a legitimate claim on the agreement of others.

Judging Values

To raise the question of values is to go to the heart of the matter between Arendt and her critics and, accordingly, to any attempt to develop a democratic theory of judgment based on the intimations of her view. How can a judgment that is not subject to validation on the basis of proofs possibly make a claim to the agreement of all? However much she criticized liberalism, Arendt's notion of opinion, rather than truth, as the sole coinage of political debate seems to invite the subjectivizing language of value qua preferences; namely, the language of value pluralism that characterizes liberalism. This "intrinsically subjectivizing vocabulary," writes Beiner, "suggests . . . that value originates not in what is admirable or worthy of being cherished in the world, but in the idiosyncrasies of our own inner life. . . . It has the effect of canceling out the claims to real validity anchored in the world; it is a self-defeating moral language. Talk of values implies that we do not find goodness in the good things there in the world, but confer value from our own subjectivity."[30] Such talk, he continues, "is inseparable from the notion of an exhaustive dichotomy between facts and values, where it is presumed that the world consists of evaluatively neutral facts that we then inject with value on the basis of our own prejudices and proclivities."[31]

I take up the problems that a subjectivist view of values raises for liberalism in chapter 3 in connection with the question of historicism in the work of Leo Strauss. Here I wish to consider how this view, far from unique to liberalism (or any other political form), is part of a larger (modern) way of thinking about the relationship of evaluative thought to the world. More specifically, it is connected to what Bernard Williams has called the "absolute conception of reality" or the "world," which distinguishes between the world as it is independent of our experience from the world as it seems to us.[32] Adherents to the absolute conception draw a sharp distinction between belief states with cognitive content, which are capable of correctly representing the world or disclosing its features, and noncognitive affective states, which are not. Rooted in a bifurcated conception of mind, which distinguishes the faculty of reason from the faculty of taste or sentiment, this view underwrites the classic distinction between subjective and objective, which, in turn, organizes most discussion of ethics, aesthetics, politics, and the difference between these and natural science. It is at the heart of noncognitivist approaches in these fields and therefore relevant to the debate about Arendt's turn to the aesthetic judgments of the third *Critique*.

According to influential noncognitivists such as J. L. Mackie, for example, variations in valuing, which form the basis for liberal pluralism, are "more readily explained by the hypothesis that [the valuings] reflect ways of life than by the hypothesis that they express perceptions . . . of objective values."[33] On Mackie's influential "error theory" of values, "value is . . . 'part of the fabric of the world,'" explains John

McDowell, but "the appearance is illusory: value is not found in the world, but projected into it, a mere reflection of subjective responses."[34] Key to dismissing the idea that evaluative thought could be anything other than the mere expression of our private inner life, just feelings that we project onto the world, as noncognitivist Simon Blackburn in a somewhat different but related approach sees it, is the definition of "objective."[35] The world is "objective" on the noncognitivist account to the extent that it "is fully describable in terms of properties that can be understood without essential reference to their effects on sentient beings."[36] This understanding of evaluative states as noncognitive and thus devoid of propositional content (that could be taken up by other judging beings), comments McDowell, rules out the possibility that "exercises of our affective or conative natures . . . [can] in some way [be] percipient, or at least [be capable of] expanding our sensitivity to how things [genuinely] are."[37]

On the noncognitivist view of evaluative thought, genuine (read: rational) disagreement over values—be it in the register of aesthetics, morality, or politics—is impossible. Ethical (or any evaluative) concepts are "mere pseudo-concepts," as classic theorists of "emotivism" such as Alfred J. Ayer and Charles L. Stevenson in their own ways argued.[38] "Emotivism is the doctrine that all evaluative judgments and more specifically all moral judgments are *nothing but* expressions of preference, expressions of attitude or feeling"—indeed, it is "a theory which professes to give an account of *all* value judgments whatsoever," according to Alasdair MacIntyre.[39] But if attitudes, feelings, and preferences are all that evaluative judgments are about, then they cannot possibly count as *judgments* at all. You might express your attitude and I mine, but how could we possibly agree or disagree about whether, say, violence against women is wrong? All we can say is: "It is wrong (or not wrong) to *me*." As Ayer states, "One really never does dispute about questions of value."[40] Or, as McDowell sarcastically puts it, "Think of the practice of expressing one's attitudes to various flavours of ice cream."[41]

How, then, are we to account for the quotidian experience of disagreeing with others about values? For Ayer (and value noncognitivists of various stripes both before, e.g., David Hume, and after, e.g., Mackie), such experience exists but is not what it seems.[42] We can argue only about facts, and any argument about facts is possible "only if some system of values is presupposed. If our opponent concurs with us in expressing moral disapproval of all actions of a given type *t*, then we may get him to condemn a particular action A, by bringing forward arguments to show that A is of type *t*. For the question whether A does or does not belong to that type is a plain question of fact."[43] In most situations in which we (mistakenly) take ourselves to be arguing about values, then, we are really arguing about facts, proceeding deductively, and expecting others to agree. "And as the people with whom we argue have generally received the same moral education as ourselves, and live in the same social order, our expectation is usually justified," notes Ayer. "But if our opponent happens to have undergone a different process of moral 'conditioning' from ourselves, so that, even when he acknowledges all the facts, he still disagrees with us about the moral value of the actions under discussion, then we abandon the attempt to convince him by argument."[44] At this point we may resort to insults, decrying the opponent's system of values as inferior, perhaps barbaric, "but we cannot bring forward any arguments to show that our system is superior. For our judgement that it is so is itself a judgement of value, and accordingly outside the scope of the argument," Ayer concludes.[45]

If the facts are logically divorced from the evaluative judgments, then disagreement in valuation is in principle interminable (for it is not genuine—i.e., rational—disagreement at all). If we do manage to bring others around to our view, then this can only be by means of (nonrational) persuasion, as Stevenson came to argue.[46] In that case, there is no substantive distinction between bringing people to change their minds on the basis of reasons and manipulating them in a way that has nothing to do with rationality. Absent any standard of correctness, there is no difference, as Habermas would put it, between "illusionary and non-illusionary convictions" ("ACCP," 225).

Unwilling to accept the idea that we cannot reason with evaluative concepts, some noncognitivists (e.g., Mackie, R. M. Hare) have suggested that the content of such concepts can contain enough descriptive material to enable us to rationally debate whose judgment is correct.[47] On this view, then, one does not have, say, genuinely *aesthetic* cognitions but only genuinely descriptive cognitions with so-called aesthetic or affective responses. This "disentangling manoeuvre," as McDowell calls it, assumes that in relation to any value concept, one can always "isolate a genuine feature of the world—by the appropriate standard of genuineness: that is, a feature that is there anyway, independently of anyone's value experience being as it is—to be that to which competent users of the concept are to be regarded as responding when they use it: that which is left in the world when one peels off the reflection of the appropriate attitude."[48]

Philosophical debates over so-called thick concepts—that is, concepts that are held to involve both a descriptive and an evaluative

13

component (e.g., fairness, kindness, courage, brutality)—bring to light what Hilary Putnam calls the deep "entanglement of fact and value."[49] A word such as *cruel*, for example, can be used in ways that we might think of as normative (e.g., "He is a cruel teacher") or it can be used more descriptively (e.g., "as when a historian writes that a certain monarch was exceptionally cruel, or that the cruelties of the regime provoked a number of rebellions").[50] "'Cruel' simply ignores the supposed fact/value dichotomy and cheerfully allows itself to be used sometimes for a normative purpose and sometimes as a descriptive term," continues Putnam.[51] The same principle can apply for a word such as *democratic*, which is typically thought to have both "thin" and "thick" connotations.[52] When asked how a certain teacher runs his classroom, I might say idiomatically, "He is not particularly democratic." But I could also answer "democratic" to the question of a particular form of regime. In either case, argues Putnam, I would have to understand the evaluative meaning of the concept to know how to apply it descriptively, which is to say, to extend it to new cases.[53]

Noncognitivist attempts to disentangle facts and values, descriptive content from evaluative content, cannot work: mastery of an aesthetic (or any evaluative) concept requires more than cognitively picking out so-called natural descriptive features of the world. As we shall see in chapter 8 when we turn to Peter Winch's "Understanding a Primitive Society," the capacity to evaluate objects in ways that can be considered rational requires the development of a certain sensibility or sensitivity, requires it in such a way that a person from another culture who failed to see the evaluative point of a thick concept, who had not learned the meaning of the concept in relation to the concerns of the human community in which it is operative—such knowledge need not be gained firsthand but might work through imaginative learning—would not be able to predict local uses of it on the basis of descriptive similarities alone. There is no "fact of the matter" to which he or she could refer that would not involve such sensitivity; or, to put the same point another way, sensitivity is what enables one to discern the existence of such a fact. "Only a creature that *can* judge of value *can* state a fact," to speak with Stanley Cavell (*CR*, 15).

Neo-Kantian ideas of public reason have various ways of managing the threat that subjectivist approaches to evaluative thought pose to the normativity of democratic debate. Whereas Rawls's would bracket public claims to the truth of value judgments that express "comprehensive doctrines" or worldviews (without directly addressing whether

such approaches get evaluative thought right), Habermas's would redeem otherwise particularistic and only incompletely cognitive or
objective value (ethical) judgments by way of the "truth analogous"
validity of moral metanorms (and show why, when it comes to *moral*
judgments, such approaches get evaluative thought wrong).[54] Political
affect theorists, for their part, press the mysterious workings of affective response deeper down in the judging subject, beneath the level of
conscious feeling as it was understood by classic emotivists (Ayer, Stevenson) or value noncognitivists (Hume, Mackie, Blackburn). We shall
examine their responses in due course.

The question for us now is why these approaches have such an uneasy grip on us, why they seem at once to speak to, and to distort, what
we are doing when we make ordinary evaluative judgments, which
are the kinds of judgment we are called on to make in a democracy
and which were clearly what Arendt had in mind when she turned to
the third *Critique*. Part of what drives us, democratic thinkers, into an
emotivist (noncognitivist or projectivist) metaphysic—regardless of
whether we have philosophical knowledge of such a thing—is something I will happily not only concede but affirm: we do not "cognize"
evaluative facts, not in the way that the rationalists or strict cognitivists would have it. And yet, notwithstanding the ordinary sense in liberal democratic societies that political judgments are not cognitions in
the strict sense of determinative rule following that "guarantees" agreement (e.g., when I say "This table is square"), but are, rather, considered
opinions that may well conflict (e.g., "This war is wrong"), it is also our
ordinary sense that not all judgments are equal, that some are better
and some worse than others, and that they are better or worse not because one has a better or worse "feeling" about a particular object but
because one either is or is not mistaken about the facts of the case. On
the latter point the emotivists were right, but they could not see how
a feeling could be world-giving, bound up with discovering the facts
and thus with rational ways of judging. "The whole idea of an emotive
meaning reckoned separately from cognitive content," writes David
Wiggins, "does insufficient justice to our feeling that divergence of attitude must itself be founded in something, and reflect a prior or co-
eval disagreement in something not itself reducible without residue to
emotive attitude (*i.e.*, in something the sentence is *about*, which is not
so far accounted for)."[55] Or, as Bertrand Russell succinctly states, "I cannot see how to refute the arguments for the subjectivity of ethical values, but I find myself incapable of believing that all that is wrong with

wanton cruelty is that I don't like it."[56] And yet not liking it is somehow connected with finding it wrong, connected in ways that are no mere "phantasm," to borrow Hume's description of evaluative thought.

By contrast with noncognitivist approaches, a democratic theory of judgment takes sensibility and affective response as world-giving, but it needs a way of talking about evaluative facts as something that we do not simply cognize, as rationalist (or strict cognitivist, e.g., Habermas) approaches to judgment would have it (and as noncognitivists, holding fast to the fact/value distinction, would too).[57] The problem of cruelty, or any other matter of common concern, is not just that Bertrand Russell (or for that matter you or I) does not like it, "but that it is not such as to call forth liking given our *actual* collectively scrutinized responses," comments Wiggins.[58] One could conceivably imagine reasons for not caring about the things that we do care about or become suspicious of ingrained habits of caring, but in the absence of such reasons, it is not necessarily question-begging to remind ourselves of why we do care (when we do). The question is how to develop that thought (about the ways in which we do or do not care and thus do or do not value certain things as right or wrong, just or unjust, better or worse) such that we can affirm the centrality of our "affective and attitudinative propensities," as McDowell puts it, to getting the world in view.[59] It is by means of these propensities that we can be brought to care about the things of this world, and brought to care in ways that are public—that is, shared. And this thought might be extended so as to refuse the (metaphysical) realism that presents itself as the only alternative to noncognitivism.

Attending to affective and attitudinative propensities will enable us to grasp what it means to agree or disagree, not just about what each of us individually or we collectively value, but in *valuation.* "Rival attempts to speak for us as a community," as Wiggins notes, "cannot be plausibly reduced to rival accounts of what, if anything, the community does already say."[60] It is not a sociological matter (of the difference between certain people or cultural groups). Surely these will always exist: that is the empirical fact of value pluralism. The empirical fact of disagreement about what we value, in other words, rests on the possibility of disagreement in valuation. But understanding the latter (with emotivists and noncognitivists) as disagreement in attitudes *expressed* does not capture what those attitudes are *about*—that is, the intentional character of judgment. We can and do ask if a particular valuational response is appropriate to its object. Human interest constitutes a particular perspective, a perspective without which there is no value to speak of. Accepting this thought while refusing subjectivism, we could hold that human perspective provides a genuine mode of access to the world. To speak with Thomas Nagel, we could resist the "voracity of the [scientistic] objective appetite," as "perhaps the best or truest view is not obtained by transcending oneself as far as possible."[61] To be in a position where we might accept such inspirational advice, however, we need first to understand why we are tempted to transcend ourselves when we judge.

Vertigo

The tenacious sense that evaluative judgments are subjective preferences is linked to the idea that to be rational and objective, they would have to conform to rules and to a mode of rule following in which rules for the correct application of concepts are fixed independently of the responses and reactions of judging subjects. This idea underwrites the noncognitivist disentangling maneuver by which the evaluative and descriptive aspects of an object can be distinguished, and a person who has no competence with the relevant evaluative concept can still pick out the relevant facts to which the concept "refers," be able to extend the concept to new cases, and communicate his or her judgments to those who have such competence. It is a view of rationality rooted in the absolute conception of the world, where science, with its established procedures, is the model. Accordingly, as Stanley Cavell observes, "the rationality of an argument depends upon its leading from premises all parties accept, in steps all can follow, to an agreement upon a conclusion which all must accept. . . . What is the significance of saying that a rational argument is one whose conclusion 'all must accept'" for thinking about evaluative judgments? (*CR*, 254)

"Aesthetic (and moral and political) judgments lack something: the arguments that support them are not conclusive the way arguments in logic are, nor rational the way arguments in science are. Indeed they are not, and if they were there would be no such subject as art (or morality [or politics]) and no such art as criticism," concedes Cavell.[62] Rather than give the cognitivists and noncognitivists what they most desire, he adds: "It does not follow, however, that such judgments are not conclusive and rational."[63] As we shall see in chapter 2, evaluative judgments on Cavell's Wittgensteinian account have a kind of "logic" or necessity and claim validity (as if they were empirical judgments), which Kant calls "'[speaking] with a universal voice.'"[64] To speak with a universal voice, as Kant describes judging aesthetically (e.g., "This rose is beautiful"), is to demand, impute, or claim agreement with our judgments, which we do not do when asserting our subjective preference, the register of what he calls the "agreeable" (e.g., "I like canary wine").[65] This necessity differs from logical reasoning and the giving of proofs—that is, as Cavell states, "arriving at conviction in such a way that anyone who can follow the argument must, unless he finds something definitely wrong with it, *accept the conclusion*, agree with it."[66] The sense of necessity that leads us to speak with a universal voice, Cavell writes, "is, partly, a matter of the *ways* a judgment is supported, the ways in which conviction in it is produced: it is only by virtue of these recurrent patterns of support that a remark will count as—will be—aesthetic, or a mere matter of taste, or moral, propagandistic, religious, magical, scientific, philosophical," or political.[67] We might think, then, about logic or rationality, comments Stephen Mulhall, as "a matter of agreement in *patterns* rather than an agreement in *conclusions*. Whether the particular patterns or procedures are such that those competent in following them are guaranteed to reach an agreed conclusion is part of what distinguishes one type or aspect of rationality from another; but what distinguishes rationality from irrationality in any domain is an agreement in—a commitment to—patterns or procedures of speaking and acting."[68]

Calling attention to agreement in "patterns of support," rather than conclusions, as the crucial element in rational argument, Cavell shows how we misunderstand the difference between evaluative judgments, on the one hand, and empirical or logical judgments, on the other hand. It cannot be reduced to the difference between cognitive and noncognitive judgments, as the debate over Arendt's turn to the third *Critique* would have us believe. In thinking about Cavell's alternative account, however, it is tempting to treat these patterns of support as if they were antecedent to anything that can rationally be said, as if they functioned like rules that laid out in advance of actual practices of speaking and judging the grammar of mutual intelligibility. It is tempting, not least because our "uses of language are pervasively, almost unimaginably, *systematic*," writes Cavell (*CR*, 29). What Wittgenstein calls "agreement not in opinions, but rather in form of life" and "not only an agreement in definitions, but (odd as it may sound) agreement in judgments [*Übereinstimmung in den Urteilen*]" is characterized by a remarkable spontaneity of intelligibility or mutual attunement in language (*PI*, §§241, 242).[69] This attunement can lead us to think that *something* must underwrite or ground our uses of words, *something* must guarantee their normativity. The very fact of our agreement in language seems to attest to the presence of a rule and to our following a rule. Is not this idea of normativity as rule-governed at the core of Wittgenstein's legacy?

Indeed, in the long-standing debate over positivism and scientism, Wittgenstein has appeared to many social and political theorists as offering an account of normativity that avoids the impossible choice between objectivism and subjectivism. Wittgenstein's account of rules and rule following, it is said, offers a third way that takes into account the (subjectivist) notion of the unique or meaningful nature of human thought and action, without relinquishing the (objectivist) idea that normativity necessarily transcends individuals, their actual practices of speaking and acting. Accordingly, Wittgenstein is seen as replacing the positivist's law-governed (nomothetic) view of human speech and action with a rule-governed account that does not reduce meaning to individual subjective states.

Habermas's early effort to develop a language-based conception of rationality, for example, credits what he takes to be Wittgenstein's rule-governed conception of language for providing an alternative to "the philosophy of consciousness" that casts normativity in objectivist law-governed terms. Wittgenstein's agent-centered approach to rules and rule following, argues Habermas, also avoids the perils of subjectivism by putting "tacit knowledge" of rules or practical competence at the heart of judging and acting. In the process of acting "knowledgeably," individuals draw on an omnipresent transcendental order of tacit rules that shape and inform their activities, securing the normativity of those activities in ways that require, rather than exclude (as did rationalist approaches), their skilled participation without their conscious knowledge or their ability to formulate an explicit discursive account of what they are able to do.[70] It is the task of the critical theorist to give this tacit knowledge of rules and rule following propositional form.

I want here to query the reception of Wittgenstein as advancing a theory of language as a framework of rules and of mutual intelligibility as dependent on rules and rule following, tacit or not. "In his later work," as Nigel Pleasants observes, "Wittgenstein tries to show that transcendental inference to hypothetical cognitive powers and tacit rules—as entities which *must* exist in order to account for the meaningfulness of human action and experience—gives a wholly delusory sense of adequate explanation."[71] A central theme in the later work "is that meaning is not '*hidden from us*,'" it is not shrouded in a mysterious tacit knowledge of a transcendental order of rules but plainly open to view in our action.[72] In section 75 of *Philosophical Investigations*, for example, Wittgenstein emphasizes that my knowledge, my possession of a concept, is completely expressed in the explanations that I could give. If the concept is "games," for example, the expression of my competence would take the form of describing a variety of games; showing how something might or might not count as a game if it shares certain features with existing games; explaining to someone that "it is only a game"; and so on.[73]

Wittgenstein does not deny that, when asked by someone in a particular situation where a particular game is in play, we may well formulate a rule to describe what we do. In the *Blue Book*, he speaks about the difference "between what one might call 'a process being *in accordance with a rule*,'" and "'a process involving a rule.'"[74] Whereas the latter refers to actions that are explicitly followed by subjects engaged in a particular practice (e.g., a novice learning how to play a game of chess), the former speaks to what an observer of any practice *might* say when asked to explain what is being done. These are perfectly ordinary ways in which we speak about what it means to follow a rule or to be guided by a rule. In neither case, however, does following a rule require that the activity is "everywhere circumscribed by rules," as Wittgenstein states (*PI*, §68).[75] And once a certain competence has been established, it seems strange to say that one is following a rule, tacitly or not. When attempting to provide a theory of linguistic meaning according to which all meaningful action and speech is governed by rules, the ordinary sense of a rule is, to speak with Steven Affeldt, "philosophically stretched out of shape."[76]

Following Cavell, I read Wittgenstein not as putting forward an alternative theory of linguistic meaning, of language as a grammatical framework of rules, but as seeking to expose misunderstandings about what kinds of structures *must* underwrite everything that humans can meaningfully do or say. This nonstandard reading is crucial for my rethinking of Wittgenstein's relevance to a democratic theory of judgment. Even as astute a scholar as Hanna Fenichel Pitkin, whose pathbreaking book, *Wittgenstein and Justice*, opened up entirely new ways of approaching basic concepts in political theory and has been a guiding inspiration for my own work, was not immune to seeing in Wittgenstein's account of language something more than a "form of action," something that transcends and guides ordinary language use.[77] Working from what she took to be Cavell's teaching, Pitkin argued that Wittgenstein's work, from the *Tractatus* to the *Philosophical Investigations*, is continuous in its "Idealist theme, the insistence that our language controls what can possibly occur in the world" and that it also "provide[s] a framework which governs the possibilities of anything we can say about reality."[78] Although Pitkin clearly recognizes that for Wittgenstein language is an "open system," the grammatical relations among concepts, she writes, "might be considered a sort of linguistic Kantianism; what Wittgenstein calls 'grammatical knowledge' very much resembles Kant's 'transcendental knowledge'; and the validity of grammar might well be said to be synthetic a priori."[79] In this sense, it is not objects but grammar that comes to "contain or govern the 'possibilities of all situations' . . . Knowing the grammar of a word, we know what kinds of things are—can be—said with it, what would count as appropriate occasions for saying them."[80] Understood as quasi-transcendental—that is, as logically "prior to any particular empirical investigation," as that which "determines a logical space of possibilities," as Stephen Mulhall in a similar interpretation of Cavell's Wittgenstein writes—"the grammar of our language" starts to look suspiciously like the very transcendental mechanisms of constraint on human action and speech that Wittgenstein sought to expose as a misunderstanding of ordinary language.[81]

The readings of Mulhall and Pitkin are instructive: they are both critically engaged with the idea of language as a prison house of sorts that determines in advance of any context of use and actual use what will count as the intelligible use of a word. They would agree, as I explain in chapter 9, that when *Philosophical Investigations* famously describes how we follow the mathematical rule "Add 2," Wittgenstein is doing more than questioning a certain way of thinking about what rule following entails (e.g., the Platonist conception of rules that are like "ideal tracks" laid out to infinity). He is "bringing to light our confusions about the normative power of rules and the fantasies concerning the nature of rules that we construct in order to account for that power as we confusedly imagine it," asserts Affeldt.[82] Wittgenstein is calling our attention to "how inessential the 'appeal to rules' is as an explanation of language," as Cavell observes, and indeed of our whole conception of normativity.[83] And yet the otherwise astute readings of Mulhall and Pitkin alert us to how the lure of the appeal may persist even in cases where we think ourselves to be deeply wary of its call. And this too Wittgenstein invites us to see. He redescribes the lure as a tenacious *"picture"* that holds us "captive" (*PI*, §115). But captive to what? a democratic theorist might ask.

As I read Wittgenstein in the chapters that follow, the picture that holds us captive is the idea of the normativity of language as a more or less fixed framework of rules. This picture matters for a democratic theory of judgment, and for at least two reasons. It matters (1) because the idea that *something* must ground mutual intelligibility in the political realm risks entangling us in fantasies concerning the nature and power of rules that lead us to lose track of our own part or voice as democratic citizens in deciding what will and what will not belong to the common world. As we shall see, it is this displacement of our political agency understood in the Arendtian terms of freedom as nonsovereignty, and not some naive noncognitivism, that animated Arendt's turn to the third *Critique*. And it matters (2) because the power we ascribe to rules is part of what animates the search for criteria that would be appropriate to public debate in a pluralistic liberal democracy, which clearly cannot adopt a scientific conception of rationality as agreement in conclusions.

The idea of public reason as a standard of correctness—of the rules that govern our uses of words, that constitute them as the specific uses they are (e.g., as political speech), and in terms of which they can be normatively assessed (e.g., as democratically legitimate)—may seem to be nontendentious (e.g., an empty rule of argumentation or a thin concept of justice as fairness). It may not put forward a clearly defined rule meant to cover all possible cases of political speech. Nevertheless, as Affeldt remarks, even a "philosophically weak conception of a standard of correctness preserves the thought that there is a job for, and that there are things that serve as, explanations or justifications of words (or actions) apart from the specific situations in which they are employed as explanations or justifications in response to specific confusions, doubts, questions, and so on."[84] Wittgenstein invites us to question not simply the idea that there could be a standard covering all cases and so all eventualities but, more important, whether something "can count as a standard of how to go on, in the absence of an actual need for some explanation of how to go on" in, say, democratic deliberation.[85] What are we doing when we provide a template of the permissible structure of normative argumentation in advance of any particular arguments?

This view of mutual intelligibility commits us to the idea that we must have criteria for every concept and for every use of a concept in judgments that are democratically legitimate. It separates out criteria from actual judgments, makes them the ground of such judgments, and in this way assumes that we have criteria for all eventualities. It assumes that a person's divergent application of a word can simply and definitively be corrected by reminding the person of its agreed criteria (e.g., not invoking one's religious views to attack or defend a particular public matter of equality) and, in this case, seeing whether it fits with the criteria for deciding whether something will count as an instance of democratic political speech. In this way, as I argue in chapter 5, Rawls maintains that the terms of one's comprehensive doctrine (e.g., belief in "God") or claims about self-evident truths will not count as proper political speech and ought to be avoided in public deliberations; and in this way, as I show in chapters 4 and 7, Habermas can argue for the radical difference between cultural values and universal norms. But what is to say that such truth words or culturally bound values cannot be projected into new contexts, public political contexts, and be heard as belonging to the patterns of support that Cavell describes as belonging to the rationality of evaluative judgments? Do we really need to have our standards or rules firmly in place for deciding what utterances will count as legitimate—that is, deserving of our response—before anything has actually been said?

Cavell's discussion of what he calls "project[ing] a word" into new contexts—using words learned in one context and with one sense in other contexts and with related but different senses—can help us see what is at stake. The projection of a word is a fundamental aspect of language use, and the ability to project a word that one has learned in one context into new contexts demonstrates one's understanding of the word. Cavell tries "to bring out, and keep in balance, two fundamental facts about human forms of life, and about the concepts formed in those forms: that any form of life and every concept integral to it has an indefinite number of instances and directions of projection; and that this variation is not arbitrary" (*CR*, 185). These two facts define the twin "condition of stability and tolerance" that characterizes our lives with language, argues Cavell. We can, for example, move from learning to "feed the kitty" or "feed the lion" to say "feed the meter" and be understood (*CR*, 181). "But though language . . . is tolerant, allows projection, not just any projection will be acceptable, i.e., will communicate," Cavell cautions. "You can 'feed peanuts to a monkey' and 'feed pennies to a meter,' but you cannot feed a monkey by stuffing pennies in its mouth, and if you mash peanuts into a coin slot you won't *be* feeding the meter" (*CR*, 182,183).

We should resist the thought that yet another regulative mechanism is in play here, determining in advance of any actual speaking in actual contexts what will count as a legitimate projection of a word *and* of our own willingness to count *this* projection in *this* context.[86] To say, as Cavell does, that the "variation" in the projection of words is not "arbitrary" is not to say that it is somehow controlled by something outside speakers of the language, what they will count, and the context in which they speak. Rather than criteria or rules that prevent us from speaking intelligibly when we project a word in this way or that determine our ability to project intelligibly, it is *our* ability to properly locate the uses of words in recognizable interests, desires, purposes, forms of life, natural reactions, and so on. Cavell explains:

> We learn and teach words in certain contexts, and then we are expected, and expect others, to be able to project them into further contexts. Nothing insures that this projection will take place (in particular, not the grasping of universals nor the grasping of books of rules), just as nothing insures that we will make, and understand, the same projections. That on the whole we do is a matter of our sharing routes of interest and feeling, modes of response, senses of humor and of significance and of fulfillment, of what is outrageous, of what is similar to what else, what a rebuke, what forgiveness, of when an utterance is an assertion, when an appeal, when an explanation—all the whirl of organism Wittgenstein calls "forms of life." Human speech and activity, sanity and community, rest upon nothing more, but nothing less, than this. It is a vision as simple as it is difficult, and as difficult as it is (and because it is) terrifying.[87]

"The terror of which Cavell writes at the end of this marvellous passage," comments McDowell, "is a sort of vertigo, induced by the thought that there is nothing that keeps our practices in line except the reactions and responses we learn in learning them."[88] Cavell seems to offer little more than a lucky convergence of subjectivities, held together by a grab bag of affective sensibilities that can hardly make a claim to normativity. How would we know that we are *really* going on in the same way? How can we know that what we are doing has any correct relationship to reality at all?

It is tempting to recoil from the vertigo into the idea of grammar as a kind of Kantian synthetic a priori or of rules that are like ideal tracks objectively there to be followed regardless of whether this felicitous convergence of subjectivities ever takes place.[89] The problem with such recoil is not only that in specifying the conditions for intelligibility we exclude the radically open aspect of language that Cavell describes as projecting a word. The problem is that we lose track of—or, worse, deny—our actual conditions of mutual intelligibility; namely, our own activity in the "whirl of organism" that Wittgenstein calls "forms of life."[90] And though we shall find "forms of life" to be one of the most deeply contentious and misunderstood phrases in Wittgenstein's entire corpus, when seen as dynamic and open, rather than (ethnographi-

cally) static and closed, it does not lead down the slippery slope of relativism, as critics charge. Instead, it opens up a way of thinking about
the imbrication of affectivity and rationality that situates subjective response at the heart of anything we consider objective. It perfectly captures the contingently necessary complex of human relations in which
knowing how to go on has its original home. Affeldt explains:

> To possess a concept, to be able to go on with a concept, is to appreciate how its
> significant employment is bound up with our interests, desires, purposes, biologi-
> cal and social forms of life, facts about our social and natural world, and the like.
> Or, in order to avoid the erroneous impression that concepts stand alone and that
> we come to possess them one by one, it is more accurate to say that to possess
> concepts, to be able to go on with them, is to appreciate the weave of connections
> both among our concepts and between our concepts and our interests, desires,
> purposes, forms of life, natural reactions, facts about our world, and so on. In com-
> ing into possession of concepts—learning to speak significantly—we are coming to
> appreciate this weave of connections. It is in this sense that coming into possession
> of concepts is becoming an initiate of forms of life. And in the matter of becoming
> initiates of forms of life light dawns gradually over the whole.[91]

The idea of "becoming initiates of forms of life" comes to displace
the focus on rules in Wittgenstein's and Cavell's thought, observes
Affeldt[92]—as it should, I shall argue, in ours. It is not that rules no
longer matter, but they can only matter as part of the larger "whirl
of organism" in which they have their life. It is only by becoming an
initiate that I so much as know what to do with any rule that presents
itself as the way to go on in a practice, be it a game of chess or a public
debate. The focus on rules occludes the crucially important role of *voice*
in anything that we can meaningfully say or judge politically. Cavell
emphasizes how saying something intelligible, something that others
may not necessarily agree with but can understand why you might say
that, requires that you speak in a way that resonates with others in the
specific context in which you speak. Surely this must be the first step in
moving to an idea of what might be "reasonable," as described by democratic thinkers such as Rawls. It is not rules that guarantee our mutual
intelligibility as democratic citizens but rather our mastery of speaking in particular public contexts. There need to "be reasons for what
you say, or be [a] point in your saying of something, if what you say is
to be comprehensible. We can understand what the *words* mean apart
from understanding why you say them; but apart from understanding
the point of your saying them we cannot understand what *you* mean,"

Cavell maintains (*CR*, 206).[93] In this sense of "to speak is to say what counts," it is to show your willingness to acknowledge certain things about the world and those to whom you speak and not to acknowledge others.[94] This focus on voice rather than rules or criteria understood as a standard of correctness for what can be intelligibly said when we speak politically will be crucial to developing a democratic theory of judgment.

To treat these natural reactions, interests, or purposes as part of the "lifeworld" (Habermas) or the "background culture" (Rawls) where the rules of public reason do not apply is to distort the grammar of mutual intelligibility. It is to treat our interests, desires, or purposes in any act of speaking intelligibly as the mere background on which the real source of that intelligibility—namely rules,—merely rests, as if the rules could be pried off that normative background. It is to evade or deny the ordinary. More precisely, to minimize the place of that normative background in judging politically reflects a continued and deep skepticism toward ordinary modes of perception and forms of subjectivity, and in a way that sustains just what contemporary neo-Kantians critique— namely, the absolute conception of the world according to which objectivity requires the elimination of every admixture of subject dependence. Consequently, the neo-Kantians remain wary toward the very condition of liberal democracy that they also celebrate: plurality. Though they are explicit critics of metaphysical realism and its singular nonperspectival ideal of truth, they remain in the grip of its basic antipathy toward any degree of dependence on our forms of subjectivity.

This evasion of the ordinary is not without costs. When rules come apart from our interests, desires, or purposes; when the locus of normativity is understood to be rules rather than our interests, desires, or purposes themselves, we are not better but rather worse able to resolve deep disagreements between speakers of a language when they arise. We are worse able because we cannot understand what a person has said and thus what we are disagreeing about without understanding it as part of those interests, desires, or purposes. We cannot just take the words uttered (e.g., "God requires us to treat people as equals") to see if they meet our criteria of public reason. "Another way to put this thought," states Affeldt, "is to say that we don't know *what* someone has said until we know what they (might have) meant—and we may misunderstand what a person has said or done because we wrongly imagine, or take for granted that we know, the interests, desires, etc. being expressed."[95] What someone might mean points not inward to some private mental realm but outward to a shared sense of reality and conditions of meaning, what Kant will describe as "sensus communis" and Arendt as a "common world."

I said earlier that the arguments for public reason claim that the rules for democratic deliberation are not inflexible and do not constitute a resolution of a disagreement (i.e., apart from the actual articulation of a disagreement). But this leaves us with little to say when intractable disagreements arise. Paradoxical though this might seem, the idea that divergent applications of a word can be corrected by reminding someone of its agreed criteria only begins to get at the real difficulty in our current conception of the problem of judgment. Even if we concede, as both Rawls and Habermas in their own ways do, that the ability of public reason to settle a disagreement cannot be decided apart from the specifics of the case, it is the job of public reason to determine whether someone's use of a word is divergent (i.e., does not conform to the criteria of public reason), which in turn assumes that we already know what the divergent speaker is trying to say. And it must be assumed because on the account I am questioning, our rules are the only way of determining what someone is doing or saying: that is the point of thinking about language as a framework of rules.[96]

Although approaching a divergent speaker in terms of our rules may seem to put us in a position of strength for ordering an otherwise "impenetrable pluralism of ultimate value orientations," as Habermas put the task of public reason, we shall find that public reason actually leaves us with little to say in the face of ways of going on, of voicing political claims, that we find problematic or unintelligible in the terms set out by our rules. If we then abandon these rules that alone render speech intelligible qua political speech, what other resources will we have to make sense of what the divergent speaker is saying? He or she will more likely remain opaque and mysterious, speaking the language of a worldview and preferences or values that we do not share. In the end, what we take to be the disagreement and its resolution will likely be wholly within the terms of our own position, notwithstanding sincere efforts to the contrary.[97]

All of this in no way suggests that taking into account the desires, interests, or purposes that I have argued to be the real conditions of political life (as of human life in general) is easy or that it guarantees mutual intelligibility or skillful judging politically—far from it. But it does allow a pathway into another way of thinking about the problem of judgment in pluralistic modern democracies than that of finding the proper criteria that would correct for the distortions associated with affective subjectivity. This is the pathway opened up by Hannah Arendt.

Judging and the Common World

For Arendt, the modern problem of judgment is not one of specifying criteria but of creating and maintaining a political space in which differences in valuation can be publicly expressed and judged. Far from embracing noncognitivism, Arendt thinks about politics and judgment outside the absolute conception of the world within which values are affectively motivated subjective preferences or projections. For her, human life takes place in the space of appearances, and appearance is not "mere" appearance. She explicitly rejects the "two-world theory," according to which there is a "metaphysical dichotomy of (true) Being and (mere) Appearance," and affirms instead "the primacy of appearance for all living creatures to whom the world appears in the mode of an it-seems-to-me [*dokei moi*]."[98] Appearance is not the epistemological veil that covers the "true world" but the genuine human mode of access to reality. Appearance is not something to be by definition mistrusted, as it is in metaphysics, or to be gotten beyond, as it is in "modern science's relentless search for the base underneath mere appearances" (*LMT*, 25). Appearance is fundamental to how human beings exist in and relate to one another and to the world. "That appearance always demands spectators and thus implies an at least potential recognition and acknowledgment has far-reaching consequences for what we, appearing beings in a world of appearances, understand by reality, our own as well as that of the world," explains Arendt (*LMT*, 46). The faith that we have in the reality of what we see, hear, taste, smell, or touch, our faith in the reality of what is given to us through the five senses, "depends entirely on the object's also appearing as such to others and being acknowledged by them [as the same]."[99]

This faith in appearance, in the "it-seems-to-me" [which qua appearance] is "open to error and illusion" (though not by definition illusory) is what Arendt calls the "prior indication of realness" (*LMT*, 49). Realness is not produced by any one of our senses taken in isolation, or by any object taken out of context. It is, rather, "guaranteed by its worldly context, which includes others who perceive as I do, on the one hand, and by the working together of my five senses on the other. What since Thomas Aquinas we call common sense, the *sensus communis*, is a kind of sixth sense needed to keep my five senses together and guarantee that it is the same object that I see, touch, taste, smell, and hear." But taken alone, she continues, common sense could not overcome "the subjectivity of the it-seems-to-me" were it not for the fact that "the same object also appears to others though its mode of appearance may be different" (*LMT*, 50). This difference in the mode of appearance, the plurality of perspectives on the same object, is crucial to our sense of realness and thus to the common world.

However important the phenomenological account of realness is to Arendt's attempt to reclaim the idea of *sensus communis* for democratic politics, it is not enough. Through the Greek idea of "learning to see politically" and the Kantian idea of "enlarged thinking," Arendt develops a conception of objectivity that goes beyond these phenomenological claims and deepens the Wittgensteinian perspective of Putnam and Cavell, which refuses philosophical and scientific conceptions of objective as something's being the case independent of how anyone would regard it. She develops a new *political* conception of objectivity for which judging in the public space is crucial to our sense of reality, of inhabiting a common world.

In claiming that Arendt develops a new political conception of objectivity based on *sensus communis*, I am aware of her tendency to put *objective* in scare quotes. I take this distancing gesture to be part of her continual struggle against a philosophical tradition that is concerned with Truth, focused on "Man in the singular," hostile to "men in the plural" and all things contingent, but nonetheless (still) held to be an authorizing metadiscourse for political theory.[100] Rather than yield the term *objective* to the philosophical tradition (or modern science), we might reclaim it for democratic theory: reclaim it as we contest noncognitive approaches to evaluative judgments without affirming cognitivism, and as we advance a practice of judging politically that resonates with Arendt's own refiguration of a humanly possible conception of objectivity in the political terms of a "common world."

For Arendt, the problem of objectivity is not—not in the first place— a question that can be addressed through various (anti-metaphysical) philosophical correctives, as important as these were in the development of her thinking. The concepts of Reality or Objectivity that metaphysics and science in their own ways forward are largely a response to skepticism or relativism understood as threats to genuine knowledge. For Arendt, however, the far greater danger lies in "radical subjectivism" or "Cartesian doubt," understood not as an epistemological problem but as the "worldlessness" or "world alienation . . . [that] has been the hallmark of the modern age."[101] Not only can this threat—which has its origin not in theories but events—not be met by various philosophical rearticulations, but it also cannot be properly understood if we remain wholly within the epistemological/philosophical paradigm in which it seems to arise.[102]

The most important consequence of "the modern age's doubt of the reality of an outer world 'objectively' given to human perception as an unchanged and unchangeable object," writes Arendt,

> was the emphasis on sensation *qua* sensation as more "real" than the "sensed" object and, at any rate, the only safe ground of experience. Against this subjectivization, which is but one aspect of the still growing world-alienation of man in the modern age, no judgments could hold out: they were all reduced to the level of sensations and ended on the level of the lowest of all sensations, the sensation of taste. Our vocabulary is a telling testimony to this degradation. All judgments not inspired by moral principle (which is felt to be old-fashioned) or not dictated by some self-interest are considered matters of "taste," and this in hardly a different sense from what we mean by saying that the preference for clam chowder over pea soup is a matter of taste. ("CH," 53)

Arendt goes on in later work to reclaim "taste" as Kant reconstructed it—namely, in terms of judgments with "subjective validity." She remained convinced, however, that, in the wake of totalitarianism and the rise of scientism and mass society, the corrosive effects of Cartesian doubt and the erosion of common sense had turned all evaluative judgments in liberal democracies into (noncognitive) subjective preferences, not because such judgments are by definition noncognitive but because the worldly conditions of their objective and shared character had been lost. In her view, this was no longer a problem of knowledge as it had arisen in early modern science but a political problem of the expansion of the social, the triumph of "life [as] our supreme and foremost concern," and the consequent decline of action and the public space ("CH," 52).[103]

What we need to grasp here is the extent to which our common sense of reality, the ordinary sense of objectivity, is *publicly* generated and sustained—not just in the crucially important sense of Wittgensteinian language games or criteria, but in the specific *political* sense of the speech and action in concert that defines the Arendtian public realm. Politically speaking, it is not just a matter of recognizing something to be an objective fact but of recognizing, counting, or acknowledging this fact as meaningful for what we do or do not have in common. That is why the withering of the public realm is so devastating in Arendt's grim view of modernity, why the corrosive effects of its disappearance go far beyond anything we might narrowly associate with political life. That is also why any restriction of what can—or how it can—be debated in the public realm in the name of saving the public realm ends up destroying it, according to Arendt. This is not to say that all subjective perspectives on the world capture things as they really are, only that any correction of a perspective would be by means of other perspectives rather than by something untainted by our affective forms of subjectivity.

The distinctively political character of objectivity, as Arendt understands it, is not restricted to the *kind* of objectivity that is proper to politics (as it is for Rawls) versus, say, the *kinds* that are proper to natural science or to ethics. As we shall see in chapter 4, these differences exist, to be sure, but Arendt's conception goes further. There is something fundamentally political to our shared sense of a common world: political, that is, in what critics find to be Arendt's rather narrow but to my mind compelling freedom-centered conception of politics, of acting and speaking in public, in the presence of one's peers. As I have argued elsewhere, for Arendt, "the raison d'etre of politics is freedom," and political freedom is based not in the "I-will" but the "I-can," which depends on other citizens who enable us to realize what we may "will."[104] Freedom is radically distinguished from "sovereignty," be it the philosophical conception of "free will" or the liberal idea of "negative freedom" (freedom *from*). Freedom is no more a state of being or a property of a subject than it is an end, something that it is the very goal or purpose of politics to secure. "It is rather the substance and meaning of all things political. In this sense, politics and freedom are identical," argues Arendt ("IP," 129).

Arendt's identification of politics with freedom includes but goes beyond "freedom of spontaneity," the Kantian idea of the human capacity to start a new series in time, which informs her conception of action as beginning anew. "Although all political freedom would forfeit its best and deepest meaning without this freedom of spontaneity, the latter is itself prepolitical" ("IP," 127), she writes. To become the I-can of Arendtian action, spontaneity must involve others, "action in concert." But because spontaneity arises from within the individual, it can survive even under conditions of tyranny and at some distance from the political realm, in her view ("IP," 127–28). Political freedom requires much more than spontaneity; it requires the freedom to speak with one another and the creation and maintenance of a "political space" within which to generate our sense of the common world ("IP," 129).

The political conception of action and freedom with speaking and acting among equals fundamentally alters our understanding of something as basic to liberal democracy as "free speech." By contrast with a narrow liberal conception, Arendt's conception of such speech as requiring a public space connects it with opinion formation, with judging as a public practice, and so with the creation and maintenance of our sense of worldly reality. Thus, what we call "free speech has always come in many different forms and with many meanings," she writes.

> The key thing, however, . . . is not that a person can say whatever he pleases, or that each of us has an inherent right to express himself just as he is. The point is, rather, that . . . no one can adequately grasp the objective world in its full reality all on his own, because the world always shows and reveals itself to him from only one perspective, which corresponds to his standpoint in the world and is determined by it. If someone wants to see and experience the world as it "really" is, he can do so only by understanding it as something that is shared by many people, lies between them, separates and links them, showing itself differently to each and comprehensible only to the extent that many people can talk *about* it and exchange their opinions and perspectives with one another, over against one another. Only in the freedom of our speaking with one another does the world, as that about which we speak, emerge in its objectivity and visibility from all sides. Living in a real world and speaking with one another about it are basically one and the same, and to the Greeks, private life seemed "idiotic" because it lacked the diversity that comes with speaking about something and thus the experience of how things really function in the world. ("IP," 128–29)

It is in this way that "political space as such realizes and guarantees both the freedom of all citizens and the reality discussed and attested to by the many," Arendt concludes ("IP," 130).

The meaning of freedom emerges in Greek society as "freedom of movement," first, in the "physical [world]" and, then, in the "mental world," argues Arendt ("IP," 168). She locates the origins of the latter, the ability "to truly *see* topics from various sides—that is, politically—" ("IP," 167) in "Homeric impartiality" which "is still the highest type of objectivity we know" ("CH," 51).[105]

Learning to see politically is to get the world in view by moving back and forth between perspectives. Were perspectives intrinsically distorting, as they are for the philosophical ideal of objectivity that Arendt (like Kant) rejects, we could not correct for one perspective by occupying other perspectives. Rather than serving as reminders of a limit, of our confinement in our human-all-too-human modes of subjectivity, perspective and affective interpretations are now taken to be the very means by which we can overcome the restrictions on seeing how things actually stand in the world that may be associated with our particular location in it. Freed from any (albeit unacknowledged) nostalgia for the metaphysical ideal of objectivity that haunts (even as it is disavowed by) many contemporary theorists of judgment, Arendt replaces "the 'extinction of the self' as the condition of [what Ranke called] 'pure vision,'" perspective untainted by anything subjective, with the ability to exchange one's own viewpoint, one's own opinion, the way the world "appears to me" and to take up the standpoints of others ("CH," 49). By "simply putting aside personal interests," she writes, we run the risk of "losing our ties to the world and our attachment to its objects and the affairs that take place in it" ("IP," 168). We lose our affective relation to the world and thus our sense of realness as something shared. The political kind of seeing that "stays in the world" is an attempt "to *understand*—not to understand one another as individual persons, but to look upon the same world from one another's standpoint, to see the same in very different and frequently opposing aspects" ("CH," 51). It concerns not what we would call the ethical practice of recognition (of the other) but the shared political practice of getting the world in view.

For Arendt, it is not the quest for objective knowledge or even truth as such that is the problem for democratic politics. This quest must in any case be part of more general practices of human flourishing. Rather, it is the mode and space in which this quest takes place. As we shall see in chapter 4, far from being hostile to the supposedly antipolitical concepts of objectivity and truth, Arendt takes them to be ordinary concepts sustained through quotidian public acts of speaking among citizens. The problem with these ordinary concepts arises when "we seek [exclusively, as it were] a meaning beyond the political realm . . . [and] like the philosophers of the polis, we choose to interact with the few rather than with the many and become convinced that speaking freely with others about something produces not reality but deception, not truth but lies" ("IP," 130). This is the idea of perspective and appearance (*dokei moi*—it-seems-to-me—opinion) as irremediably distorting that Arendt explicitly rejects. At that point, truth and objectivity become Truth and Objectivity, metaphysical ideals, the pursuit of which sets us apart from those with contrasting standpoints and thus with genuine touchstones of reality, and throws us back instead into an endless cycle of dogmatism or skepticism, animated by the fantasy of sovereignty.[106]

The plural standpoints and perspectives that make up the public realm are crucial for anything we call objective. For Arendt, to belong to a democratic political community is to have a "common world," not to share a worldview, and this common world exists only where there is a plurality of worldviews.[107]

The reality of the public realm relies on the simultaneous presence of innumerable perspectives and aspects in which the common world presents itself and for which no common measurement or denominator can ever be devised. For though the common world is the common meeting ground of all, those who are present have different locations in it, and the location of one can no more coincide with the location of another than the location of two objects. Being seen and being heard by others derive their significance from the fact that everybody sees and hears from a different position. This is the meaning of public life. . . . Only where things can be seen by many in a variety of aspects without changing their identity, so that those who are gathered around them know they see sameness in utter diversity, can worldly reality truly and reliably appear. (HC, 57)

Not only is there no common human nature that might guarantee unity in diversity, there is no "common measurement or denominator," no metacriteria according to which to adjudicate plural perspectives, only the actual public articulation of those perspectives themselves, the eliciting of ordinary criteria or "what we say," to speak with Cavell.

Our sense of what we have in common, of what is objectively given to us, can appear only when it is seen from other perspectives. These perspectives are not *mere* perspectives in the sense of irremediably distorting. Consequently, the reduction of competing perspectives results not in a world that is more shared but in a diminished sense of what we have common.[108] "If a people or nation, or even just some specific human group, which offers a unique view of the world arising from its particular position in the world—a position that . . . cannot readily be duplicated—is annihilated, it is not merely that a people or a nation or a given number of individuals perishes, but rather that a portion of our common world is destroyed, an aspect of the world that has revealed itself to us until now but can never reveal itself again," warns Arendt ("IP," 175). This is so, she adds, because "strictly speaking, politics is not so much about human beings as it is about the world that comes into being between them and endures beyond them" ("IP," 175) This world, the tangible and intangible "inter-est" or in-between whose reality emerges through acting and speaking in the shared space seen from various perspectives, is, then, quite unlike anything approaching Reality.[109]

So understood, it can sometimes sound as though the common world is given in the ontological fact of human plurality. But it is much more than that. The common world, as I wish to develop this Arendtian concept in the pages that follow, is constituted not only in and through "the fact that everybody sees and hears from a different position," but that they are also able to see from positions not their own—in short, they are able to think representatively and judge reflectively (*HC*, 57). Were the common world ontologically given, then it would be hard to see how it could ever be lost. But in Arendt's account, it surely can.[110]

Under the conditions of a common world, reality is not guaranteed primarily by the "common nature" of all men who constitute it, but rather by the fact that, differences of position and the resulting variety of perspectives notwithstanding, everybody is always concerned with the same object. If the sameness of the object can no longer be discerned, no common nature of men, least of all the unnatural conformism of a mass society, can prevent the destruction of the common world. . . . The end of the common world has come when it is seen only under one aspect and is permitted to present itself in only one perspective." (*HC*, 57–58)

However rooted the idea of plural standpoints may be in the ontological idea of human plurality, we do better to think of the common world as a political achievement requiring the creation and maintenance of public space. The common world, built as it is not only out of diverse perspectives but also out of imaginative acts of thinking and judging that take them into account, is "the space in which things become public."[111]

"If the sameness of the object can no longer be discerned, no common nature of men, least of all the unnatural conformism of a mass society, can prevent the destruction of the common world," cautions Arendt (*HC*, 58). This destruction entails the loss of plural perspectives that give us the object as the same, but it is not just that. It is a loss of the ordinary concept of perspective, according to which "perspectives are perspectives *on* something, so that *the same thing* can appear differently depending upon the perspective, from which it is viewed," as Conant describes the original concept, and the distortions in any one perspective on the same object can be corrected by other perspectives.[112] The corrosive doubt, anomie, and loneliness that characterize modern mass society, where people "are all imprisoned in the subjectivity of their own singular experience" (*HC*, 58), observes Arendt, also involves a radical change in this ordinary concept: the idea of there being a same object that is viewed from different perspectives drops out and there are only perspectives and more perspectives (understood, for example, as competing cultural or worldviews), no one any better than the other, just more entrenched, powerful, or appealing in ways that have nothing to do with rationality or better or worse ways of judging. At this point, plurality can present itself only as a threat. The task for democratic theory and public reason then becomes one of reducing the collateral damage that goes along with an ever-expanding universe of perspectives without objects.

The point at which we no longer have any sense of there being objects which we have different perspectives *on* captures the radical subjectivism that Putnam and Cavell see as the other face of an impossible objectivism. For Arendt, I have argued, such subjectivism does not so much flow *philosophically* from objectivism but is the *political* consequence of the radical shrinkage of a public space in which various perspectives can attest to the existence of a common object. It is the idea that perspectives with no object are all we have that leads us to grope around for new (albeit neutral) standards of judgment, as if they could solve the problem of relativism that attends not plural perspectives, as is commonly thought, but the loss of the objects that these perspectives are perspectives *on*. It is this loss of these objects as it is figured in our mistrust toward ordinary perspectives, rather than relativism as the immanent threat in plural perspectives, that defines the current predicament—even crisis—of judging in democratic societies.

Indeed, the scare of relativism that animates most contemporary theories of judgment does not begin to get at—but rather misconstrues —what is at stake in this radical transformation of our ordinary concept of perspective. For one thing, the idea that all perspectives are equal, that none is better than another, does not belong to the original concept of perspective, for which corrigibility by other perspectives is central. Furthermore, the erosion of our ordinary concept of perspective cannot be made good by returning to an objectivist conception of the world. It is objectivism, rather, that leads in large part to an erosion of our ordinary concept of perspective, putting in its place the impossible ideal of a perspective-free knowledge. Most important, in Arendt's account, this change in the ordinary concept of perspective is brought about not by philosophical theories of reality but by events, not by philosophical debates about objectivity but by genuine changes in the character of the modern world. Her wager is that we can recover the ordinary concept of perspective not through philosophical critique—as useful as this may be—but through the practice of acting and judging politically.

As we shall see in chapters 4 and 8, this radical alteration in our concept of perspective is what we now understand by "perspectivism," according to which "our so-called 'knowledge of the world' is never really of something independent, but consists of nothing more than our possible perspectives themselves and *nothing beyond these*," to cite Conant.[113] Consider Arthur Danto's description of the radical epistemology that he ascribes to Nietzsche:

The doctrine that there are no facts but only interpretations [is] termed *Perspectivism*. To be sure, we speak of seeing the same thing from different perspectives, and we might allow that there is no way to see the thing *save* through a perspective and, finally, that there is no one perspective privileged over any other. These would be logical features of the concept of perspective. The only difficulty here is in talking about the "same thing" on which these are distinct perspectives. Certainly we cannot say what *it* is except from one or another perspective, and we cannot speak about it as it is in itself. . . . We can meaningfully say nothing, then, about whatever it is on which these are perspectives. We cannot speak of a true perspective, but only of a perspective that prevails. Because we cannot appeal to any fact independently of its relation to the perspective it is meant to support, and we can do little more than insist on our perspective, and try, if we can, to impose it on others.[114]

Apart from the extraordinary philological acrobatics required to keep speaking of perspective when every connection with the ordinary meaning has been severed, this passage could have been written by Ayer or any of the noncognitivists described earlier—save one crucial difference: now there is no possibility of talking about a shared objective world at all. There is no "absolute conception of the world" that—so noncognitivists claim—preserves the idea of the world as it is in itself. In this way perspectivism can seem to be unflinching in its willingness to draw the sober consequences (i.e., there are only perspectives, there are no facts) of the loss of the "true world" so vividly described by Nietzsche.[115] But this is an illusion. The perspectivist idea that we are debarred from speaking about a true perspective or anything approaching a genuine glimpse of the object is just the flip side of the objectivist view of the world that it claims to reject: both accept the idea that what is objective must be free of any admixture of human subjectivity.

We have seen that Arendt's celebration of plural perspectives needs to be supplemented by a standard of judgment, critics claim, if she is to avoid the relativism that they associate with perspectivism (and which has also wrongly, as James Conant shows, been ascribed to Nietzsche).[116] Arendt did not seek such a standard, I argued in the first part of this chapter, because she was interested in the prior question of how it is that citizens get objects of judgment into view in the first place. We can now see another reason why judging was not the problem of finding common validity criteria. According to the logic of the ordinary concept of perspective as corrigible by other perspectives (to which Arendt held, even as she recognized its erosion in modernity), the philosophical problem of objectivity understood in the political terms of worldlessness represented a crisis in the variety of perspectives from which to get the world in view, not the absence of a standard according to which existing perspectives on existing objects of judgment could be adjudicated. The situation of mass society is one in which we have not too *many* but too *few* perspectives from which to see the world. Accordingly, it is not adjudication but pluralization and the expansion of the common world that should concern us. This expansion of the common world can be achieved only through the expansion of the public space, for it is in that space that genuine differences of perspective can be expressed and judged—that is, corrected by other perspectives. Once again, the articulation of multiple perspectives does not in itself guarantee critical and reflective judgment, but without them, the individual perspective from which I now see the world (i.e., partially) could never be revealed to me as *my* perspective at all; it will more likely be taken as the whole of what is real.

Working with the ordinary concept of perspective that is missing in the aforementioned critiques of her work, Arendt argues that (1) anything that can count as a perspective (*dokei moi*) must afford a view of the object (i.e., is not qua perspective "merely" subjective or illusory); (2) we need to occupy, often through the power of imagination, alternate perspectives if we wish to gain a truer view of the object; (3) we need to compare the different views afforded by different perspectives; and (4) the more views we not only can but do compare, the more objective our perspective will be.[117] It is on the basis of this ordinary concept of perspective that Arendt redescribes Kantian "enlarged thought" as representative thinking:

Political thought is representative. I form an opinion by considering a given issue from different viewpoints, by making present to my mind the standpoints of those who are absent; that is, I represent them. This process of representation does not blindly adopt the actual views of those who stand somewhere else, and hence look upon the world from a different perspective; this is a question neither of empathy, as though I tried to be or to feel like somebody else, nor of counting noses and joining a majority but of being and thinking in my own identity where actually I am not. The more people's standpoints I have present in my mind while I am pondering a given issue, and the better I can imagine how I would feel and think if I were in their place, the stronger will be my capacity for representative thinking and the more valid my final conclusions, my opinion. (It is this capacity for an "enlarged mentality" that enables men to judge; as such, it was discovered by Kant in the first part of his *Critique of Judgment*, though he did not recognize the political and moral implications of his discovery.) ("TP," 241)

To explore the democratic world-building potential of representative thinking as it will figure in subsequent chapters and our discussion of judging politically, we will need to free it from the epistemological straightjacket of perspectivism as it is *misunderstood* (i.e., as entailing the opposition "subjective versus objective"). To say with Nietzsche, "All evaluation is made from a definite perspective," is to affirm that when I call this painting "beautiful," this act "unjust," this war "wrong," I assert the perspective- or subject-dependence of my (evaluative) judgment without conceding, as the noncognitivists would have it, that aesthetic, moral, and political qualities are not genuine features of the world but merely subjective projections or affective interpretations.[118] "It is to appreciate that a property can be subjective (i.e., one whose very conception involves essential reference to how a thing which possesses such a property affects the subject) *and* objective (i.e., one that applies not only to how things seem, but to how things are)," as Conant summarizes the significance of this ordinary concept of perspective.[119]

Returning to this ordinary concept of perspective brings with it commitments for a democratic theory of judgment that may not at first be apparent. Representative thinking is not a matter of merely accumulating more and more perspectives from which to see the world, it is learning how to *count* these other perspectives as revealing something *about* the world. To approach judging through this ordinary concept of perspective is to *acknowledge* perspectives other than one's own, without denying that each perspective has blind spots of its own. As Arendt will say, judging based in representative thinking is not a matter of "counting noses," as if the democratic problem of judgment were solved through aggregation.

We may well resist revising our view of any given object based on the more expansive perspective afforded by representative thinking. The often tenacious resistance of our beliefs to rational revision based on what Arendt calls "seeing politically" (from other standpoints) is largely attributable to entrenched relations of power and hierarchy—relations that Arendt's writings do not always adequately take into account. The "unwillingness to amend immediate judgment in the light of reflection [based on evidence]," as Michael Rosen describes the puzzle that so occupied the thought of David Hume, is a genuine problem that representative thinking alone does not address but any plausible democratic theory of judgment surely must.[120]

Developing the capacity to judge politically in Arendt's critical and reflective sense would involve rational revision of our beliefs—though not all or all at once—by seeing them as connected with our unjust social practices, rather than as the consequence of our flawed psychology, as Hume and the noncognitive tradition after him has tended to view irrational belief. Recovering the ordinary concept of perspective will allow us to refigure judging beyond the view of evaluative judgments as merely subjective projections of value onto the world. Though our perspectives can distort, understanding *how* they distort requires that we first free ourselves from the thought that perspectives *always* distort, and in just this way. Let us turn now to the classic debate on the objectivity of evaluative judgments in the work of Hume and Kant.

TWO

Judging at the "End of Reasons": Rethinking the Aesthetic Turn

If one judges objects in accordance with concepts, then all representation of beauty is lost. Thus there can also be no rule in accordance with which someone could be compelled to acknowledge something as beautiful. Whether a garment, a house, a flower is beautiful: no one allows himself to be talked into his judgment about that by means of any grounds or fundamental principles. One wants to submit the object to his own eyes, just as if his satisfaction depended on sensation; and yet, if one then calls the object beautiful, one believes oneself to have a universal voice, and lays claim to the consent of everyone, whereas any private sensation would be decisive only for him alone and his satisfaction.   KANT, CRITIQUE OF JUDGMENT[1]

Kant's landmark *Critique of [the Power of] Judgment*, published in 1790, is often credited with establishing modern aesthetics as an autonomous discipline. Though many other philosophers, both before and after Kant, have taken up questions about the nature of beauty, the sublime, art, and genius, no text has had such a lasting influence nor defined the terms of the debate about aesthetic experience as the third *Critique*. This fact reflects not only Kant's intellectual standing in the Western philosophical canon but also, more important, the manner in which he at once relegated judgments of taste to the register of subjectivity, thereby excluding them, on his own terms, from any claim to knowledge, *and* insisted that such judgments, though not objective, make a claim to the agreement of all—they speak with a "universal voice."

In claiming that a judgment, "whose determining ground [*Bestimmungsgrund*] *cannot* be *other than subjective*" (*CJ*, §1, p. 44/89), can at the same time make a claim to speak for all, Kant departed from a long tradition of thinking about beauty. Philosophers before him tended to think about beauty in one of two ways: either they saw beauty as objective and judgments of taste as universally valid, or they regarded beauty as subjective and judgments about it as having no more than private validity. Carving out a third path, Kant took up aspects of both subjective and objective views of beauty, combining them into a startling claim about the "subjective universality" (*CJ*, §6, p. 54/97) of a judgment of taste.

How can a judgment that is subjective, based solely on the judging subject's feeling of pleasure in the beautiful and without the mediation of a concept, claim universal validity—demand, that is, the agreement of all?[2] This is the initial and arguably the central question raised in *The Critique of Aesthetic Judgment*, which forms the first part of the third *Critique* and which has been at the center not only of much of the secondary philosophical literature on the text but also—more important for my purposes—of the debate about the relevance of Kant's aesthetics to democratic politics. This debate, we recall, turns in large part on the so-called missing cognitive foundation for judgment, the criterial basis for redeeming validity claims which Jürgen Habermas, among other critics, protests in any political theoretical appropriation of Kantian aesthetics, most famously that of Hannah Arendt ("ACCP," 225).[3]

It is a debate that presents us with a choice between determinative versus reflective judgments, cognitive versus noncognitive judgments: judgments that are based on the rule-governed application of concepts to particulars versus judgments that are based on feeling and in which concepts are lacking. To model political judgment on aesthetic (reflective) judgment, so the critique of Arendt goes, is to relinquish any criterion according to which to adjudicate competing judgments and to invite charges of emotivism, decisionism, and irrationalism. After all, how can a judgment based on mere feeling and lacking any means of proof possibly be the subject of a public debate? How could it possibly claim validity? Does this not leave democratic theory helpless in the face of the impossible equality of judgments that David Hume ridiculed in his description of the "Ogilby-Milton phenomenon"?[4]

Hume's Answer

To appreciate what is valuable for democratic politics in Kant's idea of subjective universality, it is instructive to begin with David Hume's 1757 essay, "Of the Standard of Taste," which likewise holds beauty to be no property of objects, thus confronting the problem of subjective relativism. Hume sets out the problem in terms of two conflicting species of common sense.[5] The first accords with a certain "species of [modern] philosophy," he writes, for which "beauty is no quality in things themselves: It exists merely in the mind which contemplates them; and each mind perceives a different beauty" ("ST," 229, 230). Differences of taste are expressions not of fact but of "sentiment," for which there is no standard of correctness: "All sentiment is right; because sentiment has a reference to nothing beyond itself, and is always real, wherever a man is conscious of it" ("ST," 230). On this view, then, beauty is wholly subjective, nonrepresentational, and noncognitive; it refers only to the subject's pleasure. Accordingly, "the proverb [or species of common sense] has justly determined it to be fruitless to dispute concerning tastes" ("ST," 230); instead, "every individual ought to acquiesce in his own sentiment, without pretending to regulate those of others" ("ST," 230).[6]

Whereas the first species of common sense yields an attitude of tolerance, there is another "species of common sense which opposes it, at least serves to modify and restrain it" ("ST," 230), contends Hume. We become aware of this species when confronted with taste that "would assert an equality of genius and elegance between OGILBY and MILTON, or BUNYAN and ADDISON" ("ST," 230–31). One might as well hold "a mole-hill to be as high as TENERIFFE, or a pond as extensive as the ocean" ("ST," 231), remarks Hume. In the face of such "absurd and ridiculous" comparisons, he declares, "the principle of the natural equality of tastes is then totally forgot" ("ST," 231). True, we can grant that there is no disputing about taste in matters where the objects compared are similar or "seem near an equality," but not "where objects so disproportioned are compared together" ("ST," 231). In cases where there is already strong agreement, we can tolerate some disagreement, but not where our tastes diverge so widely as to be almost unrecognizable as belonging to the same class of objects. On what basis, then, can we adjudicate vastly disparate sentiments?

"It is natural for us to seek a *Standard of Taste*; a rule, by which the various sentiments of men may be reconciled; at least, a decision, afforded, confirming one sentiment, and condemning another" ("ST," 229), affirms Hume. Hume is committed to thinking about taste and its standard in empirical and broadly naturalistic terms. He is committed to the very "modern philosophy" (empiricism) which holds "reason" and "taste" to be irreducibly distinct faculties of mind, the former giving us genuine knowledge of objects as they really stand in nature, the latter "gilding or staining all natural objects with the colours," as Hume writes, "borrowed from internal sentiment."[7] Unfortunately, he observes, this same philosophy "represents the impossibility of ever attaining any standard of taste" ("ST," 229).

Notwithstanding his agreement with modern philosophy's bifurcated conception of mind (reason versus sentiment) and the resulting aesthetic (and more broadly evaluative) noncognitivism it entails, Hume is clearly averse to the relativity of taste that flows from its projectivist treatment of beauty. Hume sees that we do dispute taste and we do demand the agreement of others. And we rightly believe that our judgments have normative force. He sees the difference, as Kant would later put it, between the "agreeable" and the "beautiful." Hume's problem, then, is how to account for the correctness or incorrectness of a judgment that is based on sentiment, a noncognitive affective state that, by his own definition, is incapable of truth—aptly representing the world or disclosing its genuine features and therefore "not susceptible of this agreement or disagreement."[8] How can a value judgment, a judgment of beauty, be normative without relinquishing its basis in noncognitive sentiment?

Any answer to this question, argues Susan Hahn, must take seriously Hume's skepticism.[9] It is surely right to wonder why the skeptic Hume would seek, let alone find, "a *timeless* and *invariant* standard for judging beauty [e.g., rules of art, the consensus of experts]," as Hahn, with good reason, characterizes the shared verdict of otherwise diverse interpretations of Hume's aesthetics.[10] That Hume did not posit such a standard does not mean he relinquished the idea of there being a standard at all. "The very possibility of error presupposes the existence of a norm. Something must be operating at a hidden, deeper level, which is guiding our practice," Hahn writes.[11] A Pyrrhonian skeptic, Hume need only "say that this norm is unknown and unknowable on ontological/epistemological grounds," not deny its possibility.[12] Staying at a "descriptive level," he must remain "neutral . . . on the difference between repeated coincidence and a consensus that is tracking the genuinely beautiful," she adds, "exactly what one would hope for and expect from a sceptic who insisted on keeping the fact/value distinction sharp."[13] In Hahn's view, Hume presents us with a "natural deduction" that discovers a "hidden strong realist standard" of taste.[14] What this hidden standard amounts to we shall soon see.

To read Hume as presenting a *natural* deduction of taste is compelling given the way in which his text resonates with what is surely the most famous deduction of taste—namely, the *transcendental* deduction given in Kant's third *Critique*.[15] But why, we might wonder, did Hume think he needed to seek a *standard*—that is, rules or principles—of taste at all?[16] This question is all the more pressing when we consider that Hume is rightly seen as framing the problem of taste in terms of two species of common sense that can be read as foreshadowing—if not directly influencing; opinions differ—the "Antinomy of Taste" in Kant's text, which also concerns the problem of normativity but whose solution declares the very idea of a "principle of taste" to be "absolutely impossible."[17] Most attempts at an answer blame Hume's lingering entanglement in neoclassical criticism for which rules of composition were paramount.[18] Alternatively, he is said to have sought an objective standard to defend against the skepticism of his own subjectivist aesthetics, though this alchemy of subjective and objective proved to be fatal for his project.[19]

Each of these explanations has its merits. For my purposes, the important matter concerns how Hume's way of framing the problem of taste as a search for principles cannot shake free the idea that there must be something external to the human practice of judgment that would allow us to decide the question of correctness—failing that, aesthetic judgments cannot be rational. To be rational, the evaluative language employed would have to adhere to what John McDowell calls "usual paradigms of concept-application to count as expressive of judgements at all (as opposed to a kind of sounding off)."[20] In other words, what Hume detects as the albeit divergent yet nonrandom character of our aesthetic practices, justifying his claim that there *must* be a standard, would have to amount to something other than the mere coincidence of private sensations. It is a matter not, as Hahn would have it, of staying neutral on whether the repeated coincidence of tastes amounts to a consensus on what is truly beautiful but, rather, of showing that we can speak of a *judgment* of taste and agreement *in* judgments at all. If he is to seek, let alone find, a standard, Hume must show that evaluative thinking is a matter of genuine concept application—that is to say, of going on to do the same thing. The question is whether his projectivism can accommodate the idea of concept application that a standard of taste implies. Although Hume, as a good empiricist, must locate the (albeit hidden) source of normativity within human practices, as Hahn claims, his projectivist view of values is under continuous pressure to seek external grounds for judgments of taste that point beyond the affective responses that, on his own account, are the sole source of any standard of taste.

As we saw in the last chapter, this pressure is internal to a naturalism that takes for granted what Bernard Williams calls "the absolute conception of the world."[21] According to this conception, as it is expressed in the eighteenth-century philosophy of mind represented by Hume, there is a strict distinction between cognitive capacities and their exercise, on the one hand, and passions or sentiments, on the other; a radical difference, then, between empirical judgments and evaluative (aesthetic, moral, political) judgments: the former belong to the "operation of reasoning," writes Hume, in which "the mind does nothing but run over its objects, as they are supposed to stand in reality, without adding any thing to them, or diminishing any thing from them. . . . To this operation of the mind, therefore, there seems to be always a real, though often an unknown standard, in the nature of things; nor is truth or falsehood variable by the various apprehensions of mankind."[22] When we pronounce something "beautiful," however, we do not simply "run over" the objects of thought as they are supposed to stand in reality but rather add our affective reaction, which varies with our subjective natures: "nor can the same object, presented to a mind totally different, produce the same sentiment."[23] In Hume's view, as Peter Kivy parses these remarks, "we lack, in our aesthetic judgements, the 'external standard' which our factual judgements possess. The quest for a standard of taste, then, is a quest for such an external standard. The Humean programme in aesthetics is the translation of value judgements into factual judgements—judgements of sentiment into judgements of reason."[24] Beauty, were it real, would need to be intelligible from a standpoint independent of the feeling of pleasure occasioned by beautiful objects.

But of course Hume's point is not to defend the idea that beauty is real; rather, it is to show that we can speak of a standard for judging something that precisely is *not* real, with real understood, on the absolute conception, as how things are anyway, independently of our value experience of them. Now this search for a standard itself already expresses a concern about how value experience, in this case aesthetic experience, relates to the world so understood—that is what Hume's projectivism would explain. How, then, are we to understand that projectivism?

One way to think about Hume's famous metaphor of "gilding or staining" would be to follow the lead of Barry Stroud and John Mackie, both of whom (albeit in different ways and with different theoretical agendas) interpret Hume's projectivism as offering an "error theory" of value, according to which our sentiments lead us to a mistaken understanding of what is really there in the world.[25] Sentiments such as vice and virtue, heat and cold, sounds and colors, beauty and deformity are no quality of objects "as they really stand in nature" but something "new" (a sentiment) added by the mind.[26] For Hume, as Stroud succinctly puts it, "What you think to be true of the 'object' simply isn't there."[27]

There is much to be said for this reading of Hume, but it does not do justice to the spirit of his later reflections on taste.[28] Although there are several passages that endorse the "error theory," the bulk of the essay is concerned not with exposing a kind of universal human mistake in aesthetic judgments but with understanding how we can avoid the "Milton-Ogilby" problem and properly adjudicate disparate ways of evaluating aesthetic objects. Accordingly, projectivism is still an apt description of what we do when we make such judgments in Hume's view, only it cannot be adequately understood as an "error theory" but attempts instead to describe how we actually talk about such objects, a kind of grammar of aesthetic debate that will be crucial to the aesthetic theory of Kant. Following Simon Blackburn's interpretation of Hume's projectivism as an explanatory theory, we might say that rather than uncover some mistaken referential presumption in our thinking about beauty (i.e., we believe that beauty is in the object but it is not), Hume describes how we express our sentiments without falling into error: we call things beautiful while remaining quite aware that beauty is no real property of things.[29] Leaving aside for a moment the question of whether we can actually engage in a debate (agree or disagree) about something that we freely admit to be a mere "phantasm" of our affective nature, the question I want to pose now is whether, as an explanatory theory, Hume's projectivism can adequately address the problem of concept application noted earlier.

We are right to assume that a standard must exist, argues Hume, for how else could we explain agreement in judgments on things such as masterpieces? ("ST," 233).[30] But if the standard were everywhere operative, how could we explain disagreement and its defense in the old adage *de gustibus non est disputandum* (there is no disputing about taste)? Hume's answer introduces the idea of dispositional properties, the so-called secondary qualities that the "modern philosophy" distinguishes from "primary qualities" (e.g., solidity, extension, figure) by virtue of their producing certain sense-data in us, which is processed by the mind in such a way that it then projects the corresponding sentiments onto the external world as if these secondary properties were real (intrinsic) properties of objects. Accordingly, "though it be certain, that beauty and deformity . . . are not qualities in objects, but belong entirely to the sentiment . . . it must be allowed, that there are certain qualities in objects, which are fitted by nature to produce those particular feelings" ("ST," 235). Just as we speak of something's "true and real colour, even while colour is allowed to be merely a phantasm of the senses" ("ST," 234), so too we speak of real beauty as if beauty were a property of things. Here we seem to have, then, what Hahn called the "hidden strong realist standard" endorsed by Hume: the "hidden causal properties (qualities and form) in art objects [that] are causing perceivers to judge as they do."[31]

"In Hume's official theory," as David Wiggins rightly observes, "this [account of the hidden qualities of objects] is not meant to count against the Humean denial that virtue, viciousness, merit, *etc.* are in the object itself."[32] And yet the place of the object in human practices of valuation haunts Hume's quest for a standard, as we shall see. At this point in the essay, Hume struggles to make sense of what allowing for the dispositional properties of objects to cause certain sentiments in subjects can mean for explaining the lack of agreement in taste that his standard would address. On Hume's account, disagreement is to be explained in terms of "defects in the internal organs which prevent or weaken the influence of those general principles [of taste], on which depends our sentiment of beauty or deformity" ("ST," 234).[33] Some men suffer from a lack of "delicacy of taste" ("ST," 235), whether for psychological, cultural, or physical reasons, while the defective beauty sensibility in others can be traced to inadequacies in the context in which an object is viewed ("ST," 232–33). And so on. "Thus, though the principles of taste be universal, and nearly, if not entirely the same in all men; yet few are qualified to give judgment on any work of art, or establish their own sentiment as the standard of beauty" ("ST," 241), declares Hume.

The analogy Hume posits between color experience and value experience, as he makes the case for a universal (albeit in some individuals defective) beauty-sensibility, can be seen as characteristic of the Lockean distinction between primary and secondary qualities, and thus as endorsing the idea that only the former are real properties of objects.[34] "If, that is, we suppose that how things really are can be exhaustively characterized in primary quality terms," writes McDowell, "then we can explain why our colour experience is as it is without representing it as strictly veridical: the explanation reveals the extent to which the world as colour experience presents it to us is mere appearance—the extent to which colour vision fails to be a transparent mode of access to something that is there anyway."[35] What appeals in this picture is not just the thought that we have discovered an error but also the idea that one could make the case for knowing how to go on, and thus the rationality of an evaluative concept, by means of what noncognitivists, following in the steps of John Locke and Hume, claim to be "two components" of evaluative thinking: a cognitive state, which registers the presence of (primary) properties in an appearance that are really there but contain no values, and a noncognitive state, which "enriche[s that cognition of these properties] . . . with the reflection of an attitude."[36] As I argued in the last chapter, the picture is appealing because the so-called evaluative or subjective part of a value judgment (how something appears to me) can in this way "hook" onto the descriptive part (that which is not merely as it appears to me but as it is), much as a secondary property such as color hooks onto a primary quality such as extension. That is why Hume, defending the idea that there must be a standard, says that we can speak of the real and true color of a thing, knowing that color is a "phantasm."

Following McDowell, I argued in chapter 1 that this "disentangling manoeuvre" cannot work, and the thought that it can work almost inevitably leads to an attempt to isolate and cognize the descriptive feature that is there in the world, independently of anyone's value experience being what it is, by means of a conception of rules as rails.[37] We shall find this happening in Hume, but that is not the point I want to make right now. What concerns us here is that this "disentangling manoeuvre" can be brought into question from within Hume's own writing. Rather than giving his unqualified endorsement to the Lockean distinction between primary and secondary qualities, Hume can be seen as criticizing it.[38] In the *Treatise* and the *Enquiry*, Hume, taking up the distinction put forward by "modern enquirers" that secondary properties exist only in the mind, goes on—like Berkeley—to say that the same claim must be extended to primary properties:

If colours, sounds, tastes, and smells be merely perceptions, nothing we can conceive is possest of a real, continu'd, and independent existence; not even motion, extension and solidity, which are the primary qualities chiefly insisted on.[39]

We cannot disentangle primary from secondary qualities (e.g., the shape of the apple from the redness of the apple) in such a way as to sustain the reality of the former while treating the latter as mere phantasm. Thus, Hume does not, finally, accept the Lockean distinction between primary and secondary qualities, but his rejection—or at least deep questioning—of it is not to affirm, with Berkeley, that even a primary quality such as extension is mere phantasm.[40] Berkeley's radical idealism (i.e., primary properties, like secondary properties, are *mere* appearances or perceptions) is what Hume has in mind when he observes in the *Treatise* that the distinction, "instead of explaining the operations of external objects . . . we utterly annihilate all these objects, and reduce ourselves to the opinions of the most extravagant skepticism concerning them."[41]

In light of this passage, A. E. Pitson would have us read Hume's rejection of the Lockean distinction as an affirmation not of (Berkeley's) idealism but of a "commitment to the reality of *both* kinds of quality."[42] But that would be to lose track of Hume's skepticism and projectivism. I think we do better to note it as marking a tension in Hume's thought generally, a kind of long-standing struggle with the ordinary (i.e., public) character of judgment, which takes for granted an ordinary concept of perspective, according to which, as argued in the last chapter, all perspectives can distort but no one kind of perspective (e.g., related to secondary features) is irremediably distorting, as James Conant showed us.[43] Pressed by Berkeley's query as to why, given that for empiricists all experience is based on appearances, some forms of appearance refer to what is really there in the object while others do not, Hume's later reflections on taste are shot through with a deep worry: without this primal empiricist cut between primary and secondary qualities, modern philosophy's claim that "no sentiment represents what is really in the object" ("ST," 230) will leak into all appearances and so into all our judgments, and in this way impugn all perspectives as distortions of how the world really is. Consequently, we will be left with *only* the first species of common sense, *de gustibus non est disputandum*, writ large, so to speak. We will have no adequate response to the "Ogilby-Milton" problem, no hope of finding a standard of taste or for that matter anything else. Hume struggles with how to articulate the cut that is crucial to avoiding this fate but also philosophically unsustainable. It is no surprise, then, that some commentators read Hume as treating a quality such as beauty, experienced as internal sentiment, as mere phantasm, while others read him as saying that such a quality actually belongs to objects.[44] Although there are textual grounds for reading him both ways, my central claim is that Hume can never quite free himself from the logic of projectivism (even in its more appealing version as an "explanatory" [rather than an "error"] theory) because he does not have a way to talk about how affective response could be world-giving without ascribing to it the kind of objectivity that belongs to the absolute conception of the world. Consequently, Hume can never make good on his otherwise important insights into the public (i.e., normative) character of aesthetic disagreement and the subjective aspect of any objective judgment.

If the "disentangling manoeuvre" described by McDowell cannot work, what will secure the normativity of taste? The idea, we recall, was that the unknown standard that exists in the nature of things, in the world conceived as independent of any one person's particular value experience, was somehow guiding judgments of taste in such a way as to explain them *as judgments*, instances of competence with an evaluative concept, rather than a mere sounding off. The search for such a standard required that value judgments become factual judgments. This move is visible in Hume's well-known oscillation between what appear to be two standards: on the one hand, the standard is "a rule, by which the various sentiments of men may be reconciled" ("ST," 229); on the other hand, the standard is not a rule but a certain type of person, the "true judge" ("ST," 241) who is free of "defects in the internal organs which prevent or weaken the influence of those general principles [of taste], on which depends our sentiment of beauty or deformity" ("ST," 234). "Strong sense, united to delicate sentiment, improved by practice, perfected by comparison, and cleared of all prejudice, can alone entitle critics to this valuable character; and the joint verdict of such, wherever they are to be found, is the true standard of taste and beauty" ("ST," 241), declares Hume. According to the rule definition, we know who the "true judges" are by virtue of their conformity to the (universal) rules. According to the ideal critic definition, we discover what the rules are by first identifying the "true judges" independently of the rules. We learn the rules by watching the true judges judge.[45]

Hume's effort to steer a course between aesthetic relativism and aesthetic rationalism lands him, then, in what Kivy, echoing most commentators, calls "a vicious circle."[46] This circularity reflects Hume's search for something that is the proper object of a judgment, which is to say, subject to a norm of correctness. Whereas "all sentiment is right," as Hume told us, "all determinations of the understanding are not right; because they have a reference to something beyond themselves, to wit, real matter of fact; and are not always conformable to that standard" ("ST," 230). On what basis can we decide the question of the true judge? "By what marks are they to be known? How [do we] distinguish them from pretenders? These questions are embarrassing; and seem to throw us back into the same uncertainty, from which, during the course of this essay, we have endeavoured to extricate ourselves" ("ST," 241), Hume ponders, referring to the uncertainty of judgments based on sentiment. Yet Hume reassures:

But if we consider the matter aright, these are questions of fact, not of sentiment. Whether any particular person be endowed with good sense and a delicate imagination, free from prejudice, may often be the subject of dispute, and be liable to great discussion and enquiry: But that such a character is valuable and estimable will be agreed in by all mankind. Where these doubts occur, men can do no more than in other disputable questions, which are submitted to the understanding: They must produce the best arguments, that their invention suggests to them; they must acknowledge a true and decisive standard to exist somewhere, to wit, real existence and matter of fact. ("ST," 242)

Striking here, as Wiggins observes, is that Hume "takes himself to need to see [the ideal judge] as (in his terms) a real existence or matter of fact. So that it suddenly appears that, if we pass over the properties of the object itself [as Hume's projectivism requires], then a life-like philosophical subjectivism requires a *non*-subjective foundation as well as the support of a substantial conception of a nearly homogeneous human nature."[47] I have already suggested that Hume needs to make this move to an external standard of taste due to his adherence to a bifurcated conception of mind that distinguishes between cognitive belief states, which are subject to norms of correctness, and noncognitive affective states, which are not. The question is whether this move to establish the ideal judge as a matter of fact, and thus as available for *arguments* based on the understanding's application of concepts (what Kant will call "disputing"), can succeed. To anticipate the discussion that follows: In his move to so-called matters of fact, Hume occludes that which his refusal to accept the relativist consequences of the subjective character of taste has discovered—namely, that we can *quarrel* about taste, as Kant will put it, though we cannot *dispute* about it. This means that we can speak about a particular judgment as being right or wrong, though we cannot apply principles of taste as proofs.

Notwithstanding Hume's apparent satisfaction that he has kept "the fact/value distinction sharp," to speak with Hahn, it is hard to see how the judgment about who counts as a true judge could any the less involve the highly evaluative aspect that, as the projection of sentiment, can make no claim to correctness.[48] Moreover, just when we thought we had finally found the standard in the verdict of judges whose status as "true" has been confirmed as fact, Hume puts forward all manner of qualifications that undermine it. He suggests that the sentiments of young and old judges, present and past judges, European and non-European judges, and so on may well so differ (based on their places in historical time and space) that no "uniform verdicts" can arise.

Complicating the lack of agreement among the true judges, whose joint verdict was to constitute the standard, is the concern that, even in cases where such a consensus can be found, it is not obvious why anyone who is not a true judge should care. As Jerrold Levinson puts it, "Why are the works enjoyed and preferred by *ideal* critics characterized as Hume characterizes them ones that *I* should . . . aesthetically pursue?"[49] Why should their judgments, which are rooted in their sentiments, be authoritative for me? What makes the feelings of these critics "credible *indicators*" of beauty?[50] To be credible, in other words, they cannot be simply *constitutive* of the standard; they must point to something in the world. "What Hume needs, but has not quite succeeded in articulating," writes Anthony Savile, "is unabashed reference to something in the world for the good judge to detect distinct from the sentiments, yet distinct also from any supposed rules and principles [any external standard] that can be specified without reference to our sentiments and responses."[51]

Even if we accept the rules definition of the standard, it is far from certain how this would settle cases where disputes arise. Hume assumes that the critic whose judgment does not conform to the rule will be forced, based on his acceptance of the rules, to admit he is mistaken. But if pleasure can arise for us even in those cases where the rule is not followed, as Hume himself suggests when he explains how rules may change over time, then it is not clear why the critic must concede defeat. "In other words, there seems to be nothing to prevent the imagined antagonist . . . from sticking to his guns and simply adopting the position that the rule in question does not apply in the present case," writes Brent Kalar. "After all, the grounds of the rule are still held by

Hume to be ultimately empirical."[52] The tenacity of the judger, even when confronted with arguments based on rules of taste, is something that Kant will cite as evidence for his own view that the whole problem of the validity of aesthetic judgments has been misconstrued as a question of rules. Or, to put this tenacity in the Wittgensteinian terms discussed later in this chapter and in chapter 9, what is to prevent the wayward critic from insisting that he or she is in fact following the rule—to which the critic's antagonist could only reply, "But don't you *see*?"

If Hume vacillates on what the standard could possibly be, that is because he does not have a clear conception of the problem for which a standard of correctness is the solution. He is at once loath to reduce taste to what people ordinarily say or how they judge and (as a good empiricist) also unwilling to describe—as a rationalist would—a standard that exists independently of the affective responses of these ordinary judging subjects. Since he cannot conceive of their responses as anything other than "phantasms," he needs a way to bring order to what would otherwise be the mere coincidence of sensibilities. Consequently, Hume is driven to insinuate a rule that we must be following—what Hahn called the hidden realist standard—beneath the descriptions of what people actually say when they make judgments of taste. In this sense Hume's exasperated search for a standard expresses an effort to escape what (in chapter 1) Stanley Cavell called the "vertigo" that accompanies the "whirl of organism" that is the real "ground" of our mutual intelligibility in taste as it is in all judging.

The quest for a standard of taste, even if it were realized, would not settle, as Hume seems to believe it should, the problem of how conflicting parties might be brought to agree in any critical aesthetic dispute. From Kant's perspective, to accept the verdict of the "true judge" would be tantamount to "heteronomy," a failure to feel pleasure in the object and thus judge for oneself. The danger of heteronomy will animate no small part of Kant's rejection of the quest for a standard that consumes Hume.[53] But this Kantian critique, as Savile rightly observes, neglects Hume's awareness, albeit deeply buried beneath this quest, that to bring someone to share my judgment cannot be, when all is said and done, a matter of reminding him or her of the rules—which at some point leads to an infinite regress—or the true judge or any other so-called matter of fact. It must be a matter of getting the person to see what I see, to share, that is, my affective response.[54] It is a matter neither of telling the person what to believe, based on the facts, nor of merely imitating a sentiment that is not his or her own. The possibility of bringing about this shared affective response, I would add, takes for granted that the perspectives from which each of us sees the object may be distorted but are corrigible by other perspectives. I try to get you to see the same object as I see it, to see it in another way. But this whole effort would be meaningless if how each of us sees were nothing but the projection of sentiment onto a world otherwise devoid of values. It is meaningless if we cannot conceive of judgments of taste as "exercises of our affective or conative natures either as themselves in some way percipient, or at least as expanding our sensitivity to how things are," as McDowell writes.[55]

Hume's search for a standard revealed his recognition that aesthetic judgments tell us something about their objects and not just about the judging subject's mental state, but he could not free himself from the thought, fundamental to the absolute conception of the world, that whatever is not the projection of a sentiment onto an object must be independent of anyone's value experience. "Let us now abandon Hume's aspiration to secure the standard of correctness in valuation from outside the domain of values, or by sole reference to the qualified judge," to speak with Wiggins, and see how the world-giving power of aesthetic response is at once acknowledged and suppressed in Kant.[56]

Kant's Answer

On the face of it, Kant's approach to judgments of taste seems a lot like Hume's. The two species of common sense that Hume discovered are mirrored in Kant's account of what he calls two "commonplace[s] of taste" (*CJ*, §56, p. 210/214). The first, *"Everyone has his own taste,"* writes Kant, "amounts to saying that the determining ground of this judgment is merely subjective (gratification or pain), and the judgment has no right to the necessary assent of others" (*CJ*, §56, p. 210/214). The second, *"There is no disputing about taste,"* he adds, "is as much as to say that the determining ground of a judgment of taste may even be objective, but it cannot be brought to determinate concepts; consequently nothing can be *decided* about the judgment itself by means of proofs, although it is certainly possible and right to *argue* [*mit Recht gestritten werden kann; streiten*, to quarrel] about it" (*CJ*, §56, p. 210/214). Whereas the first commonplace is the means by which "everyone who lacks taste thinks to defend himself against criticism," the second "is used even by those who concede to judgments of taste the right to pronounce validly for everyone" (*CJ*, §56, p. 210/214). Kant can be seen, then, as putting forward a conflict in common sense that restates, on the one side, Hume's idea of the natural equality of taste and, on the other, the Ogilby-Milton quarrel that gives the lie to that equality.

The apparent similarity of these accounts is the basis of Paul Guyer's well-known interpretation, which reads *The Critique of Judgment* as picking up where *Of the Standard of Taste* left off.[57] According to what Brent Kalar aptly calls Guyer's "Humean reading," Kant, responding to "Hume's challenge," offers an a priori argument in the place of Hume's empirical argument as a way to explain the necessary universality of our response to beautiful objects.[58] Kant's transcendental deduction of taste, argues Guyer, aims to show that "the judgment that a particular object *x* is beautiful amounts to the claim that everyone who perceives *x* should, apart from any predication of a concept of it, take pleasure in it, or that, under ideal conditions—of noninterference from purely sensory pleasures and abstraction from any concepts that might effect an interested response—everyone who perceives *x* will take pleasure in it."[59] This prediction of agreement is akin to Hume's claim that, were it not for the "defects" that impair an otherwise universal beauty-sensibility, all men would be led to the same judgment. More specifically, the deduction must show not only that we can in principle know about the subjective states of others, but also that we can know about the particular states of particular individuals in particular circumstances. Agreeing with Hume's remark that the problem for a standard of taste arises when "critics come to particulars," Guyer claims that Kant's deduction too must come to particulars.[60] Such an analysis would have to show the de facto uniformity of our cognitive faculties in particular cases as the basis for an (albeit ideal) empirical agreement.[61] Failing to do so, the third *Critique* does not solve Hume's problem, in Guyer's view.[62]

In recent years, an array of scholars has questioned Guyer's reading, arguing that Kant puts forward the universal validity and necessity of taste neither as a theoretical claim nor as a factual prediction but as a *normative* demand: others *ought* to agree—whether they do agree is an empirical matter that is of little consequence for the transcendental philosopher.[63] Insofar as "a normative demand, as opposed to a factual prediction, is, for Kant, the content that he refers to as the universality and necessity of the judgement of taste," writes Kalar, "Kant is not dealing with quite the same problem as Hume."[64] Understood in normative rather than factual terms, Kant's approach to validity, moreover, is part of a larger transcendental question, which must bracket not only any attempt to predict agreement but also the ordinary understanding of what such agreement would be about. Thus, if Kant does not "come to particulars," as Guyer insists he must, it is because Kant's question is not, how do we decide which taste judgment is valid? (Hume's question), but, rather, with what right do we speak of the universal validity of a judgment of taste at all?

Accordingly, the normative status of a judgment of taste is restricted, in the normative reading, to the transcendental question of the conditions that must be satisfied for us to speak of a judgment of taste in Kant's sense.[65] As Eva Schaper explains, "Erroneous judgements of taste, then, are judgements erroneously thought to be taste judgements, the error or mistake lying in falsely believing that one sort of assertion has been advanced when in fact quite another sort has been made"— when we mistake a judgment about what is agreeable ("I like sparkling wine") for one about what is beautiful, for example.[66] "So a judgement of taste, when 'correct,' is so not because it can be shown to be either true or false, but because the conditions for making such a judgement have not, in Kant's words, been 'sinned against.'"[67] These are the conditions that make a judgment of taste "pure" according to Kant (e.g., disinterested; based on a feeling, not a concept; originating in the free harmony of the faculties; and subjectively purposive).

Recognizing that we might still wish to know whether "the grounds of the judgement are . . . appropriate to what we call the object of a specific judgement," Schaper sees that our question is not only about whether a judgment is a genuine judgment of taste but also "about the grounds for *this* judgement being made rather than *that*."[68] Here again she is clear:

Kant's reply would be that the further question is not one that can be asked. In matters aesthetic, what *seems* right is right for the person making the judgement—if it is correctly made: it is subjectively valid. . . . The particular judgement, once we accept it as one of taste, does not allow of further questions such as 'Is it true or false?' For its being a taste judgement leaves things just there."[69]

In my view, it is right to say that a further question arises and that this is a different question than the one that occupies Kant for most of the text, most clearly in division 1. It is, however, demonstrably wrong to say that Kant's reply would be that no further question can be asked, demonstrable because Kant himself goes on to ask it.[70]

What I have in mind is section 56 ("Representation of the antinomy of taste") at the opening of the second section ("The Dialectic of the Aesthetic Power of Judgment"), in which Kant introduces the two aforementioned commonplaces about taste (*"Everyone has his own taste"* and *"There is no disputing about taste"*) and, with them, two interlocutions: to dispute (*disputieren*) versus to argue/quarrel (*streiten*). Taken alone, however, these commonplaces would not amount to an antinomy, for they do not make antithetical claims about the "merely subjective" versus the "objective" bases of aesthetic judgments.[71] As Kant sees it, arguing and disputing have key differences but also similarities: "For *to argue* and *to dispute* are certainly alike in this, that they try to bring about unanimity in judgments through their mutual opposition, but they differ in that the latter hopes to accomplish this in accordance with determinate concepts as grounds of proofs, and so assumes *objective concepts* as grounds of the judgment. Where this is considered unfeasible, however, then disputing is also considered unfeasible" (*CJ*, §56, p. 210/214). Kant sees that the second commonplace can be expanded in such a way that it introduces the ordinary practice of arguing/quarreling about taste without denying the equally ordinary view that no proof can settle a disagreement. He then asks us to see something that is right there before our eyes, so to speak—namely, that "one proposition is missing [between these two commonplaces], which is not, to be sure, a proverb in general circulation, but which nevertheless everyone has some sense of: *It is possible to argue/quarrel [streiten] about taste* (but not to dispute [*disputieren*])" (*CJ*, §56, p. 211/214). This implied proverb contradicts the first commonplace [*"Everyone has his own taste"*], for "wherever it is supposed to be possible to argue, there must be hope of coming to mutual agreement; hence one must be able to count on grounds for the judgment that do not have merely private validity and thus are not merely subjective, which is nevertheless completely opposed to the fundamental principle *Everyone has his own taste*" (*CJ*, §56, p. 211/214).

Herein arises the antinomy:

1. *Thesis.* The judgment of taste is not based on concepts, for otherwise one could dispute about it (decide by means of proofs).

2. *Antithesis.* The judgment of taste is based on concepts, for otherwise, despite its variety, it would not even be possible to argue/quarrel about it (to lay claim to the necessary assent of others to this judgment). (*CJ*, §56, p. 210/215)

Kant's controversial attempt to solve the antinomy in section 57 by means of the "indeterminate concept" of the "supersensible substratum of humanity" (discussed subsequently) can lead one to think that the whole issue of validity is restricted (here in the opening to the second section of the third *Critique* as it was in the first section) to the transcendental question once again.[72] It is worth noting, however, that what leads us up the ineffable path to the supersensible is the philosopher's attention to the ordinary: the missing proposition that, albeit not in common use as a proverb, is still in everyone's mind; one can quarrel about taste, though one cannot dispute about it. Kant can introduce this missing proposition as an expansion of the second commonplace [*"There is no disputing about taste"*] while remaining true to the two commonplaces that it links because the conditions for a quarrel, though weaker than those for a dispute, share with the latter the conviction that there is something like a fact of the matter about which we can genuinely disagree (i.e., our views are not "merely subjective").[73]

Although Kant tells us little about what the actual practice of arguing/quarreling is supposed to be or what would count as its resolution, we can justifiably speculate on the basis of what he does say. Arguing/quarreling is introduced as a "commonplace," an ordinary activity in which we engage—namely, a debate about particulars: whether *this* or *that* is beautiful. But Kant is doing more than restating what we already know; he is reminding us of what we say when we judge *this*, rather than *that*, as beautiful. In this way, he is eliciting our criteria, to speak with Stanley Cavell, so as to bring into view our actual aesthetic practice. What Kant brings into view is just this: hope for agreement in judgments of taste animates our arguments and quarrels about taste. In a philosophical mood, we may be inclined to see such an activity as pointless, lacking any clear method for determining the right answer. Kant would remind us that *streiten* marks differences of opinion that *do* allow of right and wrong answers in the ordinary way that we anticipate, only these answers cannot be settled by way of an algorithmic decision procedure that would cover all like cases.[74] That is the reasonable if unacknowledged basis of our "hope."

Bringing this ordinary hope into view, Kant indicates that what we lack is a way of *acknowledging* what we already *know*—namely, that we do require others to agree with our particular judgment because we have *grounds* for holding our judgment to be correct. These grounds cannot be (determinate) concepts; what they are we shall soon see. At this point we need only consider that when we argue/quarrel about aesthetic judgments, we engage in what Cavell calls a "pattern of support" or justification that makes a claim to reason.[75] As argued in the last chapter, Cavell shows that in contrast to scientific rationality and the cognitive and logical judgments that are based on the exchange of proofs, aesthetic (moral and political) judgments do not proceed on the assumption that agreement in premises will lead to agreement in conclusions. If rationality can be understood as a matter of agreement in terms of patterns of support (objection and response) rather than agreement in conclusions, Cavell argues, then the interlocution Kant calls *streiten* about a judgment of taste can be at once rational and affective. Nothing prevents us from actually agreeing with another's argument in defense of such a judgment, but nothing in the nature of such argument guarantees that we will agree. If there were a guarantee based on discursive concepts, there would be no judgment of taste, but if there were no hope of reaching agreement, we would not argue/quarrel about it. The (nondeterminative) nature of the grounds, in other words, is what makes a judgment of taste at once possible and unique.

It follows, then, that our reasonable hope for reaching agreement when we argue/quarrel is based on the belief that we can say *this* and not *that* judgment is valid, even though we do not employ—not successfully, however we may try—the determinate concepts that belong to a dispute. If we have trouble acknowledging the rationality of both the first- *and* the second-order claim to validity implicit in our practice of *streiten*, it may be because, notwithstanding Cavell's key insight into types of rationality, we cannot yet see how an aesthetic debate, based on the subject's feeling of pleasure or displeasure, could be a genuine debate at all. That is why the second-order question cannot be intelligibly posed, let alone answered, without addressing the transcendental question for which such pleasure is crucial, even if the latter question also works to occlude the former from our view. That is why the Humean reading of Kant, which would foreground the second-order question as an empirical matter in no need of a first-order deduction, cannot explain the validity of taste as anything other than that on which people, in ideal conditions, actually agree.[76] So we need to keep the first-order question in play—even if we do not embrace the transcendental deduction—if we are to understand the second-order practice of *streiten*. We need to understand the second-order question as something that is irreducible to asking whether the conditions for making a judgment of taste have been satisfied, on the one hand, yet also nonsensical without an inquiry into those conditions, on the other. After all, the particular (second-order) question of whether *this* flower is beautiful would be the target of an "error theory," as it is in a certain Humean projectivism, if we thought the whole category of beauty itself to be unintelligible, a mere "phantasm."

If Kant is able to address the question of normativity at both the first- and the second-order level without becoming entangled in Hume's quest for a standard, it is because Kant sees that the kind of agreement we have a right to demand from others is much thicker than the mere coincidence of subjectivities that defines agreement in a projectivist aesthetics. The "universal validity [of a judgment of taste] is not to be grounded [*gründen*] on collecting votes and asking around among other people about the sort of sensation they have" (*CJ*, §31, p. 144/162). In other words, we argue/quarrel about taste because what we demand is not mere concurrence of private sentiments but agreement based on something shared: what Kant calls *"sensus communis"* (common sense).

In all judgments by which we declare something to be beautiful, we allow no one to be of a different opinion, without, however, grounding [*gründen*] our judgment on concepts, but only on our feeling, which we therefore make our ground [*zum Grunde legen*] not as a private feeling, but as a common one. Now this common sense cannot be grounded [*gegründet*] on experience for this purpose, for it is to justify [*berechtigen*] judgments that contain a "should": it does not say that everyone *will* concur with our judgment but that everyone *should* agree with it. (*CJ*, §22, p. 89/123)

Common sense is for Kant a sensuous capacity, inner relation, or "disposition of the cognitive powers" (understanding and imagination) that must be presupposed and be capable of being "universally communicated, for otherwise they would have no correspondence with the object; they would all be a merely subjective play of the powers of representation, just as skepticism [e.g., Hume's projectivism] insists" (*CJ*, §21, pp. 87–88/122). This disposition, crucial for cognition according to Kant, has a genuine affective quality: "this disposition cannot be determined except through . . . feeling (not by concepts)" (*CJ*, §21, p. 88/123).[77]

How common sense underwrites the strange normativity (subjective universality) of judgments of taste turns, then, in no small part on the specific role that the feeling of pleasure (or displeasure) plays in them. "The question arises whether it [the faculty of aesthetic reflection] judges only *by means* of the pleasure or displeasure which is felt in it, or whether it rather judges *about* these," writes Kant.[78] As noted in chapter 1 in relation to Arendt's idea of a *political* judgment, it is a question about how to understand the adjective *aesthetic* that qualifies the noun *judgment* in an aesthetic judgment.[79] Does *aesthetic* (which, as Werner Pluhar notes, "comes from the Greek '*aisthésthai*,' 'to sense'"

[*CJ*, p. 28, n. 30]) refer to an *object* that is prior and external to the judgment, or does *aesthetic* refer to the *means* by which the judgment proceeds? "While there is a growing consensus in recent scholarship that Kant understood the pleasure of taste not as the *object* but (somehow) the *form* of judgment," comments Joseph Tinguely, "there has been remarkably little agreement as to what, then, the proper object of such a judgment is. If pleasure is itself a judgment, what is it judging?"[80] On the most widely accepted version of the normative reading, the pleasure of taste is a judgment "about" oneself, that is, the "object" of the judgment of taste is some special state or capacity of the judging subject. In the view of Hannah Ginsborg, for example, the "free-play" of the faculties that Kant describes as part of aesthetic judging is a purely self-referential activity by which the judging subject reflects upon its mental state to see if the pleasure it feels is merely private or whether it is universally valid—that is, can with right be imputed (on the basis of common sense) to other judging subjects.[81] A judgment of taste, then, is a claim not about the object but about the validity of the subject's pleasure.[82] As Tinguely puts it, "the pleasure of taste is nothing other than the explicit, conscious awareness of the validity [that is, the universalizability] of an implicit self-referential judgment."[83]

Accounts that emphasize the self-referential structure of aesthetic judgment constitute an important response both to Humean readings (e.g., Guyer) and to attempts to bring the third *Critique* wholly within the orbit of the epistemological aims of the first (e.g., Karl Ameriks). They leave us wondering, nevertheless, how judging connects with objects of empirical experience and, further, how any object becomes a candidate for aesthetic judging in the first place.[84] And though Kant himself seems to cut off any discussion of what could be objective in an aesthetic judgment, claiming at times that it "does not pertain to the object at all" (*CJ*, §8, p. 58/100), there are other passages, observes Tinguely, that show "that Kant did not, after all, go so far as to hold the counter-intuitive idea that judgements of beauty are cut off from empirical objects altogether."[85] Although "there is room for nearly endless debate whether the referent of aesthetic judgements is a property of the object judged or rather a state of the judging subject," I would agree with Tinguely that we can take the best of both the "subjectivist" and the "objectivist" interpretations, reading Kantian taste as a way of discriminating objects in the world without falling back into the (Humean) "externalist" view that would "trace the aetiology of the feeling [of pleasure] along a causal chain back to an empirical property of an object which caused the pleasure as its natural effect."[86]

Such a reading holds "feeling to be internal to the discrimination of empirical objects," which is to say that a judgment of taste does not judge, in what amounts to a "second act," the pleasure occasioned by a "first-act" encounter with an object. Put otherwise, explains Tinguely, to say that taste judges by *means* of pleasure is to say that pleasure is not merely the "after effect of a prior intentional encounter with an object," but rather, "that the discrimination of aesthetic features of objects takes place in or through a feeling of pleasure."[87] Aesthetic objects, as Cavell observes, "are only *known by feeling*, or *in* feeling."[88] For Kant, as Tinguely expands Cavell's point, "feeling can itself be a kind of judgmental capacity."[89] I agree with Tinguely that "all that thought commits one to in the aesthetic context is that without drawing on a range of affective sensibilities one would be effectively 'blind' to what it is about a present object that merits aesthetic praise or blame in much the same way that someone who is 'tone deaf' can be unable to hear a musical performance as anything but noise."[90] As argued in chapter 1, it is by means of our affective propensities that we come to have the world in view.

In the third *Critique*, "the indeterminate norm of a common sense is really presupposed by us: our presumption in making judgments of taste proves that," asserts Kant (*CJ*, §22, p. 89/124). In Kant's account, observes Tinguely, common sense is the basis for "the emergence, out of the void between discursive rationality and total nonsense, of a new territory of rational persuasion—one which draws on and places claims upon our affective sensibilities."[91] In the case of taste, Kant argues, "the 'should', i.e., the objective necessity of the confluence of the feeling of everyone with that of each, signifies only the possibility of coming to agreement," not the guarantee of agreement based on the concepts that obtain in a cognitive judgment, "and the judgment of taste only provides an example of the application of this principle [common sense]" (*CJ*, §22, p. 90/124).

Now, the question immediately arises here: what it can possibly mean to speak about correctness when it comes to a feeling? "To claim that one is doing something correctly (or to accuse another of doing something incorrectly) while refusing to ground such claims in logical or empirical demonstration understandably raises the suspicion that one is just arbitrarily 'making it up' as she goes along, or that 'feels right' means subjectively 'feels right to me,'" observes Tinguely.[92] That is what Hume saw, and it drove him to seek a standard of taste in a "matter of fact"—that is, outside the register of affectivity and values. He could find no other way to account for feeling as normative without abandoning the absolute conception of the world that housed his projectivism. For Kant, however, "one solicits assent from everyone else because one has a ground [*Grund*] for it that is common to all" (*CJ*, §19, p. 86/121–22). We argue/quarrel with each other, demanding agreement, on the basis of shared feeling. And this shared feeling, *sensus communis*, is the subjective principle that takes the place of the objective principle that a standard of taste was, in Hume's view, to provide.

When we argue/quarrel about taste, we place demands on the feelings of others. We do not just demand that they ventriloquize our judgment, as if mouthing the words (e.g., "This painting is beautiful") constituted the kind of agreement we seek. We demand that they *feel* (the pleasure) as we do. In response to such a demand, Kant recognizes that, under the pressure of various social constraints, we may sometimes "behave as if" we like a particular object (*CJ*, §33, p. 145/164). We may even agree with arguments about why, say, *this*, and not *that*, painting is beautiful (e.g., it makes better use of color, perspective, or light). But to be persuaded that the argument is sound is not to be convinced that the painting is beautiful.

Hence a young poet does not let himself be dissuaded from his conviction that his poem is beautiful by the judgment of the public nor that of his friends, and, if he does give them a hearing, this is not because he now judges it differently, but rather because, even if (at least in his view) the entire public has a false taste, he nevertheless (even against his judgment) finds cause to accommodate himself to the common delusion in his desire for approval. Only later on, when his power of judgment has been made more acute by practice, does he depart from his previous judgment of his own free will, just as he does with those of his judgments that rest entirely on reason. Taste makes claim merely to autonomy. To make the judgments of others into the determining ground of one's own would be heteronomy. (*CJ*, §32, pp. 145–46/163)

When the subject offers a judgment as proof of his taste about some object, declares Kant, "the subject [should] judge for himself, without having to grope about by means of experience among the judgments of others" (*CJ*, §32, p. 145/163). Rather, the kind of agreement we demand here is genuine agreement in feeling, in *sensus communis*, not in the empirical sense, as we saw earlier, of "collecting votes and asking around among other people about the sort of sensations they have" (*CJ*, §31, p. 144/162). The normative reading of Kant would explain why we are warranted in our demand that others feel as we do. But when we quarrel, we express not only the hope that we can reach agreement (based on a common sense) but the expectation that we can somehow change each other's feelings.[93] This is when we do indeed "come to particulars," as Guyer would put it, only not in the Humean form of an ideal prediction but in the ordinary manner of putting forward samples of "what we say" or eliciting our criteria, to speak with Cavell.

Cavell's account helps illuminate what Kant describes as the unique kind of necessity or universality that characterizes a judgment of taste:

[It is] not a theoretical objective necessity, where it can be cognized *a priori* that everyone *will feel* this satisfaction in the object called beautiful by me, nor a practical objective necessity, where by means of concepts of a pure will, serving as rules for freely acting beings, this satisfaction is a necessary consequence of an objective law and signifies nothing other than that one absolutely (without a further aim) ought to act in a certain way. Rather, as a necessity that is thought in an aesthetic judgment, it can only be called *exemplary*, i.e., a necessity of the assent of *all* to a judgment that is regarded as an example of a universal rule that one cannot produce. (*CJ*, §18, p. 85/121)

We cannot produce or state the rule, Kant argues, because "an aesthetic judgment is not an objective and cognitive judgment." There is therefore nothing "apodictic" in exemplary necessity. "Much less can it be inferred from the universality of experience (from a complete unanimity in judgments about the beauty of a certain object). For not only would experience hardly supply sufficient evidence of this, but it is also impossible to ground any concept of the necessity of these judgments on empirical judgments" (*CJ*, §18, p. 85–86/121). There is, so to speak, nothing but the contingent expression of my judgment that makes visible the shared affective basis that alone constitutes its grounds: "Thus the common sense, of whose judgment I here offer my judgment of taste as an example and on account of which I ascribe *exemplary* validity to it, is a merely ideal norm" (*CJ*, §22, p. 89/123), concludes Kant.

Notwithstanding the nonpropositional character of a judgment of beauty, the judging person, observes Kant, "will speak of the beautiful as if beauty were a property of the object" (*CJ*, §6, 54/97).[94] Although he agrees with Hume that beauty is no such property, Kant sees, in a way that Hume never could, how it belongs to the grammar of an aesthetic judgment to talk in this way. "Then why [does Kant] not just say it *isn't* a property of an object?" asks Cavell. "I suppose there would be no reason not to say this, if we could find another way of recording our conviction that it is one, anyway that what we are pointing to is *there*, in the object," he adds. And though we know that others may disagree with what we claim to find in the object, "we think they are *missing something* if they don't [see it too]."[95] On Kant's account, aesthetic qualities do not appear to us to be in the object because they have been imposed by a subreption of the mind. We do not speak of beauty as if it were a property of things all the while ignorant of its status as mere projection, as Mackie's "error theory" Hume would have it. Nor do we speak of beauty as if it were a property of things all the while knowing that it is no property of things, as Blackburn's "quasi-realist" Hume would have it. Such ordinary talk is not to be understood as either misunderstanding or transcending the conditions of its own expression. It is rather an important clue to the peculiar "universality" that is the judgment's "remarkable feature" (*CJ*, §8, p. 57/99).

That Kant has a better grasp than Hume on what Wittgenstein would call the "grammar" of aesthetic judgment does not mean that Kant has satisfactorily explained what he claims to find. In the view of Mary Mothersill, for example, Kant ought to say that we speak about beauty as if it were a property of things because it *really is* a property of things. In this way, "the judgment of taste, like a standard perceptual judgment (perceiving a movable drop of water in a rock-crystal) 'rightly looks to everyone finding the fact as stated.' This would lead to a less strenuous and more realistic conception of what it is to 'demand' or 'require' 'universal assent' to one's judgment of taste," she writes.[96] When someone fails to respond as we do, we are apt to respond—quite rightly—with "Kantian sounding things such as "But you *must* see it!"[97] See it because there is, after all, something really there to see. And Cavell too reminds us: "It is essential to making an aesthetic judgment that at some point we be prepared to say in its support: don't you see, don't you hear, don't you dig? . . . Because if you do not see *something*, without explanation, then there is nothing further to discuss." Although I can try to instruct you to see what I see, observes Cavell, at a certain point reasons will come to an end and I will say again, perhaps more emphatically, perhaps more resigned: "This is what I see."[98]

What takes place at the point where reasons run out will become clearer when we turn to Wittgenstein's reflections on aesthetics. For now, however, both Cavell and Mothersill in their contrasting ways allow us to see that the sense of necessity described by Kant would hardly make sense if we thought that all perspectives were irremediably distorting or that there was in fact nothing there to see: no beautiful flower, for example. And yet how we go about parsing that apparently simple thought is complex. Mothersill would rightly undercut the rigid distinction between empirical and aesthetic judgments, yet it would be rash to assume that the judgment "This rose is beautiful" is no different in kind than the judgment "There is a drop of water in this rock-crystal," as she well knows. I can persuade or compel you to see the drop of water through discursive concepts, but no such concepts will get you to see—or, rather, feel—the beauty of the rose. On the one hand, if the judgment of taste made no claim to a matter of fact (i.e., the real beauty of the rose), it could not serve as the basis for a quarrel; on the other hand, if the judgment were no different than stating a fact (all roses are beautiful), we should expect the arguments that support them to be conclusive and rational in the way that arguments in logic or science are. But I have agreed with Cavell that aesthetic (and moral and political) arguments are not conclusive and rational in this same way, and yet they can be conclusive and rational.

What is at issue in the difference between the patterns of support that distinguish aesthetic (and moral and political) judgments from empirical ones is not that the former, by contrast with the latter, make no intelligible claim to an objective property. That would lead us straight back to Humean projectivism and the aesthetic noncognitivist tradition it inspired. It is rather that our argument/quarrel about taste does depend on what the judged object is like, though this question cannot be decided apart from how we are affected. The object possesses "the entirely *subjective* property of being liable to affect us (all) in certain ways, and, moreover, there is no reductive way of handling it that omits this relational reference to ourselves," comments Savile.[99] If a judgment of beauty made no reference to properties of objects, then we could not explain why we feel compelled to respond as we do; we could not explain the "ought" that a judgment of taste expresses. If such a judgment made reference only to properties of objects, then we could not explain why we feel compelled to respond as we do; we could not explain the normativity of our pleasure. We need to keep the essentially relational, both "subjective" and "objective," character of taste judgments in view at once, then, if we are to understand why we can argue/quarrel but not dispute about them.

Kant recognizes that how we find ourselves to be affected by aesthetic objects has its expression—indeed, its possibility—in how we talk about such objects. My claim to the flower's beauty, based in pleasure, neither denies nor affirms what I, as a budding "botanist," may well know: that "a flower . . . [is] the reproductive organ of the plant" (*CJ*, §16, p. 76/114). The key to reading Kantian *streiten* is neither to deny nor to reify the difference between the aesthetic and the empirical claim here; it is rather to see how it is that we elicit criteria in the one sort of judgment versus in the other when we find that we disagree. As Cavell reminds us, "criteria are 'criteria for something's being so', not in the sense that they tell us of a thing's existence, but of something like its identity, not of its *being* so, but of its being *so*." And, further, "There are no criteria for a thing's *being* so over and above the criteria for its being *so*."[100] Criteria do not just register a fact apart from a value; they express at once how something appears to me and how it is in the world.

Though "there are no criteria for determining true or false judgements of taste," as Schaper restates Kant's claim, that does not mean that there can be no attempt to *elicit* criteria that would persuade dissenting parties to agree.[101] And this eliciting can be at once rational and affective. To elicit criteria entangles us back in the criterial theory of taste that Kant rightly rejects only if we assume that criteria function as rules, where rules fully bound the practice of making judgments in such a (syllogistic) way that, if all *G* are beautiful and *F* is a *G*, then *F* is beautiful. But that is not at all how *streiten* works, not even on Kant's admittedly sparse account. Although Kant does not quite get us to the Wittgensteinian understanding of criteria that inspires Cavell, he does allow us to see that "we need to [argue]/quarrel rather than logically argue [about taste] because our aesthetic convictions are not the sort of thing that can be simply overruled by conceptual demonstration," as Tinguely observes.[102] If eliciting criteria in the hope of reaching agreement were utterly pointless, doomed because all such criteria must by definition function in the syllogistic manner previously described, then we would not bother to quarrel at all. We argue/quarrel because we believe—sometimes rightly, sometimes not—that we can bring someone to see the object as we see it and thus to feel as we do when we declare it beautiful. Thus determinate concepts may well be invoked when we quarrel, but it is not concepts as proofs that change affective response. It is a use of concepts as part of a larger strategy to light up an aspect of an object previously unseen.

If we return now to the two commonplaces, we can see how quarreling makes visible something that both the thesis and the antithesis in the antinomy share: the view that a judgment of taste must be based on a concept (it must have some objective ground). We can now see how Kant attempts to solve the antinomy by querying the sense of a concept held by the two sides of a disagreement about taste. They both agree that the validity of an aesthetic judgment requires the application of a concept, but they fail (albeit in different ways) to see that this concept need not be of only one kind:

The judgment of taste must be related to some sort of concept, for otherwise it could not lay claim to necessary validity for everyone at all. But it need not on that account be demonstrable *from* a concept, because a concept can be either determinable or else in itself indeterminate and also indeterminable. (*CJ*, §57, p. 212/215)[103]

In a judgment of taste, then, we have a concept (e.g., beauty) that is not only indeterminate but also indeterminable, a concept that is not only presently but also in principle unavailable for use in a criterial test. Were the concept under which we bring an object in a judgment of taste essentially indeterminate but not indeterminable, "the prospect might stand before us of starting out with aesthetic judgments whose truth or falsity we could not determine (settle by decision procedures already available to us), but which we might think could come to be provided with grounds of proof," observes Savile.[104] As Allison argues, "only such a 'concept' could be viewed as having the normative standing required to ground the possibility of genuine disagreement, while at the same time precluding the possibility of the determination needed to provide a rule capable of yielding a decision procedure for disputes about taste."[105] That would be to leave open the possibility, already advanced by Hume, that to grant legitimate disagreement in taste is to admit that principles of taste might be discovered someday after all—a possibility Kant vehemently denies.

Kant finds his solution to the antinomy of taste—the basis of a judgment of taste does not rest on concept, otherwise one could dispute about it (decide by means of proof), and yet it must rely on a concept (if it is to be universally valid)—by distinguishing between a determinate and an indeterminate concept: the contradiction between the two sides dissolves when it is recognized that the thesis means by concept a determinate, the antithesis an indeterminate, one.[106] But then he goes on to identify this indeterminate concept with the idea of "the supersensible substratum of humanity" (*CJ*, §57, p. 213/216), a concept at once indeterminate and indeterminable. Does this solution, asks Savile, "not promise to introduce one new and grotesque embarrassment in order to avoid another?"[107] It is as if Kant has exposed the ordinary character of aesthetic phenomena in quarreling only to hide it again in the mysterious noumenal realm; as if, like Hume, Kant too were searching for something external to the ordinary objects and practice of aesthetic judging that would guarantee the possibility of shared response in the absence of conceptual determination. Just when we thought we had glimpsed the possibility of an ordinary account of aesthetic judgments that could serve as an alternative to Hume's naturalist account, Kant's supersensible places the ordinary once again far out of reach.[108]

Notwithstanding the many criticisms that have been made of this move to the supersensible, a generous reading might look to the negative explanation of the noumenal given in the first *Critique*.[109] "The concept of a *noumenon*, i.e., of a thing that is not to be thought of as an object of the senses but rather as a thing in itself (solely through a pure understanding), . . . is merely a *boundary concept*, in order to limit the pretension of sensibility, and therefore only of negative use," Kant contends.[110] This account does not "intimate the frustrating presence over the cognitive horizon of necessarily ineffable, but true, explanations for phenomenal things, eternally closed to us. Rather, they simply serve as a reminder where the quest for explanations must come to a halt," comments Savile.[111] Though I would say—in a more Wittgensteinian key—"where our explanations just do come to a halt," I agree that Kant does not give positive meaning to the supersensible in the sense of "things in themselves." The idea of the noumenal within the theoretical philosophy, observes James Conant, "is, as Kant puts it, an 'entirely *indeterminate* concept'; and he [Kant] rightly argues that fatal confusion results when one is 'misled into treating this entirely *indeterminate* concept . . . as if it were a *determinate* concept of an entity that allows of being known in a certain [purely intelligible–i.e., humanly impossible] manner.'"[112]

Although a fuller discussion of the supersensible is beyond the scope of this chapter, I would question (with Savile and Conant) the idea that Kant held to the existence of a nonperspectival (noumenal) reality as the condition for our claims to know anything about a perspectival reality (appearance). This "pseudo-Kantian" view, argues Conant, sustains the idea that there is a way the world is from no particular point of view and thus apart from any perspective, which is precisely the view that the critical philosophy set out to attack. It sustains the absolute conception of the world but denies it to be attainable by human and therefore cognitively finite beings. If human perspective irremediably distorts or "masks the true nature of reality from view," then *streiten* would be interminable: "we can no longer compare the views afforded by alternative perspectives and thereby correct for distortion."[113] There really would be no way to decide on Kant's account *which* (aesthetic) judgment is valid, just as Schaper claimed, but only whether an *aesthetic* judgment had been made at all.

Distinguishing between a determinate and an indeterminate concept, Kant sees that we do not need to think of a concept as fixed or bounded to claim that there is a fact of the matter to which our quarrels about particular judgments of taste refer. In this way he opens the space for thinking about normativity in terms other than concepts as rules or decision procedures for determining whether a given object falls under a concept.[114] He is expanding the very idea of a concept and in this way opening the space for thinking about judging outside the rule-governed framework that his own writings are commonly taken to exemplify (and in some instances do). This is the space of a new understanding of normativity that Wittgenstein would later occupy and philosophically radicalize and Arendt would politicize.

If Kant does pose the second-order question of validity, as I have argued, does he provide us with a way to decide this question in any given case? On the one hand, the answer appears to be no. Insofar as Kant puts forward the alternative idea of a concept as that which is not only indeterminate but also indeterminable, he seems at once to underscore the idea that we can quarrel because there really is a fact of the matter and to deny that this fact can be decided (even in principle). That is why he moves to the supersensible.

And yet Kant does suggest how such a decision might be reached without turning any particular agreement about the validity of *this* rather than *that* judgment into a principle of judgment that could serve as a rule for future judgments—that would be to lose track of the *indeterminable* character of an indeterminate concept. Rather than presenting the cognitive limit of the human mind, the indeterminable aspect of a concept of beauty reminds us that when it comes to taste, as Savile comments, "we shall not ever have any mechanical decision-procedure . . . to cover all cases," and yet the claim to validity stands.[115] Focusing on this claim (the dual character of aesthetic judgment), we see that such judgments are reflective judgments, but they are not just that. As Savile argues, if all Kant wanted to show were that judgments of taste are not *determinate* but *reflective* judgments, judgments that do not bring their objects under (determinate) concepts, then, it would be hard to understand "why any antinomy about them should arise."[116] The idea of reflective judgment, which is addressed in section 4.2 of the introduction, could have easily accounted for the noncognitive character of judgments of taste. The real issue, then, is not whether we can judge without (determinate) concepts but how we can demand agreement in their absence.[117]

To hold a mechanical decision procedure necessary if quarreling on any particular aesthetic judgment is not to be interminable is to assume that rationality entails agreement in procedures and hence conclusions. All that was really required to solve the antinomy of taste, Tinguely points out, is "the possibility that there be a way of changing one another's mind, of affecting her judgment, by some means other than discursive, logical demonstration" that would still be rational.[118] We may well run up against certain limits of explanation in any given case, but the key thing to see, observes Mothersill, is that "no description of a beautiful item can convey its beauty to one who is not acquainted with the item in question."[119] You have to be within the life of the language used in any aesthetic description to be affected by its meaning—indeed, to know *where* to look when told, "But don't you *see*?"

What we hope for when we quarrel is to change each other's feelings by rearranging how the common object is viewed and creating a shared orientation. Although the third *Critique* provides clues as to how we might proceed and expand our understanding of concepts and normativity, it is Wittgenstein's reflections on aesthetics that begin to make good on the Kantian promissory note.

Wittgenstein's Answer

Wittgenstein's lectures on aesthetics might seem at first glance to split the difference between the empirical and the transcendental approach.[120] Like Hume, Wittgenstein emphasizes the historical and cultural diversity of aesthetic appreciation but denies that there is a standard to be discovered in all this variety that would yield the correct definition of beauty. Like Kant, Wittgenstein holds aesthetic judgments to be normative while mocking the idea of "a kind of science of Aesthetics" as "almost too ridiculous for words" (*LC*, 11) but disagrees that such judgments can involve no concepts as rules. "If I hadn't learnt the rules," he writes, "I wouldn't be able to make the aesthetic judgement" (*LC*, 5).[121] The question is what these rules mean and how far they bound any aesthetic practice. Treating such judgments as involving competence with concepts in an ordinary way, Wittgenstein will affirm them neither as cognitive, in the sense of proofs or an algorithmic decision procedure, nor as noncognitive, in the sense of a projection of human sentiment onto an objective aesthetic desert.

Expanding aesthetic judgments to encompass diverse practices of appreciation, which go far beyond traditional works of art to include everyday objects, on the one hand, and also beyond conventional aesthetic binary concepts such as "beautiful" and "ugly," on the other hand, Wittgenstein describes such judgments as part of diverse language games: "In order to get clear about aesthetic words you have to describe ways of living" (*LC*, 11). Utterances such as "This is beautiful" do not contain the meaning of an aesthetic judgment but are intelligible only within the larger network of human meanings and activities, interests and purposes. The use of a word such as *beautiful* is better approached as a "gesture, accompanying a complicated activity" (*LC*, 11). To understand an aesthetic judgment, then, you cannot just hear aesthetic words. You must enter into the life of the person or culture in which those words are used.

The words we call expressions of aesthetic judgement play a very complicated role, but a very definite role, in what we call a culture of a period. To describe their use or to describe what you mean by a cultured taste, you have to describe a culture. What we now call a cultured taste perhaps didn't exist in the Middle Ages. An entirely different game is played in different ages. (*LC*, 8)

Despite their blurred edges and flexible boundaries, aesthetic concepts, like all ordinary concepts on Wittgenstein's account, can be perfectly adequate for use in aesthetic judgments. Their meaning does not exist apart from who is speaking to whom and in what context, and they are not delimited as a set in the restricted way taken for granted by both Hume and Kant. "It is remarkable that in real life, when aesthetic judgements are made, aesthetic adjectives such as 'beautiful,' 'fine,' etc., play hardly any role at all" (*LC*, 3), comments Wittgenstein. In a "musical criticism" or a "poetical criticism," for example, we are more likely to say, respectively, "Look at this transition" or "His use of images is precise" (*LC*, 3). It is not as if there is a book of aesthetic adjectives at hand to be consulted when judging aesthetically. Instead we respond to the particulars of the music or the poem and to the interests of our interlocutors. There is no superconcept (e.g., "beauty") whose universal essence, if only once discovered and properly grasped, could guarantee shared meaning.

Wittgenstein can allow for the skilled use of concepts in aesthetic judgments without endorsing the Humean idea of a standard or denying the sense of necessity that it implies. It is not as if in aesthetic criticism, anything goes. "When we make an aesthetic judgement about a thing, we do not just gape at it and say: 'Oh! How marvellous!' We distinguish between a person who knows what he is talking about and a person who doesn't" (*LC*, 6), states Wittgenstein. *Pace* Hume, the normativity of aesthetic concepts does not require a standard that underwrites valid use; and *pace* Kant, such concepts do not have to be radically distinguished from rules so as not to violate what is properly aesthetic (i.e., affective) in a judgment.

Wittgenstein agrees (with both Kant and Hume) that there is a sense of necessity in aesthetic judgments that leads us to demand the agreement of others, as we do with logical or empirical judgments. We are right to detect necessity but figure this necessity in misleading terms. Consider causal explanations in ordinary aesthetic judgments. Imagine that "you design a door," suggests Wittgenstein. "If I say: 'This door is too low. Make it higher,' should we say I know the cause of my discomfort?" (*LC*, 13). But what can *cause* mean in this context? Saying "I know the cause" brings "into our mind . . . not statistics . . . but tracing a mechanism" (*LC*, 15). And soon we come around to the kinematic idea of a "super-mechanism" and "the idea of a super-hardness. 'The geometrical lever is harder than any lever can be. It can't bend.' Here you have the case of logical necessity. 'Logic is a mechanism made of an infinitely hard material. Logic cannot bend'" (*LC*, 16).

In the realm of aesthetics, Wittgenstein finds the superhard idea of causal necessity exemplified in the discipline of "experimental psychology," which some people believe will "one day . . . explain all our aesthetic judgements" (*LC*, 19), and in the way that Kant tried to rule out with his claim that such judgments are not only indeterminate but *indeterminable*. The idea here runs as follows:

Supposing it was found that all our judgements proceeded from our brain. We discovered particular kinds of mechanism in the brain, formulated general laws, etc. One could show that this sequence of notes produces this particular kind of reaction; makes a man smile and say: "Oh, how wonderful." . . . Suppose this were done, it might enable us to predict what a particular person would like and dislike. We could calculate these things. The question is whether this is the sort of explanation we should like to have when we are puzzled about aesthetic impressions. . . . The sort of explanation one is looking for when one is puzzled by an aesthetic impression is not causal explanation, not one corroborated by experience or by statistics as to how people react. (*LC*, 20, 21)

There is a singular quality to an aesthetic experience and judgment that is not reproducible across subjects in the way demanded by the scientific experiment. Not only is aesthetic judgment not governed by a law (nomothetic), it is not governed by a rule (determinative), where rule stands for a way to subsume an aesthetic experience under a known concept of aesthetics in order to judge it. There is no structure of criteria underlying the surface of an aesthetic experience that accounts for its normativity in a judgment. Both experience and judgment are bound—radically so—to the particular. "There is a tendency to talk about the 'effect of a work of art'—feelings, images, etc. Then it is natural to ask: 'Why do you hear this minuet?,' and there is a tendency to answer: 'To get this and that effect.' And doesn't the minuet itself matter?—hearing *this*: would another have done as well?" (*LC*, 29). Similarly: "You *could* select either of two poems to remind you of death, say. But supposing you had read a poem and admired it, could you say: 'Oh, read the other it will do the same'?" (*LC*, 34).

What would be the criterion that an "aesthetic explanation" (*LC*, 18) was the right one? Wittgenstein's answer is deceptively simple: the criterion for an explanation being the right one is that you agree with it.[122] What Wittgenstein calls "an entirely new account of a correct explanation" is "not one agreeing with experience, but one accepted. You have to give the explanation that is accepted. That is the whole point of the explanation" (*LC*, 18). "Here 'explanation' is on the same level as an utterance—where utterance (when you say that you have pain, for instance) is the sole criterion" (*LC*, 18n5). Explanation in aesthetic judgment becomes a transformation of our expression. We do not need to insinuate an order of rules beneath what we say (Hume's hidden standard) or leave the ordinary grammatical register of aesthetic quarreling to seek an a priori principle (Kant's *sensus communis*) to claim normativity for our judgments. We can remain at the level of the description and redescription of aesthetic phenomena. Whether we can reach agreement will be a question not of some hidden standard or a priori principle but of whether we are able to connect with the interests, desires, or purposes of the person whom we try to persuade. Only then will the explanation be satisfying and therefore convincing.

An explanation of this kind, then, does not compel agreement by means of proof—or better, *it transforms what can count as proof.* Its force lies in finding the right expression, one that I accept because it satisfies me. Wittgenstein does not limit this practice of finding the right expression to aesthetic explanation. Consider, he writes,

the Darwin upheaval. One circle of admirers who said: "Of course," and another circle [of enemies—R] who said: "Of course not." Why in the Hell should a man say "of course"? (The idea was that of monocellular organisms becoming more and more complicated until they became mammals, men, etc.) Did anyone see this process happening? No. Has anyone seen it happening now? No. . . . But there were thousands of books in which this was said to be *the* obvious solution. People were *certain* on grounds which were extremely thin. . . . This shows how you can be persuaded of a certain thing. In the end you forget entirely every question of verification, you are just sure it must have been like that. (*LC*, 26–27)

The compelling quality of the scientific theory of natural selection (or any other scientific theory) is produced through what Hilary Putnam calls "[normative] judgments of 'coherence,' 'plausibility,' 'reasonableness,' 'simplicity,' and of what Dirac famously called the beauty of a hypothesis, . . . judgments of 'what ought to be' in the case of reasoning." Theory selection cannot be reduced, as the logical positivists claimed, to an algorithm, but *"always presupposes values"* that tend to be expressed in aesthetic terms.[123]

Aesthetic quarreling works by means of persuasion, and persuasion works by aesthetic means. "If you are led by psycho-analysis to say that really you thought so and so or that really your motive was so and so, this is not a matter of discovery, but of persuasion" (*LC*, 27), observes Wittgenstein. The very sense of discovery—the "aha moment"—is the effect of persuasion: "In a different way you could have been persuaded of something different" (*LC*, 27). What persuades is not compelling proof but something (which could be the proof) that appeals: "Many of these explanations are adopted because they have a peculiar charm. The picture of people having subconscious thoughts has a charm. The idea of an underworld, a secret cellar" (*LC*, 25). It is because of its charm that we accept a certain explanation as proof. Similarly, let's say I pull a mathematical "proof to bits," but, when I'm done, writes Wittgenstein, my interlocutor says that "the proof had a charm for him. Here I could only say: 'It has no charm for me. I loathe it.'" And "I would do my utmost to show it is this charm that makes one do it. Being Mathematics or Physics it looks incontrovertible and this gives it a still greater charm. . . . I can put it in a way in which it will lose its charm for a great number of people and certainly will lose its charm for me. . . . I am . . . making propaganda for one style of thinking as opposed to another" (*LC*, 28). Wittgenstein describes this practice as "persuasion": "I am saying 'I don't want you to look at it like that'" (*LC*, 27).

From Kant's perspective, a judgment based on charm would not be a "pure" aesthetic judgment, and it would certainly have no place in empirical or logical judgments. Whereas Kant thinks charm to be "very detrimental to genuine, uncorrupted, well-grounded taste" (*CJ*, §14, p.71/109), as it is to the capacity to judge generally, Wittgenstein seems to accept it as the aesthetic basis for empirical and logical judgments. But this disagreement is more apparent than real. Even Kant concedes that charms may offer the mind more than "dry satisfaction" and can be tolerated as a supplement provided they do not "attract attention to themselves as grounds for the judging of beauty" (*CJ*, §14, p.71/109–10). And Wittgenstein, though he seems to endorse charm as more than a supplement, can also be read as explicitly calling our attention, as Kant only implicitly did, to the entanglement of aesthetics (i.e., feeling or affect) in *any* claim to knowledge in such a way as to make visible our tendency to misunderstand what we do when we try to distinguished aesthetic from empirical and logical judgments on the basis of the claim to conceptual rationality.

When Wittgenstein says, "Do not look at a proof as a procedure that compels you but as one that guides you," he is trying to persuade. He is saying, "Don't see it like that. Try to see it like this." Persuasion is a form of aesthetic reasoning that depends on finding the right expression—that is, an example that serves as an alternative explanation that satisfies. As G. E. Moore explains:

Reasons, he [Wittgenstein] said, in Aesthetics are "of the nature of further descriptions": e.g., you can make a person see what Brahms was driving at by showing him lots of different pieces by Brahms, or by comparing him with a contemporary author; and all that Aesthetics does is "to draw your attention to a thing," to "place things side by side." He said that if, by giving "reasons" of this sort, you make another person "see what you see" but it still "doesn't appeal to him," that is "an end" of the discussion.[124]

Persuasion, then, is not just a matter of bringing forward more evidence, but of "producing or deepening an example, which shows him [one's interlocutor] that *he* would not say what he says 'we' say," as Cavell explains. And "if we find we disagree about what we should say, it would make no obvious sense to attempt to confirm or disconfirm one or other of our responses by collecting data to show which of us is in fact right." It is no more a matter of collecting empirical evidence than it was for Kant a matter of collecting other people's experiences or votes. We are instead trying to get clearer about our concepts, in the meanings (i.e., the shared life) of words, that is at once affective and rational: what Wittgenstein called "agreement in judgments" and Kant "*sensus communis*." In this sense, the appeal "to everyday language," writes Cavell, is not an attempt "to convince him [one's interlocutor] without proof but to get him to prove something, test something, against himself . . . : Look and find out whether you can see what I see, wish to say what I wish to say."[125]

Richard Shusterman has usefully characterized this view of aesthetic argument as "perceptualist rather than logical or causal."[126] Reasons should be understood neither as causal explanations nor as principles of evidence that inductively or deductively support an argument. "Rather, the critic's reasons function as devices for focusing the reader's perception in such a way that he will see the work as the critic sees it. Perception is the proof."[127] This is part of the process of creating the shared orientation toward an object that Kant called quarreling and that Hume recognized as crucial but could not theorize apart from a hidden standard. The reasons advanced in such an argument do not support the aesthetic judgment discursively in the sense that they function as premises in an argument that, if accepted, would lead to agreement in conclusions. Rather, explanatory reasons for why, say, you should find Botticelli's *The Birth of Venus* beautiful might include (1) the luxuriant quality of the color, (2) the grace of the figure, or (3) the flow of the images; but none of these reasons would figure as a premise that, once accepted, would *compel* you to find the painting beautiful. These are explanatory reasons, not justificatory reasons. It is not that, given your acceptance of reason 1, 2, or 3, "there is really nothing left to think." That is why Wittgenstein describes what he does as "persuading people to change their style of thinking" (*LC*, 28). "(Much of what we are doing is a question of changing the style of thinking)," he adds (*LC*, 28).

A "style of thinking" is not aesthetic in the mere metaphorical sense denoted by Wittgenstein's choice of the word *style*. As we shall see more clearly in chapter 8 when we turn to Ian Hacking's account of "styles of reasoning," it is aesthetic in the far more complex sense of how we come to know something. Persuasion alters a style of thinking, and this altered style does not necessarily introduce new facts; it makes meaningful the facts we already know. A style of thinking, then, introduces what Cavell called "various patterns of support." These patterns of support are what underwrite the distinctive rationality of various styles. Furthermore, patterns of support count as such because, as we saw in chapter 1, there is the prior "agreement in judgments" that Wittgenstein calls "not agreement in opinions, but in form of life" (*PI*, §241). Like Kant's *sensus communis*, this agreement is normative, it is "agreement in *susceptibility* to respond thus and so [to whatever 'object' is under dispute]," as David Wiggins puts it.[128]

Although Wittgenstein's account of aesthetic argument may seem to exclude everything we normally count as crucial to making an argument, this would be a deep misreading of his view. Not every attempt to persuade will count as a pattern of support, not every such attempt will count as playing the language game of making an aesthetic argument. Surely it is crucial to draw a distinction between persuasion as *mere* assent (what Kant called "heteronomy") and persuasion as assent under certain constraints—namely, the accepted patterns of support that qualify in a particular context with particular interlocutors as an attempt to persuade in the language game of giving reasons. An aesthetic argument that is neither deductive nor inductive still relies on eliciting criteria that can count as illuminating something, lighting up an aspect, in the object that is there to be seen. The same goes for the aesthetic character of debate in other domains (e.g., science, logic).

At the heart of what Shusterman called the perceptualist account of persuasion and aesthetic argument is the view of perception as something that can be altered because it is part of an understanding of perspective as corrigible by other perspectives. "Look and see what I see" would have no persuasive force if "what I see" is no better in its ability to account for what is really there than "what you see." Wittgenstein does not embrace the relativism of all perspectives as distorted but sees them as capable of being deployed in language games of persuasion to draw out aspects of any given object and so get the world in view.

It is worth noting, as Shusterman observes, that by offering an account of perceptual persuasion Wittgenstein is not therewith excluding, in principle, the uses of traditional aesthetic argumentation (deductive, inductive, causal). He is questioning our tendency to reify what an aesthetic argument must or should be, not putting forward an alternative theory of what *all* aesthetic argumentation must or should be. Wittgenstein's account of the contextualist and plural character of aesthetic concepts would make no sense if it by definition ruled out deductive and inductive models of aesthetic argument as nonsensical. As tempting as it is to read his mocking commentary on these models in this way, we should not be lured into providing yet another account of what aesthetic argument *must* be, always and everywhere. That is what led Hume to seek a standard of taste, Kant to deny there could ever be one, and both to generate aesthetic theories that relinquished, albeit to varying degrees, the "rough ground" of the ordinary to justify (certain patterns of support for) aesthetic judgments. For Wittgenstein, the demand for certain patterns of support is perfectly in order, but only within the context of a particular language game. As Shusterman asserts, "To claim that aesthetic argument never was nor could be deductive [or inductive] is to deny that different critical games may be played at different times, which is precisely what Wittgenstein laboured so hard to establish."[129]

The distinction between aesthetic and empirical judgments that structures, in different ways, the texts of Kant and Hume is, in Wittgenstein's writings on aesthetics, best understood as a boundary that is not fixed. On the one hand, Wittgenstein grants that if we "look," we may well find "what is common to Aesthetic judgments," and that this turns out to be "an immensely complicated family of cases . . . with the highlight—the expression of admiration, a smile or a gesture, etc." (*LC*, 10). On the other hand, aesthetic judgments are not distinguished by the absence of concepts (e.g., beauty), as they are in Kant, or by the presence of concepts (e.g., beauty) as "phantasms," as they are in Hume. In general, Wittgenstein is far less concerned with drawing a boundary around a class of objects or judgments than he is with understanding the aesthetic (i.e., affective) character of our shared criteria, of what will count for us (e.g., as an object of beauty, of scientific knowledge, of psychological insight). Insofar as these criteria do not function as rules that ground or guarantee mutual intelligibility, their place in judgment is never more secure than our own ability to project a word, to bring someone to see new aspects of objects and meaning in new contexts.

Far from being limited to what is traditionally understood as the field of aesthetics with its characteristic objects, the knowing by feeling that Cavell described is also implicated in the many styles of thinking that Wittgenstein associates with the "charm" that various modes of explanation have for us. As different modes of explanation (which we accept), such styles are not restricted to aesthetic objects or judgments in the narrow sense of the term. As we have seen, there is an aesthetic character to Charles Darwin's historicogenetic explanation, which gives it its "charm" and persuaded people on grounds that were "very thin." Many people find "a peculiar charm" in Sigmund Freud's psychoanalytic "picture of people having subconscious thoughts" (*LC*, 25), as they find a charm in the "incontrovertible" character of mathematical and scientific proofs (*LC*, 28). And so on. Though Wittgenstein does not universally condone the use of charm, neither does he condemn it as one among many elements that play a role in creating a shared orientation toward a particular object. Charm can blind us to what is the case, but it can also light up an aspect of any given object that we had not seen before. We shall return to Wittgenstein's reflections on the aesthetic character of this lighting up of an aspect in the creation of a shared orientation to the world in later chapters.

We have seen that Wittgenstein, by contrast with Kant, does not exclude concepts as rules in aesthetic judging. But this difference can easily be misunderstood. Kant argues that the exemplary necessity in a judgment of taste is "a universal rule that one cannot produce" (*CJ*, §18, p. 85/121). By this he means that a rule cannot serve as an objective principle stating necessary and sufficient conditions of beauty. And with that point, Wittgenstein would agree. For both thinkers, there can be no science of the beautiful. There is no criterial test according to which we could decide in advance of actually encountering an aesthetic object that the object is beautiful. Hume thought there could—and indeed must—be such a rule if taste is to be normative at all, though he never really found his hidden standard.

What is "aesthetic" in an aesthetic judgment is for Wittgenstein, as for Kant, not an object that is external and prior to the judgment itself. "Aesthetic" is not an object but a mode of judgment. We can well entertain the *proposition* that an aesthetic object, such as "Botticelli's *The Birth of Venus* is beautiful" (based, say, on reading a book on the history of Italian art or speaking with a friend who recently saw it in the Uffizi Gallery in Florence), without *judging* it to be so. To accept such a proposition is not to judge aesthetically, for judging requires that our affective sensibilities are directly engaged, that we see with our own eyes that which we call beautiful (or not)—anything else amounts to "heteronomy." It is not the *content* of a judgment but its *mode* that characterizes a judgment of taste.[130] Likewise Wittgenstein focuses our attention not on a particular class of objects that, being aesthetic, serve as the basis for aesthetic judgments but, rather, on the aesthetic character of our response to objects. Thus the charm that plays such an important role in our acceptance of one explanation over another is not limited to a set of objects but is part and parcel of our affective response to that which strikes us as convincing.

By providing us with a more elastic understanding of aesthetic judgment, rather than the difference between a concept-guided and a non-concept-guided practice of judging, and by clarifying the aesthetic character of various styles of thinking, Wittgenstein enables us to question the strict division between aesthetic and empirical judging that is at the heart of the debate over the aesthetic turn in democratic theory. Wittgenstein's approach to normativity offers a viable alternative to thinking in terms of the difference between rule-governed (determinative) and non-rule-governed (reflective) judgments that has framed this debate. Likewise Cavell, who shifts our understanding of rationality from agreement in conclusions to agreement in patterns of support, undercuts the strict division of cognitive and noncognitive judgments, showing that each possess a kind of necessity or logic.

Wittgenstein's critical account of rule following as haunted by the specter of the "logical must" and the figure of "the machine as symbol" offers a window into our tendency to sublime all valid judgments as necessarily guided by superconcepts, lest they have no cognitive or empirical purchase at all. That is what animated Hume's search for a standard and Kant's rejection of aesthetic concepts, save the "indeterminate and indeterminable" concept of the supersensible. If concepts are not fixed, as Wittgenstein teaches, then their application can be understood as aesthetic without denying that it can also be rational. We need not escape the ordinary into either the absolute conception of the world with Hume or the supersensible with Kant in order to speak of the normativity of aesthetic judgments. We can affirm a rational practice of judgment that brings the world view through the use of our affective sensibilities.

Let us now turn to the question of how reason and affect are inflected by our deeply situated location in time and space, to the problem of judgment as it is expressed in historicism.

THREE

Historicism, Judgment, and the Limits of Liberalism: The Case of Leo Strauss

Philosophy in the original meaning of the word presupposes the liberation from historicism. I say, the *liberation* from it, and not merely its refutation. . . . The liberation from historicism requires that historical consciousness be seen to be, not a self-evident premise, but a *problem*.   LEO STRAUSS[1]

How might one take up Leo Strauss's challenge to think about historical consciousness as a problem, rather than a self-evident premise? More precisely, how might one do so without becoming entangled in the polemic that surrounds Strauss and his work? As the supposed oracle inspiring key neoconservative figures of the George W. Bush administration, Strauss has been accused of setting forth the central principles for defending the West from its own self-destruction at the hands of liberalism's blind faith in the historical relativity of values. As Shadia Drury puts it, "all neoconservatives share his [Strauss's] profound antipathy to secular liberal society (what Strauss referred to as 'modernity')."[2] This antipathy stems from Strauss's own experience with, and reflections on, the Weimar Republic, which, says Drury, convinced him that "liberal democracy is a spineless regime without any firm beliefs."[3] Caught in the web of historicism—that is, the idea that every claim to truth is relative to the society in which the claim is made—liberals are unable to defend their political values as being any better than the values of, say, an authoritarian theocracy. They cannot even defend the value of civilization over that of barbarism. It must therefore fall to a courageous elite, to those who are bold enough to state and defend their values as rational, true, and absolutely so, to rescue the achievements of the West from the ruins of liberalism.[4] If doing so involves the brazen manipulation of public opinion and the dissemination of a "noble lie"[5] (e.g., the alleged "weapons of mass destruction" justification for the 2003 US invasion of Iraq), holds Drury—so be it.

Drury's interpretation of Strauss's hostility to liberalism as a form of political society that cannot justify itself to itself, let alone to its enemies, is not without foundation in his texts. Strauss thought liberalism to be in a state of crisis whose name was "relativism" and whose origins lay in "historicism." As he writes in *Natural Right and History*, "they [liberals] appear to believe that our inability to acquire any genuine knowledge of what is intrinsically good or right compels us to be tolerant of every opinion about good or right or to recognize all preferences or all 'civilizations' as equally respectable. Only unlimited tolerance is in accordance with reason."[6] The question, however, is whether this account of the crisis of liberalism, albeit polemically stated, is that of the supposedly antiliberal Strauss (and his followers) alone. As a glance at the texts of self-declared liberals such as George Crowder, William A. Galston, John Gray, Amy Gutmann, Charles Larmore, and Martha Nussbaum suggests, it is an account that is shared in important ways by Strauss's putative opponents. In their view, there is good reason to worry because liberals—especially those who subscribe to the political liberalism of John Rawls—have been on the whole reluctant to defend their values as universally valid, which leaves them vulnerable to the attack of those (especially non-Western, nonliberal) cultures and peoples who have no such qualms about asserting the validity of their antiliberal values. Indeed, this worry, internal to the liberal camp itself, has spawned a massive literature on the crisis of liberalism.[7]

This strange convergence on the crisis of liberalism between the nonliberal Strauss and self-declared liberals points to the central problem that haunts the liberal approach to widespread value pluralism, an approach that prioritizes the right over the good and that seeks to avoid conflict and discrimination based on value differences by relegating the expression of such differences (e.g., religious belief) to the private realm. Strauss's critical stance toward liberalism, itself formed in the crucible of twentieth-century German history, expresses his view that such a political settlement does not work. The liberal principle of neutrality does not eliminate but merely relocates discrimination to the private sphere and denies it political significance. In the preface to his book on Baruch Spinoza, Strauss writes, "The liberal state cannot provide a solution to the Jewish problem, for such a solution would require a legal prohibition against every kind of 'discrimination,' i.e., the abolition of the private sphere, the denial of the difference between state and society, the destruction of the liberal state."[8] But what kind of solution would work?

If Strauss thought liberal democracy to be an irredeemably "spineless regime" that, in the case of Weimar, led directly to Auschwitz, then we should follow the advice of George Kateb: "anyone committed to modern democracy should resist the influence" of Strauss.[9] But was Strauss an enemy of liberal democracy?[10] We do better to read Strauss's quarrel with liberalism as an attempt not to refute its value but to make visible its constitutive paradoxes and blind spots.[11] "The friend of liberal democracy is not its flatterer," Strauss declares.[12] By contrast with the crisis liberals mentioned previously, Strauss does not think that the crisis of liberalism can be resolved by shoring up its foundations—that is, by declaring liberal values as the best values, as true—and thereby seeking to foreclose any genuine conflict or debate about the best possible regime. I recognize that this reading of Strauss goes against the grain of those interpretations that see him as locating the very weakness of liberalism in its unwillingness to declare its own values as true. That critique of liberalism, however, is no recipe for liberalism's salvation but an effort to expose its entanglement in the illusory neutrality with which liberals would master what they take to be an otherwise irresolvable conflict between "ultimate value orientations," to borrow Weber's phrase. In contrast to the crisis liberals, Strauss is deeply critical of the idea that it is possible to "create a society which is free of contradictions" (*SCR*, 6). It was just this idea that his critique of liberalism and its solution to the "Jewish problem" sought to question.[13]

In Strauss's view, the defense of liberal democracy as the best possible regime cannot avoid turning into dogmatism in the absence of a public debate about the best possible regime, a debate that is possible only if liberal democracy is not treated, as it is in the historicist framework in which it has its life, as the regime that is best suited to take account of the undeniable reality of value pluralism.[14] The idea that such pluralism leads to the necessity of liberalism as the best regime, which is the central argument made by liberals and crisis liberals alike, is, for Strauss, symptomatic of a way of thinking about other points of view that appears highly tolerant but is actually deeply dogmatic.

Understanding how it is that a regime that defines itself as best (because it is best able to accommodate value pluralism) could be blind to its own dogmatism is the central aim behind Strauss's claim that we need to liberate ourselves from, rather than merely refute, historicism.

What does a critique that seeks "liberation" from historicism, rather than its "refutation," look like? And why would we, Strauss's twentieth-century readers, need to be liberated from a "Weltanschauung," to borrow Karl Mannheim's characterization of the historicist outlook, which "permeate[d] everyday thinking" in Mannheim's time?[15] The "recognition that all human ideas and values are historically conditioned and subject to change," as Georg Iggers describes historicism, has its roots in the beginning of the modern period and takes the form of a "crisis" in the late nineteenth century.[16] But is it really a way of seeing things that is still with us and from which we need to be liberated? Insofar as faith in the classical historicist narrative of progressive and unitary time has been put into radical doubt by the catastrophic political events of the twentieth century, this question is all the more pressing when evaluating Strauss's project to turn historicism from a self-evident premise into a problem.

Notwithstanding these concerns, I agree with Strauss that the basic historicist insight into the relativity of values and norms is still with us. It is there not only in liberal but also other forms of contemporary political theory, and it is there in the public discourse on tolerance and multiculturalism, both global and domestic. But what does such relativity look like in the absence of faith in progress and the coherence of history? As we shall see, this was the central question that defined the late nineteenth- and early twentieth-century German debate on the "crisis of historicism" and that haunted it in the form of the threat of relativism. It was one of the important questions that Strauss would raise in his critique of liberalism's putative neutrality as symptomatic of its entanglement in historicist premises. And it is the question that continues to define the future of the liberal democratic project in the context of widespread value pluralism. Whether recognition of the diversity of worldviews necessarily leads to relativism understood as a crisis of judgment, as the "crisis liberals" seem to assume, is for us an open question.

If we grant that historicism is a self-evident premise or worldview, as Strauss claims, what would that entail? As a worldview, historicism is not something that we could test or subject to doubt; rather, it is composed of judgments that act as principles of judgment, as Wittgenstein would put it.[17] *Historicism*, as I wish to employ the term, is not a doctrine or a body of knowledge but a *"picture* that holds us captive," to paraphrase Wittgenstein, a picture of how things *must* be: values and knowledge just *are* historically relative (*PI*, §115). As Wittgenstein showed in his analysis of the various pictures that hold us captive (e.g., the skeptical picture of a doubt without end), such pictures were not available for refutation, for they were ultimately groundless. What could possibly count as proof against the historicist claim that knowledge and values change with time?

When historicism is understood to mean the view that all human knowledge and values are relative to time and place, it is easy to see why it would—and perhaps ought to—retain a hold on those of us who question claims to transcontextual criteria, external standpoints, or eternal truths. What is more, is not Isaiah Berlin (a committed liberal and full-blooded historicist, in Strauss's view) quite right to point to the empirical reality of value pluralism as proof of the historicist pudding, so to speak? Is there not much to recommend in a view that posits the relativity of values and refutes the idea that human beings can attain a standpoint from which objectivity is possible? Isn't Wittgenstein himself a "historicist"? Did not his remarks on the cultural relativity of aesthetics in the last chapter already indicate that he is? Wouldn't liberation from historicism land us right back in the arms of the dogmatic rationalism that such thinkers as Wittgenstein meant to combat? And isn't that what Strauss represents: a return to rationalism?

In this chapter I explore how a democratic theory of judgment questions historicism as a self-evident premise, how such questioning is vital to a critical but also productive interrogation of liberalism, and how it need not lead us back to rationalism, certainly not to modern rationalism, with its emphasis on foundations and certainty—that is, the "epistemological tradition sprung from Descartes," as John Gunnell writes, that Strauss "rejected very early in his life."[18] I read Strauss not as someone who puts forward a universal theory of the human condition (e.g., nonhistorical) or theses about how things stand in the world or who should rule it, but as a zetetic philosopher in search of the fundamental problems of human existence, one for whom, as Strauss says time and again, "philosophy is knowledge that one does not know" (*NRH*, 32).[19]

Strauss's approach to historicism, like his approach to liberalism and the theologicopolitical problem that liberalism claims to solve, is fundamentally therapeutic in spirit. It aims, as does the philosophy of Wittgenstein, not to refute one's opponent (historicism) or to force a choice (revelation *or* reason) but to lead us to an understanding of our entanglement in certain confusions when we seek absolute grounds for our thinking and acting or make absolute choices that exclude in principle the possible truth claims of one's opponent (e.g., Jerusalem *or* Athens) in the hopes of giving final answers to the fundamental questions, thus creating a society that is free of contradictions.[20] That this search for absolute grounds can take the paradoxical form of the liberal historicist claim that there are no absolute truths, save the historicist truth that all thought is historical, is one of the many important insights of Strauss's critique. In my view, Strauss no more aims to refute the historicist than Wittgenstein, as Stanley Cavell has shown, aims to refute the skeptic. For Wittgenstein, the point was not to invert the skeptic's claim that absolute knowledge is impossible (because there is doubt without end) but to show what the skeptic must take for granted to get the language game of radical doubt started. Just this strategy is at work in Strauss's account of historicism and, by extension, liberalism. The point is not to advance competing theses about how the world really is (e.g., there really is absolute truth) but to liberate us from the thought of how it *must* be (e.g., historically relative).

Once we recognize Strauss's aim as therapeutic, we will be better able to "recapture 'Strauss before Straussianism,'" to borrow John Gunnell's apt phrase.[21] We will see that the alternative to a historicist understanding of values and knowledge as relative is not a view of them as absolute and universal, not in the way modern rationalism would have it; that Strauss's aim in combating historicism was to contest dogmatism, not to put another dogmatic set of truths in the place of the "truth" of historicism; and that what motivates his critique is not relativism, as critics assume, but authoritarianism and the crisis of critical judgment. It is the capacity for reflective, critical judgment, not the affirmation of eternal truths or the establishment of an elite who alone can grasp them, that Strauss, a German Jew, sought to rescue from the ruins of Weimar and the political catastrophes of the twentieth century.[22]

Historicism and Its Crisis

Strauss's critique of historicism is generally treated as being of a piece with his critique of relativism. Since relativism is normally understood as the view that there are no transcendent criteria of judgment, Strauss is commonly read as attempting to refute historicism and relativism by showing that there are indeed such absolute (eternal) criteria. To critically assess this reading of Strauss, it is necessary to understand the historical background in which historicism and its crisis, which centered on the problem of relativism, arose. Doing so is not easy. Not only is the term *historicism* itself vague, accounts of both its development and its eventual crisis are highly diverse.[23] Nevertheless, insofar as Strauss (1899–1973) himself was witness to a crucial phase of the German historicist debates, it is important to gain a better understanding of the context in which his critique arose and to what extent it resembled or diverged from his contemporaries' accounts.[24] That said, what I offer here is highly schematic. My aim is to provide a general context in which we can try to make sense of Strauss's own account of the crisis brought about by historicism, which is in its own way highly partial and idiosyncratic.[25]

According to Friedrich Meinecke's *Historism* (1936), historicism has its origins in the reaction to the natural right teaching of the eighteenth century, which underwrote revolutionary movements.[26] The Enlightenment emphasized individual rights, but it never grasped the true uniqueness of individuals and cultures, argues Meinecke. Rather, it held that once people freed themselves from prejudices, they would "speak with the same voice and utter the same timeless and absolutely valid truths, which were in harmony with those prevailing in the universe as a whole."[27] It is this conception of human reason that historicism challenges.

Johann Gottfried Herder's 1774 manifesto, *Auch eine Philosophie der Geschichte zur Bildung der Menschheit* (*Yet Another Philosophy of History for the Cultivation of Humanity*), was perhaps the most powerful statement of a new historical sensibility. Herder challenged universal standards of rationality and the assumption that the course of history was unified and progressive. In Herder's text the movement of history embodied various cultural standards, each valid and comprehensible in its own context. Working off Herder, Friedrich Schleiermacher's 1799 work *Über die Religion: Reden an die Gebildeten unter ihren Verächtern* (*On Religion: Speeches to Its Despisers*) argues that truths of earlier epochs were in no way invalidated by truths of later periods. Both Schleiermacher and Herder, as Jeffrey Andrew Barash observes, make visible "the emergence of the late-eighteenth- and early-nineteenth-century conviction that, for consciousness to posit truth, the perspective of a particular historical culture is essential."[28] Barash continues, critical of the "Enlightenment faith in history as the arena of progressive application of universally valid rational norms, . . . Herder [and] Schleiermacher [nonetheless] shared the conviction that history was a meaningful, coherent whole, which, if not necessarily intelligible to human understanding, could be ascribed to what each took to be its inscrutable sacred foundation."[29]

Thinking at once about truth as historically diverse and of history as comprising a meaningful whole was given its most powerful expression in the work of G. W. F. Hegel, who invoked the historicity of truth both to vindicate the Enlightenment faith in the validity of universal standards of reason for rendering history coherent and to expose the limits of Enlightenment reason. Hegel married the universal validity of rational standards with historical diversity in a way that would deeply influence the crisis of historicism as it arose in Germany. By midcentury, Hegel's grand metaphysical synthesis came into question in the German universities. What was questioned, however, was not necessarily the idea of history as a coherent whole. Most academics simply assumed that diversity and change did not affect truth secured by the coherence of the historical process. Nevertheless, as Barash explains,

the insight into concrete historical diversity and the loss of faith in all-encompassing metaphysical syntheses left a central problem unresolved. Given the diversity of normative standards and values and their perpetual modification through history, what assurance might be adduced for coherent foundations of truth so necessary to intellectual endeavors? . . . The recognition of truth's historical diversity with no assurance that human thought could penetrate the inner depths of reality presented a perplexing challenge—how to unify the concrete foundations of the truths of different epochs into an interpenetrating totality, without which each epoch would remain locked within its specific historical context.[30]

As a debate in nineteenth- and early twentieth-century German philosophy, the basic question raised by historicism was: how is knowledge possible under conditions of flux? Thinkers as diverse as Wilhelm Dilthey and Edmund Husserl, as well as neo-Kantians such as Wilhelm Windelband and Heinrich Rickert of the Baden school and Hermann Cohen and Paul Natorp of the Marburg school, struggled in various ways with the problem of criteria for historical judgment. Their shared goal was to provide "a scientific methodology capable of overcoming the relativity of cultural values," as Charles Bambach observes.[31] All these thinkers were reacting not only to historicism but also to the naturalistic worldview that had accompanied the ascendance of the natural sciences in Germany in the 1860s and 1870s and their law-constructing methods. To defend the distinctiveness of human thought and culture, they emphasized the historicity of human knowledge, but this emphasis on historicity raised the problem of securing the foundations of such knowledge in the face of change. "The more the specificity of historical comprehension was emphasized as the method appropriate to the human sciences, the more urgent it became to establish universal criteria of coherence transcending historical individuality and the diversity of cultural perspectives," writes Paul Ricoeur.[32] Indeed, as Heidegger astutely recognized, the neo-Kantian philosophical framing of the problem of historicism as an epistemological one and the corresponding attempt to develop such universal criteria both took for granted that culture and world-historical development were primary sources of coherence that could be empirically verified.[33] The denial of universal values would have entailed a radical relativism, then, had it not been for faith in the meaningfulness of history (thanks to Providence in the form of God, *Geist*, or the state). However correct this interpretation of the debate in philosophy and the social sciences may be, argues Allan Megill, it does not really answer a crucial question: "*why*, for late nineteenth- and early twentieth-century scholars, was there a crisis of historicism?"[34] In Georg Iggers's account, the crisis was brought about by awareness on the part of philosophers and social scientists that all knowledge is "colored by subjectivity" and that there was no external standpoint from which absolute objectivity would be possible. "But why should these rather unsurprising insights lead to a crisis," especially a crisis that went beyond the small circle of philosophers and social scientists? asks Megill.[35] In his view, the roots of the crisis are to be found in the 1830s in theology and religion, specifically in Protestant theology and biblical scholarship, and not in the 1880s in historiography or philosophy. The question that arose in the 1830s, argues Megill, was not quite the one that was at the core of the 1880–1927 discussion: "How are knowledge and values possible under conditions of flux? Rather, the earlier question—which nonetheless has close relations, both theoretical and historical, to the later one—was, How is faith possible in the face of critical scientific investigation? Or, more specifically, Can Christianity survive the depredations of critical Biblical scholarship?"[36]

In Germany such scholarship was exemplified by the 1835–36 publication of David Friedrich Strauss's *Das Leben Jesu* (*The Life of Jesus*), explains Megill, which "attempted to 'historicize' (as we would say) the Gospel stories by seeing them as products of the mythical outlook that the Gospel authors shared with their time and culture: in short, the stories were the product of the unconscious poetizing of the people of that time and place. . . . [The book] gave rise to a massive controversy, for many theologians, as well as ecclesiastical and state authorities, saw Strauss's argument as destructive of Christian orthodoxy."[37] Strauss's work had the same kind of destructive effect on claims to absolute validity that preoccupied those scholars who participated in the post-1880 crisis of historicism discussion.[38] But it was here, in the realm of the eternal verities of Christian teaching, not in academic German philosophy as such, that historicism was experienced as especially corrosive.[39]

Before turning to Leo Strauss's own account of historicism, we need to ask another question—namely, as Colin Loader astutely puts it, "why did the crisis of Historicism occur when it did? Since the problem of relativism was inherent in Historicism from the very beginning, why did Historicists not perceive a crisis until the early 1920's?"[40] Although Megill's account helps make sense of the high stakes of questioning in the register of the eternal verities of Christian faith versus philosophy or social science, we are left wondering why the crisis occurred at this time and not earlier. According to Loader,

the crisis arose not from theoretical problems inherent in the doctrine of Historicism, but rather from the inadequacy of the doctrine for solving the very real problems arising from Germany's collapse in World War One and the establishment of the Weimar Republic. Or put another way, the crisis arose not because of the Historicists' inability to guarantee the existence of a universal set of values, but rather because of their inability to guarantee the existence of a *unity of values* for the German nation in the 1920s. Thus, although the Historicists expressed their crisis in *temporal* terms, in terms of the dissolution of eternal truths in the flow of history, the crisis was in fact *spatial,* resulting from their antipathy to a truly pluralistic Germany, one which was not an organic community of values.[41]

The problem of relativism did not arise as long as the historicist idea of the German nation as an organic whole stood fast. In Loader's view, "that the values of the German *Volk* might be in conflict with those of other *Völker,* did not trigger a crisis of values among early Historicists. As Heinrich von Treitschke stated: 'I write [only] for Germans.'"[42] Although there were differing opinions as to the importance of the individual vis-à-vis the state itself as the highest form of individuality, historicists as diverse as Eduard Spranger, Ernst Troeltsch, Leopold von Ranke, Heinrich von Treitschke, and Georg von Below all held that the typical Western individual, as Loader continues, "the individual who sought to satisfy his own material needs and who operated according to Bentham's calculus of pleasure and pain . . . was not practicing true individualism, but rather mere subjectivism."[43] They shared an antipathy toward the idea of "society," which, by contrast with the "state," as Treitschke wrote, was "intangible," and "composed of all manner of warring interests, which if left to themselves would soon lead to a *bellum omnium contra omnes* [war of all against all]."[44] And they saw in Marxism the paradigmatic expression of such a view.

The basic organic relationship advanced by historicists came to be questioned during the Weimar Republic. The war had already raised questions among historicists about the coherent and progressive nature of history. But it was with the advent of the republic, in which pluralism was institutionalized, that the real crisis of historicism arose. Writes Loader: "Parliamentary democracy for them [the historicists] meant 'party democracy.' Their formula was simple: the parties were institutions formed to realize the material interests of specific social groups; these interests were the product of the chaotic social sphere and not of the organic sphere of *Geist*."[45] Antipathy toward the pluralistic republic was heightened in large part because the Social Democrats were the strongest party in the early phases of the Republic, and though reformist in deed, they were Marxist in word. For the historicists, Marxism was based on the idea of society as a composite of warring material interests; it amounted to what Loader calls "a mechanistic philosophy of chaos."[46]

Most important, argues Loader, both Marxism and party democracy rejected the elitist ideas of historicism and the view that one group could speak for all.

The demise of the traditional political elite, which had been charged with the defense of the spiritual unity of the nation, naturally caused uneasy feelings among the cultural elite, among whom the Historicist world view predominated. For the first time, Historicism was forced to deal with a socio-political reality which rejected its premises. Here was the root of the crisis.[47]

Nevertheless, not all historicists perceived a crisis of historicism. For men like Below, who denounced democracy as "the devastation and waste of the nation," there was no internal weakness in the doctrine of historicism itself.[48] Rather, the problem was external. Such historicists viewed the Weimar Republic as a foreign enemy that had to be repelled with a corporatist, monarchist political program. In short, historicist premises regarding the fundamental organic unity of the nation did not need to be rethought; one needed only to wait for a resurrection of the Bismarckian state. For Max Weber, who refused the return to the iron chancellor, historicism was faced with the reality of irreconcilable conflict among diverse ultimate value orientations. The idea of national organic unity was as illusory as the claim of social science to provide ethical and political guidance. For yet other thinkers, such as Meinecke, who were not hostile to democracy as such, the fact of plural political interests did not translate into plural but equally valid worldviews. For them, domestic value pluralism was not something to be recognized and affirmed but rather overcome through the reestablishment of the organic whole. However, concludes Loader, "Since large segments of the nation rejected the basic organicist premises of Historicism, the proposed solutions to the crisis of Historicism, which were always based on these premises, were mere pipedreams."[49]

Strauss's Critique of Historicism

Taking account of the origins of the crisis of historicism will help us make sense of Strauss's own account. Far from being an academic plea for the existence of eternal truths and philosophy as the means to know those truths, Strauss's argument targets the easy acceptance of authority and tradition that, in his view, historicism enables. For Strauss, the crisis of historicism in postwar Germany was no mere crisis in philosophy or even theology; it was, above all, a political crisis. It is to grasp the political significance of this crisis that Strauss will seek a vantage point beyond liberalism from which to understand the failure of the modern liberal project.

Strauss's 1940 lecture "The Living Issues of German Postwar Philosophy," which describes, as he puts it, "the tendencies of the world in which I then was living" ("LI," 117), makes clearer the political stakes of historical consciousness for Strauss in terms of various German responses to World War I. "The large majority of the older generation and a considerable part of the younger generation naturally continued traditions which had been established in the 19th century or earlier without being disturbed by the upheaval of the war and of its aftermath" ("LI," 117). "We may call this type of men the merely academic philosophers," who had little influence on "public opinion of postwar Germany" ("LI," 117). Those who did have such influence were "thinkers who felt that the traditions of the 19th century *could* not be continued and did not *deserve* to be continued" ("LI," 117). These can be divided into two groups: "thinkers who had a direct and revolutionizing effect on . . . academic youth" (e.g., Weber) and those who worked in "relative secrecy" and who would come to be associated with a deeper revolution in thought—namely, "phenomenology" (e.g., Heidegger) ("LI," 117).

Describing the effects of the war on the thinkers with public influence, Strauss sketches in the broadest strokes historicism and its crisis. Prominent in his account is the way in which the development of historical consciousness goes hand in hand with the crisis of science and the turn away from reason to authority. Such a turn, argues Strauss, arises as a consequence of the view, mostly powerfully articulated by Weber,

that reason and argument are intrinsically incapable of giving to life a real guidance. Reason and argument cannot bridge the gulf which separates the different groups each of which is guided by a star, a value-system, of its own. Now, every human community needs some degree of agreement at least as regards the basic moral questions. Such an agreement may be supplied by a tradition; but in Germany, traditions were losing their force more and more. If reason and argument are incapable of supplying people with the minimum of mutual understanding required for living together, if mutual understanding as regards the practical basis of common life cannot be reached by reason and argument, people had no choice but to turn away from reason to *authority*. ("LI," 127)[50]

"The most visible kind of authority—most visible at least in Germany—is the *State*" ("LI," 127), adds Strauss. He goes on to explain how this turn to the authority of the state, rooted in the inability to determine which values are the right ones, is given real force in the writings of Carl Schmitt. It is often said that Strauss shared Schmitt's enmity toward bourgeois liberalism and, if anything, did not think that Schmitt went far enough in his critique.[51] This interpretation presupposes that Strauss shared Schmitt's view that by justifying obedience to the state on the basis of faith (political theology), one in effect placed such obedience beyond all possible critique. But Strauss's point was not to defend faith's immunity to critique; it was to bring into relief the failure of the kind of critique of faith generated by modern rationalism (e.g., Spinoza) and the defense of faith generated by historicism (e.g., Troeltsch and liberal theology). In Strauss's view, both rationalism and historicism took for granted the idea that belief is something that must give evidence. The search for the historical Jesus, as we saw, was supposed to provide empirical evidence for belief. But the turn to authority that concerns Strauss is precisely what occurs when evidence is lacking. "The inability of modern science or philosophy to give man an evident teaching as regards the fundamental question, the question of the right life, led people to turn from science or reason to authority, to the authority of the State or the authority of Revelation" ("LI," 129), Strauss writes.

The question Strauss raises in these passages is this: what is the basis of critical judgment? He shared Nietzsche's view that historical consciousness in Germany had led to the occlusion of judgment. "It was against 'history,' against the belief that 'history' can decide any question, that progress can ever make superfluous the discussion of the primary questions, . . . that he [Nietzsche] reasserted hypothetically the doctrine of eternal return" ("LI," 138). However much Strauss disagreed with Nietzsche on the latter doctrine, he strongly endorsed Nietzsche's critique of historicism when it came to the problem of judgment. Both rejected the idea that what comes later is by definition better, or that the victorious cause is necessarily the cause of truth.

Likewise, however critical he was of Heidegger's radical historicism, Strauss followed him in refusing the epistemological problematic as it was given by the neo-Kantians. Heidegger had radicalized historicism in large part by decisively breaking with the epistemological quest of the neo-Kantians to restore the foundations of knowledge in the face of their corrosion by historical consciousness. Because Strauss, *pace* Heidegger, emphasizes the threat to knowledge and reason posed by historicism, it may be easy to miss the fact and significance of what they share: the refusal to define the problem, or search for its solution, in the epistemic terms of the neo-Kantians. Yet that refusal is crucial to understanding Strauss's particular account of historicism and the nature of the threat to critical judgment that it posed.

The error of the neo-Kantians was to think that historical consciousness could be made compatible with modern reason and mobilized in the service of scientific knowledge. Like Heidegger, Strauss understood that this ideal of compatibility, as it was pursued in the search for historical methods, relied on belief in the coherence of history, which itself relied on the idea of progress. Now progress may appear to be an "attack on tradition" and therefore on prejudice, on unevident teachings. In fact, says Strauss, progress entails "the establishment of a new tradition." He continues,

For "progress" means that certain questions, the *basic* questions can be settled once and for all, so that the answers to these questions can be taught to children, so that the subsequent generations simply can build up on the solutions found out by earlier generations, without bothering any longer about the basic questions. I.e.: "progress" implies that the answers to the basic questions can be taken for granted, that they can be permitted to become *prejudices* for all generations after that of the founding fathers. Accordingly, the process of intellectual development during the modern centuries consists in this, that each generation *reacts* to the preceding generation and to the preceding generation *only*, without raising the question whether the whole basis on which the discussion takes place—that basis discovered by the founding fathers—is valid. ("LI," 123–24)

Entanglement in the idea of progress, otherwise necessary to stave off the corrosive effects of historical consciousness, is potentially fatal to the whole project of modern reason, whose purpose is nothing other than to expose prejudice as unevident teaching.

Thus Strauss found pointless the efforts of the neo-Kantians to reestablish the foundations of knowledge in the wake of historicist claims about its relativity. From his perspective, this was merely a continuation of the failed project of modern rationalism, which led to historicism and its crisis in the first place. The problem with the type of rationalism that historicism had rejected (i.e., that of Descartes and the Enlightenment) was, as Heidegger had shown, its reliance on subjectivity as the locus of certitude. This subjectivism constructed reality as being in principle subject to radical doubt. It easily led in the direction of its opposite, be it orthodoxy or various forms of irrationalism.[52] The kind of objectivity sought by the Neo-Kantians in modern rationalism was for Strauss, then, nothing but a pipe dream.

If Strauss accepted Nietzsche's diagnoses of the self-destruction of modern reason and Heidegger's teaching that modern rationalism, with its emphasis on the mastery of nature, led to a fatal faith in technology, then no return to modern rationalism was possible, for every return would end in yet another spectacle of self-destruction. But if modern reason cannot save us from the relativist consequences that Strauss associated with historicism or the critically debilitating consequences associated with religious orthodoxy, what idea of reason would be up to the task?

In Quest of a Nonhistoricist Understanding of Historicism

"If I have exhausted the justifications I have reached bedrock, and my spade is turned. Then I am inclined to say: 'This is simply what I do,'" writes Wittgenstein (*PI* §217). At that point one comes face-to-face with irreducible commitments as a practice, a way of going on. For Strauss, as for Wittgenstein, such recognition is not that of the *limits* of reason—as the skeptic would have us believe—but of the *limited* idea of reason as it is given in the modern rationalist notions of foundations and certainty. Strauss was not prepared to give up on the possibility of reason, for to do so would be to accept not only religious orthodoxy but any orthodoxy. Rather than "saying farewell to reason," writes Strauss in the book on Spinoza, it would be wiser to ask "whether the self-destruction of reason was not the inevitable outcome of modern rationalism as distinguished from pre-modern rationalism" (*SCR*, 31). This suspicion, already articulated in 1930, would become the basis for Strauss's critical approach to historicism: "A return to reason *which implies or presupposes a critical analysis of the genesis of historical consciousness*, necessarily is a return to reason as reason was understood in pre-modern times" ("LI," 133).[53] This approach seeks not to defeat historicism but to liberate us from the sense of its necessity by exposing as incoherent what historicism must take for granted to get its language game off the ground.

Like Wittgenstein's approach to skepticism, which gives the skeptic's irreverent questioning its due, Strauss's approach begins by acknowledging what is valuable in historicism: "Historicism refutes all systems of philosophy—by doing this, it does the cause of philosophy the greatest service: for a system of philosophy, a system of *quest* for truth, is non-sense" ("LI," 132). The emphasis here is on the idea of a "system" (à la Hegel or perhaps Kant). Philosophy is the quest for truth in Strauss's view, only such a quest is part of a quotidian and never-ending practice of critical thinking that cannot be systematized. Likewise, in *Natural Right and History*, Strauss names historicism "as an ally in our fight against dogmatism"—that is, "the inclination 'to identify the goal of our thinking with the point at which we have become tired of thinking'" (*NRH*, 22). One way in which we become tired of thinking is when we think in terms of progress, which treats the past "only as a preparation for the present" and reads past authors only in light of "the contribution of the doctrine to our beliefs."[54] Early historicists rightly criticized this approach to the past, says Strauss, recognizing that genuine interest in the past is at odds with the view that "the present is in the most important respect superior to the past."[55]

Notwithstanding its original contribution to combating dogmatism in all these forms, historicism too comes to exemplify this exhaustion with thinking: it takes its own founding idea that "all 'truths' and standards are necessarily relative to a given historical situation" ("LI," 132) as superior to all past, nonhistorical ways of thinking. "We are forced to suspect that historicism is the guise in which dogmatism likes to appear in our age" (*NRH*, 22), Strauss writes. Caught in a performative contradiction, historicism affirms that all claims to truth are historically bounded save one: the thesis that all truths are so bounded.

Historicism asserts that all human thoughts or beliefs are historical, and hence deservedly destined to perish; but historicism itself is a human thought; hence historicism can be of only temporary validity, or it cannot be simply true. To assert the historicist thesis means to doubt it and thus to transcend it. As a matter of fact, historicism claims to have brought to light a truth which has come to stay, a truth valid for all thought, for all time: however much thought has changed and will change, it will always remain historical. . . . Historicism thrives on the fact that it inconsistently exempts itself from its own verdict about all human thought. The historicist thesis is self-contradictory or absurd. We cannot see the historical character of "all" thought—that is, of all thought with the exception of the historicist insight and its implications—without transcending history, without grasping something transhistorical. (*NRH*, 25)

The historicist will object, writes Strauss, that this critique does not hold. "One does not have to transcend history in order to see the historical character of all thought: there is a privileged moment, an absolute moment in the historical process, a moment in which the essential character of all thought becomes transparent. In exempting itself from its own verdict, historicism claims merely to mirror the character of historical reality or to be true to the facts" (*NRH*, 28–29). What is the character of this reality? Being in the right place at the right time: "radical historicism asserts that the basic insight into the essential limitation of all human thought is not accessible to man as man, or that it is not the result of the progress or the labor of human thought, but that it is an unforeseeable gift of unfathomable fate. It is due to fate that the essential dependence of thought on fate is realized now, and was not realized in earlier times" (*NRH*, 28). It is because of a privileged moment in history that the truth of historicism became clear to the moderns and also that it remained something to which the ancients were blind, which reflects neither the intellectual superiority of the moderns nor the intellectual inferiority of the ancients, says the historicist, but merely their respective locations in time.[56] Needless to say, "the assumption of an absolute moment in history [that] is essential to historicism," comments Strauss, "surreptitiously follows the precedent set in a classic manner by Hegel" (*NRH*, 29), with all the consequences concerning the so-called end of history and the superiority of what comes later that this entails. And though historicism initially contested the twin ideas of progress and the end of history, says Strauss, it implicitly asserts the opposite: "no possible future change of orientation can legitimately make doubtful the decisive insight into the inescapable dependence of thought on fate" (*NRH*, 29).

The idea of fate is absolutely crucial to historicism, especially radical historicism, argues Strauss, whose thesis can be stated as follows:

All understanding, all knowledge, however limited and "scientific," presupposes a frame of reference; it presupposes a horizon, a comprehensive view within which understanding and knowing take place. Only such a comprehensive vision makes possible any seeing, any observation, any orientation. The comprehensive view of the whole cannot be validated by reasoning, since it is the basis of all reasoning. Accordingly, there is a variety of such comprehensive views, each as legitimate as any other: we have to choose such a view without any rational guidance. It is absolutely necessary to choose one; neutrality or suspension of judgment is impossible. Our choice has no support but itself . . . Strictly speaking, we cannot choose among different views. A single comprehensive view is imposed on us by fate. . . . All human thought depends on fate, on something that thought cannot master and whose workings it cannot anticipate. (*NRH*, 26–27)

This is how historicism secularizes religious orthodoxy: all knowledge comes to us not by a dispensation of God (as it does in revelation) but by fate (our contingent location in place and time). And like orthodoxy, this knowledge is at bottom no more justifiable than it is in need of justification. All thought "rests on dogmatic, that is, arbitrary premises or, more specifically, on premises that are only 'historical and relative'" (*NRH*, 30). This then becomes the dogmatic truth of historicism, which claims universality and, as Strauss observed, thereby "exempts itself from its own verdict about all human thought" (*NRH*, 25).

Whereas "philosophy in the strict sense is man's effort to liberate himself from the particular premises of any particular civilization or culture,"[57] Strauss asserts, historical consciousness holds that "a mature philosophy can raise no higher claim than that to express the spirit of the period to which it belongs" ("LI," 132). Thus radical historicism, the form that he associated with Heidegger, is fatal to critical thinking and judgment, in Strauss's view. It is fatal to philosophy as the quest for truth. But why should we not embrace the fundamental idea of historical consciousness, the idea of truth as relative to time and place? Is it not the case that, for consciousness to posit truth, the perspective of a particular culture is essential? What can it mean to liberate oneself from the particular premises of any civilization or culture? Are we to jump over our own shadow?

It can easily sound as if Strauss were calling for just such a leap, in which case he would seek the conditions of a presuppositionless judgment or context-transcendent standards from which to judge. Such conditions would mean that when critical thinking is working properly, as Nikolas Kompridis summarizes, "it subjects to rational testing and criticism not only our shared beliefs and practices but also the assumptions on which these beliefs and practices rest."[58] Such a notion of critique is, according to Kompridis, "inadequate to its task: it needs to be conjoined with rather than opposed to Heidegger's, and that is because the background assumptions of everyday practices need also to be reflectively disclosed before they can be properly thematized and criticized."[59] This need "follows from the Heideggerian/Wittgensteinian insight that we cannot render fully explicit the massive background of shared beliefs and practices no matter how public our procedures: this background resists (or withdraws from) a completely objectifying grasp," Kompridis observes.[60]

Strauss accepted Heidegger's teaching that there can be no such thing as a presuppositionless judgment which, were it possible, would turn philosophy from the search for truth into the possession of truth and thus operate wholly within the logic of progress. The judgments that function as presuppositions of judgment, however, are the prejudgments, prejudices, or *Vorurteile* that Strauss (like Wittgenstein and—we shall see—Arendt) believes we need to keep open to question, while recognizing that we cannot doubt everything all at once. Whether Heidegger is the right thinker to turn to here is not within the scope of this chapter to address. It is only necessary to recognize that Strauss is operating with certain Heideggerian—and implicitly Wittgensteinian—assumptions. In contrast with thinkers (e.g., Habermas) who, as we shall see in chapter 4, though they also hold that doubt is not without limit would renew modern reason, Strauss claims that the project of modern reason has already fully self-destructed, and no rehabilitation is possible. We need instead to return to the premodern idea of reason and try from within that horizon to think critically anew.

But how could we, situated as we are within the horizon of historicism, get critical purchase on historicism, on our own horizon of thought and knowledge, if the presuppositions of historical consciousness form the ungrounded background of our critical thinking? What would it mean to reflectively disclose these presuppositions so that they can be thematized and criticized, to borrow Kompridis's account of an enlarged critical reason? Strauss himself suggests the scope of the problem when he writes that

> the problem of historicism must first be considered from the point of view of classical philosophy, which is nonhistoricist thought in its pure form. Our most urgent need can then be satisfied only by means of historical studies which would enable us to understand classical philosophy exactly as it understood itself, and not in the way in which it presents itself on the basis of historicism. We need, in the first place, a nonhistoricist understanding of nonhistoricist philosophy. But we need no less urgently a nonhistoricist understanding of historicism, that is, an understanding of the genesis of historicism that does not take for granted the soundness of historicism. (NRH, 33)

But how does one attain a nonhistoricist understanding of nonhistoricist thought, which in turn will enable a nonhistoricist understanding of historicism, if one is always already inside the horizon of historicism? To ask this question, Strauss would argue, is to already accept the fundamental thesis of historicism—namely, that we cannot understand other cultures or past thinkers as they understood themselves.

The Limits of *Verstehen*

What does it mean to "understand"? For Strauss, to understand is to grasp the claim of one's opponent or adversary as a claim to truth, especially when reading the philosophy of the past. But such a claim can only be so grasped insofar as one accords to the author the *possibility* that what he or she claims may well be true, and not only true in a relative sense. "To understand a serious teaching, we must be seriously interested in it, we must take it seriously, *i.e.*, we must be willing to consider the possibility that it is simply true. The historicist as such denies that possibility as regards any philosophy of the past."[61] The problem with historicism, then, is that it never does accord the possibility of truth from without to any position—save its own—for it immediately identifies every claim as historically relative; that is, as true only for a particular time, place, culture, or people.

According to the idea of "sympathetic understanding" advanced in the historicist method of *Verstehen*, writes Strauss, "all positions . . . are equally true or untrue: true from within, untrue from without"

("SSH," 9). This is to treat the values of those one aims to understand "'histrionically' as the true values," to treat them in such a way that they never can call into question one's own values and one's own commitments ("SSH," 9). Such so-called "sympathetic understanding is not serious or genuine," he writes. "For genuinely to understand the value system, say, of a given society, means being deeply moved and indeed gripped by the values to which the society in question is committed and to expose one's self in earnest, with a view to one's own whole life, to the claim of those values to be the true values. Genuine understanding of other commitments is then not necessarily conducive to the reassertion of one's own initial commitment" ("SSH," 10–11). For Strauss, it would seem, to understand is to be open to the possibility that one's perspective could be radically challenged by another perspective because not all perspectives are, as perspectives, irremediably distorting; it is to be open to that which might call into question one's worldview and with it one's very being.

The humanistic historicist idea of "universal sympathetic understanding is impossible," declares Strauss ("SSH," 11). His point is to highlight the contradictions and blind spots that attend a notion of truth as historically relative and thus as based on nothing but one's commitment, which is given in one's location in time (fate). If truth were based on something other than one's commitment, it would not be historically relative, but would have a basis in nature. This idea of truth was advanced by Plato. According to the historicist position, "Plato's absolutist interpretation of his value system, as well as any other absolutism, has been refuted unqualifiedly, with finality, absolutely" ("SSH," 11). There is an absolute limit to the so-called sympathetic understanding of absolutists such as Plato. Such understanding turns out to be extended only to "the community of relativists who understand each other with great sympathy because they are united by identically the same fundamental commitment, or rather by identically the same rational insight into the truth of relativism" ("SSH," 12). Herein lies the "hidden arrogance" ("SSH," 12) of a position that presents itself as the epitome of humanistic tolerance. The occlusion of any genuine encounter with other values or worldviews, especially those that make absolute claims to truth—and are these not precisely the kinds of claims that liberals must address today?—may well be the genuine insight of Strauss's critique of the putative tolerance of the historicist position.[62]

How are we to understand Strauss's persistent objection to the idea that all thought is historical and truth is relative to time and place? Strauss is often read as attempting to prove against the historicists that there are eternal truths. Against this ostensible attempt, liberalism is put forth (e.g., by Isaiah Berlin) as a political position that rejects the idea that there is any single account of the whole truth, which could be said to exist in some ideal Platonic realm, awaiting our discovery or which could be publicly defended (John Rawls). But this reading hardens Strauss's position into a form of dogmatism, whereas his model is zetetic philosophy as Socratic practice. His point is not to put another truth in place of historicism, but rather to expose as dogmatic the historicist claim to the truth that there are no such truths.

Strauss's account of historicism's entanglement in a performative contradiction can blind us to what is really at stake for him in its critique. The issue is not simply to expose as dogmatic that which presents itself as infinitely open to alternative values as they arise in different historical contexts but also to show that this dogmatism represents a blockage of critical judgment, for it simply takes for granted the validity—thanks to fate—of its own historical view. Further, this blockage, which treats values as of equal rank save the value of historicity itself, is symptomatic of a deeper problem with the historicist worldview or, more precisely, with the modern language of value differences that historicism articulates (and liberalism, entangled as it is in historicism, adopts).

For Strauss, historicism has no rational basis from which to posit fate as providing a privileged view on how things really are (i.e., really historical). We might redescribe his critique as follows: historicism denies the corrigibility of perspectives by other perspectives. Yet it assumes that perspectives in this merely subjective sense are all we have: they do not point to anything that is really there in the world, and this begins to look rather like the "phantasm" that so bedeviled David Hume's understanding of evaluative thought. By the time we get to the early twentieth century and the historicism that troubled Strauss, however, the idea that our judgments cannot make a claim to objectivity has been extended way beyond the realm of sentiment and value where Hume, *pace* Berkeley, wanted to keep it. Now, the enduring idea that haunts perspective as irremediably distorting—namely, the idea that we are confined in our human modes of subjectivity—has been figured in the more precise terms of the necessary limits to getting the world in view posed by our cultural or historical context. In this sense, who we are and what we can know become one.

For Strauss, the language of values is intrinsically subjectivizing and at odds with our commonsense way of being in the world, where evaluative judgments are experienced as statements about how the world really is (just or unjust, beautiful or ugly, right or wrong), rather than being, according to the grammar of liberalism (and—philosophically speaking—noncognitivism), mere expressions of subjective preferences. There is an almost inevitable tendency, tracked by the development of historicism, to move from the idea that moral and political concepts of what is right and just are values that are relative to time and place, to the idea that they are merely subjective preferences, and, finally, to the inchoate idea of an infinitely large and ultimately irreconcilable conflict of timeless "ultimate values," to use Weber's phrase, whose origins dissolve into mystery.[63] Values are preferences that cannot become objects of knowledge or critical judgment, observes Strauss in his critique of Weber, whereby it follows that "there is a variety of values which are of the same rank, whose demands conflict with one another, and whose conflict cannot be solved by human reason" (*NRH*, 41–42). Subjective preferences are what Kant (as we saw in chapter 2) called "the agreeable": "I like coffee and you like tea"—what is there to debate?

For Strauss, any attempt to resurrect modern rationalism and its epistemological idea of truth as certainty as a way of solving value conflicts was doomed from the start. As we have seen, it was just such rationalism that led human beings down the road of a dangerous and self-defeating subjectivism in the first place. One could not pose "objectivity" as it was construed by modern reason in opposition to "subjectivity," for that would only land one back in the spectacle of self-destruction described by Nietzsche and Heidegger and fully accepted by Strauss. For Strauss, therefore, any attempt to counter modernity's deeply subjectivizing language of values that was at the heart of historicism demanded a return to classical reason.

The Return to Classical Reason

Strauss's effort to generate a nonhistoricist reading of nonhistoricist thought centers on the recovery of the prescientific, phenomenological or prephilosophical awareness—that is, "'the world in which we live' . . . . or the world of common sense" (*NRH*, 79). This commonsense world, however, is far less accessible to us than we think. It is not what we call "the natural world," for that too is "an abstraction" (*NRH*, 79). Indeed, "the world in which we live is already a product of science, or at any rate it is profoundly affected by the existence of science. To say nothing of technology," asserts Strauss (*NRH*, 79). If one wants to recover the natural world in which we live as "a world that is radically prescientific or prephilosophic," he adds, "one has to go back behind the first emergence of science or philosophy" (*NRH*, 79). "Extensive and necessarily hypothetical anthropological studies" (*NRH*, 80) are not necessary. What is needed is a return to classical philosophy.

Paradigmatically exemplified in Socratic dialectics, this recovery of the natural world involves the "return to common sense" (*NRH*, 123), that which modern science has defined as cognitively worthless. The question, "What is?," as Strauss explains, points to "the form or character or 'idea' of a thing, . . . [to] that which is visible to all without any particular effort or what one might call the 'surface' of the things" (*NRH*, 123).

Socrates started . . . from what is first for us, from what comes to sight first, from the phenomena. But the being of things, their What, comes first to sight, not in what we see of them, but in what is said about them or in opinions about them. Accordingly, Socrates started in his understanding of the natures of things from the opinions about their natures. For every opinion is based on some awareness . . . of something. Socrates implied that disregarding the opinions about the natures of things would amount to abandoning the most important access to reality which we have, or the most important vestiges of the truth which are within our reach. He implied that "the universal doubt" of all opinions would lead us, not into the heart of truth, but into a void. (*NRH*, 123–24)

In contrast to modern rationalism, as sprung from Descartes's practice of radical doubt, which sees in opinions only illusion and error, common sense as exemplified in Socratic dialectics or "the art of . . . friendly dispute" starts from what everyone says. Opinion is not opposed to truth but is an irreducible part of it.[64] This starting point sees in opinions "fragments of the truth" (*NRH*, 124). Common sense in the Socratic sense highlights the fallibility of opinions without undermining the idea that opinions can reach truth (i.e., not giving way either to the skeptical claim that all must be subject to doubt or to the dogmatic claim that no doubt can be raised).[65]

There is no truth on Strauss's Socratic account that is not also an opinion. We never arrive at the point where we have established the "visible hallmark which marks truth off from opinion," to speak with Hannah Arendt. It is not that any particular opinion can never be declared truthful (or not) but rather that there is no absolute criterion (or method or procedure) that would allow us to separate opinion from truth, once and for all. The Socratic approach is restricted neither to justification (e.g., Habermas) nor to disclosure (e.g., Heidegger). It is rather in the public practice of dialectics that something becomes mutually intelligible and acceptable. Any such agreement, as we shall see more clearly with Arendt's reading of Socrates in the following chapter, is subject to question, as we never reach a point where the Truth (true knowledge of the Whole) has been found. By contrast with modern rationalism, however, Socratic rationalism is not haunted by the radical skepticism that leads to an obsession with foundations and certainty. If Socrates never speaks of "values" or subjective preferences when engaging in dialectics about morals and principles of justice, as liberals do, argues Strauss, it is because in the face of every discovery that one does not know, Socratic rationalism holds out the possibility that one can know.

It can easily sound as if Strauss's insistence on natural right or the idea of the Whole as the condition of critical judging was an attempt to erect standards in the face of their collapse. He thought of natural right as the inspiring force behind our ability to form critical judgments, lest we resign ourselves, as liberalism advocates, to the intractable character of value conflicts understood as subjective preferences. "If there is no standard higher than the ideal of our society, we are utterly unable to take a critical distance from that ideal. But the mere fact that we can raise the question of the worth of the ideal of our society shows that there is something in man that is not altogether in slavery to his society, and therefore that we are able, and hence obliged, to look for a standard with reference to which we can judge of the ideals of our own as well as of any other society" (*NRH*, 3). This famous passage from *Natural Right and History* is often taken as evidence of Strauss's attempt to posit transhistorical (if not transcendent) rules of judgment anew. But that interpretation misses the zetetic character of critique. It would be more accurate to say that Strauss distinguished between truth and rational acceptability. Truth is not an epistemic concept, for it outstrips all contexts of justification, even ideal ones. This distinction between truth and justification (discussed more fully in chapter 4) is the basis for Strauss's critique of historicism. It opens up a difference between what we take to be true and what *is* true that is crucial to remaining open to the claims of other people and cultures.

To make sense of the idea of philosophy as rooted in an unending Socratic practice of questioning based at once on the distinction between truth and justification and between knowledge that one does not know and the possibility that one can know, Strauss argues, we need to see that ancient philosophy begins precisely as an attempt to arbitrate between different divine codes—that is, competing conceptions of what is good, just, and so on—which are respected by citizens of particular cities on the basis of their belief in traditional gods. By contrast with the modern historicist claim that classical rationalism had no concept of history or awareness that there are diverse values and practices, the origin of philosophy, Strauss holds, lies in just this awareness of plurality. Socratic rationalism is a response not only to the empirical reality of various conventions but also to what Strauss calls the ancient form of historicism: conventionalism. Conventionalism holds that this plurality of values and practices is fully a matter of custom and has no standard in nature.[66]

Strauss claims that, far from defeating the philosophical quest for natural right, this awareness of an open-ended pluralism is the basic condition, the incentive to gain knowledge of nature (*NRH*, 124). To arbitrate among the many divine codes and their conventions, the philosopher turns to nature, to the eternal order of the Whole, which is superior to any of the divine codes.[67] Strauss's account of this turn, and the philosophical eros that animates it, can seem to endorse the idea of an eternal order of the Whole as something that is fixed and knowable. I have already suggested that it is not and would endorse Daniel Tanguay's and Catherine Zuckert's respective arguments on that score.[68] Qua citizen, the philosopher is willing to accept the idea of the divine code as essential to political stability, but, qua philosopher, he does not accept it as true. That is why Strauss tells us that "the divine law, in the real and strict sense of the term, is only the starting point, the absolutely essential starting point, for Greek philosophy, but it is abandoned in the process." Strauss continues, "And if it [divine law] is accepted by Greek philosophy, it is accepted only politically, meaning for the education of the many, and not as something which stands independently."[69] Dogmatically held belief in divine codes—call them noble lies—for the masses, but persistent questioning for the philosophers?[70]

Judging as Care for the World

Notwithstanding his insightful understanding of the imbrication of modern rationalism in a corrosive historicism, Strauss could not translate his idea of a critical practice of judgment for ordinary citizens. For him, it appears that only philosophers were capable of sustained critical thinking, the continual questioning of whatever one holds to be true. Consequently, a certain divide between philosophy and politics emerges in his work, a divide that is at the cost of politics and the commonsense basis of political life. As Tracy Strong has argued, for the exiled philosopher Strauss, it was not "the role of the philosopher to instruct or approach the multitude." Strong continues,

He [Strauss] writes to [Alexandre] Kojève on 22 April 1957: "I do not believe in the possibility of a conversation of Socrates with the people . . . : the relation of the phi-losopher to the people is mediated by a certain kind of rhetoricians who arouse the fear of punishment after death; the philosopher can guide these rhetors but cannot do their work." So whatever the impact of philosophy on the populace is, it will have to be mediated by a group of "rhetors."[71]

In the philosopher Strauss's own case, these "rhetors" then take the form of the cult of overwhelmingly male students (as described by Drury and Norton), who formed the well-known circle around the phi-losopher and went on to spread his ideas in the absolute moral idiom that the masses could understand. Although Strauss has been accused of advocating "philosopher-kings," he actually "agrees with Aristotle, against Plato, that the philosophers should not rule but that rulers should be willing to listen to the philosophers," to borrow Arendt's for-mulation (*LKPP*, 29). Whether those in political power would listen was highly debatable, but the main point, argue critics, was to distill basic moral teachings in a simple language that the people could understand.

There is real merit in this assessment of Strauss's legacy, but my fo-cus here is not just on what Strauss may have thought of the demos and passed on to his disciples. Whatever the degree of his apparently deep-seated mistrust of the demos, the democratic problem of political judg-ment did genuinely concern him, but he was unable to recognize it, as Arendt would, as a problem for the many in large part because he could not recognize it as "care for the world." So understood, the problem of judgment is not addressed by the philosophical quest for knowledge on the model of Socrates. It is not only that Strauss expresses distrust of ordinary modes of judging on the part of ordinary citizens—and this despite his otherwise important attempt to recover common sense—but also that he does not think of the critical thinking and judging that he, like Arendt, admired in Socrates as genuinely engaged with the things of this world, which must always remain part of the Platonic cave. Despite Strauss's reference to the philosopher's concern with "po-litical things," Strauss cannot imagine Socrates as engaged in a "con-versation" with ordinary people in the agora, the place where Arendt sees the "gadfly of Athens" public engagement as a paradigm of critical practice.

Judging politically has as its object "care for the world," not knowledge of "Truth" or even the interminable quest for it that Strauss understands as the proper activity of philosophy. To borrow Arendt's account of where Kant parted ways with the classical view, we might say that Strauss agrees "with Aristotle . . . that the philosophical way of life is the highest and that the political way of life, in the last analysis, exists for the sake of the *bios theōrētikos*" (*LKPP*, 22), which is to say for the sake of philosophy itself. Indeed, it is no wonder that Strauss, by contrast with Arendt, described what he wrote not as "political theory" but as "political philosophy," which, if Strong is right, had to be distilled into an ordinary idiom by the rhetors.[72] To the extent that it even concerns itself with the *vita activa*, "'the subject-matter of modern political philosophy,'" as Arendt (citing Robert Cumming) asserts, "'is not the polis or its politics, but the relation between philosophy and politics'" (*LKPP*, 22). Notwithstanding his attention to "political things," Strauss in his approach shares this "general characteristic, a *déformation professionnelle*," as Arendt puts it, with all other practitioners of the trade (*LKPP*, 22).

Philosophical attempts to view the *vita activa* from the perspective of the *vita contemplativa* end in a radical distortion of the former, argues Arendt. And though Strauss held that the philosopher must settle for Socratic "wisdom" (the knowledge that one does not know), why would its pursuit alone facilitate the ability to judge politically? This ability, as Arendt argued, involves seeing the world from various perspectives, not because knowledge (of the world) but the world itself is at stake. And even if many of those perspectives turn out to be flawed from the standpoint of objective knowledge, they are still something that needs to be taken into account when we judge politically, for they make up (with all their flaws) what at any given moment we hold in common. As argued in chapter 1, it is the diversity of perspectives, and their corrigibility by means of other perspectives, that constitutes our sense of worldly reality.

Although Strauss emphasizes the Socratic practice of working from opinions to knowledge, judgment in Arendt's sense involves more than moving from opinions to knowledge.[73] For her, "care for the world" involves the creation of a "common world" through action and judgment: this shared reality is not, as it is for Strauss, located in the possibility of what classical political philosophy called "nature"—namely, that which is "trans-historical, trans-social, trans-moral, and trans-religious" (*NRH*, 89). For Strauss, the quest for human standards requires this regulative idea of nature, the source of all norms. And even if nature (the Whole) was not something that could ever be fully known, the possibility of knowing it is what held together the shared reality of human life, in Strauss's view.

In this way Strauss, though critical of the modern opposition of "subjective" and "objective," could never rethink their relation, as a democratic theory of judgment must, as one of mutual imbrication. Instead, he carried forward the basic premise of what James Conant calls "hidden world realism": the idea that there is a "metaphysically privileged perspective on reality—one that provides us with the means to achieve a relatively transparent mode of access to how things really are in themselves."[74] This is the philosopher's perspective, as idealized in Platonism. That the Socratic philosopher knows that he cannot know (the Whole) in Strauss's view in no way undermines the basic premise on which this metaphysical realism is built: the gnawing sense, immortalized in Plato's cave parable, that appearances are irremediably distorting and that to be human is to live in the contingent realm of illusion. It is not just a matter of distinguishing between kinds of perspective that do and those that do not involve "an inherently distorted mode of cognition" (e.g., that of the demos versus that of the philosopher), but of putting "in doubt, whether there still can be features of our ordinary experience of the world that are free of distortion," comments Conant—with the emphasis on *ordinary*.[75] Consequently, "Only with the aid of philosophy (or theology) can we enter into communion with any aspect of the 'true world'"—regardless of how partial and unending our philosophical quest may be.[76] Though Strauss held up common sense against the rampant scientism of modern (American) society, he could not free himself from the philosopher's view of ordinary perspective as irremediably distorting. The émigré Strauss could not think about politics and especially American democratic politics apart from the authorizing metadiscourse of philosophy.

Whereas Strauss turned to philosophy to save the possibility of objectivity and critical judgment, Arendt looked to the ordinary practices of acting and judging of citizens themselves to create and sustain a shared human world. For Arendt, the ability to tell right from wrong, just from unjust, was as crucially important as it was for Strauss, but the break in tradition, she argued, had already decided the question of standards in ways that Strauss did not either fully grasp or adequately address. We have seen that no return to the ancient conception of nature was possible according to Strauss; in this respect his understanding of the break in tradition was as definitive as Arendt's.[77] Nevertheless, it is hard to find in Strauss an understanding of judging as a democratic practice that takes account of precisely this insight. It was not only the

111

distinction between "the true world" and "the apparent world" that had been questioned by modern thinkers and destroyed by the catastrophic political events of the twentieth century; it was also the very idea of judging as a practice based on the application of shared rules, even when those rules are only given and valid, as historicism would have it, within one historical horizon.

The differences between Strauss and Arendt on judging can be further illuminated by reference to their critiques of historicism. Like Strauss, Arendt was fiercely critical of historicism and its debilitating effect on judgment. By stark contrast with Greek thought, historical process qua progress, she writes, "bestow[s] upon mere time-sequence an importance and dignity it never had before" ("CH," 65). Nonetheless, *pace* Strauss, observes Liisi Keedus, it was not "the loss of a universal horizon in which the particular orients itself" that concerned Arendt.[78] Rather, it was the historicist antipathy toward "single entities or individual occurrences" and the whole contingent realm of human affairs ("CH," 61). This antipathy is what historicism shared, paradoxically enough, with classical philosophy and, we might justly speculate, with Leo Strauss.[79] More precisely, as History takes on the role of objective judge, it obliterates the proper subject of critical judging in Arendt's view, which is the singular, contingent, and creative collective political practice she called "action." Further, the modern conception of history as a process with no beginning and no end, as that which alone gives meaning to whatever it happens to carry along, was for Arendt a response to the loss of the transcendent truths whose ineffable character defined the philosophical quest. By contrast with the Greeks, who sought respite from contingency in the greatness of particular events and actions, the moderns tempered what Kant called "the 'melancholy haphazardness' of historical events and developments," writes Arendt, by looking upon "history in its entirety" ("CH," 82).

The difference between Arendt and Strauss, then, concerns their contrasting conceptions of what is lost with the rise of historicism. For Strauss it is a universal or transcendent horizon of meaning (nature qua Whole), within which the particular makes sense. For Arendt it is the antipathy toward the particular itself, which is to say the very "stuff" of politics—namely, human action. But their differences go further. In Arendt's view, "the modern escape from politics into history," which is "the escape into the 'whole' . . . prompted by the meaninglessness of the particular" ("CH," 83), is itself rendered meaningless with the rise of what she calls a "strange disregard for factuality" ("CH," 87). Such disregard is characteristic of totalitarianism but also implicit in modernity's state of "radical world-alienation" and the concomitant loss of a "common world" ("CH," 89).

The modern idea of objectivity, as that which the historical process alone can reveal, is undone, in Arendt's insightful telling, by a perverse transformation of "action" into "fabrication," whereby "whenever he [man] tries to learn about things which neither are himself nor owe their existence to him, [he] will ultimately encounter nothing but himself, his own constructions, and the patterns of his own actions" ("CH," 86). In this context, there is no longer a "common object" which we can view from multiple perspectives, which, in turn, give us not only knowledge but also a sense of a shared reality. Rather, we are faced with perspectives that are no longer perspectives *on* anything, with "objects" that have been dissolved into further processes and in this way have been lost as reference points for our shared sense of an objective world. These are "hypothes[es]" that take on a life of their own, that create their own reality ("CH," 87).[80] This erosion of the common world, where a true hypothesis no longer has to tally with the facts but, rather, creates them, is definitive of totalitarian systems: "in the course of consistently guided action [i.e., action qua fabrication], the particular hypothesis will become true, will become actual, factual reality" ("CH," 87). And such "reality" eradicates, finally, the possibility of meaning, which history as process once enabled. Taken together, Arendt concludes, "thinking in terms of processes . . . and the conviction . . . that I know only what I have myself made, has led to the complete meaninglessness inevitably resulting from the insight that I can choose to do whatever I want and some kind of 'meaning' will always be the consequence" ("CH," 88).[81]

From Arendt's perspective, then, historicism as Strauss understood it was no longer the problem. Historical consciousness had been supplanted by something far more menacing to the idea of truth or objective reality and corrosive of political community than anything Strauss described. Notwithstanding their shared view of liberalism's reduction of opinions to subjective preferences and the self-annihilating character of modern reason, Arendt and Strauss radically parted ways. For Arendt, the problem was not only relativism or even nihilism. It was the radical loss of anything resembling a common world in which opinions could be treated as world-giving at all:

The modern age, with its growing world-alienation, has led to a situation where man, wherever he goes, encounters only himself. All the processes of the earth and the universe have revealed themselves either as man-made or as potentially man-made. These processes, after having devoured, as it were, the solid objectivity of the given, ended by rendering meaningless the one over-all process which originally was conceived in order to give meaning to them. . . . This is what happened to our concept of history, as it happened to our concept of nature. In the situation of radial world-alienation, neither history nor nature is at all conceivable. This twofold loss of the world—the loss of nature and the loss of human artifice in the widest sense, which would include all history—has left behind it a society of men who, without a common world which would at once relate and separate them, either live in desperate lonely separation or are pressed together into a mass. For a mass-society is nothing more than that kind of organized living which automatically establishes itself among human beings who are still related to one another but have lost the world once common to all of them. ("CH," 89–90)

By comparison with this grim picture of radical world-alienation, Strauss's worry about the relativizing effects of historicism on morality must seem curiously quaint.

Strauss's critique of historical consciousness, I have argued, is primarily therapeutic: it aims not to refute but to disclose the conditions of intelligibility that characterize modernity. In Strauss's view, liberalism is blind to the consequences of its entanglement in historicism and a failed model of tolerance (e.g., the solution to the "Jewish question"). We would be mistaken, however, to interpret the return to classical rationalism that enables this disclosure as a practical alternative to the modern rationalism that gave rise to historicism in the first place. Like Arendt, Strauss recognized that there could be no such real return.

Classical rationalism, then, provides not a destination but a departure point for Strauss—a place outside the horizon of historicism from which to gain critical purchase on historicism. We can gain such critical purchase only after we question the historicist claim that this form of rationalism had no concept of history or awareness that there are diverse values and practices. The philosophical quest for nature was based on awareness of incommensurable divine codes and conventions. Philosophy has its origins in just this awareness in Strauss's view. To accept the historicist view of the ancients is to "be forced in the end into extreme historicism," says Strauss, as if the only way to talk about historical and cultural differences of value is the historicist way. But just this awareness, we have seen, is the starting point of ancient conventionalism, the precursor of modern historicism in Strauss's account. Modern historical consciousness did not discover value differences; rather, it held these differences to be "ultimate values" in Weber's sense of the term—that is, values about which one cannot dispute for there is no way of rationally mediating differing points of view.

In the Socratic account, which sets itself at odds with the ancient conventionalist view, a natural standard of right exists against which conventional views of right need to be measured and judged. However, our *knowledge* of the standard itself does not exist apart from the quotidian practice of measuring and judging—and this is significant. To speak with Wittgenstein, the rule in Socratic dialectics does not exist apart from its application. Strauss argues that presupposing truth may lead, paradoxical though it sounds to the liberal ear, to an exchange of opinions that looks far more genuine and less in need of "tolerance" than the model derived from the modern historicist view. Whatever its difficulties, Strauss's critique of historicism has at a minimum shown that the contrary idea—namely, that there are innumerable worldviews, incommensurable but equally rational—does not necessarily lead to a less oppressive stance toward those who do not share it (e.g., the "absolutists" who do not believe in the relativity of values, be it Plato or a religious fundamentalist).

Strauss's critique of historical consciousness does not refute the thesis of the relativity of worldviews. His therapeutic approach instead invites us to see historicism, the taken-for-granted, as a problem. The problem is usually understood as relativism—and this is how the "crisis liberals" in their own way see it—but that is not the real problem that Strauss exposes, in my view. What his critique makes visible is, first, the place where a view of values as historically relative comes under intense pressure and we are called upon to make critical judgments that are not based on values understood as subjective preferences; and, second, liberalism's tendency to deny its own practice of making judgments and reliance on the idea of a standard. We need to—and simply do—make judgments about cultures and practices not our own, but we tend to misunderstand what we do when we judge. Since there is no external standard for judgment, but only the practices (Cavell's "whirl of organism" described in chapter 1) in which our criteria do or do not make sense (i.e., the norm is in the practice itself), when reasons run out in any given language game or practice in which we are engaged, we rely on "what we do." But of course that's not what we say we do. We say that all values, being preferences, are equal, but when faced with the late modern version of Hume's Ogilby-Milton problem of the relativism of taste, we say that our way of judging is "best," located as we are in history—it is merely a matter of fate.

Both Arendt and Strauss were led back to Socratic dialectics as a way of countering these tendencies in liberalism and rethinking the opposition between truth and opinion. We have seen that the origins of Strauss's return to classical rationalism in his quest for a nonhistoricist critique of historicism lay not in American debates over multiculturalism, as his admirers and critics alike seem to assume, but in the German crisis of historicism and the collapse of the Weimar Republic. So understood, the problem of historicism was the problem of authoritarianism and the failure of critical judgment. By contrast with Arendt, however, Strauss's philosophical turn of mind ultimately left democratic citizens stranded when it came to the problem of how to judge anew after the standards for judging have collapsed—a problem which his own work otherwise made clearly visible. Though she shared Strauss's view of the self-annihilating character of modern reason and wholly epistemological conception of objectivity, Arendt insisted that the capacity to judge in the absence of rules should be expected of every citizen. It is not that Arendt saw in each citizen a philosopher in Strauss's Socratic understanding of that term; rather, she sought to keep alive the revolutionary spirit, the capacity to begin anew, within democratic societies by enlarging the common world of citizens in which action is still possible and judgment can affirm free action. Unlike Strauss, she did not see her project as care for knowledge or philosophy but as care for the world.

Finally, we should be wary of Strauss's tendency to think of the predicament of modernity almost exclusively in terms of historicism and the collapse of standards. As I shall explore more fully in the next chapter, the problem is neither relativism nor the absence of standards with which to decide the truth of competing claims but the potent power of the "strange disregard for factuality" described by Arendt, whereby hypotheses, cut loose from any answerability to facts, "end in producing facts which are then 'objectively' true" in a way that cannot be disputed ("CH," 87). As we shall see, not historicism as Strauss understood it but this strange disregard for factuality in the context of radical world-alienation and the collapse of the common world—these are what should concern us.

FOUR

Objectivity, Judgment, and Freedom: Rereading Arendt's "Truth and Politics"

The really frightening thing about totalitarianism is not that it commits "atrocities" but that it attacks the concept of objective truth: it claims to control the past as well as the future. GEORGE ORWELL[1]

A writer who made the problem of truth central to his literary and nonliterary work, George Orwell controversially captured the opinion of his generation of thinkers when he identified truth as the major casualty in totalitarian regimes. But if totalitarianism spelled the death of objective truth, the threat to truth was not restricted to totalitarianism. Most scholars of Orwell's day blamed relativism, both historical and cognitive, for the rise of totalitarianism and the slowness of the Allied forces to recognize the extent and nature of the threat.[2] Relativism, as Peter Novick has argued, was seen by scholars during World War II as the equivalent of cultural and political suicide for Western liberal democracies: "Philosophers were urged [in the words of Arthur Murphy] to 'surrender the shallow indifference about ultimate truth of the debased "liberalism" of our recent past.'" Relativism was "debilitating," for it "robbed [the American] people of their convictions and their will to fight."[3] As another critic put it, cultural relativists naively "assumed implicitly that there is a kind of pre-established harmony of cultures that makes it possible for all to coexist in a pluralistic cultural world."[4] A consensus emerged among many liberal and conservative intellectuals that Western liberal democracies needed to affirm certain values as beyond dispute.

The idea that citizens in liberal democracies should put aside their differences of opinion and defend the "core values" of their society is alive and well today. In our post-9/11 political context, talk about the "clash of civilizations" has been used to undermine belief in the possible global coexistence of diverse cultures and to suppress plural opinions and political dissent within liberal democracies themselves. More to the point, the disdain for objective truth that Orwell ascribed to totalitarian societies but not to liberal democratic ones must seem misplaced if not naive. As the scandals surrounding the 2003 US invasion of Iraq demonstrated, such disdain is hardly unique to totalitarian societies. The certainty with which the George W. Bush administration declared that Saddam Hussein had "weapons of mass destruction," ignoring the counterevidence produced by its own intelligence agencies, turned out to be just the beginning of a US government–sponsored program of mendacity.

In light of this recent past, it is easy to understand why citizens would fear that truth is quickly becoming a casualty of nominally liberal democratic regimes, not just totalitarian ones. And it is also easy to understand why official investigations concerning the truthfulness of those who claim to speak in our name would provide a strange solace. Although holding public leaders accountable for the veracity of their statements is surely important and indeed essential to our belief in representative government, the question arises as to whether democratic citizens are in a position to do something with the truths that come to light as a result of such investigations. The thinker who helps us pose and perhaps answer that question, I suggest, is not George Orwell but his contemporary Hannah Arendt.

Although Arendt shares Orwell's concern about the fate of factual truths in totalitarian regimes, her response to the political catastrophes of the twentieth century is not to insist on the defense of objective truth as such but to emphasize the ability to make judgments when inherited concepts are in question or lacking. In contrast to Orwell and those scholars of her generation who decried relativism, Arendt worried about what the insistence on a singular idea of truth would mean for democracy. In "Truth and Politics," for example, she famously sets persuasive opinion against compelling truth and declares the former to be the proper mode of discourse among citizens ("TP," 232). Plural opinions are the stuff of judging politically, she argued, not absolute truth.

Arendt's account of truth as hostile to plurality and all things democratic has led well-known critics such as Jürgen Habermas to declare her understanding of political judgment to be fatally flawed, for it offers no way to ascertain the truth of statements or adjudicate competing validity claims. According to Habermas, Arendt opens a "yawning abyss between knowledge and opinion that cannot be closed with arguments" ("ACCP," 225). If we are interested in critically thinking through the politics of truth in contemporary liberal democracies, Habermas might ask, why turn to a thinker who seems to dismiss as deeply antipolitical the cognitive demand for truth?

When it comes to truth and politics, perhaps we have not given Arendt a fair reading. In previously published work, I tried to show that Arendt addresses the question of validity that occupies her critics, with one important caveat: she does not think that validity is the all-important task for political judgment—the affirmation of nonsovereign freedom is.[5] But I took for granted—or at least I did not adequately question—the idea that Arendt holds truth to be at odds with politics. That is why she turned to Kant's account of aesthetic judgments in the third *Critique*, I argued, for it posits a special kind of validity—what Kant called "subjective validity"—without an appeal to knowledge or truth. And although I still hold (and shall argue in this chapter) that freedom rather than validity or truth is the real problem that animates Arendt's entire effort to foreground the importance of the democratic capacity to judge, I want to question the central claim of her critics— namely, that she excludes truth claims from politics.

I have three reasons for questioning the idea that Arendt excludes the question of truth. First, as we shall see, Arendt was not indifferent to but deeply concerned with the increasing cynicism toward the possibility of truthfulness in political life. Not only is the obliteration of truth in public life a definitive feature of totalitarianism, just as Orwell holds, but the truthfulness of statements made by citizens or their representatives is of paramount concern in a democracy, as the current political situation makes acutely clear.

Second, if we consider the other famous Heidegger student, Hans-Georg Gadamer, and his well-known critique of Kant's "radical subjectivization" of aesthetics, we are provoked to ask whether the exclusion of truth and knowledge from politics might lead to a further sedimentation of the idea that science (with its method) is the sole claimant to and arbiter of truth and knowledge.[6] Like Gadamer, Arendt had good reason for resisting the idea that there is only one form of truth—namely, that which demands the strictest criteria of proof—because such a definition, rooted as it is in the development of modern science, would grant human practices such as art and politics and human sciences such as aesthetics and political theory their special place, while depriving them of any real authority or significance.

Third, if we deny that political claims, whatever else they are, are also claims to knowledge and truth, have we not foreclosed the possibility that such claims make demands on us that may in some ways be like but also quite unlike the demands made by truth and knowledge claims in other domains of life, such as science and even aesthetics? Perhaps the question is not whether we make such claims in politics—clearly we do—but what it means to make them, to hear them, and whether, after they enter the political realm, claims to truth can survive.

In this chapter, I want to revisit Arendt's account of the relationship between truth and politics. I do so not only with the aspiration of intervening in the reception of her work but also, especially in the final section, to show her account's relevance to the political issues just described. Qualifying certain aspects of my published work on Arendt, my argument will be that foregrounding the problem of freedom rather than the rational adjudication of validity claims as the central work of democratic political judgment does not lead Arendt—nor should it lead us—to exclude the question of truth from the political realm. Rather, it leads her—as it might lead us—both to call into question the idea that proof is our sole access to truth in the political realm and to reflect on the distinctive character of truth claims in politics and their entanglement in opinion, which Plato rejected as unworthy of serious reflection due to its inherently contingent and plural character.

Although Arendt's critics are right to say that she holds politics to be the domain of plural contingent opinions, not singular timeless truths, they are mistaken when they accuse her of setting truth and opinion fully at odds with each other. This critique assumes that Arendt excluded truth from the political realm because she had no alternative notion of truth to the Platonic one, with its characteristic contempt for all things worldly and contingent. By "alternative notion of truth" I mean not only a hermeneutical notion of truth (discussed subsequently), as it was developed by Heidegger and later by Gadamer, but a public notion of truth that Arendt (in her own idiosyncratic way) takes from both Socrates and Immanuel Kant. This notion of truth, as we shall see, requires more than a "discourse ethics" because it involves more than the ability to make public arguments and ascertain the validity of statements; it involves more than the ability to distinguish warranted public opinions from strategically manipulated ideology that animates Habermas's normative political project.

The problem that concerned Arendt and that ought to concern us is not only how to determine the truth of statements but also how to transform those truths into "publicly acceptable fact[s]," to borrow Mark Danner's phrase.[7] As we shall see, there is a difference between determining the truth content of those who claim to speak in our name and turning our knowledge of what is true into something politically significant. This next step will take us beyond the problem identified by Habermas—how to redeem validity claims—and toward the problem identified by Arendt: how to develop a public sphere in which citizens not only could tell the difference between warranted public opinion and strategically manipulated ideology but also could turn what they know to be true into something politically significant, citizens who could acknowledge what they know and draw the political consequences, so to speak.

The Truth of Opinion

Let us begin by turning not to "Truth and Politics" but to a less famous essay by Arendt, "Philosophy and Politics."[8] Here we discover that, *pace* her critics, she does not accept the founding Platonic opposition of truth and opinion and then seek merely to revalue the subordinate term (opinion) in Plato's account of absolute truth. Far from simply revaluing opinion in the ineradicable opposition between truth and opinion that Plato bequeathed to political philosophy, Arendt tries to develop instead the Socratic idea of what she calls "the truth of . . . opinion." She does so to undercut the difference that Plato drew "between those who know and do not act and those who act and do not know," for this "Platonic separation of knowing and doing" obliterates freedom and plurality; it is "at the root of all theories of domination," she observes in *The Human Condition* (*HC*, 223, 225) and a conception of politics as *Herrschaft,* or rule.

Reading Socrates against Plato, Arendt observes that the "opposition of truth and opinion was certainly the most anti-Socratic conclusion that Plato drew from Socrates' trial" ("PP," 75). In Arendt's reading, Socrates's life and teaching contravene this central Platonic opposition.

Although it is more than probable that Socrates was the first who had used *di-alegesthai* [dialectic] (talking something through with somebody) systematically, he probably did not look upon this as the opposite or even the counterpart to per-suasion [as both Plato and Aristotle did], and it is certain that he did not oppose the results of this dialectic to *doxa*, opinion. To Socrates, as to his fellow citizens, *doxa* was the formulation in speech of what *dokei moi*, that is, of what appears to me. This *doxa* had as its topic not what Aristotle called the *eikos*, the probable, the many *verisimilia* (as distinguished from the *unum verum*, the one truth, on one hand, and the limitless falsehoods, the *falsa infinita*, on the other), but comprehended the world as it opens itself to me. It was not, therefore, subjective fantasy and arbitrari-ness, but also not something absolute and valid for all. The assumption was that the world opens up differently to every man, according to his position in it; and that the "sameness" of the world, its commonness (*koinon*, as the Greeks would say, common to all) or "objectivity" (as we would say from the subjective viewpoint of modern philosophy) resides in the fact that the same world opens up to everyone and that despite all differences between men and their positions in the world—and consequently their *doxai* (opinions)—"both you and I are human." ("PP," 80)

On the one hand, Arendt emphasizes the idea that opinion, far from being merely subjective, is the source of truth and knowledge, the ba-sis for making claims with validity, the origin of what we would call "objective" and the Greeks called *koinon*, common to all. On the other hand, she contends that opinion, though in no way merely subjective, is not universal and valid for all. But what can it mean, really, to say that *doxa*, or opinion (understood as the articulation of what *dokei moi*, the "formulation in speech" of the way the world opens up or shows itself to me), is at once the source of everything we hold common or objective and not universally valid for all?

At this point we could invoke Socratic dialectic as a "method" through which opinion attains objectivity by being articulated as gen-eralizable or universal ("It appears to me as it appears to all others").[9] The danger here, however, lies precisely in thinking about Socrates's maieutic interrogative practice as if it were a "method"—that is, a means for attenuating if not eliminating the "personal" or "subjective" elements in any practice of knowing and verifying knowledge claims through rational argumentation and the giving of proofs. In that case, dialectic would yield certainty and be based on (or teach) the proper subsumption of particulars under universals (just as Plato understood it, in Arendt's view). Opinion would differ from truth as the failure of this process of subsumption.

According to Arendt, Socrates's effort "to make the city more truthful by delivering each of its citizens of their truths" proceeds neither by means of subsumption nor by leaving opinion behind ("PP," 81). To be delivered of one's truths is not to vanquish the particular or be fully released from the subjective limitations of one's standpoint; it is not to be delivered of one's opinions, as if opinion were the opposite of truth and the person most delivered of his or her truths was the one without any opinions. Rather, it is to find, by means of public debate, what in one's opinions is true. There is no truth on Arendt's Socratic account that is not also an opinion. We never arrive at the point where we have established the "visible hallmark" that marks truth from opinion, which Plato so eagerly sought but never found. It is not that any particular opinion can never be declared truthful (or not), but rather that there is no absolute criterion (or method or procedure) that would allow us to separate opinion from truth once and for all. But if the search for truth in opinion does not end with a (Platonic) declaration of the absolute difference between truth and opinion, how does one know that the opinion one holds is true?

As we saw in the last chapter, Leo Strauss also turns to Plato's Socratic dialogues to discuss the relation of opinion to truth. For him, however, there is no way to find the truth in opinion once we relinquish the idea of nature and absolute standards, for how would we seek and recognize what is true if we did not already know what is true? How could we properly subsume particulars if we had no universals under which they could be recognized as true—that is, as belonging to a specific concept? We cannot determine whether a particular action is just if we have no standard of justice by which to recognize what qualifies as just and what not. "To judge soundly one must know the true standards," declares Strauss.[10] As most people in modern liberal democracies are no longer in possession of such yardsticks (as a consequence of value pluralism and historicism), he argues, it is doubtful that citizens can "replace opinion about the nature of political things by knowledge of the nature of political things."[11] The key word here is *replace*, for opinion based in common sense, though in no way cognitively worthless as it is for social scientific conceptions of politics, is not to be preserved but overcome in the quest for truth. Opinions guide the ascent to a truth that is in principle knowable but always out of reach in Strauss's zetetic reading of the dialogues, but they are, as Strauss described them in his *Natural Right and History*, mere "fragments of the truth, soiled fragments of the pure truth" (*NRH*, 124).[12]

Strauss would have the political philosopher seek truth in Plato's Socratic dialogues, but the curious thing about those dialogues, as Arendt remarks, "is that they are all aporetic." She explains: "The argument either leads nowhere or it goes around in circles. To know what justice is you must know what knowledge is, and to know knowing you must have a previous, unexamined notion of knowledge. . . . Hence [in *Meno* we read], 'A man cannot try to discover either what he knows or what he does not know. If he knows, there is no need of inquiry; if he does not know . . . he does not even know what he is to look for.'"[13]

In his reading of the dialogues, Ernesto Grassi, another Heidegger student, also remarks on their fundamentally "aporetic" character. Like Arendt, Grassi points out that the search for truth appears to take for granted that we already know what truth is, for how else would we recognize truth when we found it? Even if we were to grant that the search for truth must have as its condition knowledge of truth, says Grassi, "the search itself seems pointless, then why would we search for something we already know?"[14] But Grassi also suggests that the dialogues show something else: that the aporetic character of the search for truth does not hold for truth as such, which is what Arendt seems to assume, but only for a certain conception of truth—namely, an objectivist (or philosophical) conception of truth. The aporia does not hold for the notion of truth that belongs to the idea of being (*das Seiende*) as becoming (*das Werdende*), which Heidegger emphasized in his return to the ancient texts. As becoming, being is both present and absent, and thus it is something for which we can search without already knowing what we are searching for. The question of truth is a matter neither of correspondence nor of subsumption but of appearance: why things show up for us as they do (*sich-zeigen*).[15] And if we recall that for the Greeks opinion (*doxa*) is the formulation in speech of what appears to me (*dokei moi*), we can begin to see how opinion and truth might be more intertwined than a certain reading of Plato allows.

Taking up Heidegger's critique of truth as correspondence and his attempt to develop the ancient idea of truth as *alètheia*, Grassi attempts to explain how things appear by redefining the problem of the *logos* in Plato's Socratic dialogues as "the originary act of *légein* [*ursprünglichen Aktes des 'légein'*]" (*VL*, 44).[16] Grassi wants to emphasize *logos*—speech, the word, reason—in a particular way: as an endless process, an ongoing act through which human beings gain access to being, to what is primordially given, and in this way create a "world" in the Heideggerian sense. To emphasize the idea of an ongoing and never-ending process, Grassi uses the verbal form of *logos*, *légein*. This *légein* act, as the Greeks (including Plato and Socrates) understood it, is the originary act of "separating, differentiating and at the same time collecting, uniting,

[and] binding [an otherwise chaotic sensible universe]" (*VL*, 44). Only through such an act does the sensible world attain objectivity for human beings.

"Does it [*légein*] have one form or many, and how are they differentiated?" asks Grassi (*VL*, 62).[17] In a variety of works Grassi tries to distinguish the various forms of *légein*. In *Vom Vorrang des Logos*, the text currently under discussion, he distinguishes (albeit in a highly schematic manner) three forms of *légein* and thus of appearance (*sichzeigen*): philosophical, aesthetic, and political. Important for our purposes here is not only the difference he draws between the philosophical *légein*, which is based on discerning universality, and the aesthetic *légein*, which is concerned with the particular, but also his insistence that the question of truth cannot be posed properly unless we distinguish among the registers in which things appear and the kinds of necessity that pertain to these registers.

"We have to ask whether out of the constraints of logic [*aus der logischen Nötigung*] a world of art ever emerged; or whether out of the constraints of logic a political reality ever originated," comments Grassi (*VL*, 214). And if the answer in both cases is no, does this mean that there is no truth in art or in politics? Like Gadamer, Grassi refuses to limit the notion of truth in this way. The ground of truth does not have the objectivist form that both logical truth and the philosophical truth advanced by Strauss's Plato must have. Truth is a question not of how things are in and of themselves but of how they appear to us, and how things appear depends in turn on the register in which they appear and the form of *légein* (e.g., philosophical, aesthetic, or political, to name but three) with which things appear.[18] Citing Machiavelli as the paradigmatic theorist of political *légein*, Grassi argues that this, like every other form of *légein*, cannot be reduced to the other forms, for each form is independent of all the others in its particular way of generating our sense of reality. To stay with the example of political *légein*, our notion of truth in the political realm is independent: though it may share with the other forms of *légein* certain features (e.g., politics is concerned with the particular just as aesthetics is, says Grassi), political *légein* is autonomous. Those who fail to see this will never understand Machiavelli but will accuse him of all that "goes under the sign 'Machiavellianism'" (*VL*, 210).

Citing the tragic attempt to impose Plato's philosophy in Sicily, Grassi does not exclude the possibility that forms of *légein* that are alien to politics could be or have been imposed on the political realm. Political actors who lose sight of the direct historical situation in which they find themselves, who fall victim to the poetic or conceptual way of seeing things, transform the political future into one guided by the maxims of aesthetics or philosophy and thereby beget a misdeed, says Grassi (*VL*, 210). Like Arendt, then, Grassi warns against the introduction of standards of truth into the political realm that are foreign to it—foreign not because truth has no place in politics (as a certain reading of Arendt holds) but because things appear differently in politics; that is, they have a particular sense of validity and are meaningful for us in ways that are not identical to how they may appear when seen as philosophical, scientific, or aesthetic objects. There is, to be sure, traffic among these realms and forms of *légein*, but each form is irreducible to the others.

Grassi helps us see that there might indeed be a form of truth in politics that is unique. This truth is not aporetic, for it is not objectivist. Contra Strauss's reading of the dialogues, we do not have to "know the true standards" to make judgments (subsume particulars under rules) about reality. Even if one were to grant that such standards are necessary for philosophical knowledge (which Grassi also refutes), politics is autonomous. Insofar as the Socratic project to find the truth in opinion takes place in the political realm, as Arendt will show us subsequently, we have good reason for resisting the introduction of standards or criteria that do not apply there. Thus we shall have good reason to be suspicious of thinkers who would assimilate politics to philosophy (or to science) and demand of political claims the same measure of truth. Likewise we shall have good reason to refute the idea that politics, if it does not meet philosophical (or scientific) standards of proof, is not concerned with truth.

If the aporia of truth described earlier pertains to an objectivist (philosophical) conception of truth but not to truth in and of itself, as Grassi has shown us, we have all the more reason to pursue the Socratic quest for the truth in opinion, for such truth would not be based on our possession of universals under which to subsume particulars or, as Strauss would have us believe, on the possibility that standards may indeed someday be found. The Socratic quest to find truth in opinion is distinguished from Plato's notion of moving from opinion to truth in ways that are inseparable from the realm in which the quest for truth takes place. First, to discover truth in opinion, one must move among the holders of opinion—that is to say, one's peers or equals—hence in the political realm. By contrast with Plato, for whom truth is—and indeed must be—a solitary affair, Socrates's activity in the agora shows that for him truth can emerge in public. The public space is not—or not always—the place to speak a truth one already knows but, rather, the condition of finding truth in one's own opinion. In her *Lectures on Kant's Political Philosophy*, Arendt observes, "What he [Socrates] actually did was to make *public*, in discourse, the thinking process—that dialogue that soundlessly goes on within me, between me and myself; he *performed* in the marketplace the way the flute-player performed at a banquet. It is sheer performance, sheer activity" (*LKPP*, 37). Socrates's practice of "maieutic," the art of midwifery (by which one brings oneself and others to find the truth in their opinion), argues Arendt, "was a political activity, a give and take, fundamentally on a basis of strict equality, the fruits of which could not be measured by the result of arriving at this or that general truth" ("PP," 81). Though one could question the claim that Socrates treated others as equals in the rigorously political manner that Arendt ascribes to him, it seems right to say that, for him, "critical thinking . . . exposes itself to 'the test of free and open examination' [as Kant put it], and this means that the more people participate in it, the better" (*LKPP*, 39). This activity is based on the conviction that "every man has his own *doxa*, his own opening to the world." Socrates must ask questions; he cannot know beforehand how the world appears to each of his fellow citizens. "Yet, just as nobody can know beforehand the other's *doxa*, so nobody can know by himself and without further effort the inherent truth of his own opinion" ("PP," 81).[19] So the kind of truth that is relevant for politics, we might conclude, requires publicity.

There is another important way in which Socrates's search for the truth in opinion differs from Plato's search for absolute truth. As Strauss makes clear, in Plato's view, opinion is something to be replaced by knowledge, whereas for Arendt's Socrates, opinion is the bearer of truth. Socrates's style of questioning is deeply critical but not "relentlessly negative," as Villa interpreting Arendt asserts, for it does not just destroy opinions but reveals what in them is true.[20] What else can it mean to find the truth in opinion, unless we settle on the purely negative or skeptical definition and say that the truth Socrates discovers in opinion is that in opinion there is no truth? But surely this is not the definition Arendt has in mind when she asserts, "For mortals [in Socrates's view] the important thing is to make *doxa* truthful, to see in every *doxa* truth and to speak in such a way that the truth of one's opinion reveals itself to oneself and to others. . . . [Socrates], in opposition to the Sophists, had discovered that *doxa* was neither subjective illusion nor arbitrary distortion but, on the contrary, that to which truth invariably adhered" ("PP," 84–5).

To see truth in every *doxa* is different from seeing error in every *doxa*, which is what the negative definition just described suggests. Furthermore, the truth Socrates helps his fellow citizens to find in their opinions is not what is left over once all the errors in their *doxa* have been revealed. That this truth in opinion is not philosophical truth (that is, the absolute truths that form the rules under which the subject as "man in the singular," seeking only to be in agreement with himself, may subsume particulars) is clear, but it is a form of truth nonetheless. To be the gadfly, as Arendt explains, is not to play the role of the philosopher who rules on the basis of knowing truth from opinion; rather, it is "to make citizens more truthful" ("PP," 81), to help them find what in their opinions is true. Let us now examine what is at stake for the political conception of truth we are trying to develop in an approach that seeks out and emphasizes what is true in opinion and not—not simply—what is false.

The Prejudice against Prejudice

If we turn now to Gadamer's reading of Socrates, we can better grasp the kind of knowledge that is at stake in the quest for the truth in opinion. Like Arendt, Gadamer identifies the Socratic art of questioning as key. The ability to ask questions, he writes, is also the ability to keep these questions from "being suppressed by the dominant opinion. *A person who possesses this art will himself search for everything in favor of an opinion. Dialectic consists not in trying to discover the weakness of what is said, but in bringing out its real strength.* It is not the art of arguing (which can make a strong case out of a weak one) but the art of thinking (which can strengthen objections by referring to the subject matter)" (*TM*, 367, my emphasis).

The art of questioning, in other words, seeks out the truth in opinion and in ordinary perspective (the formulation in speech of the "it appears to me"); it takes for granted that truth resides in what we say, in language. Not all we say is true, of course, but (contra Plato) what is true is spoken. Like Arendt, Gadamer rejects the psychologistic and subjectivist interpretation of opinion, the formulation in speech of the "it appears to me." If we think about this "it appears to me" too much in terms of the "me" (i.e., the "subject") and too little in terms of the formulation in *speech* (i.e., language) of what appears (i.e., the world), we slide into just this psychologistic conception of opinion, which leads us to think, in turn, that we need a "method" that will keep at bay our opinions, for they are the "subjective" element that hinders our quest for what is "objective."

We can grasp why this idea of opinion as subjective misunderstands what we do when we engage the opinions of others by way of the following example. Gadamer explains: "When we receive a letter [describing, say, an antiwar rally in Washington, DC] we see what is communicated through the eyes of our correspondent, but while seeing things through his eyes, it is not his personal opinions, but, rather, the event itself that we believe we ought to know by this letter. In reading a letter, to aim at the personal *thoughts* of our correspondent and not at the matters *about which* he reports is to contradict what is meant by a letter."[21] Should the description turn out to be a wildly inaccurate account of events, we might then be prompted to understand it "by recourse to a supplementary psychological or historical point of view," comments Gadamer. Although such situations surely can and often do arise (e.g., when I read an editorial by someone whose opinions I tend to distrust), we are not simply gullible to take for granted that the text "really transmits to us the *truth*. This confirms that the primordial significance of the idea of understanding is that of 'knowing about something' and that only in a derivative sense does it mean understanding the intentions of another as personal opinions" ("PHC," 154).

Although Gadamer appears to set "knowing about something" at odds with "personal opinions" here, I take him to mean what is conventionally meant by "personal opinions"—namely, that which is subjective and makes no claim to truth or knowledge. For Gadamer (as for Arendt), then, it is a mistake to think about the formulation in speech of how the world appears to someone as "mere opinion"—that is, as something purely subjective.[22] This formulation in speech of how things show up for us is no private language but an expression of common sense, of what I share with others by virtue of belonging to a particular sociohistorical culture.[23] Gadamer helps us question again the stark opposition that Plato drew between knowledge and opinion. An opinion (as expressed, for example, in a letter) makes, and is received as making, a claim to truth. Just because I can hold opinions that I (or others) may later declare mistaken does not mean that those opinions are purely subjective, as if the way the world appears to me is how it appears to me and to no other (i.e., my world is private). "Thus we come back to the original conditions of every hermeneutics: it must be a shared and comprehensible reference to the 'things in themselves'" ("PHC," 154–55). Without such a reference, argues Gadamer, no common, unified meaning, no truth, could possibly be aimed at or emerge.

According to the hermeneutical conception of knowledge advanced by Gadamer (following Heidegger), understanding has an anticipatory structure: every act of understanding presupposes preunderstanding, the elements of which are one's *Vorurteile* (prejudices or prejudgments). These "absolutely fundamental anticipations, that is, anticipations *common* to us all," are what Gadamer calls "tradition." He explains, "Hermeneutics must start from the fact that understanding is related to 'the thing itself' as manifest in the tradition, and at the same time to a tradition where 'the thing' can speak to me" ("PHC," 155).

How things speak to us through tradition can be seen in the structure of preunderstanding just mentioned, composed as it is of prejudices. Prejudice, which comes from the Latin *praejudicum,* or "judgment in advance," is "an opinion formed beforehand." A central achievement of Gadamer's magnum opus, *Truth and Method*, is "to fundamentally rehabilitate the concept of prejudice and acknowledge the fact that there are legitimate prejudices" (*TM*, 277). This is another way of saying that some prejudices or opinions are true—that is, they speak to the way things really are. Once we grant that there is such a thing as legitimate prejudice, says Gadamer, we can see that "the fundamental epistemological question for a truly historical hermeneutics [is this] . . . : what is the ground of the legitimacy of prejudices? What distinguishes legitimate prejudices from the countless others which it is the undeniable task of critical reason to overcome?" (*TM*, 277).

Arendt's account of prejudicés takes up this fundamental insight into the *Vorurteilstruktur* of understanding and the questions it raises. In her view, as expressed in her "Introduction *into* Politics" essay, "it is the task of politics to shed light upon and dispel prejudices, which is not to say that its task is to train people to be unprejudiced or that those who work towards such enlightenment are themselves free of prejudice" ("IP," 99–100). In Arendt's account, the rationalist method of dispelling prejudices often misses its mark. Such a method, premised as it is on "the prejudice against prejudice," to borrow Gadamer's felicitous description of the Enlightenment legacy, fails to grasp that prejudices are the basis (i.e., they have the anticipatory structure described earlier) for all knowledge and understanding. Arendt elaborates, "Man cannot live without prejudices, and not only because no human being's intelligence or insight would suffice to form an original judgment about everything on which he is asked to pass judgment in the course of his life, but also because such a total lack of prejudice would require a superhuman alertness" ("IP," 99).

And yet sometimes we are called on to judge anew, as when we are confronted with something we have not encountered before. Democratic citizens are called on to judge anew, in Arendt's view, largely because of the catastrophic political events of the twentieth century, which have revealed that tradition, far from being the source of continuity that it is in Gadamer's work, is characterized instead by a radical break. Arendt's claim that modernity is so characterized leads her to see in prejudices more of a threat to critical thinking and judging than Gadamer might be able to address (though he is certainly attuned to the problem). If all political thinking is essentially based in the capacity to judge, as Arendt asserts, then prejudices (*Vorurteile*) are not only enabling elements of understanding but also potentially disabling for democratic politics: prejudices are prejudgments that can substitute for (the practice of making) judgments (*Urteile*) based on current experience, and in a context characterized by the radical break just described, they often do. As shared prejudgments that appeal to what "they [people] say"—that is, to common opinion—prejudices can count on the (mostly implicit) agreement of others.[24] "If we want to dispel prejudices, we must first discover the past judgments contained within them, which is to say, we must reveal whatever truth lies within them. If we neglect to do this, whole battalions of enlightened orators and entire libraries of brochures will achieve nothing," asserts Arendt ("IP," 101).[25]

I have suggested that that are certain affinities between Gadamer's hermeneutical account of truth and prejudice and Arendt's political account. But what, if anything, is distinctive about the attempt to find truth and dispel prejudices in the political realm? And would we want to talk about this task in terms of the Socratic quest for truth, the truth in opinion that we have been discussing? Does not politics introduce concerns that suggest that such a task is not—not simply—a general philosophical question about how to distinguish legitimate from illegitimate prejudices as we distinguish truth from untruth, which is more or less what Gadamer's philosophical hermeneutics suggests?

Although Arendt adopts key aspects of the hermeneutical conception of truth, what is particularly important, as I argued in chapter 1, is the idea of a specifically public understanding of truth so conceived. Arendt follows Kant as well as Socrates in arguing that critical thinking and the search for truth require publicity. As we saw in chapter 1, questioning the received liberal understanding of free speech and thought as "the right of an individual to express himself and his opinion in order to be able to persuade others to share his viewpoint," Arendt remarks, "presupposes that I am capable of making up my mind all by myself and that the claim I have on the government is to permit me to propagandize whatever I have already fixed in my mind" (*LKPP*, 39). One could certainly question whether this view of free speech and thought can be rightly attributed to liberal thinkers such as John Stuart Mill, for whom the public exchange of opinions is as crucial to grasping the truth of any public matter, as it is for Arendt. Nevertheless, Arendt wishes to call our attention to something about freedom that tends not to be seen when we think about our right to free speech and thought in the liberal idiom of negative liberty. The public space should be understood less as the place where already formed opinions are expressed and defended and more as the actual condition of their formation, articulation, and circulation in a broader process of critical thinking and judging. It is through this process of opinion formation that facts come to have truth for us in a politically significant sense. Facts of concern for politics that lack a robust public realm in which to make sense of and articulate them as opinions are like meaningless particulars, things we may "know" but fail to acknowledge or accord value in any politically significant sense. And it is for that reason that such facts are also endangered. Absent valuation, such facts lose their objectivity for us—that is, they no longer have purchase on our sense of a shared reality. As we shall see later, even the exposure of deception or outright lies is unlikely to have real political consequences if the public realm in which to debate them is weak or deficient.

For now, it is useful to turn briefly to Habermas, who shares Arendt's understanding of the radical break in tradition and her central concern with the public practice of opinion formation and judgment. Although Habermas agrees with the basic hermeneutical point about the *Vorurteilstruktur* of understanding and acting, he is deeply critical of the idea that there is no form of discourse that would be free of prejudice or preunderstandings and prejudgments. Shunning all modern approaches to validity as expansions of scientific method and its narrow conception of objectivity, Gadamer has no way to distinguish between rational and irrational aspects of tradition, argues Habermas, and both Arendt and Gadamer have no way of distinguishing between ideological and nonideological uses of language or between illusory and nonillusory forms of belief.[26]

Part of what drives Habermas's separate critiques of the inadequate validity problematic in both Arendt and Gadamer is also what inspired the 1999 modification, in *Wahrheit and Rechtfertigung* (*Truth and Justification*), of his own discourse theory of truth: the fear of contextualism, the indexing of what is true, right, and valuable to particular forms of life. Whereas "discourse theory," based in the "communicative theory of action," held that truth is that which can be rationally warranted under ideal conditions, Habermas now argues for a distinction between truth and rational acceptability. Truth is not an epistemic concept but an absolute property "that cannot be 'lost'" (*TJ*, 250). Truth transcends every possible context of justification, even ideal ones: "a proposition is agreed to by all rational subjects because it is true; it is not true because it could be the content of a consensus attained under ideal conditions" (*TJ*, 101). Justification remains the only way to adjudicate competing claims, but truth is not reducible to what can be justified.

Habermas's later pragmatic theory of truth takes account of the lifeworld but seeks to contain what he considers to be its relativizing effects by distinguishing between objective validity and normative validity. The former pertains to truth claims, which make justification-transcendent reference to an objective world whose shared character shows up in "the more or less implicit beliefs that we take to be true against a broad background of intersubjectively shared or sufficiently overlapping beliefs" (*TJ*, 252–53), whereas moral claims make no such reference. Although "moral claims to validity lack the ontological connotations that are characteristic of claims to truth" (*TJ*, 109) moral claims are "truth-analogous" in that they have "an unconditional kind of validity" (*TJ*, 248). Whereas truth transcends every possible context of justification, even ideal ones, the universal validity of moral claims to rightness is irreducibly epistemic: "Those moral judgments that *merit* universal recognition are 'right,' and that means that in a rational discourse under approximately ideal conditions they could be agreed to by anyone concerned" (*TJ*, 229).[27]

Distinguishing between the truth of statements, which signify facts, the obtaining of a state of affairs that is known through, but never reducible to, our practices of justification, on the one side, and the warranted assertibility of moral claims to validity, on the other, Habermas has as his main concern to save truth from the contextualism of thinkers such as Richard Rorty, for whom truth is wholly epistemic (i.e., the truth of a proposition is always indexed to a context of justification). But it is also to defend against what Habermas takes to be the equally relativistic consequences of the hermeneutical conception of truth (discussed previously) that has no such epistemic pretensions but refers instead to "the doxic modality of our background, i.e., lifeworld, beliefs," as Steven Levine puts it, which inheres in shared practices.[28] In both cases, the problem for Habermas is how to defend the universal validity of moral claims; that is, how to carve out a normative register that, like truth, transcends all local contexts and thus the "realism of everyday practice," with its "huge body of beliefs that are naively taken to be true" (*TJ*, 39).

Like truth claims, writes Habermas,

Participants' [claims to moral rightness] orient themselves toward the idea of "a single correct answer," although they know they cannot go beyond the "ideal of warranted acceptability" of propositions. On the other hand, this analogy exists only on the level of argumentation. It cannot be transferred to the level of the pre-reflexive "corroboration" of beliefs. For moral beliefs do not falter against the resistance of an objective world that all participants suppose to be one and the same. Rather, they falter against the irresolubility of normative dissensus among opposing parties in a shared social world. (*TJ*, 256)

As we saw earlier, the doxic modality of belief to which the concept of truth reflectively refers is something to be accepted in the sense not of never questioned but not ever fully overcome or transcended. There is no place outside whatever we now take to be our local practices and norms from which we could articulate a presumably more inclusive conception of morality or a more objective view of the world. Although Habermas's pragmatic conception of truth allows him to see how background beliefs and certainties come to be questioned through a breakdown or failure in our everyday dealings with the world, he limits doxic certainty and its questioning to our experience of independent processes in the objective world. In other words, he denies that the background beliefs and certainties that are the formal origin of our implicit concept of truth apply to moral beliefs or have any relevance to their normative validity. But this denial has the effect of fully stripping what he calls moral knowledge from any objective purport, from its world-giving capacity in the ways that are so important to Arendt's mostly misunderstood understanding of claims to truth in political judgments.[29]

Arendt's concern with truth is based neither in ethics (Gadamer) nor morality (Habermas). It is a concern with truth and politics. This is not a small but a hugely important difference of focus. And although Habermas and (albeit it to a far lesser extent) Gadamer share certain aspects of Arendt's understanding of politics, their main foci remain, respectively, how we should orient ourselves in a just relation to the pluralistic values and beliefs of others or the classical problem of the examined life. What concerns Arendt and animates her inquiry into truth and politics, by contrast, is not care for the self or care for the other or even justice. As we saw in the last chapter, it is "care for the world." Such care entails a deep worry about truth that is in the first instance a worry about human freedom.

Freedom Saves Truth

Turning now to Arendt's discussion of truth as a problem in the modern political context, we find that what concerns her is less the rational truth sought by Plato than the factual truth of events. The "politically most relevant truths are factual," writes Arendt—and they are also the most endangered, vulnerable to human mendacity and the pursuit of political interests ("TP," 232). Like Orwell, Arendt is concerned about the fate of factual truth in totalitarian regimes, but her idea of how to save truth is different from his and from that of most intellectuals of her generation. This difference is not immediately obvious, however. Discerning precisely where it lies will help us avoid repeating the critical judgment that Arendt opposes truth to politics, as if she forbids us to make truth claims in the political realm or as if truthfulness were not important in political life.

If we carefully reread "Truth and Politics," the essay that has earned her the charge of being hostile to truth claims in the political realm, we find Arendt advancing several ideas that seem to endorse Orwell's association of totalitarianism with the destruction of objective historical truth. Arendt agrees on the need to distinguish and protect factual truths from the interpretive pen of the historian and the self-interested manipulations of the politician. But she sees such truth as vulnerable because it is political in ways that Orwell did not grasp. "Factual truth," writes Arendt, "is always related to other people: it concerns events and circumstances in which many are involved; it is established by witnesses and depends upon testimony; it exists only to the extent that it is spoken about, even if it occurs in the domain of privacy. It is political by nature" ("TP," 238). The intrinsically political character of factual truth, its irreducible connection with our (public) modes of subjectivity, raises problems for democratic politics that Orwell, focused as he was on what is objective precisely to the extent that it has no admixture of subject dependence, did not see.

Arendt raises the hermeneutical fact-value question, "But do facts, independent of opinion and interpretation, exist at all?" ("TP," 238), and answers, "Even if we admit that every generation has the right to write its own history, we admit no more than that it has the right to rearrange the facts in accordance with its own perspective; we don't admit the right to touch the factual matter itself" ("TP," 238–39). For example, "the fact that on the night of August 4, 1914 German troops crossed the frontier of Belgium" is one among those "brutally elementary data . . . whose indestructibility has been taken for granted even by the most extreme and most sophisticated believers in historicism" ("TP," 239). But to admit the "right" to alter factual truth is one thing; to recognize that such alteration occurs is quite another.

"Since everything that has actually happened in the realm of human affairs could just as well have been otherwise, the possibilities for lying are boundless," writes Arendt ("TP," 257). When not denied or twisted in some way, facts become mere matters of opinion—as if it were a matter of opinion that "Germany invaded Belgium in August 1914." Arendt worries that historical facts can be subject to the kind of historical rewritings described in Orwell's 1948 novel *Nineteen Eighty-Four*, in which the existence of undesirable historical actors and events are extinguished by "stuffing truth down the memory hole," as Orwell put it.[30] Such was the fate "of a man by the name of Trotsky, who appears in none of the Soviet Russian history books," comments Arendt ("TP," 231). But she also distances herself from thinkers such as Orwell and their idea of objective truth. The relativistic stance toward objective truth that he decries is, in Arendt's view, an inescapable risk that attaches to the contingent nature of factual truth and, even more significant, to human freedom.

As "factual truths are never compellingly true," argues Arendt, lying is not something that befalls speech from the outside, as it were.[31] Lying is not the exception to the rule of the claim to truthfulness that, say, Habermas identifies as the ontological ground of communicative action. Whereas Habermas would say that lying is a strategic form of communication that surely occurs but that is parasitic on and a deviation from speech oriented to genuine understanding, Arendt would argue that the possibility of lying inheres in the very character of factual truth itself—namely, its irreducible contingency.[32] "From this [contingency]," Arendt continues, "it follows that no factual statement can ever be beyond doubt—as secure and shielded against attack as, for instance, the statement that two and two make four" ("LP," 6). To make matters even more complicated, the possibility of lying—"that enables us to *say*, 'The sun is shining,' when it is raining cats and dogs"—is, in Arendt's account, an irreducible feature of human freedom: "If we were as thoroughly conditioned in our behavior as some philosophies have wished us to be, we would never be able to accomplish this little miracle" ("TP," 250).

Recognizing the entanglement of the question of freedom in any talk of truth, Arendt argues that the problem with factual truths arises when they are presented either as if they were necessary and incontestable, like logical truths (e.g., two plus two equals four), or as if they were relativistic and no more debatable than subjective matters of what is agreeable (e.g., "I like canary wine," to take Kant's example). On the one hand, Arendt insists on the sheer stubbornness of facts, their resistance to manipulation; if anything, facts are antipolitical, for they tend to be asserted in the manner of rational truths, which, in her view, compel us and preclude all debate. On the other hand, facts are highly vulnerable: far from "being beyond agreement, dispute, or consent," they survive as meaningful for human beings only to the extent that they are talked about.[33] "The political attitude toward facts must, indeed, tread the very narrow path between the danger of taking them as the results of some necessary development which men could not prevent and about which they can therefore do nothing and the danger of denying them, of trying to manipulate them out of the world" ("TP," 259).

More precisely, facts are not only vulnerable to being denied by human beings, they can be used to deny human freedom whenever they are presented in the manner of logical truth, with the latter's specific sense of necessity. The problem of factual truth, then, is not only that it is vulnerable to mendacity, but also that we tend to see such truth in the mode of necessity. Factual truth is crucial to the political realm, but the political challenge is how to affirm it in a manner consistent with human freedom. In Arendt's view, it is not the truth that sets you free, to cite a philosophical and religious commonplace; rather, it is a love and practice of freedom that saves truth.

Saving truth requires that we take the risk of freedom, even though freedom (i.e., contingency, not necessity, rules in human affairs) also presents grave risks for truth, which gives rise to a paradox of truth for politics. For Arendt, the possibility of lying attaches to the irreducible contingency of factual truths and to human freedom, but one needs at once to affirm truth and contingency. Any affirmation of truth that denies contingency would risk destroying freedom, and with it the distinctive nature of truth in the realm of human affairs—namely, that it could have been otherwise but was not.

From Knowing (Truth) to Acknowledging (Truth)

If we now turn to what Arendt calls "the relatively recent phenomenon of mass manipulation of fact and opinion," the paradox deepens ("TP," 252). As the Pentagon Papers show, "image-making as global policy" led to the creation of theories that were totally independent of the facts that the U.S. government itself had paid "'so many intelligence analysts to collect'" ("LP," 18, 20). "In this 'Alice in Wonderland atmosphere,'" writes Arendt, facts and decisions existed in a "nonrelation" ("LP," 20). "The facts I have in mind are publicly known, and yet the same public that knows them can successfully, and often spontaneously, taboo their public discussion" ("TP," 236). The facts or truths that everyone knows but refuses to acknowledge publicly present a significant problem for democratic politics, a problem that is not easily solved by attempts to establish normative procedures by which to "redeem" validity claims.

If we consider the search for Saddam Hussein's fabled "weapons of mass destruction" (WMD), we can see what is at stake here. "As we now know," writes Mark Danner, "the Iraqis had in fact destroyed these weapons, probably years before George W. Bush's [October 2002] ultimatum [that Iraq destroy its WMD or face war]: 'the Iraqis'—in the words of chief U.S. weapons inspector David Kay—'were telling the truth.'"[34] We also know that Kay's reporting of this truth had little political purchase.[35] As "the Downing Street memo" indicates, "by July 2002 at the latest, war had been decided on; the question at issue now was how to justify it—how to 'fix,' as it were, what Blair will later call 'the political context'" ("SWW," 5).

"What exactly does the Downing Street memo . . . and the related documents that have since appeared, prove?" asks Danner ("Reply").[36] Judging by the anemic, indeed indifferent reaction of the (mainstream) American press (which never even bothered to publish it), the story the memo tells is old hat, "nothing new" ("Reply").[37] When not ignored, the memo was viewed as being of little significance. As an example of this indifferent reception, Danner cites an article by Michael Kinsey about the memo. "Fixing intelligence and facts to fit a desired policy is the Bush II governing style," and if Bush had fixed the facts, it would be a politically significant scandal, says Kinsey. But, he continues, nothing in the memo reports actual decision makers saying they were "fixing the facts." Therefore, so Kinsey's logic goes, since they did not actually say "Let's fix the facts," we have no "proof" that they were fixing the facts: the memo proves nothing ("Reply"). Leaving aside the highly debatable claim that such "proof" would have actually produced a political scandal, if we consider Kinsey's own characterization of Bush's political style as one of deception, how are we to interpret this puzzling refusal to come to the obvious conclusion? Danner asks, "One might ask what would convince this writer, and many others, of the truth of what, apparently, they already *know*, and accept, and *acknowledge* that they know and accept? What could be said to establish 'truth'—to 'prove it'?" ("Reply," my emphasis).

Danner questions whether further evidence would have been able "to make a *publicly acceptable fact* out of what everyone now knows and accepts" ("Reply," my emphasis). Failing a tape recording of President Bush saying he "wants the facts fixed," remarks Danner, it appears that no such publicly accepted fact is possible. The discovery of the proverbial smoking gun guarantees nothing. (Was it really Bush on the tape? Maybe someone imitated his voice; maybe he was framed by the Democrats; maybe he was joking.) The real question, however, is whether proof of what was said in any form would have led to an active, rather than indifferent, public reception of the facts.

I said earlier that the facts or truths that everyone knows but refuses to acknowledge publicly present a problem for democratic politics that is not solved by procedures for redeeming validity claims. Not only is the impure domain of politics not especially "open to the possibility of 'redemption' under the normal claims of validity," as Mary Dietz puts it, but the issue that concerns us here is not even how to establish the truth of statements.[38] The issue, rather, is "how to make a publicly acceptable fact out of what everyone . . . knows and accepts." To make a fact publicly acceptable, I suggest, differs from proving or being called upon to prove that a fact is true. It is to make the truth of a fact meaningful in a politically significant way. From knowing something to be the case, it does not follow that I acknowledge that something is the case, just as "from my knowing I am late, it does not follow that I acknowledge I'm late," as Stanley Cavell succinctly puts this fundamental difference between knowing and acknowledging.[39] "Acknowledgment goes beyond knowledge. (Goes beyond not, so to speak, in the order of knowledge, but in its requirement that I *do* something or reveal something on the basis of that knowledge)," explains Cavell.[40] Even if we agree with Habermas that claims to both objective and normative validity demand argumentation to warrant them, we are still left with the question of what remains after all the reasons have been not only given but also accepted.

The problem I am trying to describe here might also be put in terms of what happens when a factual truth (e.g., the facts contained in the Downing Street memo) is revealed in the absence of an exchange of plural opinions about what might be true. One of the more curious aspects of the journalistic reporting and the public reception of the Downing Street memo was not only that its revelatory properties were questioned (as they were by Kinsey) but that, for the most part, it was simply ignored. As Danner observes, "It is a source of some irony that one of the obstacles to gaining recognition for the Downing Street memo in the American press has been the largely unspoken notion among reporters and editors that the story the memo tells is 'nothing new'" ("Reply"). It contains nothing new, so it is said, because the larger story that the memo (of July 2002) tells had already been reported by the Knight-Ridder news agency in two articles dated October 11, 2001, and February 13, 2002; namely, that President Bush had already decided to oust Saddam Hussein and had ordered the CIA, the Pentagon, and other agencies to develop a set of covert strategies to achieve that goal. Like reports on the memo after it, those Knight-Ridder articles were for the most part ignored. But the truly strange thing here, argues Danner, is this: "A story is told the first time [by Knight-Ridder] but hardly acknowledged . . . because the broader story the government is telling drowns it out. When the story is later confirmed by official documents, in this case the Downing Street memorandum, the documents are largely dismissed because they contain 'nothing new'" ("Reply").

Although I share Danner's concern with deciphering the logic of contemporary journalistic reporting on the Iraq war, the problem of what "constitutes a fact" or of how journalists can actually prove the truth of a story far exceeds the narrow frame of journalistic practices. The political problem we face here concerns not so much the ability to actually prove something is true, for that ability, I would argue, is parasitic on the very thing that the proof is meant to adjudicate or settle: the plurality of opinions. Indeed, what the curious tale of the Downing Street memo indicates is the hollowness of truth in the absence of a context of plural opinions and their exchange, for it is only in such a context that truth, when it is revealed, can reveal something to us as citizens, and further that we as citizens can reveal other aspects of the common world with the knowledge or, better, acknowledgment of that truth.

Such acknowledgement necessarily entails the entanglement of fact and value and of objective and normative validity. To take account of the fact that the events described in the Downing Street memo actually took place, we make a justification-transcendent validity claim, a claim to truth, whose reference is the objective world. But how we perceive that state of affairs is always already normatively charged, not with context-transcendent values but with the whole "whirl of organism" (to echo Cavell) of our shared practices, which inform our sense of what is valuable and should therefore be not only known but acknowledged. There is no way to decide how to act—the matter of practical reason on Habermas's account—on the basis of this fact that would not refer back to the value-laden context of the lifeworld, no deliberative process that would be free of value-laden factuality and objectivity. Rather, it is the common world rooted in a doxic mode of certainty that must be our touchstone for any critical questioning and acting.

If I am right to suggest that plural opinions are the condition of not only knowing but acknowledging something as true, perhaps we can make better sense of Arendt's brief but highly significant discussion of "representative thinking" in the third section of "Truth and Politics," which I briefly discussed in chapter 1. Often cited as one of her earliest formulations of the capacity to judge, Arendt's discussion of representative thinking emphasizes the importance of taking into account the standpoints of other people when forming an opinion. The issue, then, is not simply the existence of plural opinions but the capacity to take them into account, to acknowledge them as potentially revealing of something in the world, when forming one's own opinion or judgment. This enlarged perspective, however, does not seek to bring about the "single right answer" (*TJ*, 256) that drives Habermas's idea of moral validity.

What Habermas calls the "inclusive We-Perspective" is only apparently akin to Arendt's representative thinking, which does not find validity in judgments by abandoning the shared "reference to the world, which is also reflected in the justification-transcendent orientation toward truth," as he put the necessary condition of moral validity (*TJ*, 260). Representative thinking strives for validity by taking account of plural ordinary perspectives that alone give us a sense of an objective world that we have in common and on whose basis we can move from knowing that something is the case to acknowledging it to be the case—acknowledging it publically. We might now say that if Arendt's response to totalitarianism and the assault on truth was not to insist on objective truth in the manner of Orwell but to stress the political capacity to make judgments, it may well have been because she recognized that it is only through the practice of making judgments based on representative thinking that we can affirm the shared reality of an objective world. What we affirm when we think representatively is not just facts but the meaning these facts ought to have for what we are willing to count or acknowledge as belonging to and of concern for the public common world.

Were we to now ask of Arendt, "Is there to be no truth in politics?" we might imagine her answering, "On the contrary, there is truth in politics; however, this way of expressing truth is not simply a matter of being in agreement with oneself, but of thinking from the perspective of everyone else." We have grounds for our claims to truth in politics that provide the kind of validity that our refusal of the traditional philosophical opposition between "objective" and "subjective" throughout these past chapters has allowed us to see. This notion of truth reveals something, for it shows us what we have in common in the specific public sense of the common world that characterizes Arendt's creative formulation of a humanly possible political objectivity. And such truth cannot only survive in the political realm but can survive without destroying the plurality of opinions that are its original home. To search for the truth of opinion, as Socrates did, is to recognize this fundamental insight.

What does all this mean for the truth deficit in our current political context? One might say that as important as it is to expose lies and demand truth from those who claim to speak in our name, we also need to be able to do something political with those truths, to be able to make them into publicly acceptable facts—and this involves the ability to make judgments and acknowledge them publically. If Arendt emphasized the importance of an active citizenry debating plural opinions and paid little attention to the mechanism with which to adjudicate such debate, it was not, I suspect, because she excluded truth claims as such from the political realm but because she recognized that truth claims that are redeemed but not acknowledged (in the ways I've been discussing) have short lives. According to Danner, what remains is the "world of 'frozen scandal'—so-called scandals, that is, in which we have revelation but not a true investigation or punishment" ("Reply"), that is, citizen action that finds its end point in criminal proceedings or judicial decisions. Although Arendt would not see the end point of citizen action in law, she would surely agree that we should not confuse the politics of exposure and scandal with a vital democratic polity.

In the next chapter we will expand the understanding of a freedom-centered conception of truth and political objectivity to question the effort to bracket all truth claims in democratic politics that characterizes political liberalism.

FIVE

Value Pluralism and the "Burdens of Judgment": John Rawls's *Political Liberalism*

Few contemporary thinkers have so struggled with the problem of making judgments in the absence of a shared conception of the good or a transcendent conception of truth than has John Rawls. In light of neoconservative reactions to the putative collapse of universal standards of judgment—consider Samuel Huntington's anxious book title: *Who Are We? The Challenges to America's National Identity*—Rawls's *Political Liberalism* can seem like a sober response to the undeniable reality of social and cultural diversity.[1] In Rawls's account, "comprehensive doctrines" (religious, philosophical, and moral) are characterized at once by incompatibility and reasonability. Because people who deliberate about moral and political questions emphasize different aspects of questions and employ different methods, they will arrive at different and often irreconcilable answers. Rawls calls this free use of human reason the "burdens of judgment" and casts it as an irreducible feature of liberal democratic societies.[2] By contrast with Huntington, who sees in the demise of a coherent Anglo-American identity the loss of liberal democratic values, Rawls does not surrender the possibility that such values can be sustained. The burdens of judgment need not lead defenders of liberalism to despair: a conception of political justice can be worked out that this plurality of reasonable doctrines would endorse without succumbing to the impossible wish of reasserting one (Anglo-American) comprehensive view.

Rawls's key move within the tradition of liberal political thought is to set aside comprehensive visions of the good or the true, as they were famously articulated by thinkers such as Immanuel Kant and John Stuart Mill, to advance a "freestanding" political conception of justice as fairness. "The aim of justice as fairness as a political conception is practical, and not metaphysical or epistemological. That is, it presents itself not as a conception of justice that is true, but one that can serve as a basis of informed and willing political agreement between citizens viewed as free and equal persons," writes Rawls.[3] What matters is not whether one's views are true but whether they can be justified to others as reasonable—that is, as consistent with the core political values of justice as fairness and the view of persons as free and equal.[4] For political liberalism, reasonableness is the standard of correctness, not truth.

There is much to admire in Rawls's approach, not least his insistence on the difference between the rational and the reasonable (*PL*, 48–54) and, further, his effort to foreground the reasonable as that which matters for politics. Recognizing the dangerously coercive character of the claim to the truth of one's beliefs when it comes to shared political life, Rawls holds that "this is a claim that all equally could make; it is also a claim that cannot be made good by anyone to citizens generally. So, when we make such claims others, who are themselves reasonable, must count us unreasonable. And indeed we are, as we want to use state power, the collective power of equal citizens, to prevent the rest from affirming their not unreasonable views" (*PL*, 61). To be reasonable, he adds, is to "see that the burdens of judgment set limits on what can be reasonably justified to others" (*PL*, 61).

There is a striking similarity between Rawls's account and Arendt's critique of truth claims (as expressed in her essay "Truth and Politics"), which I have argued to be a crucial element in her understanding of judgment. Like Rawls, Arendt worries about the dogmatic character of such claims and their potentially corrosive effects on the public realm. Also like him, Arendt does not think of judging as a practice that is everywhere bounded by universally valid rules. When it comes to the realm of human affairs, she argues, the very idea that judging traffics in truth claims and appeals to universal criteria is antipolitical. In politics, plurality is the name of the game, and claims to the truth of one's beliefs, values, or judgments have no place.

Notwithstanding the important similarities in their views on truth and politics, Rawls and Arendt have significantly different perspectives on the place and importance of judging as a democratic practice. For Rawls, I will argue in this chapter, the burdens of judgment function more to set the limits on what can be discussed politically than to animate or enhance the capacity to judge in the absence of a universal rule itself. These limits are maintained through what many critics see as a highly constrained idea of public reason,[5] which is premised on what Rawls calls a "method of avoidance"—that is, avoidance of comprehensive claims to truth when speaking politically (as Rawls restrictively defines that kind of speech).[6] Agreeing with many of Rawls's critics on this score, I am also struck by Rawls's now famous answer to them in "The Idea of Public Reason Revisited." In this essay, Rawls not only strongly contests the view that public reason is—or was even meant to be—deeply restrictive in the way his critics accuse but also seems rather at a loss to explain how his work could have been so misunderstood.[7]

My own approach to this puzzle is to take Rawls at his word when he says that public reason is meant neither to define once and for all the manifest content of what citizens may debate nor to circumscribe political speech everywhere by its rule of reasonableness. If problems along these lines nevertheless persist, I argue, it is partly due to the highly constrained (though implicit) conception of meaning that guides even Rawls's more expansive account of public reason. Can we know what the effects of our speech will be—for example, will it be seen as reasonable or unreasonable; will it be affirming or destructive of liberal democratic political values—prior to any actual act of speaking? Following Wittgenstein's remarks on meaning and use, I argue in this chapter that we cannot, and that it is just this uncertainty about how our words will be taken up by others that enables judging to be not merely a boundary-securing activity, as it tends to be in Rawls's work, but a democratic world-building practice, as Arendt envisioned it.

Although public reason has been the subject of many debates within the literature on Rawls, more needs to be said about its relationship to political judgment understood in Arendt's terms as a crucial and quotidian feature of democratic citizenship.[8] As we have seen, for Arendt, the greatest threat to modern democracies lies not in the conflict among incommensurable but reasonable comprehensive doctrines, as it clearly does for Rawls, but in the loss of a common world in which significant differences of perspective can be publicly voiced and critically judged. Rather than rush to find in acts of judging citizens' nefarious designs on state power, Arendt sees the all-important world-building practice that attenuates the craving for state-centered solutions to problems of democratic citizenship.

Does not public reason's method of avoidance, though admirable for its sensitivity to a coercive and punitive (state-sanctioned) rationalism, work to undermine the development of judgment as a viable democratic political practice? And might an attenuation of the capacity to judge not in turn lead citizens to an ever greater reliance on the state to solve problems of democratic governance, notwithstanding the highly limited role granted to the state within political liberalism? Rawls's defenders could counter that political liberalism has no need of this Arendtian practice, but I shall hold that without fostering the capacity to judge, political liberalism threatens to enhance the very state power it seeks to curtail and to degenerate into the highly apolitical and stability-centered theory that its critics have claimed it to be.

To reclaim judgment as a practice of democratic citizenship, we need to think about the reasonable as something other than a mode of political speech, and a way of engaging fellow citizens, that is based on the method of avoidance. Unshackled from the constraints of public reason, the reasonable might also be understood as a form of making political judgments and claims that generates agreement on matters of common concern by enlarging our sense both of what so much as counts as a common matter and who counts as a political speaker. To judge and speak politically outside the boundaries set by public reason is always to risk unsettling what Rawls takes to be a presumably stable "overlapping consensus" about basic political principles. More than that, it is to risk being rebuffed by one's fellow citizens, treated—if not as mad—as deeply unreasonable and therefore as having nothing politically to say. But just that risk taking can constitute something new: unexpected domains and topics of legitimate democratic political debate and unanticipated speakers of political judgments and claims, which in turn generate our sense of the common world. To show how this inaugural force of political speech can work, I devote a long section of this chapter to a reading of Frederick Douglass's 1852 Fourth of July address in the context of Rawls's remarks on abolitionism and the constraints of public reason. I argue that this speech is best understood neither as a past- nor future-perfect expression of public reason under the constraints of the history of chattel slavery, which is more or less how Rawls would have us understand abolitionist speech *tout court*, but as what I call the predicative moment of politics and the world-building practice of judging.

Judgment and Public Reason

A basic difficulty with the idea of public reason, says Rawls, is that, in demanding that citizens honor its limits when "discussing and voting on the most fundamental political questions," public reason seems to limit them to an "appeal only to a public conception of justice and not to the whole truth as they see it" (*PL*, 216). Imagining the objection of an imaginary interlocutor, Rawls adds, "Surely, the most fundamental questions should be settled by appealing to the most important truths, yet these may far transcend public reason!" (*PL*, 216). At once recognizing the impulse to make comprehensive truth claims when our most fundamental political decisions are at stake and invoking the familiar interdiction on such claims that goes under the method of avoidance, Rawls imagines that he has dissolved the paradox by reminding the reader of what it means to endorse a political conception supported by an "overlapping consensus": "As reasonable and rational, and knowing that they affirm a diversity of reasonable religious and philosophical doctrines, they should be ready to explain the basis of their actions to one another in terms each could reasonably expect that others might endorse as consistent with their freedom and equality" (*PL*, 218). Reasonableness requires that "on fundamental political matters, reasons given explicitly in terms of comprehensive doctrines are never to be introduced into public reason" (*PL*, 247), for they would explain one's motivating convictions in terms of truth (*PL*, 219). "The zeal to embody the whole truth in politics is incompatible with an idea of public reason that belongs with democratic citizenship" ("IPPR," 132–33). This is "the exclusive view" of public reason (*PL*, 248), Rawls explains.

But how do we know, prior to the actual moment of speaking and judging, what another person will count as reasonable, and thus as political speech according to Rawls, in the context of a political debate? Even if we have some idea of what this might be, surely when it comes to speaking and judging politically, context is all. The importance of context to meaning is ignored not only by Rawls but also by self-declared political liberals such as Martha Nussbaum, who strongly endorses "the wisdom of the method of avoidance."[9] In her view, this method was sadly missing in founding political documents such as "the U.S. Declaration of Independence [which] uses a notion of self-evident truth, as well as a reference to the Creator, to ground its claim of inalienable rights. Political liberalism must reject this sort of language as inappropriate for the political sphere," Nussbaum holds.[10]

What does this method of avoidance assume? To take Nussbaum's example, it assumes that to declare, say, "We hold these truths to be self-evident" (e.g., the self-evident *truth* of human equality bequeathed by God), as it is elaborated in the Declaration of Independence, is to give a belief the form of a meaningful statement, and that this statement, as meaningful, could potentially cause harm, for it might offend another citizen's contrary belief. The method of avoidance recommends itself because meaning is always already contained in the statement prior to its utterance. It is thus fully poised to offend as soon as it is spoken in public. Does it make sense to talk about strings of words or sentences as having meaning in this way?

This is the kind of question addressed by Wittgenstein, perhaps most famously in *On Certainty*, where he raised concerns about G. E. Moore's attempt to answer the skeptic with the commonsense declaration (accompanied by pointing): "I know this is a hand." That statement, as Wittgenstein suggests a few sections later, is akin to:

I know that a sick man is lying here? Nonsense! I am sitting at his bedside. I am looking attentively into his face.–So I don't know, then, that there is a sick man lying here? Neither the question nor the assertion makes sense. Any more than the assertion "I am here," which I might yet use at any moment, if suitable occasion presented itself. . . . . It is only in use that the proposition has its sense.[11]

Why is it "nonsense" to say that I know that there is a sick man lying here (or I know this is a hand) when the conditions are optimal for knowing such a thing?

Wittgenstein's response, as James Conant explains, is typically understood as marking the difference between a meaningful sentence and an unsuitable context for its use.[12] "I know there is a sick man lying here" is meaningful, but to state it while sitting at the bedside of this sick man is nonsense. The context is wrong. It is just so "flamingly *obvious*," to speak with Stanley Cavell in *The Claim of Reason*, that there is a sick man lying here (*CR*, 211). On the widely accepted interpretation discussed by Conant, "Wittgenstein's complaint is not directed against *what* is said; Wittgenstein's complaint is directed rather at the idea that the 'something' in question is the kind of thing that can be asserted *here*. The charge is thus not directed against the intelligibility of what is said, but against the intelligibility of the attempt to assert 'it' on such an unsuitable occasion."[13] But Wittgenstein's objection to traditional philosophy is far more radical than that.

It is more radical because Wittgenstein's point here, writes Conant, "is that 'for a large class' of occasions of speaking there isn't anything which can properly count as asking the question 'What do the words [which have been spoken] mean?' apart from a simultaneous consideration of questions such as 'When was it said?,' 'Where?,' 'By whom?,' 'To whom?,' etc."[14] We cannot decide what words mean apart from the context in which they are spoken. "'The meaning of an expression' [e.g., "I am here"] (if by this we mean the meaning that the expression has when employed in a context of significant use) is not something which an expression possesses already on its own and which is subsequently imported into a context of use," Conant explains.[15] This context of use, in turn, is not some general category that determines in advance what a particular string of words can mean. It is not that the (generalized) context (e.g., any person sitting at the bedside of any sick man) sets the terms in which a sentence is meaningful or not, nor that the sentence ("I know that a sick man is lying here.") is meaningful apart from the (generalized) context. It is rather someone speaking a particular sentence in a particular context and to particular others that creates meaning.

The appeal to context as a way of understanding the nature of Wittgenstein's contribution to our topic, then, takes for granted that context determines what can intelligibly be said. But just this way of thinking about context remains entangled in the view of language as a framework of rules that I questioned in chapter 1. As Steven Affeldt powerfully deepens this point, it is as if "*what* the particular context [into which we speak] *is* is obvious and is determinable apart from and prior to what is (found to be) intelligibly said 'within' it. This is to treat a context as a space or a room into which words, but only some words, may be placed. We, as it were, walk into the context and by observation of its features determine which words fit the room and which do not— like so many pieces of furniture. However a context is not a room." He continues:

The fundamental problem with any appeal to a context to determine what may or may not intelligibly be said within it is that what the context is is itself determined only by what (we find) is intelligibly said. I may discover upon your making and my understanding a particular remark that the context of your (or our) conversation—in the sense of the concerns at issue—is not what I had initially imagined. And I may also discover (perhaps after the fact) that my finding something that you said unintelligible (unreasonable, pointless, irrelevant, incomprehensible, and the like) was caused by my misunderstanding, or imagining differently, the context in which we were speaking. Such experiences are familiar enough. What they show is

149

that our grasp of a context and of what someone is saying emerge together, wax and wane together.[16]

I suggest that political liberalism's method of avoidance reproduces just the assumed relationship between meaning and use, or context and intelligible meaning, that Wittgenstein would have us question.[17] If the meaning of an expression is not something that an expression possesses on its own; if it is not a manifest content that is subsequently imported into a context of use; and if we are never in the position to know in advance of any actual speaking in an actual and particular context of use what our words will mean (i.e., whether others will find them intelligible), why should we assume that the assertion "These truths are self-evident" is always already meaningful and poised to violate the principle of equal respect when spoken publicly? Or, to put the question in more felicitous terms, why should we accept the method of avoidance as the only way of saving the public realm?

For Rawls, we have seen, the rules governing public reason are consistent with the more general strategy of political liberalism, which, he writes, "removes from the political agenda the most divisive issues, serious contention about which must undermine the bases of social cooperation" (*PL*, 157). Rawls realizes that, by both excluding from debate the issues that truly divide citizens and severely limiting the terms of debate for those issues they may discuss, he has a problem explaining what political liberalism holds to be legitimate social and political change. He has a problem, for example, explaining how slavery came to be abolished, or rather how the abolition of slavery could have been justified at the time in terms of political liberalism, rather than being accepted under the aegis of "pluralism." He has a problem explaining how either the civil rights movement could have happened if its participants had embraced political liberalism and kept within the bounds of "public reason" or women's liberation could have taken place if women had recognized the lack of an overlapping consensus on women's rights.

In response to criticism along these lines, Rawls claims that, against the exclusive view of public reason discussed previously, "there is another view allowing citizens, in certain situations, to present what they regard as the basis of political values rooted in their comprehensive doctrine, provided they do this in ways that strengthen the ideal of public reason itself" (*PL*, 247). If we ask, "Did the abolitionists go against the ideal of public reason?" writes Rawls, we should view "the question conceptually and not historically" (*PL*, 250). The issue, in other words, is not a question of whether "their political agitation was a necessary political force leading to the Civil War and so to the destruction of the great evil and curse of slavery" (*PL*, 250). On that level their actions can be redeemed by history. The issue, rather, is whether such actions can be seen as conceptually consistent with the great political principles and thus redeemed by public reason. This is the "inclusive view" of public reason, which Rawls calls the more "correct" view (*PL*, 248). And not only correct but, I would add, crucially important for the fortunes of political liberalism because the inclusive view enables us to explain the social change that, under the exclusive view, must appear illegitimate. As this illegitimacy would call into question the entire project of political liberalism—why would we embrace a theory that cannot so much as account for the momentous social and political change that it holds to be legitimate?—a lot is at stake in this inclusive view. I quote at length:

> On this account the abolitionists and the leaders of the civil rights movement did not go against the ideal of public reason; or rather, they did not provided they thought, or on reflection would have thought (as they certainly could have thought), that the comprehensive reasons they appealed to were required to give sufficient strength to the political conception to be subsequently realized. To be sure, people do not normally distinguish between comprehensive and public reasons; nor do they normally affirm the ideal of public reason, as we have expressed it. Yet people can be brought to recognize these distinctions in particular cases. The abolitionists could say, for example, that they supported political values of freedom and equality for all, but that given the comprehensive doctrines they held and the doctrines current in their day, it was necessary to invoke the comprehensive grounds on which those values were widely seen to rest. Given those historical conditions, it was not unreasonable of them to act as they did for the sake of public reason itself. In this case, the ideal of public reason allows the inclusive view. (*PL*, 251)

Striking in Rawls's inclusive view of public reason is that it leaves the ideal of public reason itself wholly unchanged. Comprehensive reasons are admissible as long as they either are or (through reflection) can be seen to be consistent with public reason, which by definition excludes such reasons. Consistency is achieved through the incorporation of the "offensive" elements of these doctrines (i.e., their comprehensive moral reasoning and claims to truth) into the logic of justification. Not unlike a certain way of thinking about rights, whereby new claims to political enfranchisement are explained as the mere extension of the inherent logic of rights itself (i.e., its ever-expanding nature), Rawls's inclusive account of public reason redeems "conceptually" what were, historically, nonpublic reasons at the expense of neutralizing the political character of making judgments and claims. It is as if the logic of public reason itself determined in advance the legitimacy of claims made in the name of nonpublic reason. Thus, abolitionists' nonpublic reason, which led them to "bas[e] their arguments on religious grounds" (*PL*, 249), is redeemed as politically valid by virtue of the fact that, seen conceptually, it "supported the clear conclusions of public reason" (*PL*, 250). Likewise, the nonpublic reasons advanced by the civil rights movement, led by Martin Luther King Jr., are redeemed on a conceptual level by the "appeal . . . to the political values expressed in the Constitution correctly understood" (*PL*, 250). And so on.

But what it means to "correctly" understand the political values of the Constitution is given neither in the internal consistency of the values themselves (which would require their eventual application to all human beings, on pain of contradiction) nor by the imputation of public reason thinking to nonpublic reason claim making. The sense of correctness is generated, rather, by the very practice of making political judgments and claims. Our sense of necessity here, in other words, belongs not to any logic of expansion but to the contingent historical fact that abolitionists, civil rights activists, and suffragists claimed their freedom and equality, and their demands were eventually heard and taken up by others. It may appear as if it *had* to be that way—that such advances were already guaranteed, so to speak, by the principles inherent in the Constitution or the logic of rights—but that is the illusion created by the ideal of public reason. The achievements of abolitionism, the civil rights movement, and feminism did not have to happen at all and, as anyone familiar with the history of these struggles knows, came close to not happening at all. Rawls himself would not deny this. But the question is whether thinking about these struggles in terms of the ideal of public reason might occlude the contingency of these advances as genuine but fragile political achievements. Forged through conflict and struggle, such advances involved tremendous risk: not only the obvious risks to one's person that were known to be associated with abolitionist activities but also the less obvious risk of being rebuffed politically that I mentioned earlier. This risk of speaking outside the strictures of public reason and refusing to limit oneself to the mere extension of already legitimate political principles, we shall now see, is what made Frederick Douglass's Fourth of July address the paradigm of brilliant antislavery speeches.

Risking Unreasonableness

My point in questioning the ideal of public reason as a kind of grand narrative for making sense of the historical struggle for rights, or as a purification mechanism for making public sense of nonpublic reason, is not to deny that disenfranchised individuals and groups do in fact need to articulate their claims and judgments in a language that, far from being merely subjective, makes an appeal to some kind of universality.[18] But the question is whether thinking about that language in terms of the redemption of nonpublic reason by public reason might conceal and perhaps even distort what is at stake.

One thing that is surely at stake is how it was that a suffragist such as Elizabeth Cady Stanton or an ex-slave abolitionist such as Frederick Douglass could be so much as heard as making public judgments and claims. What Rawls observes about slaves was, albeit in a more limited form, applicable to both Stanton and Douglass: "Slaves are human beings who are not counted as sources of claims" (*PL*, 33).[19] The issue here is not whether one can speak the (English) language and be understood, but whether the language one speaks is counted as being more than merely private or subjective. The idea that one can redeem nonpublic reason with public reason assumes that one is in the position of a speaking subject who is counted as the source of claims, and who can therefore make arguments based on a conception of the reasonable, which, for political liberals, are the only game in town.

Consider Frederick Douglass's famous speech, "The Meaning of July Fourth for the Negro." Delivered on July 5, 1852, at an event commemorating the signing of the Declaration of Independence and sponsored by the Rochester Ladies' Anti-Slavery Society, this speech is widely considered to be the single most effective and important pre–Civil War speech denouncing slavery and advocating emancipation. Both the speech and the meeting itself were to provide a counter-celebration to Independence Day. Douglass was among the speakers who exposed the hypocrisy of the American Revolution and the elusive ideal of liberty for all. "This Fourth of July is *yours*, not *mine*," he told his white listeners. "*You* may rejoice, *I* must mourn." Douglass's remarks went to the heart of the crime of slavery upon which the American nation had been founded.[20]

Douglass's speech resists its redemption by the Rawlsian ideal of public reason, for it aims to expose the hypocrisy of the canons of political rationality and deliberation on which that idea is based. Invoking the voice of an imaginary interlocutor who complains that the abolitionists would do well to "argue more . . . and denounce less," Douglass questions whether the abomination of slavery can be addressed by "argument" at all.

But, I submit, where all is plain there is nothing to be argued. What point in the anti-slavery creed would you have me argue? . . . Must I undertake to prove that the slave is a man? . . . Would you have me argue that man is entitled to liberty? That he is the rightful owner of his own body? . . . Must I argue the wrongfulness of slavery? Is that a question for Republicans? Is it to be settled by the rules of logic and argumentation, as a matter beset with great difficulty, involving a doubtful application of the principle of justice, hard to be understood? . . . There is not a man beneath the canopy of heaven that does not know that slavery is wrong *for him* . . . . Must I argue that a system thus marked with blood . . . is *wrong*? No! I will not. . . . What, then, remains to be argued?[21]

As George Shulman parses this passage, the issue here is white refusal to acknowledge what is already known: "The problem is not an ignorance to be remedied by knowledge or argument, but a perception of what and who we count as real; not just a gap between our professed ideals and actual conduct, but a motivated blindness . . . about the other, about our conduct, and so about who we think we are."[22] At issue, then, is "a denial of reality so profound that every professed value seems hollow."[23] Douglass calls attention to this denial by beginning his speech with the use of the first-person pronoun "I" and then, within the space of three paragraphs, separating himself from his audience through use of the second-person "your": "This, for the purpose of this celebration, is the Fourth of July. It is the birthday of *your* National Independence, and of *your* political freedom."[24] He claims the right to speak by addressing his audience as "fellow-citizens" but also marks the hollowness of that term for free Northern black Americans including himself and the millions of slaves who were not citizens. If the central issue is that we refuse to count others as real in a political sense (as sources of claims), or if we are invested in denying the conditions that so exclude them, then Douglass must find a form of speech that makes visible his nonstatus as a credible speaker of claims.

Rather than participate in the charade of deliberative discourse that presupposes such equality of speaking subjects, Douglass declares:

At a time like this, scorching irony, not convincing argument, is needed. O! had I the ability, and could reach the nation's ear, I would, to-day, pour out a fiery stream of biting ridicule, blasting reproach, withering sarcasm, and stern rebuke. For it is not light that is needed, but fire. . . . The feeling of the nation must be quickened; the conscience of the nation must be roused; the propriety of the nation must be startled.[25]

"Quickened, roused, startled: Douglass's insights into the democratic importance of nondeliberative discourse and claims-making practices," astutely observes Jason Frank, "were not unique to him but a central component of abolition's public sphere."[26]

The point here is not to deny that Douglass makes arguments. Only these arguments come to life qua arguments through the use of "scorching irony, . . . biting ridicule, blasting reproach, withering sarcasm," and a barrage of powerful tropes and figures—in a word, through rhetoric. Rhetoric allows the arguments to come alive and the so-called manifest content of the saving principles of the Constitution to be seen. Rhetoric should be understood here as far more than the mere means of persuasion that makes it easier to absorb rational truth, as the philosophical tradition would have it. No mere "technique of an exterior persuasion," writes Ernesto Grassi, "it [rhetoric] is the basis of . . . rational thought" and "provides the framework [tropes, figures, images] within which the proof can come into existence."[27] To put this in the (Wittgensteinian) terms I used earlier, meaning is not already contained in the manifest content of Douglass's speech, which is the subject of Rawls's conceptual redemption of abolitionist moral and religious appeals by public reason. Rather, the meaning of Douglass's speech emerges in the context of his speaking: his rhetorical genius was to bring his audience to hear reasonable political judgments in the moral denouncements that his imaginary interlocutor dismissed as politically ineffective and a political liberal might call unreasonable.

The specific mode of public speaking that expresses a decisive antislavery public judgment, then, is not "based upon reasons and evidence after discussion and due reflection," which is how Rawls describes the workings of public reason (*PL*, 110). Of course Rawls also holds that "justification is not regarded simply as valid argument from listed premises, even should these premises be true. Rather, justification is addressed to others who disagree with us, and therefore it must always proceed from some consensus, that is, from premises that we and others publicly recognize as true; or better, publicly recognize as acceptable to us for the purpose of establishing a working agreement on the fundamental questions of political justice."[28] It is indeed tempting to read Douglass's speech, as Jason Frank puts it, as "a paradigmatic instance of immanent critique in the dissenting traditions of American political thought."[29] On this understanding the critic starts with commonplaces—that is, tropes and values already accepted by his audience as part of what Rawls calls public reason. "According to this approach," writes Frank, "Douglass exposes a *contradiction* between the universality of the principle and the historical particularity of its application."[30] In this way, Douglass can be seen as affirming the fundamental principles of public reason and merely asking that they be extended—as they conceptually could have been, according to Rawls—to slaves.

But Douglass's problem—which mirrors the larger problem of abolitionist struggles at that time—is not only to invoke the shared premises of the US Constitution or the Declaration of Independence to persuade those who disagree on the moral and political issue of slavery. That kind of argument had already been made—hundreds of times over, in fact. Douglass confronts an audience (hosted by an Anti-Slavery Society), many of whose members already share his judgment on the wrongs of slavery and already share core democratic premises (e.g., human equality). His problem, not unlike the one described by Mark Danner at the end of the last chapter, is not simply how to convince others on the basis of what everyone already accepts; it is how to bring them to acknowledge in their actions what they already know so that it becomes *politically*—and not just personally, morally, or religiously—significant. The point is not to endorse and merely extend the logic of the shared premises as they are expressed in the Declaration or the Constitution; it is to gain critical purchase on what each takes for granted. In this way, the premises can be subjected to critical judgment and redeployed anew.

We would miss the sheer political force of Douglass's speech if we were, with Rawls, to redeem Douglass's nonpublic reason with public reason. Douglass urges us to "hold fast" to the Declaration of Independence as the "sheet anchor" of the republic, but it could be misleading to say, as Rawls does about Martin Luther King Jr., that Douglass appeals here "to the political values expressed in the Constitution correctly understood" (*PL*, 250). Although Douglass himself, in his 1851 departure from William Lloyd Garrison's denunciation of the Constitution as a proslavery document, eventually claimed that, correctly understood, the Constitution was an antislavery document, his conversion was no mere return to what was always already there, but a creative, indeed transformative political action: an action that, together with the in-terpretations of like-minded abolitionists, redefined the meaning of the Constitution as a radical document that authorized Congress to abolish slavery. Douglass's speech can be seen as an example of what I have elsewhere called the predicative moment of politics.[31] In such moments, the claim to "we the people" does not call on an already existing subject formed through consensus on basic political principles only to affirm them. Rather, it is a form of speaking and judging that unsettles how we understand those principles and the apparent coher-ence of the "we" that denies its contingent and exclusionary character.

Speaking Truth Politically

In the case of abolitionism, Rawls sees public reason as redeeming the comprehensive reasons given by the abolitionists. But this does not alter his basic point about the intrinsically divisive character of com-prehensive claims to true beliefs. It is instructive in this regard to re-call that Douglass, though he clearly held slavery to be a moral crime against the higher law of nature and gave forceful public expression to that view, came to reject Garrisonianism, largely because of the moral righteousness of its public stance. Such righteousness, as Doug-lass saw, led to a form of political paralysis and ultimately indifference. As James Colaiaco writes, "To abolish slavery, the intractable Garrison would have gone as far as dissolving the Union, leaving two nations, one slave and one free."[32] Recognizing the fatal implications for free-dom in Garrison's uncompromising and wholly moralized approach to ending slavery, Douglass was led to advance a distinctly political ap-proach to abolition, an approach that radically altered how he thought about the relationship of absolute moral claims to politics. He did not counter Garrison by asserting the inevitable conflict between moral-ity and political expediency and, in the name of expediency, bracket claims to the moral truth of human equality (as contemporary political liberals would have us do). Rather, he saw that one can and ought to affirm as universal one's political principles, but such affirmation will always take into account political context. In this way he is engaged in building what Arendt calls a "common world." *Pace* Garrison, writes Colaiaco, Douglass saw that the refusal to make political compromises and "accept a lesser evil to avoid a greater one, can actually thwart the achievement of one's ethical goals."[33] As Douglass himself puts it, it does not follow "that what is morally right is, at all times, politically possible," but what is politically possible is the only path to the eventual attainment of what is morally right.[34]

Contrasting Douglass's deeply political way of thinking about abolitionist claims to Garrison's wholly moral view, we might wonder whether the comprehensive appeal to truth necessarily poses a risk to democracy when asserted in what Rawls calls "the public political forum" ("IPPR," 133). Arendt famously argued that it does: the appeal to an absolute truth undercuts the freedom of citizens, for it seems to lodge the authority to act politically in an extrapolitical order.[35] Moreover, this kind of truth claim poses grave dangers to democratic politics, in her view, for claims to absolute truth tend to preclude all debate. Although I implied earlier that Arendt agrees with Rawls here, we can now see that her concern is fundamentally different: she fears not the mortal combat that truth claims supposedly provoke, but the deafening silence. "Truth carries within itself an element of coercion," she writes, for any claim to truth appears to be "beyond agreement, dispute, opinion, or consent" ("TP," 239, 240). But this worry, as I argued in the last chapter, seems to forget Arendt's own insight, in the same essay, into the practice of making political claims—namely, that any claim, including claims to self-evident truths, depends in the end on agreement and consent. Thus, Thomas Jefferson may have thought that by declaring truths to be self-evident, he was putting them beyond dispute. But, writes Arendt, "by saying '*We hold* these truths to be self-evident,' he conceded, albeit without becoming aware of it, that the statement 'All men are created equal' is not self-evident but stands in need of agreement and consent—that equality, if it is to be politically relevant, is a matter of opinion and not 'the truth'" ("TP," 246) fully detached from what it is that citizens say.[36]

Nonetheless, surely there is danger in political claims and judgments that purport to embody the whole truth and therefore foreclose all debate. Aware of this danger, Douglass, though he believed in racial (and gender) equality as a deep moral truth, was willing to make political compromises that involved how he expressed or pursued the realization of that moral truth. Unlike political liberals, however, Douglass does not invoke the idea of public reason as the only legitimate way to speak to other citizens: rather, he questions that idea and advances comprehensive reasons that he then subjects to the contingent demands and exigencies of politics. Thus, Douglass can reinterpret and mobilize the Constitution as an antislavery document based on the same natural law tradition that Garrison also claimed as the basis for his rejection of the Constitution and his uncompromising moral stance.[37] It was not the claim to the truth of natural law as such that was decisive in the conflict between Garrison and Douglass but the particular way in which that claim was employed by each of them politically. Democratic politics *can* be endangered by comprehensive truth claims, but it can also be enabled—there is no guarantee, one way or the other.

Thinking about comprehensive truth claims in a political rather than a philosophical idiom, we can see that the problem facing citizens of democratic societies is how to make critical judgments in the absence of a single conception of the good. But that is not quite how Rawls understands it. For him, "the burdens of judgment" point not to the importance of developing one's capacity to judge in the absence of a transcendent rule, as it does for Arendt, but to the necessity of taking certain topics of political judgment off the table and abiding by the rules of public reason.[38] I recognize that for as many passages as one could cite that say as much, Rawls's defenders—as I learned in the course of writing this chapter—will cite others. I suggested earlier that there are certainly textual grounds for questioning just how restrictive public reason is according to Rawls. Nevertheless, it seems fair to say that although he recognized that universal rules for judgment could not be sustained in the face of deep diversity, Rawls's response was to keep judgment tethered to the authority of public reason, however capacious or narrow one understands it to be.[39] This tethering of the capacity to judge to an external authority of sorts comes at a cost: it focuses our attention on the rules of judgment or criteria of public reason, rather than inspiring us to speak and judge with reference not to universal rules but to particular contexts and interlocutors. This reflective kind of critical judgment was at the center of Arendt's different approach to her similar recognition of social and cultural diversity.

Judging as a World-Building Practice

For Arendt, I have argued, the capacity to judge reflectively (that is, in the absence of a concept or rule) is a defining feature of democratic citizenship. Such citizenship is not identical, in her view, with membership in any given nation-state. Nor is it premised on the sharing of what Rawls calls a "comprehensive doctrine" and defines as the essence of the idea of "community." Whereas Rawls and Arendt agree that unity of perspective destroys the public realm, their reasons differ. For

Rawls, a comprehensive doctrine almost always threatens to endanger liberal democratic politics when it gains public expression, for "the zeal to embody the whole truth in politics" ("IPPR," 132–33) excludes the possible legitimacy of competing views and seeks to mobilize the state in defense of a singular idea of the true. For Arendt, logical truth claims are apolitical, for they tolerate no dissent, but she also suggests that the dangerous rise of any single worldview is brought about, not hindered, by restricting the public expression of different (comprehensive) worldviews. As argued in chapter 1, to belong to a democratic political community is to have a "common world," not to share a comprehensive worldview, and this common world exists only where there is a plurality of worldviews. There is no common human nature that might guarantee unity in diversity but only the actual public articulation of those perspectives themselves. The common world is built out of diverse perspectives and the imaginative acts of thinking and judging that take them into account.

The public world we have in common for Arendt is not what political liberals mean by an "overlapping consensus." This consensus, we have seen, is premised on citizens abiding by the "method of avoidance." For Arendt, what is common for us is not some overlapping consensus, let alone some comprehensive doctrine that we all share, but rather a public space that is created out of the public expression of the plurality of comprehensive doctrines. The common world is "the space in which things become public."[40] This idea of the common world as the space in which things *become* public reminds us that the public or political character of any human practice is not given in the practice itself but is created through what Arendt calls action in concert. It was in this space that abolitionists risked being rebuffed as unreasonable and brought their fellow citizens to see slavery as a political matter subject to change, transforming their own personal moral and religious commitments to end slavery into a genuinely political and public claim.

Arendt's idea of a common world invites us to recognize that it is our practice of politics that turns value pluralism into a form of mortal combat, rather than something intrinsic to that pluralism itself. Her affirmation of plurality as something that can only appear in public, rather than, as Rawls would have it, something that is private and must be protected by a method of avoidance, is crucial for avoiding "a dreary and conservative public discourse, freed of all fundamental challenges," to speak with Veit Bader.[41] Rawls himself observes that "the forms of permissible public reason are always several," and that "new variations" may be crucial; "otherwise the claims of groups or interests arising from social change might be repressed and fail to gain their appropriate political voice" ("IPPR," 142–43). But where do these permissible forms and new variations originate if not in the violations of any existing idea of public reason? This is the risk of political speech about which I spoke earlier. People gain their political voice by taking that risk. We simply cannot know what our words will mean—or whether they will be dismissed as unreasonable, as mad, as offensive, as politically irrelevant, or some combination of these—apart from the moment of their utterance and reception. The openness to new demands that Rawls says he wants to preserve, then, cannot happen without taking that risk.

I admire political liberalism's celebration of value differences as an achievement of free liberal democratic institutions. Still, there is something awry in a political stance that construes these differences as that which likewise poses the greatest potential threat to free liberal democratic institutions, a threat that is best managed through a method of avoidance. This method leads to the occlusion of judgment as a specifically *political* practice in Arendt's sense. We find ourselves in the strange situation in which any comprehensive doctrine or stance that rejects, as Rawls writes, "the ideas of public reason and deliberative democracy" (e.g., "fundamentalist religious doctrines") will simply be shut out of legitimate public debate. "They [such doctrines] assert that the religiously true, or the philosophically true, overrides the politically reasonable. We simply say that such a doctrine is politically unreasonable. Within political liberalism nothing more need be said" ("IPPR," 178). But a lot more needs to be said—that is, if democratic citizens are not to satisfy themselves with talking publicly to people who are already part of the charmed circle of the "reasonable" and instead try to engage points of view that trouble our understanding of the reasonable. And isn't this the real political challenge that faces the democratic societies characterized by deep value pluralism today?

By contrast with Arendt, who also worries about the dogmatic character of certain kinds of truth claims and their potentially destructive effects on the public realm, Rawls ends up shrinking this realm to the point of insignificance in the name of saving it. For Rawls, acceptance of "the consequences of the burdens of judgment . . . leads to the idea of reasonable toleration" ("IPPR," 177)—which we might now say is really better understood as a deeply attenuated notion of what can be discussed politically. It is not enough to draw a distinction between the official and the background public political culture, as Rawls did in response to critics. For what is sustained in what Rawls called the *ideal* of public reason is a way of thinking about political debate that circumscribes from the start what can so much as count—what we will acknowledge—as a legitimate public object of judgment in the first place, as if the appearance of any new object (e.g., abolition, female enfranchisement, gay rights) would merely be the reappearance of objects already given in the "Constitution properly understood." It is just this prior question of how citizens come to bring new objects into view, as argued in chapter 1, that Arendt's approach to judgment would have us foreground.[42]

It is only after we recognize the place of this prior question, occluded by public reason, that the practice of judging politically comes into its own. And it is with this practice of judgment that the expression of value differences can be seen, with Arendt, not as something to be managed by the idea of the reasonable in the name of toleration and social stability, but as susceptible to becoming part of the common world, that is, as she stated in *The Human Condition*, the "inter-est, which lies between people and can therefore relate and bind them together" (*HC*, 182). How do citizens learn to think and to judge in ways that create a sense of a common world whose very possibility arises not despite but precisely because they do not share a comprehensive doctrine? Surely, it cannot be by practicing the method of avoidance.

The threat to democracy is not the deadly conflict of so-called ultimate value orientations but the deterioration of the common world in which these orientations can be expressed and judged. Plural perspectives are the lifeblood of the public realm; the means by which we come to see what is an object of common concern. They become a threat to the public realm when they are no longer expressed in the public realm. The validation of competing values expressed as political judgments and claims depends not on their redemption by some objective agency or discourse of public reason but by the reflective judgments of citizens in the practice of politics itself.

In the next chapter we shall see how this world-building practice of judging politically might be taken up by feminists confronting practices and worldviews not their own.

SIX

Relativism and the New Universalism: Feminists Claim the Right to Judge

In her well-known essay "Is Multiculturalism Bad for Women?" Susan Moller Okin takes up "the claim, made in the context of basically liberal democracies, that minority cultures or ways of life are not sufficiently protected by the practice of ensuring the individual rights of their members, and as a consequence [that] these should also be protected through special *group* rights or privileges."[1] Insofar as most (especially non-Western, nonliberal) cultures are characterized by gender practices and ideologies that strongly disadvantage women, says Okin, "group rights are potentially, and in many cases actually, antifeminist" ("IMBW," 12). Thus, she concludes, a liberal defense of human rights must give priority to the rights of individuals, not minority cultures or groups.

Proceeding in this way, it is not difficult for Okin to make a reasonable case against multiculturalism, understood as the extension of special rights to cultural groups, for the latter tend in her view to discriminate against women. But what counts as discrimination? Critics accuse Okin of an ethnocentric account of traditional cultures that is informed by contestable liberal conceptions of autonomy, freedom, and equality.[2] Persuasive though these critiques may be, at the end of the day Okin's argument cannot be easily dismissed. What continues to resonate in her essay, long after the various criticisms have been made, is something Okin herself nowhere explicitly states but nevertheless implies: we (feminists and citizens of Western democracies) need to make judgments about cultural and political practices not always our own and, where appropriate, declare them "bad for women" and refuse them our political support.

Needless to say, in the context of an American feminism that has, with some good reason, been accused of a deeply biased approach to non-Western cultures, it is difficult to imagine how political judgments could be formed that would not reproduce that bias. Okin's own practice of judgment in the essay at issue is a case in point. Okin states, "While virtually all of the world's cultures have distinctly patriarchal pasts, some—mostly, though by no means exclusively, Western liberal cultures—have departed far further from them than others" ("IMBW," 16). Although feminist Okin clearly recognizes that Western cultures still practice forms of sex discrimination, these forms pale in comparison to those practiced in non-Western cultures. Working with a familiar scale of historical progress, Okin positions Western liberal cultures way ahead of non-Western/nonliberal ones. The absolute dividing line on the scale of progress in her view lies in the fact that "women in more liberal cultures are . . . legally guaranteed many of the same freedoms and opportunities as men" ("IMBW," 16–17).

According to Azizah Y. Al-Hibri, Okin's claim about the more highly evolved status of Western liberal political cultures "is clearly written from the perspective of the dominant cultural 'I,' a Western point of view."[3] Although I would question the idea that such a unified point of view exists (any more than a single non-Western point of view exists), Okin does lack critical awareness about the cultural rootedness of her own judging practice. She simply takes for granted a whole set of judgments without so much as pausing and critically reflecting on the practice of judgment itself. Each sentence of her text is replete with judgments about what constitutes a better political system, cultural practice, form of feminism, and so on, but these judgments function as rules under which to subsume the particulars of other cultures. Notwithstanding their status as contingent artifacts of a particular historical experience and political culture (e.g., American liberal democracy), these judgments function in her text as universal standards against which to measure those other cultures and to find them lacking. The standard or rule itself (i.e., liberal cultures and practices) is barely subjected to judgment but rather is confirmed as universal—that is, as a rule that determines what will count, say, as a practice of feminism, freedom, or equality.

That Okin herself was a fierce critic of liberalism's indifference to the violation of women's rights in the private realm suggests that, when faced with the task of judging non-Western/nonliberal political cultures, she tends to lose track of her own critical feminist stance in relation to the West. This problem is not limited to the work of Okin any more than it is to the question of multiculturalism and group rights; it is a problem faced by any Western feminist who would concern herself with the situation of women in cultures not her own.

I said that Okin seems critically unaware of how her own cultural rootedness might influence or bias the nature of her judgments. If it is the case, however, that rootedness is not only a potentially limiting but also a fundamentally irreducible condition of judging, as I shall argue in this chapter, then we might well wonder, what is a feminist from the West to do? How might such a feminist mobilize the inescapability of her own embeddedness in a given cultural horizon to advance a perspective that is less myopic and self-congratulatory about Western values such as political rights without being any less critical toward the gendered cultural and political practices of non-Western, nonliberal cultures that Okin decries? For feminists, after all, critique is the name of the game. As Al-Hibri rightly notes, Okin may get a lot wrong about other cultures, but her "position has more integrity than one which views the 'natives' or 'alien immigrants' condescendingly and argues, under the guise of Western liberalism, that 'those people' should be allowed to live in accordance with their own lower standards of human rights."[4]

We would be mistaken to take Okin's ethnocentric mode of judgment as good reason for not taking the risk of judgment at all. "'Refusing to judge' issues affecting Third-World communities," writes Uma Narayan, "is often a facile and problematic attempt to compensate for a history of misjudgment. Such refusals can become simply one more 'Western' gesture that confirms the moral inequality of Third-World cultures by shielding them from the moral and political evaluations that 'Western' contexts and practices are subject to."[5] The idea that only "'Authentic Insiders'" (DC, 150)—that is, those who belong to the particular culture or engage in the particular practice that is to be judged—have the right to judge is deeply misguided, guided more by a sense of guilt over a history of Western misjudgment and misrepresentation of Third World contexts than by a genuine concern "to politically engage with the problems of individuals and groups who suffer injustice or mistreatment within these contexts" (DC, 150), Narayan contends. Furthermore, she continues, "the commitment 'not to judge'

Other cultures seems in effect to be a commitment 'not to *express* one's judgments'—which only serves to insulate these unexpressed judgments from challenges, corrections, or interrogations they might profit from" (*DC*, 150). According to Narayan, what Western feminists "need to cultivate is not a 'refusal to judge'" but an ability "to distinguish misrepresentation and 'cultural imperialism' from normatively justifiable criticisms" (*DC*, 151). The question becomes: what kind of judging practice would enable us to do just that?

Taking up these diverse calls for judgment, I want to reflect in this chapter on what it might mean to foreground the power of judgment as a central feature of critical feminist political practice. If it is at once necessary and risky to judge cultures and practices not one's own, then a Western feminist does well to ask: What am I doing, really, when I declare something "bad for women"? What gives me so much as the idea that my judgment could be, or ought to be, accepted as valid by others, especially by people who do not share my particular cultural heritage or social location?

The Ruse of Universalism

As Okin's invocation of a progress narrative suggests, the problem of judgment has been occluded in liberal political society by the idea of universalism. According to Ernesto Laclau, Western cultures typically have cast themselves as the embodiment of "a universal civilizing function" against which the resistances of other cultures are seen "as an all-embracing and epochal struggle between universality and particularisms."[6] In this struggle, non-Western cultures are cast as being without the capacity to represent the universal. Presenting itself as the model of development, the West has demanded assimilation to its own ideals, while denying at every stage their historically contingent character. What has been considered to be universal is little more than an inflated particular: Western liberal culture itself.

Universalism's entanglement with colonialism and imperialism gives it a deeply fraught legacy for contemporary feminist politics. And yet it is hard to imagine feminist politics without some appeal to universality, for politics involves forms of collective action, action in concert. As Laclau argues, pure particularism in politics is self-defeating; individuals and groups must issue judgments and claims in a language that resonates with others who do not necessarily share the same social location.[7] Classical political universalism dealt with this problem by subsuming all political identities under the one held to be the common standard for all (e.g., the proletariat, the European, man) and guaranteed by the progressive movement of history to include all subjects within a rights-based community. If this idea of a progressive universalism is no longer convincing, could we imagine another kind of universalism, a new universalism that was not a ruse through which to subsume differences?[8]

The possibility of articulating a new universalism across cultural differences is irreducibly linked to the problem of judgment. Classic universalism occluded judgment as a politically significant problem of mediating such differences. It simply took for granted shared transcontextual criteria—that is, criteria held to be valid for everyone, regardless of social or historical location, insofar as they are derived from a world of objective reality that exists independently of human beings.[9] In the face of modernity's growing awareness of value pluralism, the objectivist and rationalist idea that all individuals reasoning properly will be led to the same judgments is no longer credible, which is not to say that it is no longer tempting—the idea of perfectly attuned minds following the logic of reason dies hard, as we shall see. In any case, contemporary feminists are writing in a context of a decayed rationalism, in which the rules for judgment are no longer given or guaranteed by something outside the contingent human practice of judgment itself.

What are the consequences of this loss of classic universalism and its objectivist grounding of shared criteria of judgment? Should we think about it as precipitating a crisis of relativism, a crisis, that is, of our critical faculties when it comes to judging whatever falls outside our immediate experience and normative criteria? And if we do in fact find ourselves in the predicament of relativism, either unable or unwilling to make, let alone justify, judgments about cultures and practices not our own, would finding our way out require us to posit another universally shared standard of judgment?

In the view of Martha Nussbaum, the willingness to posit universal criteria or values is a necessary risk for any feminism that aspires to agitate on behalf of women in an increasingly globalized world. "An international feminism that is going to have any bite quickly gets involved in making normative recommendations that cross boundaries of culture, nation, religion, race, and class," she writes.[10] Problematic, as Nussbaum recognizes, is that any such normative recommendations will involve a set of judgments based on the "use [of] concepts that originate in one culture to describe and assess realities in another—and all the more problematic if the culture described has been colonized and oppressed by the describer's culture" (*WHD*, 36). Moreover, the "search for universal values" (*WHD*, 50), as Nussbaum describes her project, risks entanglement in the objectivism and rationalism of classic universalism. Aware of the deep skepticism toward universal normative approaches that characterizes feminism today, Nussbaum is adamant that her approach "yields a form of universalism that is sensitive to pluralism and cultural difference" (*WHD*, 8).

Notwithstanding her recognition of the problems associated with universalism, Nussbaum is far more worried about cultural relativism, "the idea, that is, that normative criteria must come from within the society to which they are applied" (*WHD*, 48). Relativism deeply limits feminists' capacity for critical judgment, restricting them to the "local ideas" or norms given in any particular culture, she holds, and asks, "Why should we follow the local ideas, rather than the best ideas we can find?" (*WHD*, 49). These "best ideas" become the basis for what Nussbaum, following John Rawls, calls an "overlapping consensus."[11] That the best ideas just happen to coincide with "general values, such as the dignity of the person, the integrity of the body, basic political rights and liberties" (*WHD*, 41), and so forth does not disturb Nussbaum, who appears satisfied that she has avoided conflating "universal" with "Western."

It is crucial to see how Nussbaum defends the aforementioned values as truly neutral and universal rather than Western and thus particular, since her strategy is, in my view, typical of new universalist feminist approaches to the problem of judgment in the wake of multicultural and postcolonial critiques. Cultural relativism, says Nussbaum, is based on a false, holistic view of cultures. Far from static and homogeneous, cultures are really dynamic and diverse. "As a normative thesis about how we should make moral judgments, relativism has several problems. First, it has no bite in the modern world, where the ideas of every culture turn up inside every other, through the internet and the media. The ideas of feminism, of democracy, of egalitarian welfarism, are now 'inside' every known society" (*WHD*, 49), she contends. In short, the best ideas travel; even if their origins lie in the West—a point Nussbaum also disputes—such ideas now belong to all world cultures.

In a similar move, Seyla Benhabib parses the question, "Is universalism ethnocentric?" as being premised on a false "holistic view of cultures and societies as internally coherent, seamless wholes."[12] This view is produced from "the standpoint of the social observer," not "the social agent": it is "a view from the outside that generates coherence for the purposes of understanding and control" (*CC*, 5). Failing to distinguish observers from agents, philosophers such as Richard Rorty appropriate the view of cultures as "clearly delineable wholes" (*CC*, 4) and advance a form of cultural relativism according to which "judgments of validity are 'framework relative,' whether these frameworks are defined as language games, epistemological world views, or ethnocentric traditions" (*CC*, 28).

As does Nussbaum, Benhabib rejects arguments for such relativism. Traffic across cultures is a fact of modern life, and the practice of making judgments involves a continuous negotiation of criteria whose origins are uncertain. Once we recognize the real "radical hybridity and polyvocality of all cultures" (*CC*, 25), the problem of reconciling sensitivity to the politics of culture and a strong universalist position disappears.[13] Thus Benhabib can at once make a plea for a complex cross-cultural dialogue that takes account of multicultural diversity while insisting that all political claims of culture should be adjudicated according to certain normative criteria: *"egalitarian reciprocity, voluntary self-ascription,* and *freedom of exit and association"* (*CC*, 19). That these criteria belong to the "universalist deliberative democracy model" (*CC*, 19) as it has been formulated by Jürgen Habermas does not disturb Benhabib any more than Nussbaum was disturbed by the coincidence between the "best ideas" and Western ideas.

There is, to be sure, something appealing for feminists in Nussbaum's and Benhabib's quest for universal values, a quest whose starting point is an important critique of cultures as incommensurable homogeneous wholes. Eschewing accounts that tend to pit the West against the rest, such a quest calls into question talk about the so-called clash of civilizations as a way of describing our current political predicament. Putting the otherwise static idea of culture into question by showing the flow or circulation of ideas between Western and non-Western cultures, Nussbaum and Benhabib open a space for thinking about a genuinely international practice of feminist critique.

However crucial it is for feminists to refute an essentialist view of cultures, it is also important to interrogate the new universalists' defense of cultural hybridity. Each thinker construes the problem of multiculturalism and cultural conflict as a phantom of sorts: as it turns out, cultures are hybrid and fluid, so genuine clashes, where they exist, can be adjudicated by the already shared "best ideas" (*WHD*, 49) or "norms of universal respect and egalitarian reciprocity" (*CC*, 37). By attributing (rather than exporting) these ideas or norms to non-Western cultures, both Benhabib and Nussbaum seek to evade, be it intentionally or not, the established criticisms of ethnocentrism brought by feminist, multicultural, and postcolonial theorists. The upshot of this attributive act—which presents itself in the otherwise appealing form of a feminist antiessentialist view of culture—is that Nussbaum and Benhabib, albeit in their own ways, smuggle in as universal their own judgments based on their own (Western) normative criteria. If the old universalism simply identified the universal with a form of progress that is Western, this new universalism denies its origins in the West—all the better to evade the criticisms that were made of its classic form.

The ability of Western feminists to affirm values on the basis of which to make cross-cultural judgments is important. But the new universalism of Benhabib and Nussbaum seriously underestimates the kind of political work required. Cultures surely are hybrid and open, rather than homogeneous and closed, but just as surely are they sources of politically significant local differences of identity and value that present genuine problems, but also opportunities, for feminists looking to develop the practice of making cross-cultural judgments. Although such differences may not be intractable in the sense that arguments for strong multiculturalism or cultural relativism would have it, they nonetheless need to be politically mediated in ways that tend to remain hidden when we think about Western and non-Western cultures as always already sharing the best ideas.

Notwithstanding the conscious effort to avoid it, ethnocentrism reappears in these new universalists' antiessentialist view of culture in the form of local contexts that have been rendered politically superfluous from the standpoint of any articulation of shared normative criteria. As Nussbaum explicitly argues, local ideas are tied to "local traditions," and such traditions "take themselves to be absolutely, not relatively, true" (*WHD*, 49). Thus, there could be no place within local traditions from which to begin the political process of articulating a new universalism, because aside from those "best ideas" (i.e., the truly universal universals in non-Western cultures), traditions are closed.[14] Consequently, it becomes hard to see local ideas and values both as potential sources of progressive change and as presenting a potential challenge to any given understanding of the best ideas. That which is not already universal (the best ideas) but marked, rather, as culturally particular (local ideas) appears unworthy of our critical attention—that is, as a potential interrogation of what we hold to be the best or properly universal ideas.

Just because a particular claim (local idea) does not achieve articulation as universal (best idea) and in this way come to stand for the aspirations of political women across national borders does not make it either meaningless (with no relation to universality) or dangerous (an instance of particularism and relativism) in the way that Nussbaum assumes. There are numbers of claims that have never attained such status (e.g., the ongoing political claims of women or of sexual minorities today), yet their particularity may well harbor another way of thinking about what counts as universal. Holding that the best ideas (the universal) are always already shared across cultural borders, in other words, excludes local ideas (the particular) as critically relevant and makes it seem, to speak with Judith Butler, as if there can be no "competing versions of universality."[15]

What would it mean to take the contexts of local particularity as a starting point for a critical political encounter in which the universal criteria for cross-cultural judgments could be articulated rather than assumed? The problem, after all, is not the ongoing search for universal values (Nussbaum) or "normative principles to guide our judgments and deliberations in complex human situations" (CC, 37) but the presumption that this search will discover something that is always already there (shared by Western and non-Western cultures alike). Instead of thinking about our political practice in terms of either cultural exportation (as the old universalism understood it) or cultural attribution (as the new universalism suggests), we might think about it with Butler in terms of cultural translation.

Such translation is a political practice of making cross-cultural judgments and claims in an idiom that others can come to recognize as shared. Translation is necessary, explains Butler, because in each cultural context "there is an establishing rhetoric for the assertion of universality and a set of norms that are invoked in the recognition of such claims. . . . Thus, for the claim to work, for it . . . to enact the very universality it enunciates, it must undergo a set of translations into the various rhetorical and cultural contexts in which the meaning and force of universal claims are made."[16] These contexts are irreducibly local. Local ideas may be the source of arguments for cultural relativism, but they are also the main vehicle through which cross-cultural agreements about values are reached. To understand the search for universal values as an act of cultural translation rather than exportation (the old universalism) or attribution (the new universalism) is to refuse to assume from the start an agreement that needs to be worked out politically. And it is to treat the local or particular as a potential source of new iterations of universality, where the very idea of the universal will not be decided once and for all but will always remain open to further political interrogation.

Had Nussbaum and Benhabib acknowledged that the values they endorse are Western rather than the expression of some shared core across cultures, they might have recognized the need for cultural translation. We begin to suspect that their respective antiessentialist views of culture and cases for a new universalism are ultimately in the service of the old universalism or, more precisely, a revived rationalism. The necessity of this revived rationalism follows from the terms in which each thinker casts the entire political problem of judgment—namely, as an epistemological problem of relativism, a problem that is defined, and can only be solved, by philosophy and the search for first principles—as the bottom line beyond which no political claim to culture dare go. If relativism is "a position holding . . . the view that one belief or value is as good as another . . . entailing descent down a slippery slope toward moral and intellectual quiescence," as John Gunnell puts it,[17] then no feminist would ever be a self-declared relativist. (But then again, are there any self-declared relativists, feminist or not?) And because no feminist would declare herself a relativist according to that definition, it is easy to be seduced by the thought of a saving universalism that comes wrapped in the aura of respect for cultural hybridity and difference. This new universalism, then, is akin to the proverbial wolf in sheep's clothing.

What the charge of relativism expresses, as Gunnell explains, is the "worry . . . that there are no transcontexual grounds for truth claims [as the old universalism would have it], that is, that the criteria of valid judgment in any practice or activity are necessarily indigenous in both a de facto and a de jure sense."[18] The worry here is directly connected to the recognition of value pluralism—and yet, concede Nussbaum and Benhabib, feminists writing in the wake of multiculturalism must take account of plurality. The problem is how to square the need to take account of plurality with the pressing need to judge. Once we become not only aware of but also affirm human plurality, it becomes difficult to decide which values or practices are best. Thus the acknowledgment of plurality leads directly into the crisis of relativism—or so it would seem. And the crisis of relativism can be overcome, as it turns out, only through the suppression of plurality—that is, through a revived rationalism. But are these our only choices?

If, as Gunnell observes, "the defense of 'rationality' against 'relativism' is often . . . a defense of contemporary Western science, common sense, and culture against alien images,"[19] then feminists do well to question the terms in which the problem of judgment is posed. Why should acknowledgement of value pluralism lead to a crisis of relativism? Nussbaum and Benhabib—and they are hardly alone here—would have us believe that the presence of multicultural differences and the absence of transcontextual criteria for adjudicating claims represent a real danger to practical judgment and lead to political quietism. Their antiessentialist view of culture, I have argued, would neutralize these differences with the idea of cultural hybridity, but that turns out to be in the service of a revived rationalism. Rather than sign on to the crisis of relativism that is the other face of this revived rationalism, we do better to ask what kind of work the problem of relativism might be doing in their newfangled universalism and, more generally, how it might constrain our understanding of judgment and its place in a critical feminism. More precisely, what other sort of problem might the problem of relativism conceal?

The Ruse of Relativism

The extent to which the threat of relativism has insinuated itself into feminist theory and defined the terms in which the entire problem of judgment is framed can hardly be overstated. Already with the rise of standpoint theory in the 1970s, feminist theorists were preoccupied with warding off the danger of relativism that was seen to arise once the objectivist account of knowledge was put into question. What kept standpoint theory tethered to the problem of relativism was precisely its parsing of the problem that I am examining here; namely, on what basis can (Western) feminists claim that their cross-cultural judgments are not merely the expression of subjective or ethnocentric preferences?

The problem with standpoint theory's parsing is that it took the question of judgment to express a problem that could be both defined and solved in epistemological terms. Nancy Hartsock, for example, initially attempted to escape the charge of relativism that was quickly associated with standpoint theory's subject-centered, perspectival view of knowledge production by holding onto the idea of objectivity and claiming epistemic privilege for oppressed groups such as women.[20] This solution, which failed to account for differences among women, as inside critics such as Sandra Harding would later argue, remained trapped within the very epistemological framing of the problem that standpoint theory's otherwise deep political concern with issues of power sought to question.[21] The idea of epistemic privilege conceded to the rationalism under dispute the crucial point about the claim to knowledge and truth: it must be guaranteed by something outside the practice of judgment itself (in this case, the social location of women in relation to power).

In its more self-critical iterations, standpoint theory rightly recognized the imbrication of relativism and rationalism and that the relativist charge, if accepted as a genuine political danger, would drive feminists back into the arms of the objectivism they sought to question. As Donna Haraway puts it, "Relativism is the perfect mirror twin of totalization in the ideologies of objectivity; both deny the stakes in location, embodiment, and partial perspective; both make it impossible to see well."[22] What both objectivism and relativism share, then, is a denial of responsibility for knowledge claims. Thus, Haraway writes, the alternative to both objectivism and relativism "is partial, locatable, critical knowledges sustaining the possibility of webs of connections called solidarity in politics and shared conversations in epistemology."[23]

As an alternative epistemology that makes visible the irreducible relations of power in claims to knowledge, there is much to recommend in Haraway's notion of "limited location and situated knowledge," as there is in other iterations of standpoint theory.[24] The question, however, is whether the problem of judgment that concerns us here—namely, cross-cultural judgment as a practical problem of feminist politics—can be properly addressed if we hold to the idea that such judgment is fundamentally a problem of having a (more) critical epistemology. An affirmative answer to this question would assume that political problems are fundamentally philosophical/epistemological ones and, further, that the basis of feminism as a critical enterprise is epistemology.

As much as I appreciate the contributions of standpoint theory, I resist framing the political problem of judgment in epistemological terms, though I too am concerned with the problem of rearticulating a conception of political objectivity, as Hannah Arendt has throughout these pages enabled us to do. Not only do such terms continually land feminists, notwithstanding their cogent rebuttals, back in if not the crisis, then the problem of relativism and thus rationalism, but they are also terms that keep us from seeing judgment as a practical problem of a first-order discourse—namely, politics, which has no philosophical/epistemological second-order solution.[25] This is not because no claims to knowledge and truth are at stake in politics—as argued in previous chapters, surely they are—but rather because whether a claim is critical or dogmatic, accepted as valid or not, is a practical "matter of . . . actions and historical context and not abstract issues of epistemic privilege."[26] It simply cannot be settled at the level of philosophy/epistemology, as if once we have the rules or criteria for deciding the question of validity we will be able to adjudicate the significant kinds of practical challenges that are associated with making judgments in the global context of widespread value pluralism. This is the mistake made by Benhabib and Nussbaum, who took for granted that feminist judgments in the register of politics need philosophy/epistemology to underwrite them. In this way, Benhabib and Nussbaum not only felt that they had to defeat cultural relativism as a kind of epistemological claim but also missed what is really at stake in making cross-cultural judgments—namely, an ability to form an opinion about the particular qua particular precisely in the absence of known rules.

If we understand our predicament in terms of relativism, we shall continually be tempted, notwithstanding awareness of the dangers of rationalism, to seek transcontextual criteria and grounds for political judgment lest we be critically impaired, utterly unable to judge. The threat that relativism supposedly poses to our ability to make judgments in the first-order discourses that concern us, then, is something we do well to question. It is a "picture that holds us captive," to paraphrase Wittgenstein, because our epistemologically and philosophically inflected language of politics repeats it to us inexorably (*PI*, §115). But what would it mean to think about the problem of judgment in terms other than the threat of relativism?

Beyond Relativism

Let us try to bypass the crisis of relativism, and the entire epistemological problematic in which it arises, by returning to the thought of Arendt. As we saw in chapter 1, for Arendt, judgment emerges as a problem in the wake of the collapse of inherited criteria for judgment, or what she calls the final "break in tradition" that marked the definitive political event of the twentieth century: totalitarianism.[27] In her view, however, the collapse of the shared criteria of judgment represents a practical, first-order problem that has no philosophical, second-order solution. It is not a problem of relativism in the sense of a loss of criteria of judgment that can be solved through the reestablishment of such criteria. On the contrary, it is the idea that criteria must be given as universal rules governing from above the application of concepts to the particulars of political life that has led partly to the breakdown of the capacity to judge critically in the first place. And it is only with the breakdown of such criteria, she argues, that the power of critical judgment can come into its own. Thus, where others see relativism and a crisis of judgment, Arendt sees the chance to practice judgment critically anew.

Arendt's effort to foreground judgment as a critical capacity of democratic citizenship precisely once the rules for judgment have collapsed (*LKPP*), we have seen, leads to her radical rereading of Immanuel Kant's third *Critique* (*CJ*). She questions the idea that judgment is the faculty of subsuming particulars under known rules (which is how Kant defined the determinative judgment that he associated with cognitive judgments). Judging is less an act of subsuming, argues Arendt, and more an act of discerning and differentiating (which is how Kant defined the reflective judgment that he associated with aesthetic judgments).[28] Arendt's point is not to contest the idea that we often do subsume particulars under rules (e.g., "this is a war"), but rather to foreground the features of judgment that characterize it as critical evaluative judgment (e.g., "this war is unjust"). The act of mere subsumption that is at stake in a determinative judgment, though far from easy, is not fully reflective and critical, for it mobilizes particulars to confirm the generality of concepts. Lost is the particularity of the particular itself, the "this" that refers to *this* war and to no other.

In the realm of politics, as Arendt showed us in chapters 1 and 4, we have always to do with opinion and thus with evaluative judgments that cannot be adjudicated by an appeal to the objective truth criteria and the ability to give proofs that are at stake in the validity of cognitive (determinative) judgments. Following Kant's account of judgments of taste, Arendt holds that if political judgments are not objective in the aforementioned sense, neither are they merely subjective, matters of individual or cultural preference (*LKPP*). As we saw with Kant in chapter 2, the judgment "this painting is beautiful" differs from the claim "I like sparkling wine"; it would be ridiculous to say, this painting "is beautiful *for* me"; the judgment of beauty posits or, more precisely, anticipates the agreement of others (*CJ*, §7). Likewise, if I say, "sex and gender-based inequality is unjust," I do not mean it is unjust for me but that others too ought to find it unjust. Whether others find it so is another matter, one that cannot be settled by claims to epistemic authority or privilege (knowing which criteria to apply and how to apply them) but that must be worked out in the difficult first-order practice of politics itself—that is, by means of persuasion and the exchange of opinions. Judging politically solicits the agreement of all, but it cannot compel it, as the philosophers and epistemologists would have us believe, in the manner of giving proofs.

To argue, as the rationalist tradition has, that practical judgment will be fully paralyzed in the absence of transcontextual criteria of application is to accept the top-down conception of judgment as a practice of subsumption that Arendt would have us question. The real threat of nihilism is not the loss of standards as such but the refusal to accept the consequences of that loss. The idea that by holding fast to universal criteria we shall avoid a crisis of critical judging neglects the real possibility that such rules can function as a mental crutch that inhibits our capacity to judge critically. What matters from the perspective of our critical capacities is not the content of the rules as such but the dependence on rules ("TMC," 436). Rules are like a banister to which we hold fast for fear of losing our footing and not being able to judge at all. The problem with this top-down understanding of judgment is that it leaves whatever rules we employ more or less unexamined; their normativity becomes the taken-for-granted basis for every claim to validity. We then risk not only ethnocentricism but also loss of the critical purchase that the act of judging might give us on our own rules and standards.

Put another way, the temptation here is to employ our own concepts as rules or standards by which to judge other practices and cultures. But then the question arises as to whether we have engaged in the act of critical judging—or have we, rather, applied the rules of "our" culture to the particulars of "theirs," all the better to confirm what we already know and claim to be? With this question arises another temptation; namely, if we reject such a rule-governed practice of judgment as, say, uncritical and ethnocentric, then perhaps we really cannot avoid the dilemma of subjectivism, at least at the cultural level, and have little choice but to adopt the position of the relativist. Since radically divergent views can be equally valid depending on one's standpoint and membership in any particular culture, so this relativist holds, it is best not to judge at all. Who are we—outsiders—to judge?

"Outsideness" as a Condition of Judging

The question of whether firsthand experience is the condition of judging politically is crucial, for it is here that the now pervasive scare of relativism in our political thinking gets its force. It is also, significantly enough, the central assumption behind feminist standpoint arguments for the epistemic privilege of women. And though there is something crucial about taking the standpoint of the judging subject into account (especially to contest the "view from nowhere"), such a standpoint is by no means the whole of judgment, nor the ground for its validity. Even if we grant not only that standpoint matters but that subjugated standpoints are more likely to be savvy about how things really stand in the world, it is still the case, as Haraway recognizes, that "*how* to see from below is a problem."[29] More specifically, it is a problem of learning "how to see faithfully from another's point of view"[30]—but not too faithfully, or so I will argue.

If we hold that criteria of judgment are indigenous rather than transcontextual—as we must, lest we give hostage to the rationalist fantasy of a shared core—then being a "native" (or being able to "go native") would seem to follow as the very condition of judgment. Such a view gives rise to the problems Narayan associates with the idea of the authentic insider—namely, a relinquishment of any responsibility for making judgments about cultures not one's own or, more often, an unwillingness to subject "unexpressed judgments" (*DC*, 150) to the critical scrutiny of others. Or it may give rise to a certain self-satisfied ethnocentrism—that is, a stance according to which one simply assumes that it is not possible to see things from cultural perspectives other than one's own.

Although ethnocentrism is always a risk when we seek to judge other cultures or practices, it is not the inevitable consequence of being rooted in a particular culture. "To believe that this rootedness is *only* negative and that one should and actually could get rid of it through some infinite purification of reason," writes Cornelius Castoriadis, "is the illusion of a naive rationalism. It is not simply that this rootedness is the condition of our knowledge . . . it is also a *positive* condition, for it is our own particularity which allows us access to the universal. It is because we are attached to a given view, categorial structure, and project that we are able to say something meaningful about the past" and about other cultures and practices.[31] But if rationalism is an illusion, it is equally illusory to think that every attempt to understand and judge other cultures must be from a "native" perspective. Should an ethnologist wish to study the Bororo, to take Castoriadis's example, he or she should try to see their world through their eyes, but then he or she will need to judge it from his or her own standpoint, enlarged by what he or she has seen, or not judge it at all. "The ethnologist who has so thoroughly assimilated the Bororo's view of the world that he or she can no longer see the world any other way, is no longer an ethnologist but a Bororo. . . . The ethnologist's *raison d'être* is not to be assimilated to the Bororo's but to explain to the Parisians, the Londoners, and the New Yorkers in 1965 the other humanity represented by the Bororos." And this he can do only through the "categorial system of the Parisians, the Londoners and so forth."[32]

We might better grasp Castoriadis's point here in terms of the old joke, elaborated by Mikhail Bakhtin, that "the ancient Greeks did not know . . . that they were *ancient* Greeks."[33] It is we who have made them "ancient" Greeks, projecting our own modernity backward into antiquity. For Bakhtin, as for Castoriadis, however, it is precisely such projection that creates meaning and discovers something to which the Greeks, as Greeks, were blind. Bakhtin continues:

There exists a very strong, but one-sided and thus untrustworthy, idea that in order better to understand a foreign culture, one must enter into it, forgetting one's own, and view the world through the eyes of this foreign culture. . . . Of course, a certain entry as a living being into a foreign culture, the possibility of seeing the world through its eyes, is a necessary part of the process of understanding it; but if this were the only aspect of this understanding, it would merely be duplication and would not entail anything new or enriching. *Creative understanding* does not renounce itself, its own place in time, its own culture; and it forgets nothing. In order to understand, it is immensely important for the person who understands to be *located outside* the object of his or her creative understanding—in time, in space, in culture. . . . In the realm of culture, outsideness is a most powerful factor in understanding.[34]

Understanding and judging require striking a balance between the tendency to project our own values onto a foreign culture, on the one side, and the fantasy that one could "go native," on the other side. What interests us in other cultures are "other human possibilities in their absolute singularity"—that is, the opening of the world to us through human plurality.[35] This singularity, the particular, is visible to us on the condition that we not subsume it under either a transcendent rule or a rule given by our own culture. And yet we must judge it from the place where we stand, from our own social, historical, and cultural location.

Following Castoriadis and Bakhtin, we might think about outsideness as the enabling condition of political understanding and judgment of other cultures and practices. Outsideness, I hasten to emphasize, is not the Archimedean standpoint coveted by rationalism. Rather, it is a way of expressing the specificity of one's own rootedness elsewhere as the condition of understanding and judging what is not here, perhaps foreign. I would therefore question the idea, put forward by Benhabib, that the standpoint of the social observer (the outsider) inevitably generates a distorted, because overly homogeneous, view of a particular culture or cultural practice. Although the imposition of a false "coherence on cultures as observed entities" (*CC*, 5) is always a risk of the outsider perspective (e.g., it is we who see the Greeks as ancient Greeks), such a perspective can also yield a form of understanding that is not available to an insider, for the element of strangeness is missing. Such strangeness can be generated from inside one's culture in the form of a defamiliarization, but that requires an engagement with other cultures that does not reduce to a confirmation of one's own criteria of judgment.

Just this defamiliarization is at stake in Arendt's account of judging. Like Bakhtin and Castoriadis, Arendt resists the idea that only an authentic insider can judge. In her Kant lectures, Arendt argues that it is the spectator, not the actor, who occupies the position from which it is possible to critically judge the objects of the common world (*LKPP*). To form an opinion is to see the world from more than the insider perspective given in a historically and culturally situated human subjectivity. The position of the spectator is associated with a form of rooted but impartial seeing; it is not the view from nowhere but the view from somewhere enlarged by taking account of other views. The ability to form an opinion is political, and its name, as we have seen, is "representative thinking."

I form an opinion by considering a given issue from different view points, by making present to my mind the standpoints of those who are absent; that is, I represent them. This process of representation does not blindly adopt the actual views of those who stand some where else, and hence look upon the world from a different perspective; this is a question neither of empathy, as though I tried to be or to feel like somebody else, nor of counting noses and joining a majority but of being and thinking in my own identity where actually I am not. The more people's standpoints I have present in my mind while I am pondering a given issue, and the better I can imagine how I would feel and think if I were in their place, the stronger will be my capacity for representative thinking and the more valid my final conclusions, my opinion. ("TP," 241)

Arendt distinguishes what she (citing Kant) calls "enlarged thought" from any form of identification: "To accept what goes on in the minds of those whose 'standpoint' (actually, the place where they stand, the conditions they are subject to, which always differ from one class or group as compared to another) is not my own would mean no more than passively to accept their thought, that is, to exchange their prejudices for the prejudices proper to my own station" (*LKPP*, 43). Besides, such empathy creates a sense of familiarity (albeit false), whereas what is at stake in judging is a kind of distance that is completely unlike the external standpoint. But what is the difference between saying that representative thinking does not entail "try[ing] to be or to feel like somebody else," on the one hand, and saying that representing to myself various people's standpoints involves the effort to "imagine how I would feel and think if I were in their place," on the other hand?

Feminists might interpret Arendt's account of representative thinking as a call for the mutual recognition of diverse identities and their worldly standpoints. But where, then, would be the actual moment of judgment? As Narayan observes, "The goal of a feminist politics is seldom merely to come to a refined and sensitive understanding of various points of view held by those immediately affected by an issue. In the broadest sense, feminist political projects involve commitments to normative and political inquiry, which calls for questioning, assessing, analyzing, and criticizing various points of view" (*DC*, 151). Thinking from the place of the other is best understood, then, not as a practice of identification but as an attempt to see from multiple standpoints in order to form a critical opinion and to make a judgment. It takes for granted that the plural perspectives from which one endeavors to see the world might actually provide a glimpse of the world as it is: perspectives are not irremediably distorting.

Rooted in an uneasy confrontation with the opinions of others, the ability to judge critically must be differentiated from the capacity for identification, recognition, or empathy. Although "other-regard" may play a role in a practice of judgment, we should not confuse an ethical stance (other-regard) with a political practice (representative thinking). As argued in chapter 1, it is important to put oneself in the place of the other, not because ethics calls for it (though it well may) but because seeing the world from other perspectives is the political condition of impartiality and objectivity. We should try to see from other perspectives because those perspectives open the world up to us; they give us more worldly reality. Judging involves neither becoming identical with you, nor for that matter with myself, but "thinking in my own identity where actually I am not." One is in this way, then, always situated in relation to the objects of judgment but also outside them in some important sense, and this outsideness puts one in a potentially critical relation to oneself and one's own criteria of judgment.

Rather than search for a universal (shared) core, occupy the place of the other, or sanctify the idea that no outsider is in a position to understand or judge the other, outsideness suggests that we understand and judge from a position that is neither identical nor incommensurable but rather mediated, at once separate from and related to that which we judge. Outsideness works both ways: just as we raise questions for a foreign culture (or people) that it does not raise for itself, so that foreign culture (or people) raises questions for us—if we allow it to do so. Outsideness as a condition of judging, then, entails a willingness to allow the encounter with others to raise questions about our own norms and practices.

I began this chapter with Okin, who rightly calls for making judgments but does not properly consider how Western feminists might do so while remaining critical in relation to their own cultural norms. Although Benhabib and Nussbaum are sensitive to this challenge, we have seen that their new universalism attributes to non-Western cultures the very Western values that are in question. Preoccupied with the threat of relativism, these new universalists do not escape the problems with the old universalism that they otherwise criticize.

I have argued that relativism is a false problem that leads us to misunderstand what we do when we judge politically. If accepted, the charge of relativism almost inevitably lands feminists, as it did Nussbaum and Benhabib, back in the very rationalism they would dispute. Understood in a loose sense, the threat of relativism may resonate with feminists as a real problem insofar as when we are engaged in politics, we may well—and indeed often do well to—experience a sense of uncertainty about the legitimacy of our criteria and thus our judgments. Furthermore, criteria of judgment may well give way under the weight of history, as Arendt argues about life after totalitarianism. That said, practical problems of judgment look nothing like the picture given to us in philosophical discussions of relativism, such as those that guide Benhabib and Nussbaum. In these discussions, which typically feature a complete paralysis of our critical faculties, what is at stake is not really practical judgment in first-order discourses such as politics; at stake, rather, is "the ability of philosophy to posit a metatheoretical basis of judgment with respect to such practices."[36] Whenever such an ability—or, more precisely, the "right"—of philosophy to adjudicate matters of practical concern is put into question, as it was in many multicultural, postcolonial, and feminist texts, there inevitably follows the charge of relativism.

The real problem of judgment in the context of widespread (value) pluralism is not relativism, the inability to judge cultures and practices not our own, but the failure to take genuine account of the strangeness of what we are judging. As Arendt once remarked, armed with rules and their correct application, we tend to take refuge in our own criteria, "denying that we saw anything new at all, . . . pretending that something similar is already known to us."[37] Finding solace in our own norms cannot possibly count as critical judging—and yet the threat of relativism leaves us with little other choice.

To say farewell to relativism as the threat that names the whole political problem of judgment in the context of modernity's value pluralism, as I suggest we do, is to refuse to frame political problems in epistemological/philosophical terms without conceding the impossibility of speaking about a shared reality. In the interest of reviving the problem of judgment as it arises for us in everyday contexts, I have suggested that we rethink political judgments as fundamentally anticipatory rather than antecedent (justificatory) in structure. When I judge political things, I say more than how it appears to me (as subjectivism would have it), for (as Arendt and Kant argue) I have taken the standpoints of others into account. My judgment anticipates your agreement, but it cannot compel it with proofs (as objectivism would hold). There simply is no extrapolitical guarantee (e.g., epistemic privilege) that my judgment is valid or that it will be accepted by others or that it ought to be.

To think in this political idiom about the problem of judgment is to take leave of the new universalists and their insistence on first principles as the condition of cross-cultural judgments but without relinquishing the idea of universality as a political achievement. Understood in a political rather than philosophical idiom, universality is an achievement that is deeply dependent on practical context and thus fragile. Rather than see this fragility as a failure of sorts, we might see it as an opportunity, for it means that apparently settled and stark differences of value, especially when it comes to the varying situations of women in a global context, can be disturbed and reconfigured in productive new ways, giving form to new shared objects of judgment and meaning.

In the next chapter we shall explore further how shared objects of judgment can arise for us through the practice of judging itself, especially as the latter seeks meaning in political events.

SEVEN

From Willing to Judging: Arendt, Habermas, and the Question of '68

In light of the events that go under the sign of 9/11 and its aftermath, it would seem that *On Violence* would be among the most relevant of Arendt's writings for us today.[1] Yet receptions of Arendt's text suggest just the opposite: because she defined violence as nonpolitical, so the dominant reception of her work goes, Arendt has little to contribute to any debate on violence and politics. Not unlike her view of the social question, Arendt's reflections on violence speak to her narrow idea of what can count as political.[2] Reduced to the praxis of those who talk to each other about issues of no material concern, Arendt's exceedingly Greek conception of politics, argues Jürgen Habermas, categorically excludes not only all socioeconomic matters but all forms of strategic action (which she defines as force), including fully normalized and institutionalized expressions of "the strategic competition for political power and . . . the employment of power within the political system" ("ACCP," 224).[3] In the spirit of redeeming what might still be valuable in Arendt's work, declares Habermas, we must first acknowledge the ways in which she is hostage to a concept of politics that is inapplicable to modern conditions.

Before signing on to such a verdict (and the redemptive project it underwrites), we do well to revisit *On Violence* and see whether Arendt's supposedly outdated conception of politics might not be connected in some way with the things that she gets right about 1968—and brilliantly right, in my view. Simply stated, the particular problem that provoked Arendt's text was how to explain the "undeniable glorification of violence by the student movement" and other social movements around 1968 (*OV*, 19). "It would be futile to say that only the 'extremists' are yielding to a glorification of violence," writes Arendt (*OV*, 14). Denouncing "the new militants . . . as anarchists, nihilists, red fascists, Nazis, and . . . 'Luddite machine smashers,'" or blaming their behavior, as most commentators of Arendt's generation did, "on all kinds of social and psychological factors," such as "too much permissiveness in their upbringing in America" or "too much authority in Germany and Japan" is equally futile (*OV*, 15). Refuting all these familiar explanations, what Arendt got brilliantly right was that "the present glorification of violence is caused by severe frustration of the faculty of action in the modern world. It is simply true that riots in the ghettos and rebellions on the campuses make 'people feel they are acting together in a way that they rarely can' [as Herbert J. Gans put it]" (*OV*, 83).

For Arendt, the student movement in particular was best understood in terms of its own slogan, "the claim for 'participatory democracy'" (*OV*, 22), a claim that, in her view, embodied the originary demand for political freedom that lay at the heart of the American Revolution.[4] That demand came face-to-face with the failure of the American founders and those who came after to preserve the "revolutionary spirit"—to preserve, that is, spaces and contexts in which events become occasions for response and action makes sense. The eruption of this demand in the sixties could not have been predicted, says Arendt, and, in fact, constituted a set of "events" in the specific sense she gives to that term—namely, "occurrences that interrupt routine processes and routine procedures" (*OV*, 7).[5] "We do not know if these occurrences are the beginnings of something new—the 'new example'—or the death pangs of a faculty [action] that mankind is about to lose" (*OV*, 83–84), she remarks.

Put otherwise, there simply is no guarantee that what the actors of 1968 experienced as a new beginning is in fact the beginning of something new. Time alone will not tell, for it is never history that decides, in Arendt's view. Fundamentally, it is a problem of judgment. Not unlike Immanuel Kant, whose own spectatorial state of fascinated horror at the French Revolution was a central topic in her Kant lectures at the New School for Social Research, so too did Hannah Arendt watch the events of 1968 with deeply mixed feelings about their meaning for the future of democracy in the United States and abroad.[6] What worried her was that not only the actors but the spectators of 1968—including those, like ourselves, who ponder and judge these events from a certain historical distance—would conclude that violence, whatever its costs, is the only way to bring about genuine social and political change.[7] Deeply concerned to contest this ascription of new beginnings to the use of force, Arendt challenged the entire tradition of thinking about violence, not by excluding violence from the register of politics—in order to preserve the latter's putative Greek purity—but to think about violence politically. And though that may not seem like a particularly original project, it is.

The project of thinking about violence politically is original because "to raise the question of violence in the political realm" (*OV*, 35), as Arendt describes her project in *On Violence*, is to take leave of received understandings of violence, including those that dismiss violence as "irrational," as far too episodic and arbitrary to be studied seriously, or that describe violence in what Arendt calls "non-political, biological terms" (*OV*, 75).[8] Arendt's effort to think about violence politically radically questions the "consensus among political theorists from Left to Right to the effect that violence is nothing more than the most flagrant manifestation of power" (*OV*, 35) and that "power . . . is an instrument of rule, while rule, we are told, owes its existence to the 'instinct of domination.'" Thus, "we read in [Bertrand de] Jouvenel that 'a man feels himself more of a man when he is imposing himself and making others the instruments of his will,' which gives him 'incomparable pleasure'" (*OV*, 36).

Against this naturalization of power as one man's (natural desire to) rule over others, Arendt writes:

Power corresponds to the human ability not just to act but to act in concert. Power is never the property of an individual; it belongs to a group and remains in existence only so long as the group keeps together. When we say of somebody that he is "in power" we actually refer to his being empowered by a certain number of people to act in their name. (*OV*, 44)

Commenting on this passage from *On Violence*, Habermas remarks, "The fundamental phenomenon of power is not the instrumentalization of *another's* will, but the formation of a *common* will in a communication directed to reaching agreement" ("ACCP," 212). Arendt's "communications concept of power [*Kommunikationsbegriff der Macht*]" ("ACCP," 214)—his phrase, not hers—is to be applauded for breaking with instrumentalist and functionalist accounts of power (e.g., Max

Weber's and Talcott Parson's). It is to be applauded for recalling the origins of legitimate political institutions in, as Arendt describes it, "an opinion upon which many publicly are in agreement" (quoted in "ACCP," 213). But it is to be strongly criticized for offering no means by which to decide whether the formation of any particular will is rational or not, or whether those who are empowered to act and speak in the name of the people do in fact express an opinion on which many were publicly in agreement. Arendt's view lacks the normative criteria by which to determine the validity of competing claims and, therefore, to transform mere collective will-formation into *rational* will-formation.[9] Absent any "critical standard" for distinguishing between "illusionary and nonillusionary convictions" ("ACCP," 225), writes Habermas, we would be left with nothing but an arbitrary and incontestable act of will as the ground of political validity. Although Arendt would oppose such decisionism,[10] Habermas concedes, she is unable to grasp the "structural violence" by which communication is blocked, ideologies are formed, and "subjects deceive themselves about themselves and their situation" ("ACCP," 224, 224–25).[11] Just this is what happened to the student movement, in Habermas's view.[12]

According to Habermas, then, Arendt fails to see that "basic institutions and structures which are stabilized through political rule could only in rare cases be the expression of an 'opinion on which many were publicly in agreement'" ("ACCP," 224). "Politics cannot, as with Arendt, be identified with the praxis of those who talk together in order to act in common" ("ACCP," 224); it is also "a strategic competition" ("ACCP," 224) for various forms of power within the political system. If we want to bring together both of these insights, we need an account of political rule that grasps how power can come to manifest itself not only as force or violence but as false ideological convictions. We would require a normative procedure for distinguishing between legitimate and illegitimate claims based on the aforementioned standard according to which such claims might be adjudicated. Arendt cannot provide such a procedure or standard, argues Habermas, because she clings to a radical distinction between opinion and truth that prevents her "from comprehending the process of reaching agreement about practical [political] questions as rational discourse" ("ACCP," 225).

In chapter 4 I argued that it is too simplistic to read Arendt as treating all claims to truth as fundamentally apolitical and, indeed, that factual truth is by definition political in her view, for it is always constituted in relation to the world of human affairs. The issue for her is not truth claims as such but the manner in which they are presented and debated. Habermas believes he has solved the problem of the dogmatic assertion of truth by (1) distinguishing sharply between theoretical and practical reason, (2) refusing to restrict practical reason to its pragmatic (strategic or instrumental) use, and (3) restricting the democratic use of practical reason to moral rather than ethical validity claims. In other words, the particularistic claims of an ethical community rooted in a taken-for-granted background understanding that operates below the level of reason is radically distinguished from the universal moral claims that form the basis of "democratic procedures [that] are meant to institutionalize the forms of communication necessary for rational will-formation."[13] So understood, the normative use of practical reason is capable of distinguishing between "ideologies, [which] are, after all, illusions that are outfitted with the power of common convictions," on the one hand, and "common convictions" that have "a cognitive foundation," on the other hand ("ACCP," 225).

In this way, then, Habermas sees himself as redeeming Arendt's insight into the communicative nature of power in an effort to clarify and elaborate what such procedures must look like if practical reason is to be reformulated and rational will-formation achieved. As I elaborate in this chapter, we might wonder whether the supposedly more realistic version of "communicative power" that Habermas proposes with his critical moral standard is not in fact a far more radical departure from Arendt's idea of power as action in concert than he claims.

Pace Habermas, Arendt's conception of the so-called communicative power that underwrites democratic politics is not an attempt to reformulate Kantian practical reason to give it a dialogic or communicative dimension consistent with the linguistic turn. That she did not see her project in terms of the reformulation of Kantian practical reason (and hence the moral law) reflects neither her acceptance of an "antiquated concept of theoretical knowledge" ("ACCP," 225) nor her acceptance of the Kantian transcendental model of practical reason that houses human freedom in the noumenal realm. Arendt's concern is not with reason understood as either theoretical or practical. It is with the critical and reflective faculty of judgment as she found it elaborated not in Kant's second but his third *Critique*. Her concern, then, is not with judgment as it is connected with practical reason, moral validity, and rational will-formation but with judgment as the capacity to affirm political freedom, as the human capacity to act in concert, on the one hand, and judgment as the capacity to distinguish politics as genuine acts of freedom from politics as rule, on the other hand. As we shall see in this chapter, judgment discerns universal validity not in adherence to a neutral procedure devoid of all substantive ethical import but in the manifestation of what Arendt (following Montesquieu) calls "principles" (such as "honor or glory, [or] love of equality," but also "fear or distrust or hatred")[14] that have their roots in the lifeworld that Habermas's practical reason and rational will-formation would leave behind.

Was Arendt really blind to the threat of decisionism and structural violence that her theory of power supposedly countenanced? To answer this question, we need a clearer sense of what was at stake in her critique of the will, keeping in mind that, in Habermas's account, it is not the will as such that is problematic for democratic politics but the will unguided by communicative practical reason. At the end of *Willing* (published as volume 2 of *The Life of the Mind*), Arendt explicitly announces the need to write a section on "judging" in order to respond to the impasses in every philosophy of the will, especially as it bears on democratic theory and practice (*LMW*, 217).[15] In the philosophy of the will, Arendt identified the central aporia of democratic action: how to think and affirm plurality and a nonsovereign concept of freedom. Indeed, the word *aporia*, which comes from the Greek *aporos* and means literally "without passage," best describes what Arendt discovered in her reflections on the faculty of the will: there is no way to move from the idea of the will as free (which is to say, sovereign) to the idea of membership in a democratic community. For the freedom of the will, as Friedrich Nietzsche recognized, is irreducibly bound to the logic of obedience and command: "What is called 'freedom of the will' is essentially a passionate superiority toward a someone who must obey. 'I am free; "he" must obey'—the consciousness of this is the very willing" (quoted in *LMW*, 161). It is "strange indeed that the faculty of the will whose essential activity consists in dictate and command should be [so it is said] the harborer of freedom," as Arendt remarks elsewhere.[16] And not only strange but bearing "fatal consequences for political theory." Indeed, "this equation of freedom with the human capacity to will," she explains, is "one of the causes why even today we almost automatically equate power with oppression or, at least, with rule over others."[17] Freedom as freedom of the will/freedom as sovereignty, as she writes in *On Violence*, is bound up with the idea of power as rule/force—"making others act as I choose," to speak with Voltaire (*OV*, 36).

All of Arendt's writings, but especially *On Violence* and the unfinished work on judging, can be understood as an attempt to break with the entire modern philosophy of the will in which the twin ideas of power as rule/force and freedom as sovereignty have been housed. This break is far more radical than anything proposed by Habermas, who is certainly deeply critical of the same tradition of thought but who would rearticulate democratic will-formation as rational will-formation by means of his accounts of communicative action and discourse ethics.[18] He questions not the faculty of the will as having a legitimate role to play in democratic politics but its mute, solitary character and groundless exercise. By describing Arendt's notion of power as "communicative power" and redescribing the latter as "collective will-formation," Habermas can then criticize her for failing to provide the mechanisms of rational will-formation, the normative criteria according to which we judge. In my view, Arendt's conception of power and politics neither dismisses nor invites decisionism—that is, the notion that political actions and principles require no valid reasons but are simply the expressions of a groundless will—because, in breaking with the philosophy of the will, Arendt breaks with the very idea of democratic politics as will-formation, rational or not.[19]

As I argue in what follows, Arendt breaks not only with the idea of the will that yields the permanent threat of decisionism (just as rationalism yields the permanent threat of skepticism; and objectivism yields subjectivism) but also with certain assumptions about human action that keep the possibility of beginning tied to the power of the will. Refuting the will as the origin of action and human freedom in the distinctively *political* sense that she understood the power of beginning (i.e., precisely not as Kantian spontaneity, which is the ambivalent achievement of "Man in the singular," but as being with "men in the plural" in word and deed), Arendt goes on to refigure this possibility in relation to the power of judgment.[20]

Once we question, with Arendt, the idea that rational will-formation is the aim of democratic politics, and with it the notion that political actions can and need to be justified in the strict cognitive sense demanded by Habermas, decisionism ceases to present itself as a genuine political problem.[21] Arendt's so-called failure to generate the normative criteria according to which power is the formation not just of a common will but a will that is rational turns out to be part of a genuine innovation; an innovation, I suggest, that amounts to a virtual Copernican revolution in political theorizing—namely, an unprecedented break with the philosophy of the will in the history of political thought. This break is Copernican in spirit because it reveals that the claim to free action that the will arrogates to itself depends on the power of judgment. Although foregrounded in the work of philosophers such as Nietzsche, Henri Bergson, and Martin Heidegger, each of whom questioned the will as the locus of freedom, it was Hannah

Arendt herself who first recognized the implications of such a break for our understanding of democratic politics.

Is Power "Collective Will-Formation"?

Habermas credits Arendt with breaking with "the philosophy of consciousness," (which he ascribes not only to the paradigmatic figures of Kant and René Descartes but also to G. W. F. Hegel, Karl Marx, Heidegger, Theodor Adorno, Max Horkheimer, and even Jacques Derrida). In *Between Facts and Norms*, he marshals his earlier account of Arendtian "communicative power" to elaborate an argument about political autonomy as part of a larger argument about the cooriginality of law and power. What Habermas finds appealing in Arendt is the idea that "both law and communicative power have their co-original source in the 'opinion upon which many publicly were in agreement'" (*BFN*, 147). If law is not to stand as an alien force that is permanently at odds with "the people," so Habermas argues, its origin cannot be imposed from above. He continues, "If the sources of justice from which the law itself draws its legitimacy are not to run dry, then a jurisgenerative communicative power must underlie the administrative power of the government. This concept, introduced dogmatically by Hannah Arendt, requires further clarification" (*BFN*, 147).

Why? From Habermas's perspective, the Arendtian concept of "communicative power" (once again, his phrase, not hers) needs elaboration because it does not in itself satisfy the demand of legitimacy; people talking to one another must form not only a common will but also a common will that is rational. If we are to make good on Arendt's otherwise useful account of "communicative power," he argues, we need a deliberative procedure—which, we shall shortly see, is already implicit in the normative know-how of speaking subjects—in order to distinguish "valid norms of action [which] obligate their addressees equally and without exception to satisfy generalized behavioral expectations . . . [from] values . . . understood as intersubjectively shared preferences" (*BFN*, 255). But that demand to form in this or any other way a common rational will is Habermas's, not Arendt's.

As Habermas reads her, "Arendt conceives political power . . . as an *authorizing* force expressed in 'jurisgenesis'—the creation of legitimate law—and in the founding of institutions" (*BFN*, 148). Although Arendt would agree that law ought to have its origins in political action, it is hard to see how her account of power in *The Human Condition* lends itself to Habermas's definition of power as common will-formation, especially understood as sorting (particularistic) values from (universal moral) norms. Save one reference to "the unreliable and only temporary agreement of many wills and intentions" and another to the modern age's idea of the "will to power," Arendt never discusses the will in her account of power (*HC*, 201, 203). And even the first reference tends to highlight the event-like character of wills coming to share some common purpose, not a normative agreement on the order that Habermas suggests.

To redescribe Arendt's notion of acting in concert in terms of common will-formation risks losing sight of the contingency of action qua action without which, after all, power would not exist. "Power is what keeps the public realm, the potential space of appearance between acting and speaking men, in existence" (*HC*, 200), but there is no power in the absence of those "acting and speaking men." Arendt continues, "If power were more than this potentiality in being together, if it could be possessed like strength or applied like force instead of dependent upon the unreliable and only temporary agreement of many wills and intentions, omnipotence would be a concrete human possibility" (*HC*, 201). The emphasis here is less on the creation of political organizations, let alone the preconditions of law, than on the fact that no one individual can have power or act alone. "And whoever, for whatever reasons, isolates himself and does not partake in such being together, forfeits power and becomes impotent, no matter how great his strength and how valid his reasons" (*HC*, 201). To lose sight of this, as I shall argue subsequently, is to break the all-important link between the principle of democratic beginning and the ongoing relations of democratic rule.

Nonetheless, there is an ambiguity in Arendt's account that may well contribute to Habermas's interpretation of power as something rather more purposive or directed (will-like) than action. On the one hand, Arendt tells us that "the space of appearance comes into being wherever men are together in the manner of speech and action," and that "its peculiarity is that, unlike the spaces which are the work of our hands, it does not survive the actuality of the movement which brought it into being, but disappears not only with the dispersal of men—as in the case of great catastrophes when the body politic of a people is destroyed—but with the disappearance or arrest of the activities themselves. Wherever people gather together, it is potentially there, but only potentially, not necessarily and not forever" (*HC*, 199). The creature of action rather than fabrication, such a space would be as ephemeral as action is fleeting were it not for power. As Arendt puts it, "Power is what keeps the public realm, the potential space of appearance between acting and speaking men, in existence" (*HC*, 200). Here power seems more durable than action indeed. Before ascribing to power the durability that action lacks, which Habermas tries to capture with the idea of power as common will-formation and which Arendt's own prose here seems to promise, let us consider the passage that immediately follows:

> The word [*power*] itself, its Greek equivalent *dynamis*, like the Latin *potentia* with its various modern derivatives or the German *Macht* (which derives from *mögen* and *möglich*, not from *machen*), indicates its "potential" character. Power is always, as we would say, a power potential and not an unchangeable, measurable, and reliable entity like force or strength. While strength is the natural quality of an individual seen in isolation, *power springs up between men when they act together and vanishes the moment they disperse.* (*HC*, 200, my emphasis)

If power vanishes the moment men stop acting in concert, it is hard to see how power could sustain the space of appearance, which is itself nothing but the site of men acting in concert. Power, when all is said and done, is hardly distinguishable from action and, like action, it opens up a field of possibilities. To cast Arendt's account of power in terms of collective will-formation, as Habermas repeatedly does, risks losing sight of the potential eventfulness of power—that is, the fact that power is, when all is said and done, nothing more than action in concert. Habermas both needs this potential eventfulness, in order to counter positivistic and objectivist accounts of law, and fears it, for it threatens to overwhelm the normative work of communicative power—namely, rational will-formation.

It is important to see what happens when the Arendtian conception of power is framed by the legitimation problematic that dominates the thought of Habermas: action—and the passions, values, and beliefs that inspire it—disappears. What remains is what Habermas, speaking about the "new beginnings" represented by the constitutional assemblies of Philadelphia and Paris, calls the "*reasonable* trace" (emphasis in the original). As Bonnie Honig has argued, emphasizing the reasonable trace of these world-historical events, "Habermas here tries to take advantage of the exemplary power of the event without forsaking the transcontextual rationalism of discourse theory."[22] His commitment to grounding democratic principles in the practices of speaking subjects, rather than imposing them in a top-down application, requires that he find them in actual events. As Honig contends, "Habermas needs Philadelphia and Paris to motivate his 'constitutional patriotism.'"[23]

The problem, however, is that the "place names" of Philadelphia and Paris, as Honig observes, open a "Pandora's box." With them come "not simply 'constitutionalism,'" she writes, "but two distinct revolutions and foundings, each characterized by its own unique, contingent drama, intrigue, public spiritedness, and remnants." She continues,

In the U.S. case, "Philadelphia" conjures not only the assembly that produced the new national constitution but also the many competing conceptions of the American experiment that were sidelined or minoritized by the assembly and its constitution. The revolution, the Articles of Confederation, the constitutional assembly in Philadelphia, the resulting constitution itself, the antifederalists who fought it, the diverse crowds considered too unruly to be part of the deliberations, the various practices of popular constitutionalism delegitimated over the years, and the confederal practices of some native peoples are all the origins of contemporary American constitutional democracy. . . . If they are unrecollected in Habermas's invocation of "Philadelphia," that is because they are not, for him, part of its "reasonable trace." It is the trace, not the event, that he seeks to recollect.[24]

The disappearance of the political event in the rational trace, I would argue, is part and parcel of Habermas's interpretation of Arendt's view of "power as the potential of a *common will* formed in noncoercive communication" (*BFN*, 147).[25] Making power into collective will-formation, Habermas occludes its ongoing or continuous character and casts it as a point of absolute beginning, thus setting up what Honig calls "the chicken and egg problem" of what came first, the rule of law (constitutionalism) or the communicative power of the people (democracy), which his thesis of cooriginality is designed to solve.[26] Arendt's account, by contrast, emphasizes the background conditions of world-historical events such as the American Revolution. As Honig observes, these conditions included "decades of acculturation in democratic habits, mindsets, practices, law, and institutions . . . made possible by their contingent distance from sovereign power."[27] One could say, in other words, that the American Revolution did not come out of nowhere but had as its condition the space of appearances kept in existence by power. Fully aware of the importance of the "lifeworld," Habermas would not deny this notion. As we saw in chapter 4, however, the role played by the variety of practices, preunderstandings, and prejudgments that characterize the lifeworld is drastically curtailed in

Habermas's normative theory of democracy. He sharply distinguishes ethical-practical discourses, which arise within and belong to any particular form of life, from moral practical discourses, which are universal in scope.

Commenting on Jean-Jacques Rousseau's "republican tradition that binds the citizen's political practice to the ethos of an already integrated community," Habermas writes:

An interpretation along the lines of discourse theory, by contrast, insists on the fact that democratic will-formation does not draw its legitimating force from the prior convergence of settled ethical convictions. Rather, the source of legitimacy includes, on the one hand, the communicative presuppositions that allow the better arguments to come into play in various forms of deliberation and, on the other, procedures that secure fair bargaining conditions. Discourse theory breaks with an ethical conception of civic autonomy, and thus it does not have to reserve the mode of deliberative politics to exceptional conditions. (*BFN*, 278–79)

According to Richard Bernstein, this sharp distinction between ethics and morality works to radically attenuate if not deny the importance of the substantive-ethical commitments (values and beliefs) that are created through shared practices in the lifeworld. Yet Habermas's discourse theory is in fact dependent on those commitments, on a "democratic ethos," in ways that he explicitly excludes: "Even Habermas's references to good reasons and 'the force of the better argument' presupposes such an ethos where participants debate and agree with each other in good faith."[28] Habermas's invocation of "Philadelphia" and the "reasonable trace" is just one example of this denied dependence.

I agree with the critiques of Bernstein and others (e.g., Hilary Putnam[29]) regarding the highly abstract character of discourse ethics, but I want to resist—for reasons that will become clearer in the concluding chapter—the move to restrict the autonomy of politics by grounding it in a democratic ethos. Such autonomy is fundamental to Arendt's account of democracy and judging politically. I recognize the dangers of what Habermas calls "the *exceptionalist description* of political practice—how it really ought to be" (*BFN*, 278). Exceptionalist formulations of citizenship in "strong" or "thick" ethical terms have often tended, as he observes, to construe participation in the public sphere as "striving for the collective good" understood in the terms of "the hermeneutic appropriation of 'constitutive traditions.' According to this view, it is only the ascribed membership in an intersubjectively shared form of life and the conscious appropriation of antecedent traditions that explain why citizens are able to achieve any consensus at all about how to solve problems on the agenda—and about what standards should define the 'best' solution in each case" (*BFN*, 279). And I agree with Habermas in his assertion that "the ethical particularism characteristic of an unproblematic background consensus does not sit well with the conditions of cultural and societal pluralism that distinguish modern societies" (*BFN*, 279). That said, "this 'thick' or 'strong' understanding of substantial-ethical commitments must *not* be confused or identified with the 'thin'—but crucial—substantial-ethical dispositions and virtues required for engaging in democratic procedural practices," as Bernstein reminds us.[30] If taken to mean "the decades of acculturation in democratic habits, mindsets, practices," and the like as elaborated in Honig's account of the background conditions of the American Revolution, I would agree.[31] But we should not confuse this contextualist account with one that limits in advance of action what can appear in the world, for that would deny action the novelty that defines it in Arendt's view. And we should be wary—as Arendt was—of every attempt to reintroduce evaluative standards into the political realm that seek to legislate for democratic politics from the perspective of moral philosophy, even when this takes the form of a far more contextualized conception of a democratic ethos.

We should also be wary of Habermas's claim that proceduralism will in fact guard against exceptionalist accounts of democratic citizenship. It is not clear why "discourse ethics," as it redescribes rational democratic will-formation, is not equally exceptionalist in its account of what political practice ought to be. It conceals this exceptionalism by claiming to give mere propositional form to what citizens, as competent speakers of a language, must already presuppose, whether they know it or not, when they communicate with each other.[32] This is the tacit knowledge of rules that Habermas claimed to find in the work of Wittgenstein, as we saw in chapter 1. In response to critics, Habermas denies that his "rational reconstruction" of "argumentation as such" is an idealization that he posits as foundational for liberal democracy. But it is hard to see how the "priority of the right over the good," which ought to guide democratic will-formation on his universalist view, could get any traction whatsoever if it were not grounded in the supposedly irrefutable normativity of everyday communicative action. It is one thing to put forward this principle of universalization as a political or even a moral principle. It would then be something about which we could have public arguments, form opinions, and make judgments. But, as Nigel Pleasants observes, Habermas engages in a "conjuring trick" by which he "tries to pass off his own moral and political views as 'valid universally.'"[33] What secures the mutual intelligibility and rationality of communicative action, as Habermas writes, is not politics or even epistemology, it is ontology: "the inescapability of the general presuppositions that *always already* underlie the communicative practice of everyday life."[34]

One way to think about "the 'transcendental' lure for a proper [ontological] *grounding*" and "Habermas's hankering after a purified discourse theory which is not tainted by any substantial-ethical commitments," argues Bernstein, is as an effort to avoid the "'vicious' circularity" of presupposing that which it sets out to justify.[35] The problem, however, could also be stated in the explicitly political terms of Rousseau's famous paradox of founding, according to which, as Honig formulates it, "you cannot have good laws without good people, and you cannot have good people without good laws."[36] It is, in other words, not only a problem of the hermeneutical circle (described in chapter 4) or how to ground one's own critique—two related problems that have haunted Habermas (and critical theory) from the beginning—but, more important, a problem of how to ground the rule of law in a way that does not mistake facticity for validity, what is for what ought to be, but finds justice in the rule of law, and finds it at its origin, in the founding.

Now it may be the case that any thinker working with the notion of common (rational) will-formation as the ground of democratic politics will find a tension between facticity and validity—*Faktizität und Geltung*, as the German title suggests—and be tempted to think about democratic origins in terms that wrench apart the principle of beginning from the principle of rule. Such a thinker would then more than likely find him- or herself, as does Habermas, engaged in the reconstructive project of bringing rule and beginning back together. In the next section I try to elaborate an account of action as beginning that avoids the usual pitfalls of thinking about beginning as a radically unconditioned event and also tries to situate the idea of beginning in relation to the power of judgment rather than will.

What Counts as a "Beginning"?

In the volume on willing, Arendt explicitly addresses what Kant called "the embarrassment of 'speculative reason in dealing with the question of the freedom of the will . . . [namely, with] a power of *spontaneously* beginning a series of successive things or states'" (*LMW* 20).

Kant sets this power of spontaneously beginning against the idea that there is no freedom in the world; everything in the world takes place in accordance with the laws of nature in the "third antinomy" in *The Critique of Pure Reason*.[37] "What is so very troublesome is the notion of an *absolute* beginning," writes Arendt, citing Kant, "for 'a series occurring in the world can have only a relatively first beginning, being always preceded by some other state of things'" (*LMW*, 29). Save divine creation ex nihilo, beginning must always be relative: it is a beginning only in relation to something that came before it, which is another way of saying that beginning, at least for human beings, is always conditioned. The problem is how to think of beginning as conditioned but not determined.

Arendt insists that "a characteristic of human action is that it always begins something new, and this does not mean that it is ever permitted to start *ab ovo*, to create *ex nihilio*" ("LP," 5). This point has been lost on many of her interpreters, who tend to read her theory of action as an attempt to redeem the idea of spontaneity that Kant found embarrassing and to make it relevant for the political realm. And once you make Kantian spontaneity, which is the act of a groundless will, the model of Arendtian action, it is easy to see how you might begin to think about action in terms of the problem of rational will-formation.[38] The task would be to make what is spontaneous and groundless into something rational. Just this task defined Habermas's appropriation of Arendt's communicative conception of power. I have already suggested some of the problems associated with reading Arendt's notion of power as collective will-formation. Now, I would like to elaborate the ways in which thinking about democratic politics in terms of the will tends to produce an opposition between the principle of beginning and that of rule (the problem, that is, that Habermas's cooriginality thesis sets out to solve).

"The main problem with the politics of the will as politics of unconstrained creation *ex nihilio*," as Nadia Urbinati explains, "is that it assumes constitution-making as an act of freedom renunciation rather than of freedom constitution or *the institution of the space and time of politics*."[39] According to the idea of politics that equates freedom, the will, and sovereignty, freedom is a prepolitical condition that coexists with politics only in the moment of founding or constitution making. Whatever comes later is by definition not political action in the strong sense. Urbinati continues, "The paradox of this view (whose 'democratic' rendering is direct popular sovereignty) is that it grounds politics in an exquisite non- or antipolitical act of unbounded will or liberty . . . [which] makes politics so absolute as to make it inactive."[40] We are left with the impossible choice of the "authentic" extraordinary politics of permanent revolution or the "inauthentic" ordinary politics of electoral democracy. Urbinati is concerned with teasing out some of the problems that inhere in democratic theory's approach to the question of rule. More specifically, she wishes to interrogate the widely held idea that representative democracy is an "oxymoron" and at best "a pragmatic alternative to something that we, modern citizens, can no longer have, namely direct democracy."[41] This critique attempts to recover judgment as a mediated practice that offers an alternative to unmediated sovereign will as the basis for democracy. Urbinati does not oppose the idea of will-formation as such; she attempts to refigure it through judgment and opinion. In this respect her project is friendly to Habermas's, with one crucial difference: she does not think that expelling substantial ethical commitments, rhetoric, and partisanship from politics (by subjecting them to a procedural conception of justice, i.e., rule of argumentation) ought to define our understanding of the deliberative project.

Although he does not directly address the question of the will, Patchen Markell too has examined the problem of thinking rule and beginning together in an effort to interrogate the dominant interpretation of rule in democratic theory. For the most part, he argues, democratic theorists have accepted the idea that rule involves obedience and command, as well as stability and closure. The only question that arises is, who rules? And in a democracy it will be "the people." This way of thinking about rule, argues Markell, immediately raises the problem of how to account for more inaugural political practices—that is, practices that put into question constituted political forms, as did the student movement of 1968. Such is the objection of Sheldon Wolin, for whom the very idea of democracy as involving relations of rule excludes the constitutive power of the people, their ability to subvert existing institutions and practices and to create things anew. Although Markell welcomes this objection, he perceptively notes that it opens a space "structured by a series of stark oppositions between those phenomena rule is supposed to enable, such as stability, order, closure, and continuity, and those it is supposed to inhibit, such as change, interruption, openness, and novelty."[42] Consequently, democracy is cast "as a constitutively paradoxical enterprise, caught between the ideal of popular sovereignty, in which the people jointly exercise control over their collective destiny, and the ideal of popular insurgency, in which the people spontaneously shatter the bonds of established political forms"

("RP," 2) The result is that it is hard to see how any democratic political order could make a claim to its decisions, institutions, and practices without negating itself as a democracy.

Markell's effort to loosen the paradox that arises with this way of thinking about rule centers on rereading Arendt's etymological account of "the Greek *archê* and *archein*, [which] meant not only 'rule' and 'to rule' but also 'beginning' and 'to begin'" ("RP," 2; see *HC*, 177). Arendt's recovery of this original ambiguity in the meaning of rule, Markell argues, not only throws into question our automatic association of rule with *Herrschaft* (that is, the assumption that to rule means that some command and others obey) but also opens the space in which to rethink what it means to begin.[43] Rather than set beginning (which Arendt associates with action) at odds with rule (understood in conventional terms as the sedimented relations of order, stability, and closure), Markell astutely observes that, for Arendt, "novelty inheres in all events, even those that are expected or predicted"("RP," 2). This interpretation turns on thinking about beginning less as a radical break with all that came before (e.g., the instituted political forms and practices of democracy) and more as a certain responsiveness or attunement to the irrevocability of an event. What has happened and cannot be changed—the event itself—becomes "a new point of departure," observes Markell ("RP," 7).[44]

What would it mean to think about beginning as "a feature of *all* events" ("RP," 6), rather than as a "particular subset of human acts" ("RP," 6)? Surely Markell does not want to counter the idea of beginning as a rarefied feature of some events with the idea of beginning as a property that inheres in all events qua events. How do we determine whether something counts as a beginning? How do we determine, for that matter, whether any given happening is an event to which we might respond, rather than one of an endless flow of occurrences? What makes one occurrence stand out for us from an indefinite background of occurrences as an event that is both irrevocable and a point of departure? And, finally, if it is not a break with all that has come before that characterizes beginning, what does distinguish it?

We can seek answers to these questions by turning to Markell's notion of "attunement," which he describes as a certain perspective or stance one takes toward what has happened.[45] Saying as much, however, immediately raises the question not only of "Whose 'attunement?'" and "What is attunement, anyway?" ("RP," 8), but also of whether something counts as a case of beginning if the one who acts thinks it does. Rightly concerned to guard against such an agent- or subject-centered view of action, Markell does not want to treat beginning as a mental state. Beginning may be "a feature of all events" in Markell's view, but it is more in the way of a potential that must be actualized by others than a substance that inheres in all events. What makes one happening or occurrence count as an event that calls for our response, in other words, is how other citizens take it up. Beginning as a feature of all events must be actualized, and this actualization turns on whether others take up an event as an occasion for response. In Markell's view, "there is no way to undo what has been done, no way *not* to suffer it—but you can do more than *merely* suffer it: you can take it as your point of departure" ("RP," 10).

This attempt to undo what has been done is the option that Nietzsche diagnosed as belonging to the experience of the will as it confronts the "It was." The will's relationship to the stubborn "It was" takes the destructive because impossible form of a wish to will backward, which treats events not as points of departure but as occasions for rancor. I agree with Markell that "the novelty of a new beginning" turns "on an agent's attunement to its [the act's or event's] character as an irrevocable event, and therefore also as a new point of departure." ("RP," 7). But, if Nietzsche is right, such attunement is perhaps more difficult than Markell may have led us to believe. If we want to avoid treating attunement as a kind of mental state and think about it rather as an activity or a practice, as Markell clearly invites us to do, then we must ask: what kind of activity or practice enables me to treat an event as "irrevocable" and as a "point of departure," rather than as undoable and as an occasion for ressentiment? Although Markell does not directly pose this question, he begins to suggest how we might answer it when he writes:

Importantly, identifying breakdowns of the nexus of event and response is not a matter of the top-down application of an authoritative philosophical criterion: just as, for Arendt, the status of human activity as "action" cannot be apprehended from the disengaged stance of the classifier, the significance of events is also a matter of judgment, and, often enough, a matter for dispute, undertaken within the horizons of practical engagement. ("RP," 12–13)

Whether something counts as an instance of beginning depends not on some intrinsic property of the event qua event, then, but on how we respond. Whether we respond (i.e., are attuned) in a way that affirms an event as irrevocable and as a beginning, rather than, say, as an occasion to try to undo what has been done, as I would now extend

Markell's point, depends on the capacity to judge—more specifically, to judge an event in its freedom. In such a judgment an event calls forth an acceptance of the "It was" (what has been given and cannot be changed), rather than the impossible wish to will backward. For Nietzsche, to be genuine the acceptance must take the form of an affirmation: "To redeem what is past and transform every 'It was' into 'Thus I would have it'—that's what I take to be redemption."[46] Once again, to redeem the past (Nietzsche) or to treat it as a point of departure rather than merely suffer it (Markell's Arendt) is not to discover something that inheres in the event qua event but rather to alter one's relationship to it.

Judgment is needed if events are not to serve as an occasion for rancor in the way Nietzsche described. But judgment is also necessary because the transition from "the not-yet" to the "already" (which, says Markell, is the crucial difference that all events share, regardless of whether they were in some sense expected or unexpected) brings with it the specter of causality and necessity. Our ability to take an event as a departure point is related to our ability to see in it something that could have been otherwise. The point here is not to exclude events that were or could have been anticipated or foreseen. Rather, it is to emphasize the power of judgment that allows us to affirm contingency in events, even those that were anticipated or foreseen.[47] When Kant spoke of the French Revolution as a historical sign indicating the hope for humanity's moral progress, he was referring not to something in the events themselves but to the judgment of spectators like himself. It was they who found in the events the opening of what was possible. What they saw was not unlike what Arendt saw when she watched the events of 1968: power understood as the action in concert that is a beginning insofar as it is taken up as an occasion for response.

Judging 1968

"Some of the most important work of democratic politics," writes Markell, "consists in the interpretation of particular events; that is, in the re-presentation of happenings that, although they may or may not be widely known as matters of fact, are not (as) widely experienced as practically significant" ("RP," 13). Returning in this way to the events we associate with 1968, we might say that the problem here is not that the events are unknown but that they are so well known that we no longer take them as a point of departure. I said at the start of this chapter that the question of whether these events represent "the beginnings of something new—the 'new example'—or the death pangs of a faculty [the capacity to begin] that mankind is about to lose" (*OV*, 83–84), as Arendt put it, is fundamentally a question of judgment. It is our judgment, and not something that inheres in 1968 as an event qua event (or set of events), that makes of 1968 a beginning—that is, a point of departure for our own action. The same goes for those far less well-known happenings both before and after 1968—many of which are only now starting to get the attention of scholars—that tend to get occluded from our judgment of the past when we think about beginning as an absolute break with all that has come before.[48]

On what basis, then, can we judge '68? "If [Arendtian] action really does constitute a radically new beginning that 'breaks through the commonly accepted,' it surely cannot be judged according to any evaluative criteria determined in advance," asserts Lucy Cane.[49] Even if we temper this more familiar account of Arendt with Markell's description of new beginnings as ongoing points of departure, the introduction of standards external to any particular event to ground judgment will always remain alien to politics on Arendt's view. We have seen, however, that for Habermas, Arendt's refusal to specify the regulative moral criteria for judgment leaves her account of politics vulnerable to irrationalism and decisionism. Furthermore, looking back on the movements that exploded in the violence of 1968 from where we stand in time, it is easy to find naive what Arendt described as the students' "astounding will to action, and . . . no less astounding confidence in the possibility of change" (*OV*, 16).[50] As Max Elbaum observes, "The dominant view [of this period] even in progressive circles is that the young people who embraced revolutionary ideas after 1968 had essentially 'gone crazy' and that the early 'good sixties' were replaced by a later 'bad sixties' characterized by political madness."[51]

On Violence was written neither to define nor to redeem what would later be called the "bad sixties," but rather to understand why violence exploded as it did and, finally, to judge. Arendt's effort to understand and to judge, we have seen, involves a radical rethinking of power and a break with the philosophy of the will. Refusing the idea that power is power over others, the power to make others act in accordance with one's will, she advances a notion of power as acting in concert. This idea of power goes against every political and philosophical tradition, save one:

When the Athenian city-state called its constitution an isonomy, or the Romans spoke of the *civitas* as their form of government, they had in mind a concept of power and law whose essence did not rely on the command-obedience relationship and which did not identify power and rule or law and command. (*OV*, 40)

This Greco-Roman tradition, for which politics and power are not a form of rule, is the one that Arendt sees the students as reviving. Unfortunately, not unlike the American men of revolution who, though they turned to this tradition, seeking to "to put an end to the rule of man over man, . . . still talked about obedience—obedience to laws instead of to men" (*OV*, 40), so too did the student movement and other movements of the period get caught in the very logic of politics as rule that their action in concert otherwise sought to challenge. Their turn to violence was at once an expression of the frustration of action in the modern world—especially the forcible closing of the spaces of action opened up by the students as they found their protests increasingly met with police brutality—and "the conviction that the most crucial political issue is, and always has been, the question of Who rules Whom?" (*OV*, 43). From there, Arendt remarks, it was but a short step to affirming (with Mao Tse-tung) that "power grows out of the barrel of a gun" (*OV*, 11).

If we wish to make sense of and ultimately to judge the students' claim to isonomy as well as their fall back into violence and the politics of rule, we need to grasp their action not in terms of the extrapolitical standards of rational will-formation that guide Habermas's critique of 1968 but in terms of what Arendt (following but also strongly modifying "Montesquieu's famous analysis of forms of government"), calls "a principle."[52] As noted earlier, it is the principle that guides action by which action can be judged on Arendt's view. Arendt does not provide a clear account of how we can discern the particular principles at work in a given action. Nevertheless, as Cane notes, we may speculate that attending to an action's "context, slogans, and tactics . . . as well as the goals it articulates in its earliest stages," as Arendt clearly did in the case of the student movement, will provide keys to what those principles might be.[53] Indeed, far from excluding motives or goals as forms of strategic action (as Habermas accuses),

she [Arendt] claims that any particular goal of action "can be judged *in the light of its principle once the act has been started*." To judge a goal in this way is not to assess whether that goal has been achieved, or how useful it is in relation to other ends. It is rather, I submit, to discern the extent to which a particular goal exemplifies and sustains a principle. This particular judgment escapes means-ends reasoning, as a goal is viewed neither as an end, nor as a means to further ends, but simply as an *example* of a principle in action. In other words, the goals of an action matter for Arendt, because it is partly through them that the action manifests a principle and so acquires meaning and greatness.[54]

To grasp "how principles operate [in Arendt's thought] as evaluative standards facilitating critical judgments," as Cane writes, without falling into the trap of turning them into the same extrapolitical criteria that Arendt's critique of the philosophy of the will (and any moral grounding of politics) was meant to expose, we need to think of any particular judgment made on the basis of principles as examples, not rules.[55] This means not only that principles are not rules under which to subsume a particular action when judging it, for that position can easily be accommodated by more critical neo-Kantian thinkers such as Seyla Benhabib. Although Benhabib eschews the subsumptive model of Kantian moral judgment, she holds fast to the idea that judging is first and foremost a "moral faculty."[56]

In chapter 2 we saw that Kant refused the idea of a principle of taste and argued instead for the importance of examples in figuring, demonstrating, and eliciting agreement in judgments of taste. Arendt does not eschew the idea of a principle because principles for her do not function as rules of any kind, let alone as universal moral criteria that transcend any particular context and according to which particular actions must adhere. Although Benhabib grants that "such criteria [do not arise out of nowhere but] are going to be embodied in some or another tradition or in some or another practice," it is crucial to her modified neo-Kantianism that universal moral criteria be used to legislate political action and ground judgment.[57] For Arendt, however, such criteria represent yet another attempt within the Western tradition to understand and ultimately regulate politics from the perspective of (moral) philosophy. Holding to the autonomy of politics and judging politically, Arendt argues that it is only in and through action that principles are realized and discerned; they have no status qua moral principles that "reflect a universalistic morality," as Benhabib would read them. Rather than set principles in a universalistic moral idiom that then legislates over what Benhabib calls a "situational [political] casuistic,"[58] Arendt, observes Cane, "characterizes principles as 'general' and even 'universal,' not in the sense that they are somehow valid for all political actors but rather in the sense that they are 'not bound to any particular person or to any particular group.'"[59]

Thus, "principles can be repeated time and again," asserts Arendt, and the repetition is what sustains the vitality of the political realm.[60] "However, the manifestation of principles comes about only through action, they are manifest in the world only as long as the action lasts, but no longer," she adds.[61] These principles, then, are not at all like the ones that Hume ascribed to his "hidden standard" of taste whose possible discovery, either now or in the future, Kant vehemently denied. The principles that guide action and by which we judge action cannot be discovered in this or any other transcontexualist sense but can only be manifested through action.

Here we find the key difference between Arendt's explicitly political understanding of a principle and Habermas's more philosophical one, but also the difference between Arendt's understanding and the idea of a principle in more context-sensitive neo-Kantians such as Benhabib. As we saw in her feminist response to "the claims of culture" in chapter 6, Benhabib holds that principles, to be universal, must transcend the practices in which they nonetheless have their origin. We might think of this difference in terms of the distinction between criteria and the conventional sense of standards described by Cavell in chapter 1, where standards are understood to be separate from criteria and both exist from the actual language game in which they are being employed. More precisely, we might say that it is only in our activity, in what Cavell called the "whirl of organism" of our form of life, that principles have their life, that we become so much as aware of them as principles. Like criteria in this Cavellian sense, principles are not only open to rearticulation but also are claimed as *our* principles, as "what we say," only in being rearticulated in action and then subjected to judgment. More precisely, principles are claimed by each one of us when we claim to speak publicly for "what we say," though we may well discover—by way not of philosophy, epistemology, or ontology but engaged democratic politics—that the claim is refused by those on whose part we claim to speak and elaborate a shared principle.

This necessary rearticulation does not exclude the idea that principles can be "preserved" through institutions or various cultural artifacts, though they would be reduced to empty words without the continual reanimation that only action provides and judgment makes visible. Institutions and the stories we tell ourselves about the American founding, for example, often provide the template from which to rearticulate principles in light of the exigencies of the present. As articulated in its "claim for 'participatory democracy'" (OV, 22), the student movement can in this way be understood as having reanimated the principle of isonomy that once guided not only the ancient city-state but also the American Revolution. In search of what Arendt called the latter's "lost treasure," the students were gripped by "the revolutionary spirit" that the founders had failed to give enduring form—namely, those quotidian institutional spaces of freedom in which postrevolutionary citizens too could enact, through their action, the founding principles of freedom, equality, and public happiness.

In conclusion, we can say that to make reflective, critical judgments about the student movement and the events of 1968 is to move outside the philosophy of the will, its framework of rule, and the standards of moral philosophy. According to Arendt, "It is only after one ceases to reduce public affairs to the business of domination that the original data in the realm of human affairs will appear, or, rather, reappear in their authentic diversity" (*OV*, 43–44). I hope to have shown that these original data do not constitute democratic rational will-formation but power understood in Arendt's specific sense as action in concert, which can be judged not on the basis of transcontextual moral standards but only by means of the principles that inspire and guide action itself.

EIGHT

What on Earth Is a "Form of Life"? Judging "Alien" Cultures According to Peter Winch

The problem of judgment that we have been exploring from various angles throughout this book is perhaps nowhere more starkly posed than in cases where we seem to be dealing with incommensurable worldviews not only within one national culture (the subject of Rawls's *Political Liberalism* and Habermas's *Between Facts and Norms*) but between cultures located at disparate points in time and space. Although Strauss's critique of historicism engaged the problem of judgment at this level, it did not really wrestle with the question of what it would mean to be confronted with a worldview so radically different from one's own that it seemed as if we could no longer speak of anything like a minimally shared sense of what is real. Just this problem is taken up in Peter Winch's controversial essay, "Understanding a Primitive Society."

I say "controversial" because the common charge leveled against Winch is that he is a relativist who denies that we can legitimately judge other cultures. Not unlike the feminist new universalists examined in chapter 6, Winch's critics too are faced with the problem of how to judge competing worldviews without incurring the charge of (Western) ethnocentrism. Once we acknowledge "that

the ways in which human minds conceptualize and apprehend reality are plural and not single, and that culture and language appear to
play a major role in shaping categories we recognize," as Martha Nussbaum elaborates the challenge posed by a variety of worldviews, then
we seem to "focus increasingly on the relativity of all judgments to a
conceptual scheme, and on the human and cultural-historical character of conceptual schemes."[1] But just what is a conceptual scheme or
a worldview? Before turning to Winch himself, let's see if we can get
some clarity about what is at stake in the radical cultural differences
that he powerfully described but, in the view of critics, either could not
or refused to judge.

On Incommensurability

The idea of a conceptual scheme as a way of thinking about value-
centered knowing and judging has been at the heart of many debates
in philosophy, anthropology, philosophy of science, and linguistics. As
its most renowned critic, Donald Davidson, explains:

Conceptual schemes, we are told, are ways of organizing experience; they are systems of categories that give form to the data of sensation; they are points of view
from which individuals, cultures, or periods survey the passing scene. There may be
no translating from one scheme to another, in which case the beliefs, desires, hopes
and bits of knowledge that characterize one person have no true counterparts for
the subscriber to another scheme. Reality itself is relative to a scheme: what counts
as real in one system may not in another.[2]

Originally derived from a certain reading of Kant and later given a
nominalist twist in the work of W. V. O. Quine, the scheme/content
distinction—indeed, the very idea of conceptual scheme relativism —is
incoherent, argues Davidson. The condition of recognizing a putatively
alternative conceptual scheme is our ability to translate it into our own
language. But if we are able to translate it, then we cannot coherently
maintain that it is an *alternative* conceptual scheme: there must be
some common frame of reference for translation to get started.[3]

Challenged in Davidson's essay is a picture of the relation of language and world that takes language to comprise a scheme of concepts
that organizes and gives meaning to the otherwise meaningless sensory input of the empirical world. Davidson asserts, "It is essential to

this idea [of a scheme-content dualism] that there be something neutral and common that lies outside all [conceptual] schemes"—namely, the content, which the scheme organizes in a certain way.[4] This picture presupposes what Hilary Putnam called the "disastrous idea that has haunted Western philosophy since the seventeenth century, the idea that perception involves an interface between the mind and the 'external' objects we perceive."[5] Within the frame of this picture, the moment we take into account the plurality of languages held to structure multiple worldviews, as historicism did, it can easily seem that we are right back to the problem of untranslatability. *Language, worldview, culture*, and other terms come to be synonyms for the often radical incommensurability of perspectives on an object whose status qua object can no longer—as it was in the original, ordinary conception of perspective discussed in chapter 1—be assumed. What there is (empirical content) will depend on what scheme (concepts) is applied.[6]

Davidson shows the unintelligibility of "the concept of an uninterpreted reality, something outside all schemes," and in so doing appears to rule out the possibility that we could ever be "in a position to judge that others had concepts or beliefs radically different from our own."[7] Although his critique starts as a powerful argument against the idea of "the total unintelligibility of beings we nevertheless recognize as agents," comments Charles Taylor, it does not do justice to the moments when we meet up with strange beliefs or practices and really cannot recognize in them anything we would call rational.[8] Davidson exhibits what Taylor calls "the standing ethnocentric temptation . . . to make too quick sense of the stranger, that is, sense in one's own terms."[9] I fully share Taylor's concern, but what terms other than our own for making sense do we have?

Responding to this question and to the relativism that the idea of incommensurable conceptual schemes is seen to present, a wide array of critics has turned to Wittgenstein, who famously associates language with a worldview and a form of life. The passages around which the discussion circles include the following:

The limits of my language mean the limits of my world.
—*TRACTATUS LOGICO-PHILOSOPHICUS* 5.6

It is easy to imagine a language consisting only of orders and reports in battle.—Or a language consisting only of questions and expressions for answering yes and no. And innumerable others.—And to imagine a language is to imagine a form of life.
—*PHILOSOPHICAL INVESTIGATIONS* §19

"So you are saying that human agreement decides what is true and what is false?"—
It is what human beings *say* that is true and false; and they agree in the *language*
they use. That is not agreement in opinions but in form of life.
—*PHILOSOPHICAL INVESTIGATIONS* §241

"Language" is for us a name for a collection, and I understand it as including German, English and so on, and further various systems of signs which have more or
less affinity with these languages.
—*ZETTEL* §322

Among the many questions we might raise, I shall focus initially
on the issue of plurality. Whereas *Philosophical Investigations* section 19
suggests that there can be many languages and thus many forms of life,
as Donald Barry observes, *Zettel* section 322 has been taken to imply
that "'Language' would mean any humanly recognisable language, and
so imagining this language would be to imagine the distinctively human form of life."[10] Though Wittgenstein speaks of innumerable languages in section 19, the only ones we can really imagine are those
quite like our own (English, French, German, and related sign systems),
which are collected under the group called "language" in section 322.
"There is no interesting sense in which I must imagine different *forms*
of life when I think of French and German," asserts Newton Garver.[11]

According to the transcendental (Kantian) readings of Garver, Bernard Williams, and Jonathan Lear, different forms of life are not really
possible for us; we cannot so much as grasp them. Wittgenstein's many
examples of people who do things in ways that radically differ from our
own ways (e.g., price wood according to the ground area it covers; continue the series "add 2" beyond 1,000 with 1,004 or 1,008) are intended
not to present us with actual empirical possibilities but to show us how
it is that *we* employ our concepts, how *we* go on. Hence, the examples
"are not alternatives *to* us; they are alternatives *for* us," comments Williams.[12] Seeing in Wittgenstein's later work a continuation and transformation of the idealism of the *Tractatus*, Williams observes, "The limits of *our* language mean the limits of *our* world [not simply, as it had
in the earlier work, *my* world]."[13] Likewise Lear, endorsing Davidson's
claim "that the idea of an alternative conceptual scheme is incoherent,"
supplements it with the supposedly Kantian concept of "mindedness":

Let us say that a person is *minded* in a certain way, if he has the perceptions of salience, routes of interest, feelings of naturalness, in following a rule, etc. that constitute being part of a certain form of life."[14]

From Wittgenstein's (Kantian perspective), "the notion of people be-ing 'other-minded' is not something on which we can get any grasp. The possibility of there being persons who are minded in any way at all is the possibility of their being minded as we are," Lear concludes.[15] The transcendental reading, then, construes Wittgenstein's references to "form of life" as the "Human Form," notes Barry, as "a kind of uni-fied subjectivity."[16]

Yet other scholars find in Wittgenstein a "theory of meaning" that can serve as a prophylactic against criticism of "our form of life," while granting that there may be multiple forms of life that are likewise immune to criticism. Insofar as Wittgenstein holds that the account-ability of meaning to the world cannot be understood apart from our concepts, he is seen as advancing "the implausible claim," comments Alice Crary, that "we are never in a position from which it makes sense to talk about the adequacy or inadequacy of our discourses to the nature of what we are talking about" or to criticize the adequacy or inadequacy of the discourses of others.[17] When we encounter people with other values and worldviews, "we should conceive the distances in question, not as disagreements which can be settled through ra-tional conversation, but rather as differences resistant to all efforts at reasoned resolution."[18] Working from just this understanding ac-cording to which "traditions cannot be [rationally] judged," J. C. Nyri commends Wittgenstein for advancing "a conservative stance toward our own practices and tolerance toward those of others."[19] Speaking for other critics, Ernest Gellner condemns Wittgenstein's view of lan-guage for trapping each individual culture in "a cozy, self-contained conceptual cocoon," a hermetically sealed worldview that deprives us of shared epistemic grounds for resolving scientific disputes and value conflicts.[20]

Where Gellner finds a troubling quietism, Richard Rorty invokes Wittgenstein to argue for socially progressive liberal arguments free of self-defeating liberal guilt. When Wittgenstein writes, "What has to be accepted, the given, is—so one could say—*forms of life*" (*PI*, §226), argues Rorty, he teaches us that "ethnocentricism," understood as an epistemological position, is "an inescapable condition—roughly syn-onymous with 'human finitude.'"[21] Liberal projects that seek to justify our moral standards to people who do not share our form of life are doomed from the start. Liberal justifications will inevitably run out and, reaching "bedrock," we will be forced to conclude with Wittgen-stein: "This is what I do."[22] Refusing to accept the inescapable fact of epistemological ethnocentrism, "wet liberals," argues Rorty, agonize over making judgments across cultural divides.[23] Acting "as if giving grounds did not come to an end sometime," as Wittgenstein describes the problem of endless justification in *On Certainty*, "wet liberals" persist in the metaphysical dream of Reason and transcendent criteria of correctness.[24] Turning to what he takes to be Wittgenstein's critique of objectivity, Rorty develops his "'anti-anti-ethnocentric' stand as a way of freeing wet liberals from this imaginary problem," Farid Abdel-Nour observes.[25] Once objectivity is exposed as a metaphysical pipe dream, we can stop worrying, as Hilary Putnam critically comments, about whether "some value judgments are reasonable and some are unreasonable, or some views are true and some false, or some words refer and some do not."[26] We can stop worrying about whether what counts as valid for us is just our ethnocentric opinion. At that place where we agree in our judgments, justification is not only impossible but also unnecessary. We can certainly try to "persuade" those who do not share our concepts, but the persuasion won't be "right" or "wrong"—it will not have rational grounds.

Rorty's interpretation of Wittgenstein is irksome to many a fellow philosopher, but is it not also plausible? As Elizabeth Anscombe succinctly states,

In his [Wittgenstein's] work up to *On Certainty* we might think we could discern a straightforward thesis: there can be no such thing as "rational grounds" for our criticizing practices and beliefs that are so different from our own. These alien practices and language games are simply there. They are not ours, we cannot move in them.[27]

Before it was associated with Rortian relativism, the supposedly Wittgensteinian idea that one would have to be inside a particular worldview to criticize its practices was most closely associated with the equally controversial interpretation of Peter Winch.

Language and Reality

In "Understanding a Primitive Society," Winch attacked E. E. Evans-Pritchard's 1937 account of the African tribe of the Azande, also known as Zande.[28] For Evans-Pritchard, Zande practices such as witchcraft and belief in oracles were based on a conception of reality that has been shown by modern science to be false:

Scientific notions are those which accord with objective reality both with regard to the validity of their premises and to the inferences drawn from their propositions. . . . Logical notions are those in which according to the rules of thought inferences would be true were the premises true, the truth of the premises being irrelevant . . .

A pot has broken during firing. This is probably due to grit. Let us examine the pot and see if this is the cause. That is logical and scientific thought. Sickness is due to witchcraft. A man is sick. Let us consult the oracles to discover who is the witch responsible. That is logical and unscientific thought.[29]

In the same spirit with which Wittgenstein attacked James Frazer's nineteenth-century European account of primitive ritual practice as bad science,[30] Winch accuses Evans-Pritchard of illegitimately applying European criteria of judgment to judge a worldview that is utterly different from that of modern science. Evans-Pritchard does not see that different languages establish different relationships to reality and establish the ungrounded framework for deciding what is true and what is false. Winch writes:

Reality is not what gives language sense. What is real and what is unreal shows itself *in* the sense that language has. Further, both the distinction between the real and the unreal and the concept of agreement with reality, themselves belong to our language. I will not say that they are concepts of the language like any other, since it is clear that they occupy a commanding, and in a sense a limiting, position there. We can imagine a language with no concept of, say, wetness, but hardly one in which there is no way of distinguishing the real from the unreal. Nevertheless we could not in fact distinguish the real from the unreal without understanding the way the distinction operates in the language. If then we wish to understand the significance of these concepts, we must examine the use they actually do have—*in* the language. ("UPS," 309)

For Winch, you cannot judge one conception of reality (the Zande) wholly using another conception of reality (the European modern scientific). That is far worse than the adage about "comparing apples and oranges," for the latter assumes we agree that they both are "fruit." Missing are shared standards of evidence and proof. Evans-Pritchard claims this right to judge on the basis of the untenable assumption, contends Winch, that

the conception of "reality" must be regarded as intelligible and applicable *outside* the context of scientific reasoning itself, since it is that to which scientific notions do, and unscientific notions do not, have a relation. Evans-Pritchard, although he emphasizes that a member of scientific culture has a different conception of reality from that of a Zande believer in magic, wants to go beyond merely registering this fact and making the differences explicit, and to say, finally, that the scientific conception agrees with what reality actually is like, whereas the magical conception does not. ("UPS," 308)

Winch accuses Evans-Pritchard not of failing to recognize the *coherence* of the Zande worldview but of judging it wrong from a standpoint fully outside it. This external standpoint, as we saw in chapter 1, is the one Williams described as belonging to the "absolute conception of the world"; namely, the distinction between the world as it is independent of our experience and the world as it seems to us—that is, the world as it seems *peculiarly* to us. With the reduction of our affective propensities to the peculiar (i.e., limited by those propensities) way in which we humans see the world, "the absolute conception will, correspondingly, be a conception of the world that might be arrived at by any investigators, even if they were very different from us," as Williams explains.[31] Winch contends, on the contrary, that such a standpoint is fully illusory:

Evans-Pritchard . . . is trying to work with a conception of reality which is *not* determined by its actual use in the language. He wants something against which that use can itself be appraised. But this is not possible; and no more possible in the case of scientific discourse than it is in any other. We may ask whether a particular scientific hypothesis agrees with reality and test this by observation and experiment. . . . But the general nature of the data revealed by the experiment can only be specified in terms of the criteria built into the methods of experiment employed and these, in turn, make sense only to someone who is conversant with the kind of scientific activity within which they are employed. ("UPS," 309)

Winch gives an example of a "scientific illiterate," who wanders into a physics laboratory and is asked to describe the results of the experiment that he has just observed. But this he could not do, says Winch, not in terms that were "relevant to the hypothesis tested." Evans-Pritchard cannot see this because, for him,

the criteria applied in scientific experimentation constitute a true link between our ideas and an independent reality, whereas those characteristic of other systems of thought—in particular, magical methods of thought—do not. It is evident that the expressions "true link" and "independent reality" . . . cannot themselves be explained by reference to the scientific universe of discourse, as this would beg the question. We have then to ask how, by reference to what established universe of discourse, the use of those expressions *is* to be explained; and it is clear that Evans-Pritchard has not answered this question. ("UPS," 309)

The very concepts at issue here, in other words, depend for their meaning on the language game of the modern scientific experiment.

Winch implicitly draws here on Wittgenstein's remark, in section 105 of *On Certainty*:

All testing, all confirmation and disconfirmation of a hypothesis takes place already within a system. And this system is not a more or less arbitrary and doubtful point of departure for all our arguments: no, it belongs to the essence of what we call an argument. The system is not so much the point of departure, as the element in which arguments have their life.

The suggestion that arguments only make sense within a system; that all testing of hypotheses already presupposes an ungrounded frame of reference apart from which there can be no question of the true or the false, the real or the unreal, the rational or the irrational, can appear to exclude the possibility of learning anything whose basic premises are not already accounted for by the system, the "universe of discourse" to which Winch referred. And could not what Wittgenstein writes in section 94—"I did not get my picture of the world by satisfying myself of its correctness; nor do I have it because I am satisfied of its correctness. No: it is the inherited background against which I distinguish between true and false."—be seen to underscore the view of the many critics who accuse him and Winch of quietism and relativism?

In general agreement with Winch's exposure of scientism but critical of the fall into form-of-life relativism, Habermas in *The Theory of Communicative Action* remarks that Winch "bases his objections to Evans-Pritchard on a culturalistic concept of language inspired by Wittgenstein."[32] Before we can see what Winch (and the culturalistic concept) gets wrong, says Habermas, we should appreciate what he gets right. Like Wittgenstein, Winch rightly sees that there are such things as worldviews and that they "refer to something particular" (i.e., there are many "forms of life") but also to "totalities; for members of the same culture the limits of their language are the limits of the world. They can broaden the horizon of their form of life in an ad hoc manner, but they cannot step out of it; to this extent, every interpretation is also an assimilation." Haberma continues:

Inasmuch as worldviews refer to totalities, we cannot get behind them as articulations of an understanding of the world, even if they can be revised. In this respect, they [worldviews] are like a portrait that claims to represent a person as whole. A portrait is neither a *mapping* that can be exact or inexact, nor a *rendering of the facts* in the sense of a proposition that can be true or false. A portrait offers rather an angle of vision from which the person represented appears in a certain way. Thus there can be numerous portraits of the same person; they can make the character appear in quite different aspects, and yet they can all be experienced as accurate, authentic, or adequate. Similarly, worldviews lay down the framework of fundamental concepts within which we interpret everything that appears in the world in a specific way as something. Worldviews can no more be true or false than can portraits. (*TCA*, 58)

Worldviews, then, are totalizing particularistic frames of reference that can nonetheless have the same object in view, though each worldview sees or discloses it differently (i.e., renders the object qua object as always already having a certain meaning), just as different portraits render different aspects of the character of the same person. The question arises: how, from within any totality, any particular worldview, could one discern that the object, as it is seen from another totality, another equally particular worldview, is in fact the same?

This problem of shared reference in the absence of shared meaning is one that bedevils Habermas's own acceptance of the "world-disclosing" hermeneutic conception of language that he attributes to Winch (and, more generally, to Heidegger and Wittgenstein). According to this conception, writes Cristina Lafont, "meaning determines reference" (i.e., the preunderstandings of the "lifeworld" gives us objects as things we can refer to because we already know their meaning: the "as-structure" implicit in all prepredicative seeing).[33] How, then, could we refer to something on whose meaning we did not already agree? It is this implicit theory of "indirect reference" that belongs to the "hermeneutic conception of language," argues the otherwise sympathetic Lafont, that bedevils Habermas;[34] bedevils him in such a way that he would narrate the traffic between worldviews and the transformation of particular worldviews (modernity) as our ability to rise *above* the worldview that Winch has otherwise rightly told us we cannot get "*behind*," thus foreclosing the possibility of legitimate internal critique and outside criticism.

Habermas's version of language as "world-disclosure" is so totalizing, writes Lafont, that he is unable "to find an adequate alternative to the contextualism [or relativism] inherent [in that conception]."[35] But of course he did think he had found one. Though Habermas's version did not (like the transcendental version of Lear, Garver, and Williams) hold that there could be only one form of life, the Human Form, or deny that we could so much as coherently posit the existence of alternative worldviews, he joined them in finding something truly universal that would mitigate the relativistic consequences of worldview pluralism: an ontological account of communicative competence which holds that adherence to the intersubjective rules of communicative action is common across diverse cultures. Although Habermas ascribes what he found "right" in Winch to a shared Wittgensteinian-inspired linguistic and pragmatic turn, the normative presuppositions that make "every subject competent in speech and action" capable of "criticizable validity claims" are untainted by anything Winch's Wittgenstein would call ordinary—namely, that which belongs to a particular worldview (e.g., belief in oracles or in science). That is the difference, we will recall from chapter 4, between "morality" and "ethics"; a difference between universal norms that are fully procedural and particular values that express a communal conception of the good. We have good reason to suspect that it may not be Winch (let alone Wittgenstein) but Habermas himself who ascribes to language an all-powerful reality creating power that inevitably makes worldviews immune to criticism, save by means of a highly idealized conception of the development of communicative competence.

It is no surprise, then, that what Habermas finds wrong in Winch's account is the failure to recognize that the question of "the cognitive adequacy of worldviews—that is, the coherence and the truth of the statements possible in them as well as the effectiveness of the plans of action dependent on them"—is a legitimate one (*TCA*, 60). We can and should ask with Evans-Pritchard whether the contradictions that emerge within the Zande worldview and their "tolerance for a higher level of contradiction, [might be] a sign of a more irrational conduct of life," writes Habermas (*TCA*, 60). Only we should not do this—and here Winch was right and Evans-Pritchard, among others (e.g., Robin Horton), was wrong—according to whether they reflect science as the sole arbiter of the real or "promote a scientific mentality" (*TCA*, 62). To press the Zande to be more consistent is no "category mistake" (*TCA*, 60), as Winch called it, if it is done with an eye not to confirming "an uncritical self-interpretation of the modern world that is fixated on knowing and mastering external nature" (*TCA*, 66) but rather to being part of "learning-processes" (*TCA* 67). Such learning, as Jean Piaget teaches, "decenters" the "interpreted lifeworld" that is otherwise "im-

mune from critique," argues Habermas, and takes "the risk of disagreement that arises with every actual process of reaching understanding;
for communicative actors can achieve an understanding only by way
of taking yes/no positions on criticizable validity claims" (*TCA*, 70).

If Winch had addressed, as Habermas thinks he should have, "the
cognitive adequacy of worldviews," he would have been forced to conclude, with Evans-Pritchard, that the tolerance for contradiction exhibited by the Zande is grounds for judging their worldview irrational—irrational not because unscientific but because lacking in the capacity
for learning that is a distinctive mark of communicative rationality, in
Habermas's account. The question for Winch, however, is this: "What
criteria have we for saying that something does, or does not, make
sense?" ("UPS," 312). Although he would agree with Habermas that "a
set of beliefs and practices cannot make sense insofar as they involve
contradictions" ("UPS," 312), Winch is fully at odds with Habermas
about how these might be discerned. It is not, as Habermas claims, that
Winch believes it to be "illegitimate to press the demand for consistency further than the Azande of *themselves* do" (*TCA*, 60). That would
be to affirm the hermetically sealed idea of a worldview that Winch
(and Winch's Wittgenstein) will not underwrite but undermine. It is
that Winch does not believe, as Habermas clearly does, that it is possible and indeed necessary "to provide a *context-independent standard for
the rationality of worldviews*" (*TCA*, 62), albeit one that would not be
scientistic.

Understanding as Representative Thinking

To see why Winch's refusal to seek a context-independent standard
does not amount to entrapment in form-of-life relativism, let us return
to the title of Winch's essay, "Understanding a Primitive Society." The
call for *understanding* offers the key to what Winch took—and we might
take—to be the aim of his inquiry. Habermas himself momentarily recognizes this possibility when he observes that

after Winch's arguments have been examined and defused, something of his pa-
thos survives, to which we have not given its due: [quoting Winch] "My aim is not
to engage in moralizing, but to suggest that the concept of 'learning from' which is
involved in the study of other cultures is closely linked with the concept of *wisdom*."
Can't we who belong to modern societies learn something from understanding alternative, particularly premodern forms of life? Shouldn't we, beyond all romanti-

cizing of superseded stages of development, beyond all exotic stimulation from the contents of alien cultures, recall the losses required by our own path to the modern world? (*TCA*, 65)

Habermas recognizes, only to neutralize, what is at stake for Winch in not assimilating "learning from" the study of other cultures to learning how to take "yes/no positions on criticizable validity claims." Although he briefly cites Robin Horton on a similar point, for Habermas what is to be learned from Winch's general teaching, once the relativistic consequences of his argument "have been diffused," is that we should gain critical perspective on the "pattern of cultural and societal rationalization that helps cognitive-instrumental rationality to achieve a one-sided dominance not only in our dealings with external nature, but also in our understanding of the world and the communicative practice of everyday life." The problem of Western culture, in other words, "is not scientific rationality as such, but its hypostatization" (*TCA*, 66). That is what we can learn from the study of other cultures.

To say that this is a misreading would be to understate what is at stake. It is certainly true that the presumptions of modern science guided Evans-Pritchard, just as they had guided Frazer. But for both Winch and Wittgenstein there was much more involved in the critique of these anthropologists than exposing their scientism, just as there was much more involved in understanding the temptation of seeking the external standpoint that science held out. Scientism is not only the view that science and its method alone can produce knowledge and discern what is real; it is also a certain style of reasoning that leads us to think that we can somehow attain—and would need to attain— a place outside our own practices from which to see them as rational or not. There could be no place from inside our practice, language, or worldview, from which to judge. It was this understanding of scientism that led Evans-Pritchard and Frazer to assume that understanding a primitive society or its rituals was nothing other than deciding the question of whether one has the *right* based on legitimate qua external *grounds* to judge.

For Winch and Wittgenstein, the blatant scientism of Evans-Pritchard and Frazer covered over the failure to *understand* the alien cultures they studied, which in turn led to a failure of critical reflective judgment. To judge in this way, one must first attempt to understand an alien practice on its own terms, as difficult and partial as this may be from an outside perspective (i.e., one cannot "go native"). The irreducibility of understanding to judging is visible in Winch's response to Alasdair MacIntyre's interpretation of Evans-Pritchard and Frazer, which also figures in Habermas's account. Though critical of their scientism, MacIntyre endorses the idea that the rationality of Zande forms of life must be evaluated, explains Winch, "in terms of certain specific forms of life to be found in our culture" ("UPS," 319). As I have imagined Winch's possible response to Habermas's demand for a "context-independent standard," so too Winch responds to MacIntyre by saying that we simply do not have the criteria with which to judge.

Winch poses the question: how can we judge Zande magic to be riddled with contradictions if "*we* do not initially have a category that looks at all like the Zande category of magic"? ("UPS," 319). The Zande concept of magic is not at all like the Western concept of magic, which is defined in relation to a scientific conception of the world that the Zande lack.[36] But that is not what MacIntyre sees, or what we see. Assuming a symmetry if not identity of an abstract concept ("magic"), MacIntyre takes for granted that the Zande magical concept of "*A affecting B'*" is, according to Winch, "a sort of *hypothesis* like, e.g., an Englishman's belief that all the heavy rain we have been having is due to atomic explosions" ("UPS," 320). It is crucial to see here that Winch's critique goes to the heart of what is at issue for him in the purported attempt to understand a "primitive" culture. At issue is not that we have our conception of reality (e.g., of magic) and the Zande have theirs. It is that we cannot begin to understand the Zande conception—or our own—apart from its applications in the actual practical language games in which it is used. It is there in actual practice—and there only—that concepts can even be said to constitute our sense of reality. At the level of abstract concepts, wrenched from the contexts and practices in which they alone have meaning, we are misled to think we see identity where there may well be radical difference. As Evans-Pritchard himself said, Winch reports, "When a Zande speaks of witchcraft he does not speak of it as we speak of the weird witchcraft of our own history. Witchcraft is to him a commonplace happening and he seldom passes a day without mentioning it. . . . To us witchcraft is something which haunted and disgusted our credulous forefathers" ("UPC," 310). Though Evans-Pritchard sees that the Azande use the concept "witchcraft" in a radically different way than "we" do, he could not draw the consequences for his conception of reality. Instead, as Winch wrote, he "is trying to work with a conception of reality which is *not* determined by its actual use in language" ("UPS," 309). To admit the contrary—the constitutive relation between meaning and use that Evans-Pritchard implicitly recognized—would have deprived Evans-Pritchard of what his absolute conception of the world desperately needs, as Winch notes: "something against which that use can itself be appraised" ("UPS," 309). Only something external to the use of the concept and to the actual practices of its (scientific) appraisal could provide legitimate grounds with which to judge. But this, Winch shows, is illusory.

Winch's critique of Evans-Pritchard does not relinquish the possibility of judging an alien practice, assuming of course that judging begins with understanding, and understanding involves something other than *unreflectively* applying our conception of rationality, our criteria. Winch cautions, "But I do not want to say that we are quite powerless to find ways of thinking in our own society that will help us see the Zande institution in a clearer light. I only think that the direction in which we should look is quite different from what MacIntyre suggests" ("UPS," 320). For Winch, what Mikhail Bakhtin (as we saw in chapter 6) called "outsideness" is an enabling condition of critical judging; firsthand experience is not the irreducible condition for the "right" to judge. To paraphrase Cornelius Castoriadis's related remarks (in chapter 6), the ethnologist's raison d'être, according to Winch, is not to be assimilated to the Azande but to explain to the Parisians, the Londoners, and the New Yorkers of his own time the other humanity represented by the Azande. And this he can do only through the conceptual system of the Parisians, Londoners, and New Yorkers.[37] The task of Evans-Pritchard, in Winch's view, then, was never to "go native," as if judging the Azande practice of magic required jumping over one's own shadow.[38]

To suggest that Winch and Wittgenstein were primarily concerned with the question of whether we do (or do not) have a *right* to judge is already to prejudice our reading of them. Foregrounded in the notion of a "right" and its "grounds," as John Gunnell astutely observes of Evans-Pritchard and MacIntyre, is the idea that *"understanding an alien society required judging the extent to which its conception of the world was right or wrong."*[39] Let us hear this important remark in the right key, the key in which understanding is assimilated to judging and judging to deciding "right" or "wrong" (yes/no). The issue here is not only, as Gunnell rightly observes, that we can hardly avoid such a judgment when "we confront ideas that are outside our view [of] the world, and even abhorrent to us." As we saw with Susan Okin in chapter 6, the refusal to judge cultures not one's own is often politically untenable. Nor is it simply to be reminded that the central question is "whether the philosopher or other social investigator could call upon a neutral standard of judgment in deciding about the rationality of the values and beliefs of a particular society," as Gunnell likewise rightly contends.[40] The really radical question posed by both Winch and Wittgenstein, I submit, was not whether we have a right to judge or even whether we have neutral grounds; it was why we were inclined to think that *"understanding an alien society required judging the extent to which its conception of the world was right or wrong."* Was not this demand itself symptomatic of the very failure to understand, and ultimately properly to judge (critically and reflectively), in the first place?

Judging from Outside

To see how difficult it is to move outside the frame of reference in which the threat of relativism and the adjudication imperative (deciding the *right* to judge and on what *grounds*) structure what we take judging to entail, I now turn to Cora Diamond's essay, "Criticising from 'Outside.'" Diamond also accuses Winch of advancing form-of-life relativism, but in contrast to both Habermas and MacIntyre, she holds this account of worldviews to be unfaithful to Wittgenstein's own.[41] Anscombe's previous remark about Wittgenstein's stance toward alien language games and practices, argues Diamond, was not to underwrite but to contest the idea that, for him, a "conflict of irreconcilable principles" ("CO," 115) or worldviews can never be described in terms of a genuine (rational) disagreement or that "one would have no right to call erroneous the view that people in that other culture take" ("CO," 116). In short, "Wittgenstein is not committed to the view that you have to be 'moving within the system' [of an alien form of life] to call something that 'they' say error" ("CO," 116). But neither, I would add, was Winch—the real question is whether the claim to your "right" and "grounds" to judge something an error is based on a prior effort to understand alien concepts; that is, "the use they actually do have—*in* the language" ("UPS," 309).

Diamond's "Anscombian" example of principles that clash comes from *On Certainty*, and it describes (as did Winch's critique of Evans-Pritchard's encounter with the Azande) an encounter between someone who believes in the modern scientific principles of physics, which he holds to provide a comprehensive grammar of worldly explanation based on the ability to give a "good ground" for one's view, with people who consult oracles. Wittgenstein wonders:

Is it wrong for them to consult an oracle and be guided by it?—If we call this "wrong" aren't we using our language-game as a base from which to *combat* theirs?

And are we right or wrong to combat it? Of course there are all sorts of slogans which will be used to support our proceedings.

Where two principles really do meet which cannot be reconciled with one another, then each man declares the other a fool and heretic.

I said I would "combat" the other man,—but wouldn't I give him *reasons*? Certainly; but how far do they go? At the end of reasons comes *persuasion*. (Think what happens when missionaries convert natives.)[42]

Drawing out the absolute conflict that Wittgenstein describes "when two principles really do meet"—"The verb translated as 'meet' is *treffen*, so the image is of principles that hit each other; they do not miss each other; they do not pass each other by" ("CO," 119)—Diamond proceeds to describe what we are doing as a refiguration of the conflict in terms that create a new sense of reality and with it new grounds for moving beyond mere persuasion and for rationally judging which party to the conflict is right. Although each of the two principles belongs to a particular worldview, she writes,

In taking the two principles to *meet*, in taking them to be *irreconcilable*, we are giving a logical shape to the conflict; we are making a conception of reality, of what is real, that is not internal to either of the two forms of thought that provide the initial understanding of the conflict-situation. That is, we can take the situation here to be one in which what is real is contested; and this idea of *reality as contested* is a different notion of reality from that which is involved in either of the two forms of thought themselves. If the conflict is understood in this way, the *space* for the dispute between the two forms of thought is not given in advance; it is not provided by either of the two modes of thought that are in conflict. The articulation of what is at stake in the "meeting" of two irreconcilable principles is what *gives* the space. ("CO," 119)[43]

Claiming that "what counts as a reason in thinking about such conflict-cases is not given in advance of the conflict itself" ("CO," 128), Diamond affirms the "right" to judge an alien culture by rethinking what the rational grounds for external criticism might be. These grounds would originate wholly in neither of the two cultures whose principles clash but instead would be constituted in the attempt to make sense of the conflict. She compares this to a new mathematical proof in which we develop compelling reasons in puzzling through a problem: "The new method of proof is not there to be a standard in advance of the proof" ("CO," 120).

Diamond is not focused here on a particular belief in the sense of an opinion. She is concerned with the way in which contrasting conceptions of reality come into view and are questioned, and how other conceptions of reality emerge. She is tracking how we bring into our field of vision what Wittgenstein called the "hinge propositions" that form the ungrounded ground of our language of true and false. More precisely, Diamond would foreground how "hardened riverbed propositions" ("CO," 121) made of rock come to be less hardened ones made of sand and so on into something as fluid as the water itself, just as Wittgenstein's metaphor of how certainty can eventually turn into doubt suggests. For example, the belief in witches in parts of contemporary Africa, she argues, is part of a conception of reality according to which people are understood as having occult powers and being able to do things that we would characterize as a "system of false beliefs about what human agents can do" ("CO," 124). On that basis we would judge punishing witches "unjust": they cannot possibly have done what they are accused of doing. But this judgment is itself made possible by changes in the riverbed of European thought, according to which a principle that once was held fast by all that was around it yielded to developments that challenged not so much the belief in witches but the idea of human agency that underwrote that belief, that held it fast.

"I have not argued that the grounds for taking our worldview to be right vis-à-vis the witch-fearing, witch-finding cultures are grounds that would be found persuasive to all of *us*" ("CO," 128), writes Diamond. In other words, "the rational grounds for such a view" ("CO," 128) are not universal in the strong sense demanded by what Habermas called a *"context-independent standard for the rationality of worldviews"* (*TCA*, 62): they do not "have to be taken to be good grounds by anyone who understood them" ("CO," 128). But neither are such rational grounds immanent to what Winch says McIntyre called "specific forms of life to be found in our culture" ("UPS," 319), or so Diamond would claim. And they are certainly not immanent to the alien culture whose "universe of discourse" becomes, she argues, the sole standard of judgment for Winch.

Diamond leaves us wondering why the rational grounds she claims to create with her new conception of reality should be considered legitimate by anyone who did not already share them, not least the people whose (witchcraft) practice we judge "unjust." The assumption that such grounds *must* be accepted might provide a certain satisfaction for those involved in the new creation, but it is hard to see how it would actually alter the fraught political and social reality in which what is judged unjust actually takes place. Thus, Gunnell rightly wonders "who the 'we' is" here: who is the subject developing the different conception of reality that can serve as novel but compelling grounds for a judgment in Diamond's account?[44] He suspects that it is once again the philosopher who is tasked with "construct[ing] a mediating vision of reality."[45] I agree that the familiar image of philosopher as master adjudicator of social and political conflict lurks in the background of Diamond's scenario, but the problem may run even deeper.

Although Diamond claims that "what can be taken to be 'rational grounds' for criticising a worldview do not depend upon appeal to standards of what counts as rational available independently of and prior to the articulation of thought about conflicting worldviews" ("CO," 129), she falls prey to the same sleight of hand of which Winch accused both Evans-Pritchard and MacIntyre: a surreptitious equation of our conception of rationality for what rationality *is*. This happens despite Diamond's conscious effort *not* to impose a preexisting standard and her explicit rejection of the external standard as it is envisioned in the absolute conception of the world. Despite, because in her attempt to ask of Winch, "Why should there have to be an 'established universe of discourse?' Why can one not be making, giving articulation to, a kind of thought about reality *in thinking about the conflict* [of irreconcilable principles]?" ("CO," 119), Diamond wrenches these principles (whatever they might be) out of "the [practical and material] use they actually do have—*in* the language," as Winch put it ("UPS," 309), and sets them in a kind of Weberian war of the gods of ultimate values. The difference between Diamond and Max Weber, of course, is that Weber thought the conflict interminable because forever lacking rational grounds, whereas Diamond believes she has created those grounds with her new conception of reality.

Although Diamond's reading points in the direction of grasping how our conceptions of reality might be enlarged by understanding another culture, it yields, finally, to the traditional philosophical demand for grounds and drifts curiously into a kind of mentalist construal of what the creation of such grounds would actually entail. That a justly renowned Wittgenstein scholar such as Diamond too thought she needed to expose Winch's form-of-life relativism and develop the idea of "criticizing from the 'outside'" from within Wittgenstein's texts speaks to the tenacity of the adjudication imperative that I have argued to be the virtually undisputed frame of reference for the whole problem of judgment in modernity. Notwithstanding her lapse into the very idea of rationality that she would denounce, Diamond helps us see, as Weber never could, that there can be changes in our conception of what is real and what unreal, rational and irrational, and that such changes can come about through the experience of conflicting worldviews. With that prospect in mind, let us return to the idea of persuasion.

Persuading as Reasoning

Diamond's "Anscombian" critique of Winch began with a question about whether the persuasion that comes at the end of reasons could be considered right or wrong—that is, rationally grounded. Although she could have moved to an argument about the ways in which persuasion calls into question a certain philosophical conception of what rationality is, that is not what Diamond does. Instead she tries to save persuasion from its supposedly inferior status by folding it into what I have argued to be a fairly traditional conception of rational grounds. To move outside the framework in which understanding is assimilated to judging and judging becomes a search for rational grounds, then, we need to rethink the implicit demotion of persuasion in Diamond's reading of Wittgenstein—and she is far from alone here—to the mode of discourse we may adopt when we run out of rational grounds. Writes Gunnell:

Wittgenstein never suggested that when matters of disagreement arise, and we reach the end of our reasons and turn to persuasion, that persuasion is a move into some realm devoid of rationality, but only that we have reached the point where our prior reasons run out. Sometimes when missionaries sought to convert others to Christianity they turned to force, but other times they simply attempted to make their doctrines appealing to or even compatible with indigenous beliefs.[46]

To see how persuasion can remain rational while not figuring a ground in the traditional philosophical sense, we can turn briefly to Ernesto Grassi, who has critically discussed the place of rhetoric in the Western philosophical tradition. According to that tradition, when not viewed as outright deception that fully bypasses our reason, "to resort to images and metaphors, to the full set of implements proper to rhetoric," writes Grassi, "merely serves to make it 'easier' to absorb rational truth."[47] This is the view of rhetoric that has structured the critique of persuasion in Wittgenstein's work. Turning the tables on the tradition, Grassi questions both the claim that rhetorical speech is inferior to rational speech and the idea that there could be rational speech that was not itself based in rhetoric.

To prove [apo-deiknumi] means to *show* something to be something, on the basis of something. . . . Apodictic, demonstrative speech is the kind of speech which establishes the definition of phenomenon by tracing it back to ultimate principles, or *archai*. It is clear that the first *archai* of any proof and hence of knowledge cannot be proved themselves because they cannot be the object of apodictic, demonstrative, logical speech; otherwise they would not be the first assertions. . . . But if the original assertions are not demonstrable, what is the character of the speech in which we express them? Obviously this type of speech cannot have a rational-theoretical character.[48]

According to Grassi, "the indicative or allusive [*semeinein*] speech" that grounds philosophical or rational speech "provides the very framework within which the proof can come into existence" at all. This indicative speech, he continues, "is immediately a 'showing'— and for this reason 'figurative' or 'imaginative,' and thus in the original sense 'theoretical' [*theorein*—i.e., to see]. It is metaphorical; it shows something which has a sense and this means that to the figure, to that which is shown, the speech transfers [*metapherein*] a signification." Such speech "'leads before the eyes' [*phainesthai*] a significance." The basis of rational speech, then, "is and must be in its structure an imaginative language."[49] This conclusion radically alters the relationship of rational speech and rhetorical speech: "The term 'rhetoric' assumes a fundamentally new significance; 'rhetoric' is not . . . the technique of an exterior persuasion; it is rather the speech which is the basis of the rational thought."[50]

The rhetorical basis of rational speech, argues Grassi, is *sensus communis*: an agreement in judgments (not in opinion but in form of life) that is creative. *Sensus communis* "lies outside the rational process, within the sphere of ingenuity, so that it assumes an inventive character";[51] it is based on "the activity of *ingenium* [which] consists in catching sight of relationships, of *similitudines* among things."[52] These relationships are not given in the things themselves but are created through reasoning based in rhetoric. They "are *never eternally valid*, never absolutely 'true,' because they always emerge within limited situations bound in space and time; i.e., they are probable and seem to be true [*verisimile*], true only within the confines of 'here' and 'now,' in which the needs and problems that confront human beings are met," writes Grassi.[53] Whereas the deductive activity of logical reasoning "must restrict itself to finding what already is contained in the premises," *ingenium* is the art of invention.[54] It is the basis of persuasive reasoning whose ground is aesthetic.

With the rhetorical and material basis of rational speech in mind, we can now better understand what Wittgenstein means when he writes, "at the end of reasons comes *persuasion*." Persuasion comes after reasons, we might now justly speculate, not because persuasion is not rational but because what is rational has its figurative or aesthetic "ground" in what persuades. Perhaps this is why the original German reads: *"Am Ende der Gründe steht die Überredung"* (At the end of reasons stands persuasion). Persuasion does not so much *come after* reasons run out but *stands* there, as it were, where it always was: as the ungrounded ground of the reasons we give. We do not take refuge in persuasion because we have run out of reasons, as if persuasion were by definition a derivative and ultimately vastly inferior form of argumentation. Should one insist on thinking about the relation in linear terms, persuasion is not what comes after but what comes before; it is what lends the reasons we give their reasonableness—that is, their convincing character. Where reasons cannot convince, come to an end, we have no longer a figure that can persuade as part of a practice in which, as Grassi put it, "the needs and problems that confront human beings are met."

Ian Hacking's essays in *Historical Ontology* on "styles of reasoning" offer a related lens through which we might further pursue this alternative account of persuasion.[55] Though Hacking does not elucidate the figurative element in any particular style of reason, his emphasis on style foregrounds the creative character of reasoning akin to Grassi's rhetorical conception. It also provides an alternative to Davidson's analytic philosophical critique of conceptual schemes, which Hacking (like Taylor) fears are "founded upon a lack of concern for alternative interests" (*HO*, 172). Davidson's focus on the truth of sentences and their translatability into another language, observes Hacking, neglects how it is that something becomes a candidate for truth in the first place: "for part of our language, and perhaps as part of any language, being true-or-false is a property of sentences only because we reason about those sentences in certain ways" (*HO*, 174). Indeed, the "truth of a proposition in no way explains our discovery of it," or its status as "a standard item of knowledge. Nor does being a fact, nor reality, nor the way the world is" (*HO*, 192). Rather, the truth of a sentence (of a kind introduced by a style of reasoning) is what we find out by reasoning using that style. Styles become standards of objectivity because they get at the truth. But a sentence of that kind is a candidate for truth or falsehood only in the context of the style. *(HO, 191)*[56]

Hacking strongly distinguishes his account from "constructivism," for which facts are not there to be discovered until constructed as such. For Hacking, by contrast, "if a sentence is a candidate for truth or falsehood, then by using the appropriate style of reasoning we may find out whether it is true or false" *(HO, 191–92)*.

There are ways of thinking whose style of reasoning are so radically different from our own that "we cannot even recognize their objects. The renaissance medical, alchemical, and astrological doctrines of resemblance and similitude are well-nigh incomprehensible" *(HO, 170)*. The same can be said, adds Hacking, of "witchcraft" *(HO, 195)*. These now "dead" or "extinct" styles are not so much incommensurable with our modern scientific styles of reasoning in the sense that the truth of propositions do not match up with our own; rather, "the way the propositions are proposed and defended is entirely alien to us" *(HO, 170)*. How propositions are defended takes us not to the abstract concepts of, say, "magic" or "witchcraft" that occupied the energies of Evans-Pritchard and his many critics (save Winch), but rather to the concept as it is actually used *in* the language as part of a style of reasoning from which it gains and gives meaning. Alien to us are what Cavell (as we saw in chapters 1 and 2) called the "patterns" (of objection and support) that make various discourses (e.g., scientific, aesthetic, political, and moral) rational—rational, that is, as we have come to understand it through our own engagement with those patterns in everyday contexts. In other words, we are unable to recognize the process of reasoning qua reasoning; we cannot see how what "they" call reasoning could yield an objective account of reality.

Undaunted by the relativist scare, Hacking boldly asserts what I take Wittgenstein and Winch to have been arguing:

We cannot reason as to whether alternative systems of reasoning are better or worse than ours, because the propositions to which we reason get their sense only from the method of reasoning employed. The propositions have no existence independent of the ways of reasoning towards them. *(HO, 175)*

To those (such as Habermas) who would seek a "context-independent standard," Hacking says: there can be "no external justification" for any style of reasoning, "an independent way of showing that the style gets at the truth" (HO, 175, 175–76).

The question arises as to whether Hacking has pulled the rug out from under any attempt to defend the possibility of criticizing an "alien" society or "alien" styles of reasoning. When cast in the now familiar terms of the adjudication imperative that has framed the debate over judging, the answer must be yes. But if seen through the lens of understanding that Winch proposed—which I would now align with the "creative understanding" described by Mikhail Bakhtin (discussed in chapter 6)—then the possibility of criticizing what is "alien" or simply strange can be soundly affirmed. Understanding an "alien" society is not reducible to "judging the extent to which its conception of the world was right or wrong," as MacIntyre and Evans-Pritchard assumed; it is grasping, initially through an act of imagination and later through new practical efforts, the different style of reasoning that generates candidates for judgments of what is true and what is false.[57] As Hacking explains,

Understanding the sufficiently strange is a matter of recognizing new possibilities for truth-or-falsehood, and of learning how to conduct other styles of reasoning that bear on those new possibilities. The achievement of understanding is not exactly a difficulty of translation, although foreign styles will make translation difficult. It is certainly not a matter of designating translations which preserve as much truth as possible, because what is true-or-false in one way of talking may not make much sense in another until one has learned how to reason in a new way. One kind of understanding is learning how to reason. (HO, 171)

Understanding the style of reasoning that guided the Zande belief in oracles or witches, for example, is not comparing the propositions that "match ill with our modern sciences" (HO, 170). Winch's and Wittgenstein's respective critiques of the shared scientism of Evans-Pritchard and Frazer, we recall, recognized that it covered over a more general failure of imagination and understanding. This failure was surely ethical, but it also marked a cognitive (read: rational) inability to grasp what the real differences in propositions and conceptions of reality were. Thus it failed, and failed even on its own terms of affirming what was objectively real. Rather than compare what the Zande took for true with what we "moderns" take for true, we need to "recreate the thought" of those whom we wish to understand, writes Hacking. We need to enter into the lives in which words alone have meaning. Only by grasping their chains and styles of reasoning can we make visible "the inherited background" of our picture of the world, as Wittgenstein put it, "against which I distinguish between true and false."

When we take account of different styles of reasoning and in this way try to understand the worldviews in which they have their life, we are not placed wholly outside the system of concepts we are trying to understand. The picture that holds us captive here, explains John McDowell, looks like this:

> When we work at making someone else intelligible, we exploit relations we can already discern between the world and something already in view as a system of concepts within which the other person thinks; so that as we come to fathom the content of the initially opaque conceptual capacities that are operative within the system, we are filling in detail in a sideways-on picture—here the conceptual system, there the world—that has been available all along, though at first only in outline.[58]

Such a picture underwrote the idea of worldviews as virtual prison houses of language and leads back to the idea of a conceptual scheme with which we began. It portrays a general philosophical misunderstanding of how we come to acquire the ability to understand alien concepts. But the world is not something "out there" to be "represented" by concepts whose incommensurability we at once see and try to make sense of; rather, the world is already in view. McDowell continues:

> The mistake is not to give proper weight to this fact: in the innocuous sideways-on picture, the person we do not yet understand figures as a thinker only in the most abstract and indeterminate way. When the specific character of her thinking starts to come into view for us, we are not filling in blanks in a pre-existing sideways-on picture of how her thought bears on the world, but coming to share with her a standpoint *within* a system of concepts, a standpoint from which we can join her in directing a shared attention at the world, without needing to break out through a boundary that encloses the system of concepts.[59]

Just this way of understanding a primitive society is what Winch, *pace* his many critics, thought we could do and should do. And his guide in these matters was Wittgenstein.

Beyond Form-of-Life Relativism

The idea of a worldview as *internally* composed of different styles of reasoning undercuts the static prison-house-of-language account of worldviews that drove the critique of Winch as a relativist. If "each style introduces a great many novelties, including new types of objects . . . [and] ways of being a candidate for truth or falsehood" (*HO*, 189), as Hacking contends, then the notion of a worldview as something closed, something that cannot be questioned from within its own standards of rationality, must be untenable. Winch too questions the idea, which he ascribes to MacIntyre, that what can count as intelligible within any particular worldview is limited to a particular inherited "stock of descriptions" for making sense of human action. If we want to understand how the stock of descriptions can change over time—a point MacIntyre's account of "the thread of rational criticism in human history" (quoted in "UPS," 316) seeks to explain—we need only look to "the further development of rules and principles already implicit in the previous ways of acting and talking" ("UPS," 316). A worldview is open to changes in what can count as intelligible. What Wittgenstein called "grammar" is not a closed set of descriptions but an open structure of meaning, insists Winch, through which "new ways of talking and acting . . . may be introduced" ("UPS," 316). Novelty is possible because, as Cavell showed us in chapter 1, to speak a language is to be able to project a word into new contexts. The point is not that "anything goes," and we are free to make things up as we go along. It is rather to "emphasize the *open* character of the 'rules,'" explains Winch, such that "the intelligibility of anything new said or done does depend in a certain way on what already has been said or done and understood" ("UPS," 316), without limiting what *can* emerge to what already *is* (or, to what grammar via some shared subjectivity or universal human "mindedness" makes possible in logical space).

To say that "worldviews have the power to structure a whole life" and that "the kind of dissensus that can *reasonably* be expected" is one that makes "any further attempt to reach a consensus after all meaningless or even dangerous" (*TJ*, 227), as Habermas does (and as Rawls's idea of "comprehensive doctrines," examined in chapter 5, also assumes), is to foreclose the possibility that we could transform the style of reasoning and so also the rhetorical basis that holds particular bedrock judgments fast. Though we cannot doubt an entire worldview as such (for the condition of all doubt is certainty), surely our sense of what is true and what false, what is real and what unreal, what counts as evidence, and so on, is not static.

The idea that worldviews are uncriticizable "cozy, self-contained conceptual cocoon[s]," as Gellner accused, is what Wittgenstein's image of certainty as a riverbed composed of varying degrees of hard rock, softer sand, and flowing water contests. "There is not a sharp division of the one from the other," Wittgenstein wrote, suggesting that there is no proposition so fundamental, so hardened, that it could never be understood by a stranger, or subject to critique and change, from within or without.[60] As Putnam states,

Recognizing that there are certain places where one's spade is turned; recognizing, with Wittgenstein, that there are places where our explanations run out, isn't saying that any particular place is *permanently* fated to be "bedrock", or that any particular belief is forever immune from criticism. This is where my spade is turned *now*. This is where my justifications and explanations stop *now*. To recognize that a loyal human being is better than a disloyal human being, . . . that a person capable of a sense of community, of citizenship in a *polis*, is better than a person who is incapable of a sense of community or of citizenship in a *polis*, and so forth, is not to say that any one of these values . . . is final, in the sense, of being exclusively or exhaustively correct.[61]

Looking for where justification *actually* runs dry, rather than positing a kind of intracultural uniformity at bedrock (be it based in a unified human subjectivity, the common behavior of humankind, or any other overly unifying concept) and the form-of-life-relativism it implies, requires that we look in specific contexts and in dialogue with specific interlocutors, learn new styles of reasoning. As Barry observes, there is no good reason to assume that justification will reach its limit at the same level. "It is much more reasonable to suppose that the different forms of life ('narrowly construed' [i.e., as different language games]) will each reach their own limit of justification and that there are, therefore, thresholds of access between them."[62] These thresholds of access among different forms of life "are put into interaction with each other by *people* (not 'subjects'). This is to use the notion of a 'person' as more open and less philosophically constrained than that of a 'subject,'" Barry adds.[63]

Thinking about a form of life as a closed subjectivity on the order of the philosophical conception of "Man in the singular," as Arendt put it, can lead us to assume that for there to be any intelligible traffic between different forms of life, there must be something they already have in common before we so much as look and see what they might have in common. And though Wittgenstein and Winch (no more than Arendt) would not rule out the possibility that there certainly are common features to human life (e.g., the capacity for language, the ability to hope, the basic structure of our bodies) and certain rudimentary responses, neither of them casts these as foundational in the sense of guaranteeing understanding across cultures or a unified "we." In other words, the transcendental idea of the human as a sort of "mindedness," as exhibiting the shared "perceptions of salience, routes of interest, etc.," need not be seized on to ward off form-of-life relativism. Instead, we can think of forms of life with Cavell as a "whirl of organism."

As we saw in chapter 1, Cavell described this "whirl of organism" in terms of the plurality of language games whose standards of correctness are immanent to the actual human practices or activities themselves. Though it is the justified source of our confidence in our ability to make sense, to know how to go on and thus to act rationally, this whirl of organism tends to incite a sense of vertigo, as John McDowell put it, "induced by the thought that there is nothing that keeps our practices in line except the reactions and responses we learn in learning them."[64] By contrast with the idea of mindedness (and all the other unifying concepts in the philosophical arsenal against form-of-life relativism), Cavell, I argued, seemed to offer little more than a lucky convergence of subjectivities, held together by a grab bag of affective sensibilities that can hardly make a claim to the kind of objectivity required to speak of following a rule as a normative practice. How would we know that we are *really* going on in the same way? How can we know that what we are doing has any correct relationship to reality at all?

Returning to this "whirl of organism," we can now see why it would indeed be better "not to have felt the vertigo in the first place," as McDowell wryly notes, for it almost inevitably leads to self-defeating attempts to transcend that whirl of organism in some kind of artificial unity.[65] Winch did not feel the vertigo—perhaps that alone irritates his critics most. He defended the idea that "a primitive system of magic, like that of the Azande, constitutes a coherent universe of discourse like science, in terms of which an intelligible conception of reality and clear ways of deciding what beliefs are and are not in agreement with this reality," while maintaining that this defense, as he states, "would not commit me to accepting as rational all beliefs couched in magical concepts or all procedures practiced in the name of such beliefs" ("UPS," 309). And though Winch rightly pointed out that such a commitment was "no more necessary than is the corresponding proposition that all procedures 'justified' in the name of science are immune from rational criticism" ("UPS," 309), critics will still want to know on what basis can he possibly claim to have the right to his critique, to his judgment: what, in short, are his grounds?

Like Cavell, Winch finds in Wittgenstein an alternative to the idea that there is only one way of making sense, which had been expressed in the *Tractatus* in terms of the general form of propositions: "This is how things *are*." The demand that something must guarantee normativity that led readers such as Habermas to think of a form of life as ethnographically static, rather than as dynamic and potentiality world-opening, is once again what Wittgenstein sets out to question as he moves away from what Winch sees as the earlier view. Such a unified understanding of rational meaning, argues Winch, is what guided Evans-Pritchard's judgment that "the European is right and the Zande is wrong" ("UPS," 313), which Winch found "illegitimate" and as exhibiting a genuine failure to understand. Winch explains:

By the time Wittgenstein composed the *Investigations* he had come to reject the whole idea that there must be a general form of propositions. He emphasized the indefinite number of different uses that language may have and tried to show that these different uses neither need, nor in fact do, all have something in common, in the sense intended in the *Tractatus*. He also tried to show that what counts as "agreement or disagreement with reality" takes on as many different forms as there are different uses of language and cannot, therefore, be taken as given *prior* to the detailed investigation of the use that is in question. ("UPS," 313)

Questioning his earlier tendency to speak "of 'language,' as if all language is fundamentally of the same kind and must have the same kind of 'relation to reality'" ("UPS," 313), as Winch describes it, Wittgenstein would famously admonish philosophers not to assume that there *is* something in common, but rather to "Look and See!"

Far from endorsing form-of-life relativism, denying the right or the grounds to judge other cultures, Winch's self-declared attempt "to make intelligible in our [modern] terms institutions belonging to a primitive culture, whose standards of rationality and intelligibility are apparently quite at odds with our own" ("UPS," 315), rests in the end on an account of language and rules that is radically more creative and open than those of his critics, including Diamond. It is interesting to note that Diamond, claiming to go beyond Winch's relativism, overlooks the way in which Winch himself attempts to bring an "alien" concept of intelligibility into dialogue with "our" concept of intelligibility. Winch writes:

We have to create a new unity for the concept of intelligibility, having a relation to our old one and perhaps requiring a considerable realignment of our categories. We are not seeking a state in which things will appear to us just as they do to members of S [an "alien" society], and perhaps such a state is unattainable anyway. But we *are* seeking a way of looking at things which goes beyond our previous way in that it has in some way taken account of and incorporated the other way that members of S have of looking at things. Seriously to study another way of life is necessarily to seek to extend our own—not simply to bring the other way within the existing boundaries of our own, because the point about the latter in their present form is that they *ex hypothesi* exclude the other. ("UPS," 317–18)

Winch's effort at "grasping forms of rationality different from ours in an alien culture" ("UPS," 318)—in a word, understanding—is directed not (not at first) at judging whose form is correct but, rather, at getting the shared world in view. But doing so requires seeing it from other points of view, thinking representatively: seeing Zande magic, for example, not as an irrational instrument to manage, say, crop production, but as a way of responding to life's "contingencies"—that is, the "recognition that one's life is subject to contingencies, rather than an attempt to control these" ("UPS," 321). Viewed in these terms, Zande magic might give us critical purchase on the principles of consumption and mastery that organize our own relation to external nature that include but go beyond the critique of scientism. Such seeing might lead us to grasp "ways of dealing with misfortunes" that, though they do not include magic, turn on the shared problem of how to respond to the "disruptive effect[s] . . . [that contingencies and misfortunes have] on a man's relations with his fellows, [and] with ways in which life can go on despite such disruption" ("UPS," 321).

The inability to see Zande magic as anything but primitive science or an irrational attempt to control external events is a kind of "aspect blindness," to borrow Wittgenstein's phrase, an inability to "see something as something" that reflects not only a failure of imagination and effort to understand a "primitive" society on its own terms but a more general failure of critical self-reflection (*PI*, p. 213). Winch clarifies:

MacIntyre speaks as though our own rules and conventions are somehow a paradigm of what it is for rules and conventions to have a point, so that the only problem that arises is in accounting for the point of the rules and conventions in some other society. But in fact, of course, the problem is the same in relation to our own society as it is in relation to any other; no more than anyone else's are *our* rules and conventions immune from the danger of being or becoming pointless. ("UPS," 321)

Far from a brief for cultural relativism and a declaration of incommensurable rationalities or forms of life, "Understanding a Primitive Society" should be read as a call for us to reflect critically on our own practices and norms. We should recognize them as bound up with our own interests and desires and yet subject to rational critique and judgment. For a growing group of contemporary political theorists, as we shall see in the next chapter, just this assumption should be questioned.

NINE

The Turn to Affect and the Problem of Judgment: Making Political Sense of the Nonconceptual

The approaches to judgment that we have explored in previous chapters differ in a number of ways, yet they all share the conception of judgment as a fundamentally rational practice. And though what counts as rationality varies, thinkers from Kant to Winch take for granted that our affective propensities work in tandem with our reason in judging. This assumption has been questioned throughout the history of philosophy and political theory by skeptics and noncognitivists, who argue that some judgments (e.g., value judgments) or even all judgments lack rationality. But they held to the conception of rationality that Bernard Williams described as the absolute conception of the world, which is to say that they still had an operative conception of rationality to which a judgment must conform if it is to count as rational.

In a certain strand of contemporary theory, the entire idea of rationality as the basis for judgment is questioned if not rejected as wholly illusory. As we saw in chapter 1, the recoil from rationalist approaches to judgment, especially neo-Kantian accounts, has been characterized as an "affective turn." Among other sites of inquiry, affect theorists unsettle strict cognitivist conceptions of the liberal subject and rationalist ideals of politics. In an effort to account for the tenacity of entrenched forms of (gender, racial, and class) power in an era of formal legal and political equality, they explore the nonrational bases of political attachments that impede progressive social transformation.[1]

As a feminist critic of strict cognitivist models of politics, I appreciate aspects of the recent extension of the affective turn into my own field of political theory.[2] I recognize as important the challenge to conceptions of liberal democratic and feminist politics that rely on exaggerated ideas of human autonomy and reason and that remain in the grip of what ordinary-language philosopher Stanley Cavell has called the "epistemological quest." Like ordinary-language philosophy, affect theory rightly questions the inherited Western philosophical idea that the fundamental relation of human beings to the world and to others is one of knowing—or at least what we think of as knowing. Exposing the complex ways in which citizens as embodied beings practically navigate their built environments, both schools of thought complicate this inherited view of human thought and action and open a space for imagining practices of democratic citizenship in terms that diverge from those laid down by the rationalist (neo-Kantian) approaches that continue to dominate contemporary political thinking.

In this chapter I explore how the approaches to judgment advanced in theories of affect both resonate with and, in certain ontological iterations, depart from the conception of judging elaborated in the ordinary language philosophy that I have associated with the philosophical tradition after Wittgenstein as developed and extended by Cavell.[3] My aim here is not to provide a comprehensive review of the now extensive literature in affect theory, nor is it to engage closely with any particular thinker. Rather, it is to draw out the intimations of the more recent ontological turn to affect for critiques of the epistemological ideal described by Cavell or what, following ordinary language philosopher Gilbert Ryle, I referred to in previous chapters as "intellectualism" or the "intellectualist doctrine." Bequeathed by Descartes, it is a doctrine, we recall, that tends to treat all aspects of human thought and action in terms of cognition. Accordingly, our orientation to the world is wholly conceptual, with *conceptual* understood here in the specific sense of the mental grasping of true propositions: practical knowledge (knowing how) is reducible to conscious theoretical knowledge (knowing that). On this view, you must *consciously* know that something is the case before you can know how to do it. I am interested in how a certain way of formulating and responding to the problem of intellectualism animates approaches that go under the sign of affect theory.

Far from the radical departure from modern philosophical accounts of human action and judgment that its advocates often claim it to be, affect theory can be read as another chapter in a familiar debate about the relationship between conceptual and nonconceptual modes of orientation to the world. More precisely, affect theory extends a critique of conceptual rationality as inherently situation-independent and disembodied that has roots in the phenomenological tradition.

Rather than equate conceptual rationality with what phenomenologist Hubert Dreyfus calls "the Myth of the Mental," ordinary language philosophy offers a way to refute intellectualism without sliding into a philosophically debatable and politically fraught nonconceptualism.[4] A ordinary-language critique of intellectualism, as I shall try to develop it further in this chapter, would advance an understanding of intelligent action and judgment in which affect and reason are understood to be mutually imbricated in modes of conceptuality, rather than distinct. To see them as distinct—or, as I shall put it, as occupying separate ontological layers—is to remain entangled in the Cartesian conception of the subject as a disembodied intellect that affect theory and phenomenology would have us refuse. Ordinary-language philosophy allows us to see that there are better and worse ways of arguing the anti-intellectualist case and, in so doing, to raise pressing questions about the stakes for democratic feminist politics in the idea that "much of perception and judgment is prior to consciousness," as political theorist William Connolly puts it.[5]

"Knowing That," "Knowing How," and the Critique of Cartesian Dualism

The critique of the intellectualist view of judging (and acting) that serves as the departure point for affect theorists of all stripes has deep roots in the phenomenological tradition. Martin Heidegger and Maurice Merleau-Ponty, to name just two legendary figures, are said to have foregrounded what Dreyfus, speaking on behalf of that tradition, calls "the nonconceptual embodied coping skills we share with animals and infants."[6] According to Dreyfus's architectural metaphor, "overcoming the myth of the mental" entails a challenge to the intellectualist conceit that "philosophers [can] successfully describe the conceptual upper floors of the edifice of knowledge while ignoring the embodied coping going on on the ground floor; in effect declaring that human experience is upper stories all the way down." Contemporary neo-

Kantians such as John McDowell, argues Dreyfus, "claim that perception is conceptual 'all the way out'" and in this way remain trapped in the intellectualist inheritance. Any serious response to this inheritance would affirm conceptuality to be an "upper story" that is supported by a "ground floor" of nonconceptual but intelligent bodily experience.[7]

Dreyfus's claim that the mind is simply absent at the basic level of embodied experience—that is, that in unreflective, practical activity, mental functions yield to a more fundamental, bodily, and nonconceptual mode of orientation to the world—seems to resonate with the work of Ryle, who famously attacked "the intellectualist legend" in his 1949 tour de force, *The Concept of Mind*. According to intellectualism, human capacities count as enabling of intelligent behavior only if they are "somehow piloted by the intellectual grasp of true propositions" (*CM*, 26). The intellectualist assimilation of "knowing how" to "knowing that," argued Ryle, is caught in a vicious regress, whereby "acting intelligently requires a prior action of considering a proposition, and considering a proposition intelligently requires a prior action of considering a proposition intelligently," and so on in an infinite number of prior actions, as Jason Stanley summarizes Ryle's account.[8] Sarcastically noting that "intelligent practice is not a step-child of theory" (*CM*, 26), Ryle went on to distinguish knowing how from knowing that. Intelligent action of some kind (e.g., knowing how to swim, how to cook, how to play chess) does not require that we engage in a prior mental act of consulting a proposition, in Ryle's view (and in the view of the now extensive literature in epistemology, philosophy of mind, critical theory, and political theory that has taken up some version of the knowing that versus knowing how distinction).

Ryle's distinction between knowing how and knowing that represents an enduring contribution to debates on rule following and the ongoing critique of Cartesian dualism, which finds two of its most important contemporary expressions in neurobiology (in science) and affect theory (in the humanities). Broadly speaking, these critiques of the intellectualist model extend—even as they radically transform— Ryle's insight. As affect theory critic Clive Barnett argues, they are based on "a widely shared intuition that propositional 'knowing-that' is a function of embodied 'knowing-how.' Once it is acknowledged that 'knowing-how' involves all sorts of learned, embodied dispositions that are inscribed in various types of 'unconscious' disposition of anticipation and response, then theoretical traditions that are too partial to a picture of a social world governed by rules, principles and practices of reason seem constricted or even wrong-headed."[9]

On the face of it, then, the recent turn to affect takes place on the larger historical terrain carved out by an otherwise diverse group of postfoundational thinkers, including existential phenomenologists and ordinary-language philosophers, all of whom conceive of propositional knowledge (knowing that) as connected to a indefinitely heterogeneous complex of dispositions and abilities (knowing how).[10] This shared background, however, obscures what I shall argue to be crucial differences regarding the idea of nonconceptuality or embodied coping as the proper response to intellectualism.

The idea of knowing how as embodied coping has had great appeal for feminists (including me) who are interested in how social norms are taken up and reproduced through the repetition of unconscious ordinary modes of skilled embodied comportment.[11] The knowing that/ knowing how distinction offers a valuable vocabulary for challenging rationalist approaches to power and social identities by making visible the everyday practices through which heteronormative ideals of gender are reproduced and challenged in embodied experience. Attention to knowing how or the attainment and exercise of skilled bodily comportment can facilitate critiques of the atmosphere of naturalness in which normative gender identities are housed.

As important as the idea of embodied knowing how has been for interrogating rationalist models, I now think democratic and feminist thinkers should question it. Claims about "the nonconceptuality of social norms" that characterize phenomenological accounts of intelligent behavior have given way to an unbounded celebration of nonconceptualism in affect theory, with reason playing an increasingly minimal and in any case ineffective role in critical judgment.[12] Could it be that what was once a useful corrective to intellectualist accounts of human practice has become yet another "picture that holds us captive," to paraphrase Wittgenstein, to the way things *must* be?

To open a space in which we might better assess the consequences of embracing nonconceptualism as if it were the only alternative to intellectualism, I want to question the assimilation of ordinary-language philosopher Ryle's knowing that/knowing how distinction to Dreyfus's phenomenological difference between mentalism and embodied coping. We could read Ryle as arguing that cases of knowing how do not fit the strictly intellectualist picture of propositional knowledge, not because knowing how is nonconceptual but because the strictly intellectualist conception is a wrongheaded account of conceptuality or propositional knowledge that mistakes a narrow range of cases of knowledge with the general case.[13]

The Concept of Mind does not so much refute the idea that conceptual or cognitive capacities are at work in knowing how as it rejects the intellectualist conception of what the use of those capacities entails. On this more unfamiliar reading, Ryle's main target is not propositional knowledge or conceptualism as such but, as Robert Stalnaker writes, "an intellectualist picture of propositional knowledge—one that tends to identify propositional knowledge with conscious awareness of a linguistic expression of a proposition that corresponds to the fact that one knows."[14] It is just this intellectualist picture of conceptualism that holds us captive—captive to the nonconceptualist alternative that is really the flip side of the intellectualist idea that the concepts involved in propositional knowledge must be consciously grasped by the mind before any action can be taken. Keeping open the possibility that our conceptual or cognitive capacities normally do not require conscious awareness, we will be able both to appreciate the specific ways in which affect theory and ordinary-language philosophy criticize the intellectualist view and to question the stark distinction between affect and reason that characterizes affect theory in some of its ontological iterations and—of particular interest to me here—feminist and democratic appropriations.[15]

Within the ordinary-language strand of theory represented by Ryle and (albeit differently, as we shall see) by Wittgenstein, we do not have concepts as mental entities. We learn what things are through action. To know that *this* is a chair is to know how to do things with chairs: how to sit on them, arrange them in a circle, offer them to guests, decorate one's space with them, and so on. By foregrounding the background of "affective dispositions and desires" against which such practical reasoning takes place, affect theory (as one among many postfoundational theories) "could be expected to reconfigure what, following Ryle, we might call 'the logical geography of action [and judgment],'" writes Barnett ("PA," 188).[16] And in certain iterations of affect theory, this reconfiguration not only obtains but is deepened to take a far more nuanced account of affective dispositions than most postfoundational thinkers have done, and certainly more than Ryle ever did.

Within the feminist affect theory literature, for example, the groundbreaking writing of Eve Kosofsky Sedgwick complicates the debate over queer publics and the need to develop reparative practices of reading in relation to affects such as shame.[17] Lauren Berlant develops a historical and literary account of the formation of affective publics that brilliantly tracks how attachments to certain objects can facilitate but also cripple emancipatory projects—what she has most recently called "cruel optimism."[18] And Sara Ahmed, in her essay "Happy Objects" in *The Affect Theory Reader*, powerfully explores how feelings of happiness and unhappiness, "good feelings" and "bad feelings," can carve out an affective landscape that allows "historical forms of injustice to disappear" (*AT*, 50). These and related affect theorists, such as Heather Love and Ann Cvetkovich, can productively be read in tandem with the extensive literature in feminist and democratic political theory that explores the nonrational emotions and sentiments that influence the formation of democratic publics, political judgment, and practices of legitimation.[19] Notwithstanding important differences, affect as a field of study shares with this literature a concern to expose the lingering Cartesian assumptions that shape modern theory, keeping it tethered to an unwarranted dualism of body and mind, affect and reason. The shared critique of rationalist models does not create a new hierarchy (affect over reason) but rather insists on the irreducible entanglement of thinking and feeling, knowing that and knowing how, propositional and nonpropositional knowledge.

Put another way, the aforementioned authors "all focus on the affective aspects of life *without* adopting a vocabulary of ontological layers," to speak with Barnett ("PA," 189). It is just this vocabulary that distinguishes the rather different form of affect theory that shall concern me in the next part of this chapter.

Layer-Cake Ontologies of Affect and Reason

The productive overlap described in the previous section between affect theory and democratic political theory on the central role played by nonrational sentiments and feelings in political life indicates a shared understanding of the affective character of reason and cognition that is seen by some affect theorists as interesting but not innovative. When understood as an attempt to theorize embodied subjectivity, certain iterations of the affective turn, argues Patricia Clough in her essay "The Affective Turn" in *The Affect Theory Reader*, "extended [rather than transformed] discussions about culture, subjectivity, identity, and bodies begun in critical theory and cultural criticism under the influence of poststructuralism and deconstruction" (*AT*, 206).[20] Indeed, "in the early to mid-1990s," Clough continues, "many of the critics and theorists who turned to affect often focused on the circuit from affect to emotion, ending up with subjectively felt states of emotion—a return to the subject as the subject of emotion" (*AT,* 207). Rather than make a clean break with these already established attempts to foreground "the subject's discontinuity with itself," affect theory may have deepened but in any case continued them (*AT,* 206).

The real challenge to Cartesian intellectualism, or so it would seem, was not the work of thinkers who turned to affect qua emotion but those who understood, as Clough describes it, "affect as pre-individual bodily forces augmenting or diminishing a body's capacity to act and who critically engage those technologies that are making it possible to grasp and to manipulate the imperceptible dynamism of affect" (*AT,* 207). Inspired primarily by the work of Gilles Deleuze (and his reading of Baruch Spinoza), "the most provocative and enduring contribution of the affective turn," argues Clough, is to be found in the work of those writers who focus on affect but do not follow "the circuit from affect to emotion, ending with subjectively felt states of emotion" (*AT,* 207). Whatever their differences, the "autonomy of affect"—a phrase coined by Brian Massumi and associated variously with the nonrepresentationalist theory of Nigel Thrift; with the political affect theory of John Protevi and the neuropolitics of Connolly; and with the new materialist sexual difference theory of Elizabeth Grosz, the neurological body of Elizabeth A. Wilson, and the biomediated body theory of Clough herself, among other thinkers—does not simply deepen but radically refigures the critique of intellectualism as described thus far.[21] Its distinguishing mark is its ontology.

Broadly speaking, the ontological innovation that breaks the circuit tying affect theory to poststructuralism and other theoretical predecessors is what Barnett (citing Robert Brandom) calls a "layer-cake interpretation of the relationship between practice and expression."

Layer-cake interpretations present propositional intentionality as resting upon a more basic level of pre-conceptual, practical intentionality in such a way as to present propositional intentionality as derivative of this layer of practical attunement. On this view, the practical presupposition of the available, ready-at-hand qualities of environments in embodied actions that treat these environments as merely occurrent, or present-at-hand, is interpreted as implying an order of *conceptual priority* of the practical. This model of conceptual priority puts in place a view of practical attunement as a stratum that is autonomous of propositional intentionality. It is treated as a layer [as Brandom writes] that "could be in place before, or otherwise in the absence of the particular linguistic practices that permit anything to show up or be represented as merely *there*." ("PA," 188)[22]

The reinterpretation of the postfoundationalist foregrounding of "knowing how" against the intellectualist focus on "knowing that" in terms of layer-cake ontologies of practice, then, involves a crucial departure from the thought of ordinary-language philosophers and existential phenomenologists, who show not only that propositional intentionality is entangled in and unthinkable apart from practical intentionality but also that there is no sharp line between unarticulated knowing how and explicit knowledge. As I have already suggested in relation to Ryle and shall develop more closely with Wittgenstein, what is unarticulated (i.e., prepredicative), however, is not by definition non-conceptual, not in the way that Dreyfus argued it to be for the phenomenological tradition (about which there can be some dispute). The key point I wish to develop now is that affect theory has radicalized the phenomenological idea of nonconceptual embodied coping, radicalized it in such a way that the latter no longer supports but instead undermines rational judgment and claims to knowledge.

According to this layer-cake version of affect theory, affect is not a synonym for feeling, emotion, or sentiment, expressions of which are semiotically mediated and at once public and personal (as Wittgenstein shows in his private language argument).[23] That was the so-called error of theorists who turned to affect only to reinstate the subject as the subject of emotion. Affects are not understood in this ordinary sense. Expressions of autonomic bodily response, affects take place below the threshold of conscious awareness and are, to speak with Donald Nathanson, "completely free of inherent meaning or association to their triggering source."[24] Affect theory critic Ruth Leys explains:

For both the new affect theorists and the neuroscientists from whom they variously borrow . . . affect is a matter of autonomic responses that are held to occur below the threshold of consciousness and cognition and to be rooted in the body. What the new affect theorists and the neuroscientists share is a commitment to the idea that there is a gap between the subject's affect and its cognition or appraisal of the affective situation or object, such that cognition or thinking comes "too late" for reasons, beliefs, intentions, and meanings to play the role in action and behavior usually accorded to them. The result is that action and behavior are held to be determined by affective dispositions that are independent of consciousness and the mind's control. ("TA," 443)

Affect is seen, then, as a distinct layer of experience that is both prior to and beneath language and intentional consciousness, an irreducibly bodily and autonomic force that shapes, without the subject's awareness, conscious judgment. As Connolly puts it, "Affect is a wild card in the layered game of thinking [acting and judging]."[25]

Affect matters politically in the view of Thrift, Connolly, and Protevi because it forms a new means through which "masses of people become primed to act."[26] All three thinkers agree that the determining force of affect on cognition and judgment takes place in "the half-second delay between action and cognition."[27] The manipulation of affect, then, becomes the central mechanism for securing the status quo. If a striking feature of any false ideology is its resistance to rational revision, one can see why this account of affect as a form of unconscious priming would have significant explanatory power, not least for feminists, who have struggled to make sense of the tenacity of gender oppression in the face of increasing critiques of prevailing gender norms.[28]

The problem is not that oppressed groups consider feeling or its availability for manipulation when accounting for such tenacity—that is something that feminists in particular have been doing in their various ways for decades, and rightly so. Instead, the problem is that the theory of affects as radically outside meaning and signification and free of their triggering source leaves us with no way to link an affect to the judgment the affect presumably primes.[29] "Tactical work on dispositions installed below consciousness" and the "application of techniques" to populations with the aim of promoting new forms of responsiveness, which is put forward as a strategy of resistance, must pale in the face of the kind of manipulation that is described.[30] Indeed, it is difficult to see how there could be any political resistance at all. The "wild card" of affect has lost any connection to our power of judgment: affect and cognition are posited as being two different systems, entirely distinct. This is the shared anti-intentionalism that Leys has identified as being at the nexus of neuroscience and affect theory, exemplified in the work of Connolly. Insofar as intentionality entails the relationship of thought to the world or the power of the mind to represent and be about something in the world (properties, states of affairs, etc.), the radical separation of cognition and affect, argues Leys, leaves us with no way to connect affective experience to anything in the world that could possibly be symbolized or shared by others. *Affect* would be in this view no better than a private language in Wittgenstein's critical understanding of that term, on the order of the classical philosophical conception of pain.

When we think about propositional intentionality as derivative of practical attunement, as the layer-cake model of affect theory invites us to do, we are drawn into a way of thinking about action and judgment as the mere effects of already primed dispositions, for which the giving of reasons is little more than window dressing on what was going to happen in any case. The layer-cake model fully elides the aspect of embodied knowing that involves the capacity to take part in the language game of giving and asking for reasons. Affect theorists such as Connolly, argues Barnett, are "cryptonormativists"—that is, individuals who have political views (such as the value of democracy) that they cannot defend in any meaningful way because reasons, in their account, always trail after affect-driven preferences ("PA," 195). Leys, too, is critical of the politics of affect theory, although she sees the problem as one of an inability to take a normative position at all ("TA," 452). Preferring democracy to despotism or feminism to patriarchy is like preferring coffee to tea; there is no rational basis from which we could possibly agree or disagree. An affect-driven preference, then, is really no better than an avowal, a merely subjective matter of taste—only now the subject of taste itself has been dissolved into the inhuman anonymity of affective forces.

Problems with the Critique of Anti-Intentionalism

I agree with Leys that the anti-intentionalism of affect theory wrongly reduces cognitivism to "the human capacity for producing linguistic propositions" ("TA," 470). But if we want to understand the break with the earlier theorizations of affect in which the relation to conceptuality still played some role, we need a clearer account of this misconception—what Ryle called "intellectualism"—than what is offered by either Leys or Barnett.

Leys—and the same could be said for Barnett—seems to think that the corrective response to affect theory would reaffirm a proper understanding of intentionality. Replying to Connolly's response to her essay, Leys writes, "From my perspective, intentionality involves concept-possession; the term *intentionality* carries with it the idea that thoughts and feelings are directed to conceptually and cognitively appraised and meaningful objects in the world. The general aim of my paper is to propose that affective neuroscientists and the new affect theorists are thus making a mistake when they suggest that emotion or affect can be defined in nonconceptual or nonintentional terms."[31] Commenting on Leys's reply, Charles Altieri remarks that "one does not have to share William Connolly's vitalist affiliations" to question her account of intentionalism, which refuses to countenance the possibility that "there are diverse and valuable forms of nonconceptual emotions and that these are present in moods and in esthetic experiences."[32]

Why does Altieri (or any of the related theorists we have been discussing) think he *has* to insist on experiences outside the sphere of the conceptual? Responding to the anti-intentionalism of affect theory by insisting on the irreducibility and ubiquity of intentionality qua concept possession, Leys never seriously entertains this question and more or less ignores the worries that pull affect theorists, like phenomenologists, in the direction of nonconceptualism.[33]

Leys's critics would affirm the reality of experiences that exceed our conceptual capacities. For them, it simply cannot be that "to have the ability to notice a sort of thing is already to have the concept of that sort of thing," as Wilfrid Sellars famously put the Kantian idea of intentionality as concept possession.[34] Our ability to discern fine shades of color, for example, when having the aesthetic experience of gazing at, say, Claude Monet's *The Gardens at Giverny*, seems far more capacious than our ability to name what we see. Surely our perceptual experience exceeds color concepts such as "red," "green," "lilac," or even "burnt sienna." The intentional encounter with an object elaborated by Sellars seems to involve the situation-independent subsumption of an intuition under a concept in what Kant calls a determinative judgment.[35] The judged particular ("*this* shade") is the mere instantiation of a general kind ("red"). Regarding this Kantian picture of intentionality as concept possession, how would we know whether our concepts are really responsive to the heterogeneous, embodied character of human experience, truly open to the world? How could we ever come to discern anything new in the world at all? These are the sorts of worries that are raised in affect theory, just as they are in phenomenology. Although ordinary-language philosophy will help us answer them without taking flight into nonconceptualism, such worries must first be understood as expressions of long-standing philosophical issues about the relationship of "mind and world" that are not answered by reiterating intentionality as concept possession.

These issues (of the new, of singular reference, of embodied responsiveness) circle around the central question of what it means to-be-in-the-world and to-be-open-to-the-world. Though the anti-intentionalism Leys decries was surely radicalized in layer-cake ontologies of affect, I have suggested that its roots lie in the nonconceptualism of the embodied coping celebrated by Dreyfus as the lasting achievement of the phenomenological tradition and ascribed—wrongly, in my view—

to ordinary-language philosophers such as Wittgenstein, Cavell, and Ryle. (I also think it is ascribed wrongly to existential phenomenologists such as Heidegger, but that is another story.) The key difference is that in theories of affect, nonconceptual embodied coping is no longer in the service of any rational action or judgment at all. But that danger was in some sense implicit in the architectural model of understanding proposed by Dreyfus, according to which the upper conceptual floor of human understanding rests on a ground floor of "absorbed coping" that is outside the scope of conceptual rationality.

The danger was already implicit because, as Dreyfus sees it, the upper floor is not continuous with the ground floor but is rather a radical transformation of it.[36] Although this phenomenological account of the relationship between conceptuality and nonconceptuality does not adopt the ontological layers of affect theory—that is, in keeping with the metaphor, there are stairs leading up from the embodied realm of mute attunement to the rational mental space of concepts—it nonetheless claims that what takes place on those upper floors amounts to "situation-independent" or "detached" rule following. Given this understanding of conceptuality as strictly intellectualist, it follows that any attempt to foreground the role played by our embodied affective propensities would require a radical undoing of the notion of rational conceptuality itself. Put another way, it is not just a matter of questioning whether "all intelligibility [is] *rational* intelligibility, or is there a form of intelligibility characteristic of our skilled bodily engagement with the world that falls outside the reach of reason," to borrow Joseph Schear's formulation of what is at issue in the McDowell–Dreyfus debate.[37] Any answer to that question will be based on what one thinks "rational intelligibility" or "conceptuality" necessarily entails. Only then will we be able to make sense of Leys's claim that "intentionality involves concept possession."

Though I too question the view of affect and embodied coping skills as nonconceptual—and here I agree both with Leys against her critics and with McDowell against Dreyfus—we need a better understanding of the temptation to embrace nonconceptuality as the *only* adequate response to intellectualism. If the fascination with neuroscience, for example, that characterizes the work of affect theorist Connolly is shared by phenomenologist Dreyfus, that may well be because both are responding to similar concerns about what conceptualist models of intelligent action and judgment must entail. For both thinkers, what is conceptualist is by definition strictly intellectualist (i.e., fully detached from embodied affective propensities). Can ordinary-language philosophy respond to these concerns without yielding to the temptation of nonconceptualism as the only real response to intellectualism?

The temptation to posit a nonconceptual given as the basis—either enabling or not—of intelligent action and judgment, I have argued, stands as the shared response of affect theorists and phenomenologists to what they both take to be the situation-independent and detached quality of conceptual rationality. Within phenomenology, the nonconceptual given would include those forms of skilled bodily engagement with the world for which we have and need no words; within affect theory, the nonconceptual includes "all those processes that are separate from meaning, belief or cognition and that occur at the level of autonomic, pre-conscious bodily reactions, responses and resonances," as Lisa Blackman puts it.[38]

Now if intentionalism involves a mode of concept possession that does not necessarily entail intellectualism, what might that be? Can we speak of affective propensities in ways that are conceptualist but nonintellectualist? Taking the basic case of perception, we might turn to Wittgenstein's reflections on the phenomenon of aspect dawning in part 2 of *Philosophical Investigations*, which offers a way to describe the conceptual character of our prepredicative mode of being in the world. Wittgenstein's remarks on aspects takes up the startling experience of seeing a (gestalt) figure suddenly as, say, a duck when one has seen it all along as a rabbit. Since the object has not changed, how can we explain our change in view?

Wittgenstein's account takes up various explanatory models including physiological, empiricist, and subjectivist. None of these approaches adequately explains the peculiar experience of what he calls "noticing an aspect." Against the empiricist, for example, Wittgenstein argues that the change in perception does not originate with a genuine change in the object. He also counters the view that ordinary acts of perception (expressed in the statement "I see a picture rabbit") entail interpretation ("I am seeing the picture rabbit as a picture rabbit")— that is, the application of concepts to a bare given. As Stephen Mulhall explains, what appeared at first to be an investigation into an extraordinary experience of aspect dawning (suddenly seeing the rabbit as a duck) turns out to be a critical examination into the ordinary practice of seeing, one that brings out the irreducibly conceptual character of all embodied experience.[39]

Wittgenstein shows how we simply take for granted the status of certain objects; that is, we continually see them under an aspect (e.g., a rabbit or a duck) in an entirely unmediated way. We do not normally interpret what we see ("I see it as a duck but it could also be a rabbit") but immediately grasp the object before us. Situations may arise in which we interpret (e.g., when the lighting is bad, when playing a game with gestalt figures), but in the normal course of events, we simply see the duck or the rabbit. The idea that we must interpret what we see, that there is something that mediates an indirect relationship of mind to world (inner images or representations, for example) is part of an idea of intentionality that Wittgenstein shows to be illusory: "One doesn't 'take' what one recognizes as the cutlery at a meal *for* cutlery; any more than one ordinarily tries to move one's mouth as one eats, or aims at moving it" (*PI*, II, xi, §123).

The immediate grasping of objects can appear to be nonconceptual; after all, we are hardly seeing things neutrally and then bringing them under concepts in what Kant called a "determinative judgment." The very idea of judgment here can seem out of place. There is a skilled embodied comportment at work when one uses cutlery, not a detached practice of rule following. Just this thought leads thinkers such as Dreyfus, Charles Taylor, and others to assimilate Wittgenstein to the phenomenological tradition of embodied coping. And although it is right to say that the use of cutlery does not involve a subsumptive practice of rule following, it does not necessarily follow that the skilled ability to eat with a fork and a knife is nonconceptual.

The conceptuality of embodied coping is what Wittgenstein reveals through the initially nonordinary example of the gestalt figure. The dawning of an aspect (e.g., "Now it's a rabbit!"), Wittgenstein shows, is based not on a change in the object but in the use of another concept. On the nonconceptual reading, this nonordinary example is when concepts come first into play. But this reading misses what Mulhall shows to be the crucial insight afforded by way of the nonordinary example. That I *now* see the picture as a rabbit reveals that I *had* been seeing it as a duck all along—that is, according to a concept. Ordinary embodied coping involves seeing and dealing with things continually under aspects—that is to say, conceptually. That the use of concepts that belongs to the prepredicative act of seeing is not intellectualist (in the way criticized by Ryle and associated with all conceptual thought by Dreyfus) becomes clear in the distinction Wittgenstein draws between interpreting and seeing. As Mulhall explains, "It is one of the fundamental aims of Wittgenstein's treatment of aspect perception to show that aspect-dawning and continuous aspect perception are a matter of seeing *rather than* interpretation. For Wittgenstein, the notion of interpretation carries connotations of making inferences, forming hypotheses or drawing conclusions—as if when someone sees a friendly glance in another's eye, what really happens is the direct perception of shapes, colours, and movement which are then interpreted to mean that the glance is a friendly one."[40] We see the friendliness of the gaze as immediately as we see the color of the eye. Interpretation happens when our dealings with the world turn intellectualist, not conceptualist.[41] Interpretation is the making explicit of the as-structure that already accompanies our otherwise ordinary skillful and conceptual embodied coping. Interpretation is, as it were, the intellectualist case of being-in-the-world that gets mistaken for the ordinary case.

That our ordinary embodied coping is conceptual does not mean that we have words ready at hand to describe the practice in which we are engaged. The capacity to predicate our experience of continuous aspect seeing is just that: a capacity, not a condition of the seeing itself. To say that our experience already possesses the "as-structure" is just to say that it is conceptual, not that it must be immediately available in propositional form, as cognitivism would have it. The idea that our everyday affective experiences must be strictly propositional to be conceptual is tied to a way of thinking about rules and rule following that Wittgenstein questions: "There is a way of grasping a rule which is *not* an *interpretation*, but which is exhibited in what we call 'obeying the rule' and 'going against it' in actual cases" (*PI*, §201).

Intellectualism and Rule Following

The pervasive sense that affective embodied coping is nonconceptual is linked to the idea that to be conceptual, the correct application of concepts would have to follow rules that are fixed independently of the affective responses and reactions of judging subjects. This view of rule following is at the core of the intellectualist legend that Ryle mocked as the untenable idea that prior deliberation or interpretation is necessary for embodied rational action, which in his view leads to an infinite regress of rules.

Competence with a concept in any intelligible judgment entails the practice of going on to do the same thing. As already suggested in chapter 1, the classic temptation here is to think about this practice as fixed by rules that are like ideal tracks or rails along which any correct rule-governed activity must run. Taking the hard case of mathematical necessity (the "logical *must*"), Wittgenstein first exposes and then undermines the mistaken source of our confidence in thinking that anyone who understood the rule (e.g., "Add two") would be compelled to go on in the right way. Following the view in question, once the rule is properly grasped (i.e., the judging subject's psychological mechanism engages the rails of the rule), it is a mere mechanical matter of churning out the correct answers for the extension of a series. Whether conceptualized with the rationalist (as transcendent forms) or with the empiricist (as contingent learned behavior), the view here is that if a pupil has understood the instruction "Add two"—that is, if the pupil starts the series with 100 and continues with 102, 104, 106 . . . and that is what "to understand" means—then the pupil is not free to continue in some other way, say, with 110. To claim that 110 is the correct next step is illogical, for the pupil has already demonstrated an understanding of the rule (i.e., the pupil's mental wheels have been engaged). Thus on pain of logical contradiction, the pupil *must* write 108. In response to the construal of the errant pupil as mistaken, perverse, or insane, Wittgenstein explains, "If my reply is: 'O yes of course, *that* is how I was applying it!' or: 'Oh! *That's* how I ought to have applied it—!'; then I am playing your game. But if I simply reply: 'Different?—But this surely *isn't* different!'—what will you do? That is: somebody may reply like a rational person and yet not be playing our game."[42]

In this passage, comments Barry Stroud, Wittgenstein "tries to show that not all cases of deviating from what we expect or from what we all do in continuing the series can be put down to simple misunderstanding, stupidity, or deliberate perversity on the part of the pupil."[43] The point is not to question the awry calculator's mental state, let alone to set in motion a familiar philosophical skepticism about "other minds" (i.e., the possibility that the rule-following behavior of others might come adrift). It is to show that the confidence we have in the outcome of the rule "Add two" is not based on the existence of a psychological mechanism that grasps an independently existing rule—but that does not mean we are wrong to be confident, only that the source of our confidence is misplaced.

The problem, then, is how to get the proper ground of our justified confidence in view, and doing so requires interrogating the traditional intellectualist conception of what could possibly count as the ground of going on to do the same thing. Cavell has urged us to understand the basis and nature of our confidence in terms of the "whirl of organism" Wittgenstein calls "forms of life."[44] And though it would appear to embrace just this "whirl of organism," the nonconceptualist understanding of embodied coping ends up curiously denying that affective sensibilities could play any normative (conceptual) role in judgments at all. Where there is judgment, there is no affect—or, to put the same point another way, where there is affect, there is no judgment. Intellectualism holds that "judgment is everywhere pure sensation is not, which is to say everywhere," according to Maurice Merleau-Ponty.[45] But this, too, is illusory. Both the intellectualist and the nonconceptualist positions are hostage to the same idealized view of rules and rule following: what *must* be the case for judgment to get off the ground. It expresses our being captive to the picture that to judge is to follow rules and the rules really must be independent rails, or they are nothing at all.

What Wittgenstein teaches us is not to deny the "logical *must*," mathematical necessity, as a mere phantasm of a sensation of compulsion. It is not to deny that 1,002 really does follow 1,000 according to the rule "Add two." Rather, it is not to misunderstand the source of necessity or the perspective from which it is discernible. We are engaged in a practice, and it is from within the midst of this embodied affective practice, this "whirl of organism," that we rightly expect 1,002 to come after 1,000 and that we can so much as recognize the correct move as such. Our reliance on forms of instruction that appeal to our contingent, affective responses seems like a departure from conceptual rationality only if we assume that we could occupy an abstract vantage point from which all such responses could be seen as intrinsically distorting.[46] The intellectualist denies that feeling can be normative at all. Wittgenstein and Cavell give us a contrasting view.

"Knowing by Feeling"

The idea that affects and emotions should be theorized in nonintentional terms, we have seen, is shared by certain iterations of affect theory and phenomenology. Although I have agreed with Leys that one does not need to treat all thought as conscious to retain the idea of intentionality, I am also concerned with complicating the intellectualist understanding of conceptual rationality that mistakes one narrow case for the general case.

Returning to the problem of judgment, we recall that anti-intentionalism threatened to reduce all judgments to subjective preferences. And yet affect theorists such as Connolly who defend the nonconceptual character of experience clearly see themselves as advancing critical accounts of the ways in which the nonconceptual character of affect is manipulated to uphold the status quo. Rather than accuse them of being "cryptonomativists," we might try to understand how the attempt to foreground the affective dimension of judgment need not require denying the place of concepts in embodied experience. The question left unanswered by affect theorists is how a judgment based on feeling could possibly be normative.

The relationship between affect and normativity animates Kant's account of aesthetic judgments in the third *Critique*. Aesthetic objects, as Cavell showed us in chapter 2, "are *known by feeling*, or *in* feeling."[47] Working through the ordinary-language idea of "what we say," Cavell was struck by the similar sense of necessity that accompanies claims to taste—that is, judgments whose peculiar validity is based not on a property of the object but only on the feeling of pleasure or displeasure in the judging subject. The claim "I like canary wine," Kant explains, expresses what is "agreeable," a merely subjective preference. By contrast, the claim "This painting is beautiful" posits the assent of all: everyone who sees *this* painting *ought* to agree. It would be "ridiculous," writes Kant, to say that it "is beautiful *for me*"—for then one should not use the word "beautiful" (*CJ*, §7, p. 55/98). The expectation of universal assent belongs to the grammar of an aesthetic judgment just as it does to the ordinary-language philosopher's claim to what we say.

The "subjective validity" described in the third *Critique*, I have argued with Cavell, is not unique to taste but belongs to all evaluative judgments. Calling attention to agreement in "patterns of support," rather than conclusions, as the crucial element in rational argument, Cavell showed us how we misunderstand the difference between evaluative judgments, on the one hand, and empirical or logical judgments, on the other. "Our ability to judge a priori the communicability of the feelings that (without the mediation by a concept) are connected with a given presentation" (*CJ*, §40, p. 162/176), as Kant initially defines the reflective judging that characterizes taste and Cavell then extends to describe all evaluative judging, should not be understood as nonconceptual. For reflective judging is rational: "A judgment of taste is indeed based on a concept, but on an *indeterminate* one" (*CJ*, §57, p. 213/216), as Kant clarifies his earlier point. Rather than being subsumed under a determinate concept, a particular intuition has the form of what Kant calls a "concept in general" or a "concept as such." In other words, it exhibits something akin to the prepredicative as-structure that characterizes Wittgenstein's notion of seeing an aspect.

There is ample room for creative work on the rational role played by affective propensities in conceptualist accounts of being open to the world.[48] The problem of singular reference mentioned earlier, for example, need not follow from the conceptualist view that I have been trying to defend. Among other concerns, affect theorists and phenomenologists worry about the loss of the particular in its subsumption under a concept; with this worry in mind, they defend a nonconceptualist approach to human practice and judgment. As we have seen, the sense is that there are experiences that fall outside the sphere of the conceptual, experiences that concepts either cannot accommodate or—worse—distort.

In answer to my earlier question about why phenomenologists and affect theorists think they need to locate experiences outside the sphere of the conceptual, I have argued that their worries (about novelty, singular reference, embodied responsiveness) are important but based on a misunderstanding of what conceptual rationality entails. To return to the example of color sensibility, the worry about singular reference need not lead us to object to the idea that unique perceptual episodes are conceptually articulated because the general nature of concepts does not by definition exclude the possibility that concepts can be as "fine-grained" as any particular shade of color. What makes the experience of a particular color shade "conceptual," as McDowell explains, is not that it can be captured by a general concept such as "red" or even "burnt sienna," but that when we speak of *"that* shade," we have in mind something that is just as "fine-grained" as our perception of the color sample; we attend to that shade as having the general form of a concept.[49] This ability to recognize *"that* shade" is no private language but a conceptual capacity, he continues, that "can in principle persist beyond the duration of the experience itself. . . . into the future . . . and that, having persisted, it can be used also in thoughts about what is by then the past."[50] In this way we use *"that* shade" normatively to go on to do the same thing, to follow a rule in Wittgenstein's ordinary sense.

In concluding this chapter, I would like to speak directly to the question of what ordinary-language philosophy might offer feminist and democratic thinkers, many of whom have embraced various versions of nonconceptualism as it is presented in phenomenology and in affect theory. I suggested earlier that the idea of embodied coping and a nonconceptual know how or practical knowledge has played an important role in critical efforts to explain the tenacity of regimes of power, including heteronormative gender difference. There is something fundamentally unconscious about the ways in which individuals conform to and thus reproduce normative concepts of identity. And yet the assumption that what is not conscious, present in the form of propositional knowledge, must be nonconceptual remains tethered to an intellectualist view of what conceptuality entails. By contrast with affect theory, ordinary-language philosophy offers no new ontology but instead brings to light the misunderstandings upon which our sense of the need for this new ontology is based. Just because our affective experiences do not take propositional form does not mean that these experiences are nonconceptual. The thought that they must be nonconceptual is captive to an intellectualist conception of what conceptuality must entail—namely, the kind of detached rule following that Dreyfus associated with the "Myth of the Mental." Likewise critical of Cartesian dualism, ordinary-language philosophy invites us to think of affectivity as the irreducible element in the "whirl of organism" that Cavell showed us to characterize not the nonconceptual but the normative dimension of embodied thought and action.

Drawing on the resources of ordinary-language philosophy, we need to think about the stakes for feminist and democratic politics in the idea that much of perception and judgment takes place without our conscious awareness. It is not as if no discourse prior to affect theory ever asserted such a thing—psychoanalysis comes to mind—but the manner in which this idea of what is subthreshold is formulated has radically changed.[51] That change in manner is partly because the idea of affect as something working behind our backs, as it were, structuring or even determining our judgments before we so much as know that we are making them, was not conceptualized in such radically anti-intentionalist terms—that is to say, as devoid of meaning or signification. For affect theorists, affect and cognition are two entirely different systems. But does this split view not rely on an entirely false picture of the mind/body relation, one that turns out to be parasitic on the very dualistic account that it would undercut?

Ryle memorably characterized the Cartesian image of the human as the "dogma of the Ghost in the Machine," a bifurcated thinking yet embodied being living "two lives" and in "two worlds" (CM, 15–16, 12). "In consciousness, self-consciousness and introspection," such a being remains "fully authoritative." Although this being "may have great or small uncertainties about concurrent and adjacent episodes in the physical world ['including his own body']," writes Ryle, he "can have none about . . . what is momentarily occupying his mind" (CM, 12). In their ongoing efforts to criticize this ghostly figure, critical thinkers such as feminists, affect theorists, and phenomenologists might draw on the resources of ordinary-language philosophy to avoid unwitting entanglement in it and wrestle instead with investigating the conceptual dimensions of embodied experience.

Although I have agreed with Leys and other critics that affect theory remains entangled in Cartesian dualism and its many intellectualist temptations, I hope to have shown that a critical response must do more than reaffirm intentionality—the relation of thought to its objects—in one or another of the ways now familiar in the philosophy of mind. Affect theory is an attempt to explain the tenacity of oppressive social norms and to hold out the possibility of a novel and politically progressive response. It raises the key question (mentioned earlier) that preoccupied David Hume: why are some of our beliefs resistant to rational revision? Affect theory provides a plausible account of affective priming that certainly has foundation in broader literatures such as social psychology.[52] The basic argument about priming, in other words, is neither new nor controversial; it is, rather, how this idea of priming is understood.

The "layer-cake" strand of affect theory remains caught in the Humean view that irrational thought and belief reflect our psychological makeup, even as it would dispute Hume's claim that genuinely rational thought in certain realms of life is still possible. Although it does not adopt the absolute view of the world on which the fact/value distinction is based, affect theory nevertheless takes for granted that our affective nature and response leads us into the arms of false ideologies. While trying to explain the persistence of social injustice, however, affect theory formulates the problem in terms of a kind of unconscious priming that loses track of whatever it is in the world that primes us thus. This is because, I submit, in affect theory the material status of objects has fully given way to the subjectivist idea that all we have are our perspectives or affective interpretations. Whereas Hume's embrace of the distinction between primary and secondary qualities made comparatively clear the distinction between "what in my experience of an object is a function of my perspective and what in my experience of it is not due to perspective," as James Conant writes, by the time we get to (post-poststructuralist) affect theory, this distinction has long been lost.[53] The self-proclaimed project of recovering the materiality of affect in the face of poststructuralist reductions of everything to language enters a discursive philosophical space in which the very idea of a cut between what is merely subjective and what belongs to the fabric of reality no longer exists. And not just the idea of this cut, which belongs to the absolute conception of the world that Hume embraced and a democratic theory of judgment must reject, but the idea that something could be objective that can only be experienced as subjective—that is, in terms of its effects on sentient beings.

To conclude, we might say that because it then fully severs the link between affect and judgment, save as a fundamentally unknowable relation of priming, affect theory leaves us stranded when it comes to judging politically understood as entailing the revision of irrational beliefs, especially democratically problematic beliefs such as those that undermine basic political principles of equality, freedom, and social justice. We should remain skeptical, as Claire Hemmings cautions, of the "theoretical celebration of affect as uniquely situated to achieve this [politically progressive] end."[54] The unpredictability of affect, its lack of connection with any object, raises pressing questions about its role in a critical political practice.

We can pursue the idea advanced by affect theorists that judging cannot be understood as a disembodied practice, as the intellectualist doctrine would have it. But if reflective judging is a kind of knowing by feeling or in feeling, as Cavell parsed the Kantian account, it does not proceed nonconceptually. Affect and cognition are not two different systems but radically entangled. To see this entanglement, we need to rethink knowing how as a form of knowing that, to speak with Ryle, but also knowing that as a practice of knowing how. Can we describe the radical entanglement of affect and conceptual rationality in a way that keeps their mutual imbrication from sliding into always already affectively primed responses, on the one hand, or always already conceptually determined responses, on the other hand? This is the real problem—the problem of critical judgment—raised at once by and for affect theory.

Judging as a Democratic World-Building Practice

In a July 11, 2010, *New York Times* editorial titled "Veiled Threats," Martha Nussbaum addresses the controversy around European bans on headscarves, full-face or full-body veils, and specifically the burqa.[1] Such legislation, she argues, violates the fundamental liberal democratic principle that "all human beings are equal bearers of human dignity" who ought to be treated with equal respect. Freedom of conscience includes "both freedom of belief and freedom of expression and practice," she asserts. Arguments about the importance of revealing one's face in a democracy or about security (e.g., bank robbers or terrorists disguised in burqas) don't stand up to comparative analysis.

What is wrong with both of these arguments is that they are applied inconsistently. It gets very cold in Chicago—as, indeed, in many parts of Europe. Along the streets we walk, hats pulled down over ears and brows, scarves wound tightly around noses and mouths. No problem of either transparency or security is thought to exist, nor are we forbidden to enter public buildings so insulated. Moreover, many beloved and trusted professionals cover their faces all year round: surgeons, dentists, (American) football players, skiers and skaters. What inspires fear and mistrust in Europe, clearly, is not covering per se, but Muslim covering.[2]

Arguments about the degradation or physical well-being of women are similarly suspect. If comfort is the issue, then let us ban "high heels, delicious as they are"; if the burqa is held to be a "degrading prison," what of our own "degrading prison of plastic surgery?" And so on. "Once again, then, the opponents of the burqa are utterly inconsistent, betraying a fear of the different that is discriminatory and unworthy of a liberal democracy. The way to deal with sexism is by persuasion and example, not by removing liberty," concludes Nussbaum.[3]

Striking in Nussbaum's response is how her own judgment of full-cover veils as implements of (Islamic) "sexism" is itself concealed in a comparative feminist list of the undeniable sexism that is rampant in the West. The problem is not that her list exemplifies the "relativism" that we have already (in chapter 6) seen Nussbaum attack but that it takes for granted that we are dealing with similar objects. Is the burqa really *like* high heels or plastic surgery? Is it *like* the face coverings of dentists or Chicagoans wrapped up in winter scarves? And, finally, is wearing a burqa really *like* the practical expression of "freedom of conscience" that belongs to "human dignity" in a liberal democratic society? To ask these questions is not to deny that such comparisons might work as part of a deliberate and compelling Western feminist rhetorical strategy to get critical purchase on one's own practices. Rather, it is to suggest that Nussbaum's approach to judging might fully bypass the problem of understanding practices of veiling and in turn occlude the basis of the judgment whose ethnocentricism and sexism such comparisons were meant to illuminate.

The theoretical framework of Nussbaum's argument is the political liberalism of John Rawls. Since we live in a society characterized by the empirical "fact of a plurality of reasonable but incompatible comprehensive doctrines," as Rawls states in his *Political Liberalism*, it is not "reasonable" for any one "community" (i.e., people who share a worldview, a "comprehensive doctrine") to declare publically their beliefs as true (*PL*, xvii). As we saw in chapter 5, this is a core element of the "burdens of judgment" in modern liberal democracies, and it is central to the political liberal conception of objectivity based on what is reasonable according to the principle of justice as fairness. When it comes to what really matters, however, the interdiction on public claims to the truth of one's belief can be hard to practice and almost inevitably invites its own violation. "For of course I do believe that men and women are truly metaphysically equal, and that the equality of black and white is a *fact*, and so on," writes Nussbaum. "Why shouldn't we say that this political judgment is grounded on deep facts about what human beings are?"[4] She explains:

I believe that the equality of male and female is a metaphysical fact, but if some-one's religion says otherwise, I believe this view should be respected, *provided that* this person is prepared to sign on to (and genuinely, not just grudgingly, affirm) the political doctrine that men and women are fully equal as citizens—with all that follows from that, including fully fair equality of opportunity, guarantees of nondis-crimination even in private employment, equal access to the basic goods of life, and so forth.[5]

Why must the affirmation of political equality be endorsed "genu-inely, not just grudgingly"? As Nussbaum observes, to sign on to politi-cal equality genuinely means you affirm it "as reasonable basis for po-litical life," whereas to sign on to it grudgingly means you affirm it as a mere *"modus vivendi."*[6] A modus vivendi is too thin a basis on which to support equality; it rests agreement about political principles not on justice but on self-interest.[7] One might wonder, however, what the *gen-uine* affirmation of gender equality can mean for someone who thinks, in accordance with a particular comprehensive doctrine, that men and women are not equal. One can imagine why such a person might *be-have* in accordance with the equality principle in those spheres of life where not to do so is to risk public sanction, but that leaves in place the so-called private realm in which gender discrimination has its original home. One can also imagine how someone who does not believe that men and women are equal might come to believe otherwise, but that would require a far more robust form of public debate than political liberalism allows.

Advocates of the aforementioned ban would argue that just this equality of citizenship between men and women is at stake. Nussbaum is not exactly deaf to their view, but she cannot countenance it as an exercise of state power, which defines for her more or less the full scope of the political matter at hand. Although she rightly cautions that sex-ism must be addressed through "persuasion and example, not by re-moving liberty,"[8] it is hard to see how the political liberalism Nuss-baum endorses could facilitate the public exchange of opinions and judgments that must be part of any effort to persuade that is not merely private. The issue, in other words, is whether the focus on the legiti-mate exercise of state power, and the idea of the "burdens of judgment" connected to it, might work to hinder the very practice of persuasion, opinion formation, and judgment that Nussbaum would endorse.[9]

On its own terms, Nussbaum's political liberal argument against the ban is sound, but it neglects what I have called judging politically.

From her perspective, once we have our political and ethical principles in place—and that is the task of constructing ideal theory in the manner of Rawls—then we know how to judge and ultimately to act. It is a matter of applying the principles given by the theory.[10] More or less reducing the question of restrictions on women's clothing to the correct application of the ideal principles for regulating state power, Nussbaum suggests that once reasonable pluralism is upheld as the irreducible basis of liberal democratic societies, and once all the related arguments about the violation of a woman's freedom of conscience have been made (i.e., by way of the relativizing moves just discussed), the issue is settled: every "reasonable" person—as defined by Rawls—must agree. From the perspective of political liberalism, there is nothing left to be said.

I recognize that Nussbaum is dealing with the question of state power and that the immanent exercise and pernicious effects of this power are real: the French ban on face-covering veils was upheld in July 2014 by the European Union's Human Rights Court, and, based on this nonappealable judicial decision, other countries are expected to follow suit if they have not already.[11] Nevertheless, rather than rush to see the ban exclusively as a question of the legitimate exercise of state power, we might pause to consider whether there is a question of judgment here that is not so reducible. To do so would be to ask what it means to belong to a political community in terms other than those of the state, what it means to be a citizen in Arendt's sense of being a participator in government, broadly construed.

For Arendt, the capacity to judge reflectively, in the absence of a concept or rule, is a defining feature of democratic citizenship. Such citizenship is not identical with membership in any given nation-state. Nor is it premised, as we saw in chapter 5, on the sharing of what Rawls calls a "comprehensive doctrine" and defines as the essence of the idea of "community" that stands in a deeply fraught relation to his vision of a liberal democratic society (PL, 42). For Arendt, to belong to a democratic political community is to have a "common world," not to share a worldview, and this common world exists only where there is a plurality of worldviews. Our sense of what is common, "the sameness of the object," can appear only when it is seen from multiple perspectives. Consequently, the loss of competing perspectives results not in a world that is shared but in a loss of what we have common, that which can be seen only through an encounter with different points of view. The common world is "the space in which things become public."[12]

The Adjudication Imperative

If it is difficult for some democratic thinkers to see how Arendt's idea of a common world might serve as a framework for understanding the challenges facing multiethnic and multiracial democratic societies, that may well be because they think of those challenges primarily as a problem of adjudicating value differences. What if the threat to democracy were not the conflict of "ultimate value orientations" (Habermas)[13] but the deterioration of the common world that can only be sustained and enlarged through the expression of plural perspectives? As argued in chapter 1, this is the wager of Arendt, for whom the danger to democracy is not the conflict of worldviews that looms in a world characterized by value pluralism but the possibility that such pluralism, and the common world it sustains and that sustains it, could come to an end, as it did under totalitarianism and as it well could under current conditions of mass society.

Surely one obstacle to seeing the destruction of the common world, rather than the adjudication of value pluralism, as the real problem of judgment today, is the tendency to figure pluralism in Weberian terms as the "unending struggle between . . . [the] 'gods'" of the different systems and values or worldviews.[14] Writing in the context of the crisis of historicism debate described in chapter 3, Weber held all values to be relative to time and place, all cultural phenomena to be value laden, and the study of a society to be guided by a comprehension of its worldview. "Ultimate possible attitudes towards life" cannot be adjudicated by social science, philosophy, or any exercise of human reason, for they are fundamentally groundless. Claims to absolute truth and knowledge, argues Weber, rest not on evident premises but on faith. Science itself cannot provide a justification of its own value.[15]

For neo-Kantian democratic theorists, Weber's fundamental insight into the moment where giving grounds comes to an end opens up the threat of relativism, decisionism, and emotivism. As we have seen, in their work the historicist critique of transcendent standards of judgment, which is figured in Weber's image of eternal value conflict, becomes the departure point for the urgent need to "ground a conception of justice in something more universal than the considered convictions of our [or any particular] political culture," as Thomas McCarthy observes.[16] Apart from the question of whether this task is realizable, what might formulating the problem of judgment as a quest for (truly) universal criteria take for granted and what might it occlude?

Judging politically, I have argued, involves more than the adjudication of criticizable validity claims and a rethinking of what the criteria of adjudication might be. We are not just giving a yes/no answer to such claims, as if they presented us only with a problem of the validity of concepts we currently grasp. Instead we are learning new meanings for words, new ways in which objects can be disclosed, and in this way enlarging our sense of worldly reality. In chapter 1 we saw that for Arendt judging is political, not because it is about political objects that are prior and external to it but because it proceeds by taking into account the perspectives of others. What we count as "political" arises in, is internal to, the very process of judging itself. Understood in this way, judging is an activity that constitutes the space in which the objects of judgment can appear. Rather than think of judgment as the adjudication of value conflicts in the absence of a universal idea of the good, Arendt focused our attention on the prior question of what it means to have a world in common, a world in which value differences present themselves not as preferences but as politically relevant objects for judgment in the first place. The problem of judgment is not simply how to judge in the absence of shared rules but also how to recognize common objects as candidates for judgment, objects on which our considered opinions might very well diverge. We need to recognize them not simply as versions of objects we already count (e.g., be it Zande magic as being *like* primitive science, or the burqa as being *like* high heels) but as appearances that press us to test our existing criteria, our concepts. In some cases judging politically "expands the concept itself in an unlimited way," to speak with Kant (*CJ* §49, p. 183/193).

Shifting our understanding of the democratic problem of judgment, we need to recover the ordinary concept of perspective, according to which perspectives are perspectives *on* something—that is, they share a common object and are corrigible by other perspectives (through representative thinking). In the contemporary debate over judgment, this ordinary concept has given way to more or less intractable worldviews that have lost their common objects—indeed, the relation to any worldly object at all. That is why what currently goes under the sign of multiculturalism is so often seen as harboring relativism: in the absence of common objects, "multicultural perspectives" or worldviews are all we have. As merely subjective affective and value-laden interpretations, how could they possibly be brought into any kind of rational debate? The loss of this ordinary concept of perspective animates the worry shared by many democratic thinkers that plurality, though clearly an achievement of liberal democracy, is also its greatest threat.

If plurality generates an "impenetrable pluralism of ultimate value ori-entations" (Habermas) or "comprehensive doctrines" (Rawls) in the ab-sence of shared political criteria, it is easy to see how relativism would arise as the central threat to democratic order and how addressing rela-tivism would involve democratic theory in a quest for a conception of justice grounded in a substantively neutral (and supposedly universal) adjudicative mechanism such as public reason.

My point is not that democratic thinkers deny the existence of ob-jects on which we have perspectives (i.e., as if they were advancing a skeptical or idealist stance), it is that the ordinary concept of per-spective, and thus our ordinary modes of judging, has in some way been lost for them—as it never was for Arendt—as a means to correct distorted perspectives. If they admire Arendt's account of representa-tive thinking but fault her for failing to provide criteria with which to adjudicate competing perspectives, that is because perspectives for them have already been cut loose from the objects on which they are perspectives. Recall Arthur Danto's account of the epistemology of perspectivism (discussed in chapter 1), according to which we can no longer speak of what we have a perspective on "except from one or another perspective, and we cannot speak about it as it is in itself. . . . We can meaningfully say nothing, then, about whatever it is on which these are perspectives. We cannot speak of a true perspective, but only of a perspective that prevails. Because we cannot appeal to any fact independently of its relation to the perspectives it is meant to support, and we can do little more than insist on our perspective, and try, if we can, to impose it on others."[17] Although it is surely right to say that we cannot speak of what something *is* apart from human perspective, as an absolute conception of the world would have it, it is also true that the very concept of perspective is meaningless absent an object on which it is a perspective. This is the dynamic interplay between subjectivity and objectivity that underwrites representative thinking to which I shall return shortly.

Neo-Kantian democratic theorists do not openly endorse the episte-mology of perspectivism, but they are nonetheless in its grip. The strict cognitivism of Jürgen Habermas, for example, needs to be understood in relation to the loss of the ordinary idea of perspective. Cognitiv-ism is the other face of the loss of something independent that belongs to the ordinary concept. Cognitivism is a reactive stance toward the threat that the loss of common objects presents for rational judging. So too is any democratic theory that takes the affective and value-laden interpretations that characterize human perspective as an immanent threat to the public realm. The loss of the ordinary idea of perspective indicates the extent to which the late modern conception of a "world-view" as determining of our "conception of reality" has made it difficult to imagine a critical practice of judging as rooted in the exchange of ordinary perspectives, perspectives that have not been "purified" by public reason. If worldviews are hermeneutically bounded by their own "conceptual schemes" and "concepts of reality," how could a rational exchange between speakers of different worldviews (within any society or across national cultures) be possible, let alone a candidate for democratic debate? How could anyone "outside" the worldview criticize it in ways considered valid by those within it? And, not least, how could someone within a particular worldview gain critical purchase on his or her own "concept of reality"?

Dynamic Forms of Life

As argued in chapter 8, Ludwig Wittgenstein is often associated with a totalizing idea of a worldview, as are many of the thinkers who base their work on his philosophy. Following the pioneering interpretations of Stanley Cavell, Hanna Pitkin, and Peter Winch, I have maintained that for Wittgenstein forms of life are not static but dynamic. Rather than cast forms of life in narrow ethnographic terms, as if they stood for cultures with incommensurable conceptions of reality, Wittgenstein calls our attention to the complexity and depth of our agreement in language. But the creative and open-ended character of that agreement is often hard for us to see. "'So you are saying that human agreement [*die Übereinstimmung der Menschen*] decides what is true and what is false?'" asked the imaginary interlocutor in section 241 of *Philosophical Investigations*. "It is what human beings *say* that is true and false and they agree in the *language* they use [*in der Sprache stimmen die Menschen überein*]. This is not agreement in opinions [*Übereinstimmung der Meinungen*] but in form of life [*sondern der Lebensform*]," answered Wittgenstein. As Cavell comments, "the idea of agreement here is not that of coming to or arriving at an agreement on a given occasion, but of being in agreement throughout, being in harmony, like pitches or tones, or clocks, or weighing scales, or columns of figures. That a group of human beings *stimmen* in their language *überein* says, so to speak, that they are mutually voiced with respect to it, mutually *attuned* top to bottom" (*CR*, 32).[18] We agree not *on* but *in* a form of life, which is to say that agreement should not be thought of as conventionalist or contractual, as if it could be abrogated at will. But that does not mean that you are either inside or outside a particular form of life, either mutually attuned or mutually unintelligible.

Another way to put the problem presented by the idea of a form of life is in terms of the moment when reasons run out, and we fall back on an unjustified and unjustifiable appeal to what *we* already do. Does this not suggest that rational justification is limited to what the community says is right? Wittgenstein writes:

"How am I able to obey a rule?"—if this is not a question about causes, then it is about the justification for my following the rule in the way I do.

If I have exhausted the justifications, I have reached bedrock, and my spade is turned. Then I am inclined to say: "This is simply what I do." (*PI*, §217)

As we saw in chapter 8, Richard Rorty interprets the idea of bedrock in terms of our right to "epistemological ethnocentrism." We cannot justify our practices to people who are not already within our form of life, what *we* do or say. Likewise, Saul Kripke reads Wittgenstein's philosophy as one of simple deference to some "form of life" determined by a community. "In Wittgenstein's own model," he writes, "if the community all agrees on an answer and persists in its views, no one [in the community] can correct it. . . . If the corrector were outside the community, on Wittgenstein's view, he has no 'right' to make any correction."[19]

I have contested the view of Wittgenstein (and Cavell and Winch) as endorsing this narrow communal and consensus theory of justification. That would be to argue, quite "absurdly," as an understandably irritated Winch responds to critics, that the "ways men live together can never be criticized, . . . [and] that a way of living can never be characterized as in any sense 'irrational' . . . [or] that men who belong to one culture can 'never understand' lives led in another culture."[20] We do not encounter a different form of life as an enclosure to which we have no access or right of critique. Rather, we are tasked with the challenge of recognizing in practices not our own the interests, purposes, and desires that make them humanly intelligible. Without understanding a primitive culture, as Winch put it, we cannot judge a primitive culture. Evans-Pritchard had no "right" to judge the Azande as he did, not because he was an outsider but because he never actually tried to understand the Azande. Instead, he applied the scientific concept of rationality (i.e., agreement in procedures leads to agreement in conclusions) to practices (e.g., magic) in which that concept had no place.

Consequently, like James George Frazer before him in Wittgenstein's biting account, he could find in primitive magic nothing other than a flawed primitive science.

To deny that the scientific model of rationality can be extended to all registers of human practice and judgment is not to concede an untenable relativism. Pointing to agreement in patterns of support rather than conclusions as a better way to characterize rationality in all realms (including science), Cavell helped us question this narrow conception of rationality that continues to have a hold on democratic theory, notwithstanding the latter's own important critiques of scientism, objectivism, and the fact/value distinction. The sense that *something* must take the place of the scientific conception if we are to speak of rationality at all, but also that this something cannot be the acquired sensitivities so crucial to recognizing the patterns of argument that belong to a particular practice (e.g., aesthetic, moral, and political), leaves democratic theorists unable to think about the "whirl of organism" that is forms of life as anything other than a significant distraction or—worse—a genuine impediment to judging politically.

The view of a form of life as disabling for critical judgment, a virtual prison house of language, is symptomatic of thinking about language as a framework of rules in which our affective propensities play a minimal role. According to this view, as we saw in chapter 1, all intelligible and rational human speech and behavior is rule-governed, be the rules consciously articulated (e.g., Ryle's "intellectualist legend") or tacitly followed (e.g., Habermas's ontological conditions of "communicative action"). In Cavell's account, writes Steven Affeldt, "the idea of our becoming initiates of forms of life *displaces* the appeal to rules."[21] If critics see in a form of life a closed system, it is because they see there a system of rules and mostly rules that "leave no loopholes open," rules that determine in advance of any actual instances of speaking and acting what people within that form of life can meaningfully do or say. It is not the idea of form of life that should trouble us but the reduction of *Lebensform*—let's translate that as "way of life" or, better, way of living, an activity, not a state—to a practice of following rules, and an ethnographic one at that. As Lisa Wedeen has rightly argued, this static conception of culture, which persists in our political thinking and in the various disciplines of social science, fully occludes the ongoing dynamic or "dialectical" relationship of practices to signifying systems and blinds us to "how symbols operate in practice, why meanings generate action, and why actions produce meanings, when they do."[22] Whatever it may be, a "form of life" is not a *form* in the literal sense of that term: it is not "the shape and structure of something as distinguished from its material," as *Merriam-Webster's* tells us,[23] the purely formal container for what is material. And it is just as surely not language as a framework of rules. It is a messy, affect-laden and world-giving "whirl of organism" in which whatever becomes intelligible to us has its life. That is where future rewritings of a democratic theory of judgment should begin.

If a form of life is composed of shared practices, structures of salience, routes of interest and feeling, and so on, then understanding and judging must start with an awareness of the ways in which our affective sensibilities are involved in "the discovery of properties or the lighting up of properties that are there [in the world]," as David Wiggins puts it.[24] It is our affective responses that indicate the direction for the finer perceptions that attune us to how other people see the world. Sharing a form of life, far from a guarantee of mutual intelligibility, is only the occasion to discover what we actually do and do not share with others and on what things we agree or disagree. Affect, then, is crucial for this kind of discovery, but it should be understood in relation to conceptual rationality, rather than reduced to an unknowable mechanism of psychological priming, as it is was in many of the affect theories examined in chapter 9. The idea of judgment primed by inscrutable affect remains tethered to untenable philosophical ideals of what judging must be to count as rational.

We remain in the grip of a philosophical ideal of objectivity that most democratic theorists would adamantly refuse: "the identification of objectivity with the elimination of every admixture of subject-dependence," as James Conant observes. "It is this identification that blocks the possibility of the sort of interplay between the moments of subjectivity and objectivity in our experience that any coherent (literal or metaphorical) employment of the concept of perspective presupposes." He continues:

As long as this philosophical block remains in place, with its misplaced horror of the very forms of subjectivity we cannot do without, an oscillation is bound to ensue between an insistence upon a vacuous conception of objectivity [e.g., metaphysical realism] and a misdirected recoil into a celebration of just the sorts of subjectivity we can do without [i.e., skepticism or radical subjectivism].[25]

This oscillation between an impossible Objectivism and an impossible Subjectivism, I have argued, characterizes the debate over judgment in the work of many deliberative democrats and political affect theorists. It is a reaction to the "vertigo" experienced when faced with the thought that nothing secures the intelligible projection of words into new contexts, nothing secures mutual intelligibility. Rules alone, apart from human interests, desires, and purposes, cannot circumvent this problem of what Cavell called "voice." We are thrown back on our own ordinary and quotidian—sometimes immediate, sometimes fraught, sometimes futile—efforts to speak, listen, understand, and be understood.

"To possess a concept, to be able to go on with a concept, is to appreciate how its significant employment is bound up with our interests, desires, purposes, biological and social forms of life, facts about our social and natural world, and the like," observes Affeldt.[26] Thinking about normativity in this way, we can see how the acquired sensibilities that belong to a form of life might be central to rethinking procedural rule following (and not only its scientific version) as the sine qua non of rational judging. We can grasp how evaluative judgments (aesthetic, moral, political) involve our affective propensities without relinquishing their rationality. And we can recover a conception of objectivity and agreement that is appropriate to democratic politics, just as Arendt invites us to do—yet we have also seen that this is far from easy.

"What happens when we feel that realms like ethics or aesthetics [or politics] are arbitrary and subjective is that we compare our actual use of standards and judgment in these realms with an incorrect idealization of what goes on in science or mathematics—an ideal of standards free of any convention, absolute, capable of being invoked without the possibility of contradiction and therefore without responsibility or commitment. But that ideal does not exist in reality," contends Hanna Pitkin.[27] Even in these realms, in which agreement in procedures seems to guarantee agreement in conclusions, we find that "there are assumptions and conventions guaranteed only by our commitment to them, the way we use them."[28] It is not that deviant positions in science and mathematics are "impossible," she observes, but that they are not "acceptable" as positions in these fields. "The fact that someone gets a different answer in arithmetic does not shake our faith in the existence of 'right answers' in that field, even for an instant."[29] If we are so shaken when we get divergent answers in politics, if we begin to lose faith in the possibilities of democratic politics when our judgments are not aligned, as they often are not, it may well be not only because we wish that agreement in politics would be more like that in mathematics or science but also because we have idealized what secures agreement in those latter fields.

The possibilities of disagreement, conflict, and misunderstanding in attempts to reach agreement about what belongs in the common world are intrinsic to democratic politics, and no theory of judgment can render itself immune from them. "We should not tumble over ourselves to assert that there is irresolvable substantive disagreement. We should simply respect the possibility of such disagreement," remarks Wiggins, "and in respecting it register the case for a measure of cognitive underdetermination." Rather than assume an interminable war of "comprehensive doctrines" or "ultimate value orientations," we do better to affirm our ordinary capacities for "reasoning, conversion, and criticism—without guarantees of success, which are almost as needless as they are unobtainable."[30] And, I would add, too often antipolitical.

Judging Politically Is Not a Moral Faculty

Pursuing the intimations of Arendt's reflections on judging, I have highlighted the political character of her distinctive contribution, a contribution that resonates with but also deepens and expands philosophical arguments made by Wittgenstein, Winch, and Cavell. My aim has been to show how the focus on freedom as action that is affirmed by judging involves a creative *political* rethinking of objectivity that is valuable for democratic and feminist theory. We act—and only when we act are we free, according to Arendt. But it is our capacity to judge reflectively, as we saw in chapter 7, that allows us to affirm the freedom of action, to see in action not necessity and not just contingency either—as a certain strand of postmodern theory would have it—but our collective activity as world building: as sustaining, renewing, and expanding the network of tangible and intangible relations, of what counts as an object of shared concern, not just in the sense of our shared view of it but also our awareness of the different perspectives in which the object can be seen and understood.

In this way, acting and judging are not two distinct activities, the former belonging to the *vita activa*, the latter to the *vita contemplativa*, as Ronald Beiner (among other commentators) interprets Arendt's later work.[31] Judging does not represent a withdrawal from the world of appearances but is an exercise in affirming the worldliness, realness, or objectivity of appearances. The "mental activity" of judging that Beiner identifies as belonging to the life of the mind actually belongs, in Arendt's account, to the public practice of freedom; judging is the ability to move in "the mental realm" just as one is able to move in "the physical realm," as she put it in her discussion of the Greek practice of seeing politically. This mental movement or capacity for critical thought takes place not in the solitary life of the mind but in the plural spaces of politics. As we saw in chapter 1, this is the "freedom to speak with one another," which is only possible in interaction with others and in the public space. Freedom of thought is for Arendt so completely bound up with the public space that the first institutionalized retreat from it—the [Platonic] Academy—is in her view deeply antipolitical and as such highly fragile.[32]

Although judging does require stepping back, as it were, to consider what one has learned by attending, whether in actual practice or though imagination, to different points of view, this is a far cry from the philosophical *vita contemplativa*, which Arendt consistently characterized—not least in volume 1 of *The Life of the Mind*—as being indifferent if not hostile to opinion, to *doxa* (opinion) and the *dokei moi* (it-appears-to-me).[33] By contrast with "thinking," which is concerned with "invisibles," the "objects" of "judging" (and "willing"), writes Arendt, "are particulars with an established home in the appearing world, from which the willing or judging mind removes itself only temporarily and with the intention of a later return."[34] As we saw in chapter 4, if Socrates is spared in Arendt's critique of the philosopher's *vita contemplativa*, that is because he begins the quest for truth in the agora, hearing and weighing the opinions of others, before proceeding to judge.

My approach takes issue not only with the view that judging represents a retreat from politics into the life of the mind but also that judging is for Arendt—or should be for us—a "moral faculty." The latter position, already implicit in Habermas's 1976 critique of Arendt's failure to provide criteria of judgment, is articulated most forcefully a decade later by Seyla Benhabib, who holds that "an unusually narrow concept of morality" blinded Arendt to her own topic and led her to mistakenly separate (rather than connect as she could have) morality and politics.[35] "Arendt herself never made good on the 'attempt to arrive at a halfway plausible theory of ethics' and instead called judgment 'the most political' of all our cognitive faculties," observes Benhabib.[36] As we saw in chapters 6 and 7, this interpretation of Arendtian judging as a moral faculty led Benhabib and Habermas to propose various supplements to Arendt's account (e.g., moral criteria for judging and representative thinking), all the while claiming to remain true to the basic participatory spirit of her politics.

The claim that judging is a moral faculty has seemed to many a critic to be intuitively correct. After all, in the wake of the Adolf Eichmann Nazi war crimes trial, Arendt talked about judging as the ability "to tell right from wrong" and linked it to "the inability to think" and "a disastrous failure of what we call conscience."[37] Furthermore, even if Arendt herself did not properly account for the moral character of judgment, it would seem that a democratic theory of judgment would have to foreground morality: morality not so much in the Kantian rule-governed sense of knowing right from wrong but in the contemporary sense of posttraditional justice as it is formulated by Habermas. "The fundamental question of morality consists in how we can legitimately regulate interpersonal relationships," Habermas states, adding that in the context of the widespread pluralism that characterizes modernity, "justice recedes from the concrete contexts in which it is embedded into forms of an inclusive and impartial judgment formation" (*TJ*, 261).

Even if one does not agree that justice must in this way "take on a proceduralist form" (*TJ*, 261), it can be tempting to assimilate Arendtian judging and representative thinking (as both Habermas and Benhabib each in their own ways do—but they are far from alone) to the formation of what Habermas calls an enlarged "We-perspective by means of mutually taking one another's perspectives" (*TJ*, 260), which both generates and is governed by universal moral criteria. But this assimilation of representative thinking to what Benhabib calls "a procedure for ascertaining intersubjective validity in the public realm," as argued in chapters 4 and 7, misconstrues what is at stake for a democratic theory of judgment by seeking to legislate for politics from the perspective of moral philosophy.[38] The formation of a "we" perspective through Arendtian representative thinking does not transcend the "merely" ordinary lifeworld of values or conceptions of the good. The "We-perspective," as Arendt understands it, is not "enlarged" because it has employed an empty rule of argumentation to keep these values and conceptions from blocking our presumably more universal understanding of what is "morally right."

Even if one were to try with Benhabib to situate and contextualize the deontological model of Kantian morality to bring it in line with the situated character of political life (and thereby refuse what she takes to be the "two-world metaphysic" of Kant), we should resist the idea that Arendtian representative thinking needs to be guided by this rewriting of the moral law: "Act in such a way that the maxim of your actions takes into account the perspective of everyone else in such a way that you would be in a position to 'woo their consent.'"[39] For Benhabib, "such a procedure of enlarged thought and contextual moral judgment are not at all incompatible," but in my understanding of Arendt, they remain so.[40] What ought to animate the spirit and practice of representative thinking is not the "moral respect [owed to 'each person'] to consider their standpoint," as laudable as that may be in itself for working through our complicated modern lives with others who are often strangers.[41] It is not just the nagging question of whether "a universalist moral standpoint must be formalistic, a prioristic and context insensitive," as Benhabib denies but Arendt would maintain.[42] Worrisome here is not just the classic Kantian *imperative* form of the demand but its *addressee*: the subject and its relation to the other. This self–other relation, foregrounded in the moral rewriting of representative thinking, risks losing track of the really important *political* thing at stake for Arendt and so for a democratic theory of judgment: the relation that each of us has to the world and, through the world we have in common, to each other.

To foreground judging as a political rather than a moral or an ethical faculty is not to declare morality or ethics as irrelevant for political life.[43] It is to keep "care for the world" in view and to resist the kind of "shift of interest away from the world [and its fragility] and toward man [and his irrational, self-centered, or parochial tendencies]" that Arendt saw as characteristic of all moral (and, I would argue, most contemporary ethical) approaches to politics and of the modern despair toward politics. For Arendt, "one thing is certain: any response that places man in the center of our current worries and suggests he must be changed before any relief is to be found is profoundly unpolitical" ("IP," 105–6). Not only is the focus on "man" a distraction from what we share (which, for Arendt, is always the world and not "human nature," whether [neuro]biologically or socially understood), it also misconstrues what is at issue in judging critically and reflectively.

In this way too we might take distance from the many thinkers examined in this book who would make sense of beliefs resistant to rational revision as symptomatic of an intrinsic problem with the way in which our subjective endowments impair our capacity to think and to judge. Concern with the unwillingness to amend immediate judgment in light of reflection, which characterized for Hume and his descendants flawed belief, should direct our attention outward toward the world, for it is something about the world that leads to the distortion of perspective that impairs our critical political abilities, our capacity to think representatively, not human perspective as such.[44] "If we want to change an institution, an organization, some public body existing within the world, we can only revise its constitution, its laws, its statutes and hope that all the rest will take care of itself" ("IP," 106), asserts Arendt. This blunt remark may seem small solace for those of us who have come to think of democratic politics in terms of what I have elsewhere called "the subject question."[45] I will nonetheless invoke it here as one more reason to remain appropriately cautious about contemporary forms of ideal theory, especially as they have dominated our understanding of judging politically. The problem with politics as "applied ethics" is not only that it starts with "people as they ideally should be, not as they are," as Raymond Guess puts it,[46] but that it starts with what Arendt called "man" rather than "the world." Although these (mostly self-ascribed neo-Kantian) forms of ideal theory claim no direct interest in subjectivity (save for making certain ontological "observations," e.g., Habermas, or explicitly sociohistorical and political ones, e.g., Rawls), many put forward adjudicative mechanisms born out of a disavowed nostalgia for a philosophical ideal of objectivity and often enough a picture of human thought and judgment as confined in its current modes of subjectivity—save the saving supplement of ideal theory.

Arendt did not misunderstand her own topic, which was never to provide "a halfway plausible theory of ethics." She explicitly and with good reason called judgment our most political faculty. Should we choose to take the risk—it is a risk—and develop her view, we shall find it to be no "incomplete doctrine" in need of a moral (or any other ideal) supplement, for judging politically, as Arendt understood it, could be based on no doctrine at all. If politics for her was never "applied ethics," it was because Arendt was admirably alert to the well-established tendency in Western philosophy to transcend the contingent and chaotic world of ordinary human affairs, to turn our attention away from this unpredictable and messy world in which we simply cannot know what we do before we act and judge politically, and redirect our gaze toward the stable "true world" of classical thought, the private inner world of Christian thought, or the other-directed ethical world of so much contemporary democratic theory.

Arendt's insistence that at the center of politics is not "man" but the world, and that judging takes place not in the life of the mind but "in the space between men, that is the world," holds plurality to be a political relation (rather than an ontological condition) characterized by distance and proximity, relation and separation. "To live together in the world means essentially that a world of things is between those who have it in common, as a table is located between those who sit around it; the world, like every in-between, relates and separates men at the same time," she writes. And so it is that the common world "gathers us together and yet prevents our falling over each other, so to speak" (*HC*, 52). The common world in which plurality is so constituted and acknowledged, then, is a potentially potent way of talking about and refiguring our understanding of democratic political space and the place of judging in its constitution and renewal. "It is the space between them that unites them, rather than some quality inside each of them," as Margaret Canovan beautifully describes what citizens have in common according to Arendt.[47] Judging politically we constitute and renew our relations as citizens, not in terms of identity (or sameness) and not even of difference (or alterity) as these are typically understood, but of political relation based on distance and proximity.

A democratic theory of judgment takes the ordinary perspectives that generate the space of democratic politics to be world giving, but it does not blindly celebrate differences, as if plural perspectives were not in need of our judgment. Rather, such a theory calls for the development of a robust quotidian practice of judging that takes politics on its own terms, beginning with the recognition that "politics is based on the fact of human plurality" ("IP, 93). This deceptively simple claim, repeated time and again in Arendt's work, is a stark counterpoint to philosophy's concern "with *man* [in the singular]," which prevents it from being able to give a legitimate "answer to the question: What is politics?" ("IP," 93). Every attempt at an answer has taken for granted that there "were only one or two men or only identical men" ("IP," 93), Arendt remarks. Arendt's claim about plurality conceals an equally simple but also not readily understood insight into the autonomy of "the faculty of judgment, which has far more to do with man's ability to make distinctions than with his ability to organize and subsume [under a rule]" ("IP," 102). Judging, the ability to discern differences and *also* similarities without the mediation of a concept, allows us to affirm the political space of relation—distance and proximity—that is the common world.

This book has attempted to keep both plurality and the democratic need to judge in balance by showing with Arendt that the condition for judging politically is plurality. Judging is a practice through which citizens can enlarge their sense of what belongs in the common world, but it is clearly not a practice of endless liberal tolerance. Tolerance in this form is what we are left with when plurality is treated as a kind of immanent threat to democracy, something that we claim to celebrate but think best remain a shadow figure in our public debates. The limits we set to the (mode of) expression of the plural perspectives from which we see the world restrict our sense of what is real and also, most important, of what we will count as part of the common world, acknowledge as meaningful for democratic public life. Judging is a continual testing of "what we say" to find the always contingent limits of democratic community as they exist for us right now.

Arendt did not concern herself with the various means for adjudicating competing worldviews that consume the energies of contemporary democratic theorists. This indifference indicates not a blindness to the genuine problem of judging in the absence of universal criteria but an awareness, which has guided my own project, that it is the shrinkage of the common world in which plural perspectives can be voiced, and not the otherwise "impenetrable pluralism of ultimate value orientations" absent some ordering mechanism, that is the real problem of judgment in modern democracies. There is no guarantee that more perspectives will yield a more realistic account of how things stand in the world, only the promissory note that without exposure to multiple perspectives in public spaces of debate, critical judgment (i.e., judgment that questions ideas and beliefs previously resistant to rational revision on the basis of knowledge, evidence, or facts) will not even get off the ground.

"Anyone who goes beyond procedural questions of a discourse theory of morality and ethics and, in a normative attitude . . . embarks on a theory of the well-ordered, or even emancipated, society will very quickly run up against the limits of his own historical situation," observes Habermas.[48] A democratic theory of judgment and the ordinary activity of judging politically, as I understand them, would stubbornly refuse this warning regarding normative political visions of what we hold to be right, just, or good. What democratic citizens need now are not theories that shirk the task of providing a substantive critique of real world power relations, let alone an alternative normative conception of what social relations might be. The pressing issue is not how to justify the very idea of political critique as such that tends to guide the ideal theory of deliberative democrats; it is, rather, how to return to the animating force behind democratic practices of critique—namely, the crucial connection between critique and social/political transformation. To speak with Cornelius Castoriadis, how might we, democratic theorists and citizens, refigure democratic theory and practice as "critical" (of what exists) by means of its capacity to posit "new forms/figures of the thinkable"?[49] This too is where I hope future rewritings of a democratic theory of judgment will begin.

This book has not resolved all the puzzles and problems it has described. I hope to have provided alternative pathways for making sense of our current political predicament, though I recognize that some readers will have wished for a work more on the order of the ideal theory that I find lacking for thinking about the real problem of judgment today. In doing so, I have sought to make visible the picture that holds us captive: judging figured wholly as a problem of the adjudication of competing validity claims in the absence of a universal conception of the good. Only when we first recognize the steady grip that this picture has on our political imaginations can we begin to understand the limitations it imposes on our thinking and acting, and in ways that make it harder to see and to forward the wide range of possibilities that an engaged democratic politics can open for us.

Should we seek release from this picture, let us return to the rough ground of our ordinary practices. Let us affirm what we value: affirm it not as mere subjective preference but as an aspect of objective worldly reality. Let us remain unmoved by the philosophers who chide us about the "queer" status of that claim. Let us put forward substantive public visions of what we hold to be right and just and debate these without the aid of the newfangled democratic criteria created in the academic laboratories of ideal theory. Finally, let us trust instead that what we seek when we judge politically is, as Wittgenstein put it, "already in plain view. For *this* is what we seem in some sense not to understand" (*PI*, §89).

Abbreviations

"PHC"	Hans-Georg Gadamer, "The Problem of Historical Consciousness"
PI	Ludwig Wittgenstein, *Philosophical Investigations*
PL	John Rawls, *Political Liberalism*
"PP"	Hannah Arendt, "Philosophy and Politics"
"Reply"	Mark Danner, "Reply" to "The Secret Way to War: An Exchange"
"RP"	Patchen Markell, "The Rule of the People"
SCR	Leo Strauss, *Spinoza's Critique of Religion*
"SSH"	Leo Strauss, "Social Science and Humanism"
"ST"	David Hume, "Of the Standard of Taste"
"SWW"	Mark Danner, "The Secret Way to War"
"TA"	Ruth Leys, "The Turn to Affect"
TCA	Jürgen Habermas, *The Theory of Communicative Action*
TJ	Jürgen Habermas, *Truth and Justification*
TM	Hans-Georg Gadamer, *Truth and Method*
"TMC"	Hannah Arendt, "Thinking and Moral Considerations"
"TP"	Hannah Arendt, "Truth and Politics"
"UPS"	Peter Winch, "Understanding a Primitive Society"
VL	Ernesto Grassi, *Vom Vorrang des Logos*
WHD	Martha Nussbaum, *Women and Human Development*

Notes

1. Hannah Arendt, "Introduction *into* Politics," in *The Promise of Politics*, ed. Jerome Kohn (New York: Schocken, 2005), 104 (hereafter cited in text and notes as "IP").

2. See Jürgen Habermas, "Hannah Arendt's Communications Concept of Power," in *Hannah Arendt, Critical Essays*, ed. Lewis Hinchman and Sandra Hinchman (Albany: State University of New York Press, 1994), 211–30 (hereafter cited as "ACCP"); Albrecht Wellmer, "Hannah Arendt on Judgment: The Unwritten Doctrine of Reason," in *Judgment, Imagination, and Politics: Themes from Kant and Arendt*, ed. Ronald Beiner and Jennifer Nedelsky (Boston: Rowman and Littlefield, 2001), 165–81; Seyla Benhabib, *The Reluctant Modernism of Hannah Arendt* (Thousand Oaks, CA: Sage, 1996). Benhabib finds in Arendt's "disturbing" turn to Kant's third *Critique* further evidence of Arendt's failure to provide a normative foundation for politics from which it would be possible to assess competing validity claims (*Reluctant Modernism*, 193–94). I discuss these critiques in Linda M. G. Zerilli, "'We Feel Our Freedom': Imagination and Judgment in the Thought of Hannah Arendt," *Political Theory* 33, no. 2 (April 2005): 158–88.

3. John Rawls, *Political Liberalism* (New York: Columbia University Press, 1993), xvi.

4. Key works on judgment in democratic theory include F. R. Ankersmit, *Aesthetic Politics: Political Philosophy beyond Fact and Value* (Stanford, CA: Stanford University Press, 1996); Ronald Beiner, *Political Judgment* (Chicago: University of Chicago Press, 1983); Albena Azmanova, *The Scandal of*

Reason: A Critical Theory of Political Judgment (New York: Columbia University Press, 2012); Kennan Ferguson, *The Politics of Judgment: Aesthetics, Identity, and Political Theory* (Lanham, MD: Lexington Books, 1999); Alessandro Ferrara, *Justice and Judgment: The Rise and the Prospect of the Judgment Model in Contemporary Political Philosophy* (Thousand Oaks, CA: Sage, 1999); Alessandro Ferrara, *The Force of the Example: Explorations in the Paradigm of Judgment* (New York: Columbia University Press, 2008); Peter J. Steinberger, *The Concept of Political Judgment* (Chicago: University of Chicago Press, 1993); Leslie Paul Thiele, *The Heart of Judgment: Practical Wisdom, Neuroscience, and Narrative* (Cambridge: Cambridge University Press, 2006); Ronald Beiner and Jennifer Nedelsky, eds., *Judgment, Imagination, and Politics: Themes from Kant and Arendt* (Boston: Rowman and Littlefield, 2001).

5. Although there is no single idea of the good that can or ought to be defended in the neo-Kantian view, there can and ought to be agreement about the ground rules for debate. In the case of Rawls, we can agree to disagree and leave the most divisive topics off the public table. What we do agree to debate can in principle be discussed rationally through the use of shared concepts (justice as fairness) and norms (e.g., reasonableness). Habermas, by contrast, believes that all topics can in principle be on the table if subjected to certain procedural norms of argumentation, for implicit in all human communication, regardless of cultural particularity, is an orientation toward rational legitimation. Universality in public matters is thus based on agreement or rational consensus achieved at the end of a "discourse of reasons" (or public debate) to which various individuals take part. Implicit in our discursive practices is an assurance that the claims we make are capable of being validated with respect to the truth of what they assert, their appropriateness to the situation, and our sincerity in uttering them.

6. Habermas writes:

> The limits of a decisionistic treatment of practical questions are overcome as soon as argumentation is expected to treat the generaliz*ability* of interests, instead of being resigned to an impenetrable pluralism of apparently ultimate value orientations (or belief-acts or attitudes). It is not the fact of this pluralism that is here disputed, but the assertion that it is impossible to separate by argumentation generalizable interests from those that are and remain particular.

Jürgen Habermas, *Legitimation Crisis*, trans. Thomas McCarthy (Boston: Beacon, 1975), 108.

7. Jürgen Habermas, *The Inclusion of the Other: Studies in Political Theory*, ed. Ciaran Cronin and Pablo De Greiff (1998; repr., Cambridge, MA: MIT Press, 2000), 37.

8. William Connolly, *Neuropolitics: Thinking, Culture, Speed* (Minneapolis:

University of Minnesota Press, 2002); Thiele, *Heart of Judgment*; John Protevi, *Political Affect: Connecting the Social and the Somatic* (Minneapolis: University of Minnesota Press, 2009). For other examples of the ontological turn to affect (and, in some cases, cognitive neuroscience) in political theory, see Jane Bennett, *Vibrant Matter: A Political Ecology of Things* (Durham, NC: Duke University Press, 2010); Davide Panagia, *The Political Life of Sensation* (Durham, NC: Duke University Press, 2009); Jennifer Nedelsky, "Receptivity and Judgment," *Ethics and Global Politics* 4, no. 4 (2011): 231–54. For a critique of Connolly, see Alexander Livingston, "Avoiding Deliberative Democracy? Micropolitics, Manipulation, and the Public Sphere," *Philosophy and Rhetoric* 45, no. 3 (2012): 269–94. For an excellent critique of the turn to cognitive neuroscience and affect in political theory, see John G. Gunnell, "Unpacking Emotional Baggage in Political Inquiry," in *Essays on Neuroscience and Political Theory: Thinking the Body Politic*, ed. Frank Vander Valk (New York: Routledge, 2012), 91–116; John G. Gunnell, "Are We Losing Our Minds? Cognitive Science and the Study of Politics," *Political Theory* 35, no. 6 (2007): 704–31.

9. As we shall see in chapter 9, there is an extensive feminist literature (e.g., the work of Lauren Berlant and Sarah Ahmed) dealing with the importance of affect for understanding political and public sphere formations that extends and in some cases significantly deepens the work on emotion in feminist political theory. Within the political theory literature, see Sharon R. Krause, *Civil Passions: Moral Sentiment and Democratic Deliberation* (Princeton, NJ: Princeton University Press, 2008); Susan Bickford, "Emotion Talk and Political Judgment," *Journal of Politics* 73, no. 4 (October 2011): 1025–37; Cheryl Hall, "Recognizing the Passion in Deliberation: Toward a More Democratic Theory of Deliberative Democracy," *Hypatia* 22, no. 4 (2007): 81–95; Lynn M. Sanders, "Against Deliberation," *Political Theory* 25, no. 3 (1997): 347–76.

10. Connolly, *Neuropolitics*, 90.

11. James Conant, "The Dialectic of Perspectivism, I," *Sats: Nordic Journal of Philosophy* 6, no. 2 (2005): 5–50. Conant distinguishes what he calls "naïve perspectivism," which he associates with an ordinary idea of perspective, from the various philosophical stages of perspective in which perspective comes to involve "irremediable distortion" (ibid., 23). My discussion of perspective in this chapter is deeply indebted to Conant's work.

12. Ibid., 12.

13. Ibid., 43.

14. Wilfrid Sellars, *Empiricism and the Philosophy of Mind* (Cambridge, MA: Harvard University Press, 1997), 76.

15. Ludwig Wittgenstein, *Philosophical Investigations*, 2nd ed., trans. G. E. M. Anscombe (1953; repr., Malden, MA: Blackwell, 1997), §81 (hereafter cited as *PI*). "But if you say that our languages only *approximate* to such calculi, you are standing on the very brink of a misunderstanding" (ibid.). This

brink is where I place the attenuated form of the intellectualist account of judging that characterizes contemporary democratic theory. The intellectualist idea was powerfully criticized by Gilbert Ryle, *The Concept of Mind* (Chicago: University of Chicago Press, 2002; hereafter cited as *CM*). I discuss Ryle in chapter 9.

16. See especially Hannah Arendt, *Lectures on Kant's Political Philosophy*, ed. Ronald Beiner (Chicago: University of Chicago Press, 1992; hereafter cited as *LKPP*).

17. Ronald Beiner, "Hannah Arendt on Judging," in *LKPP*, 89–156, at 137. "The problem with this exclusion of knowledge from political judgment is that it renders one incapable of speaking of 'uninformed' judgment and of distinguishing differential capacities for knowledge so that some persons may be recognized as more qualified, and some as less qualified, to judge" (ibid., 136). This is just the kind of qualification that Arendt, following Kant's insights on the peculiar nature of aesthetic judging, would have us question. Question, not because all judgments are of equal rank, but because the capacity to judge politically should be learned by and expected from each and every democratic citizen.

18. Ibid., 138. In her later work, what "Arendt seeks from Kant," writes Beiner, "is no longer a theory of *political* judgment, for, as she now conceives the matter, there is only *one* faculty of judgment, unitary and indivisible, which is present in various circumstances—in the verdict of an aesthetic critic, the verdict of a historical observer, the tragic verdict of a storyteller or poet—and the variety of circumstance does not relevantly affect the character of the faculty thus instantiated" (ibid).

19. Ibid.

20. I have discussed certain aspects of the critique of Arendt's "noncognitivism" in Zerilli, "'We Feel Our Freedom.'"

21. I borrow this example from Joseph Tinguely, whose excellent dissertation on Kantian aesthetics I discuss in chapter 2. Joseph Tinguely, "Orientation: Kant and the Aesthetic Content of Cognition" (PhD diss., New School for Social Research, 2011), 99. Tinguely uses this example of diplomatic policy to make a similar point about the way to understand two senses of the adjective *aesthetic* in the phrase "aesthetic judgment" in Kant's work.

22. A survey of Arendt's entire corpus shows that she speaks of "political judgment" only six times. Thanks to Sarah Johnson for this information. The real issue of course is not how many times she actually mentions *political* judgment but what the adjective *political* means: does it signify the object which is being judged, or does it signify the mode by which judgment proceeds?

23. Hannah Arendt, "The Crisis in Culture: Its Social and Political Significance," in *Between Past and Future: Eight Essays in Political Thought* (New York: Penguin, 1993), 197–226, at 221.

24. Ibid., 220.

25. Arendt translates Kant's phrase as an "enlarged mentality." Ibid., 220. For Arendt's remarks on "representative thinking" see Hannah Arendt, "Truth and Politics," in *Between Past and Future*, 227–64, esp. 241 (hereafter cited as "TP").

26. In "The Crisis in Culture," Arendt writes, "The power of judgment rests on a potential agreement with others, and the thinking process which is active in judging something is not, like the thought process of pure reasoning, a dialogue between me and myself, but finds itself always and primarily, even if I am quite alone in making up my mind, in an antici-pated communication with others with whom I know I must finally come to some agreement" (220).

27. Ibid., 221.

28. I use the term *objects* here in a loose sense. What comes into view for us in evaluative judgments is not necessarily an "object" at all. That way of thinking about evaluative judgments (aesthetic, ethical, political) is con-nected with a metaphysical conception of objectivity that rejects the idea that value judgments, since they do not refer to objects that can count as facts, could be objective. Hence, Hilary Putnam will argue for "objectivity without objects" when it comes to such judgments. Hilary Putnam, *Ethics without Ontology* (Cambridge, MA: Harvard University Press, 2004), 52–70.

29. Habermas, *Legitimation Crisis*, 108.

30. Ronald Beiner, *What's the Matter with Liberalism?* (Berkeley: University of California Press, 1992), 40–41.

31. Ibid., 41.

32. Bernard Williams, *Descartes: The Project of Pure Enquiry*, rev. ed. (New York: Routledge, 2005), esp. 49–50.

33. J. L. Mackie, *Ethics: Inventing Right and Wrong* (1977; repr., New York: Penguin, 1990), 37. Also quoted in John McDowell, "Aesthetic Value, Objectivity, and the Fabric of the World," in *Mind, Value, and Reality* (1998; repr., Cambridge, MA: Harvard University Press, 2002), 112–30, at 114–15, although McDowell mistakenly substituted the word *reflect* where Mackie had originally written *express*, as shown here.

34. McDowell, "Aesthetic Value," 112. Mackie's error theory of moral judg-ment shows him to be both a moral cognitivist *and* a moral realist. He thinks that since no moral properties exist, no moral judgment can be true. All positive moral judgments are false. I discuss Mackie's error theory in chapter 2.

35. Simon Blackburn, *Spreading the Word: Groundings in the Philosophy of Lan-guage* (New York: Oxford University Press, 2004). I discuss the differences between Mackie's and Blackburn's respective accounts of emotivism and projectivism in chapter 2.

36. McDowell, "Aesthetic Value," 114.

37. John McDowell, "Non-Cognitivism and Rule-Following," in *Mind, Value, and Reality* 198–218, at 200.

38. Alfred J. Ayer, *Language, Truth, and Logic*, 2nd edition (New York: Dover, 2012); Charles L. Stevenson, *Ethics and Language* (New Haven, CT: Yale University Press, 1944). In the sixth chapter of his logical positivist tract, Ayer argued for an antirealist "emotivist" theory of ethics, which rejected the idea that ethical expressions fit into one of two categories of genuine (literally meaningful) propositions: analytic propositions (tautologies) and synthetic propositions (empirical). Ayer attacked, on the one hand, the absolutist view of ethics, whose statements of value admit of no empirical test, as well as naturalistic theories of ethics that attempt to translate statements of ethical values into statements of empirical fact in an effort to make ethical utterances into something they are not—namely, statements or judgments that are subject to testing. Moral pronouncements are expressions of emotion that cannot be verified. Likewise Stevenson argues that facts are logically divorced from evaluations, hence the latter are not subject to rational debate, and moral disagreements are in principle interminable. For a critique of the emotivism of Ayer and especially Stevenson, see Stanley Cavell, *The Claim of Reason: Wittgenstein, Skepticism, Morality, and Tragedy* (New York: Oxford University Press, 1982), chaps. 9–10 (hereafter cited as *CR*); Alasdair MacIntyre, *After Virtue: A Study in Moral Theory*, 3rd ed. (London: Gerald Duckworth, 2007). MacIntyre argues that the emotivist theory of ethics is the expression of the final stage in a long development of ethical thinking from the Greeks through to the early twentieth century. It is based on the fact/value distinction and the ought/is distinction. However, the distinction should be seen as historical rather than intrinsic to the nature of morality as such. It is based on the rejection of human nature, interests, and desires as the basis for ethics. Whether this basis can be recovered is an open question.

39. MacIntyre, *After Virtue*, 11–12.

40. Ayer, *Language, Truth, and Logic*, 110.

41. John McDowell, "Projection and Truth in Ethics," in *Mind, Value, and Reality*, 151–66, at. 154.

42. Hilary Putnam observes:

> Ever since Hume, the fact that there are many kinds of value judgment that are not themselves of an ethical (or "moral") variety tends to get sidelined in philosophical discussions of the relation between (so-called) values and (so-called) facts. This is especially true of the positivists. Carnap generally speaks not of "value judgments" but only of the statements of "regulative ethics" (or sometimes "normative ethics"). Reichenbach, when he turns to the "value" side of the fact/value dichotomy writes of "The Nature of Ethics." And in Charles Stevenson's book *Facts and Values* there is not a single reference to any value judgments outside of ethics! It is not that these authors would deny

that, say, aesthetic judgments are cases of value judgments, but, for the most part, their real target is the supposed objectivity or rationality of ethics, and in disposing of this topic, they take themselves to have provided an account that covers all other kinds of value judgment as well.

Hilary Putnam, "The Empiricist Background," in *The Collapse of the Fact/Value Dichotomy and Other Essays* (2002; repr., Cambridge, MA: Harvard University Press, 2004), 7–27, at 19.

43. Ayer, *Language, Truth, and Logic*, 111.

44. Ibid.

45. Ibid.

46. "When ethical disagreement is not rooted in disagreement in belief, is there *any* method by which it may be settled? If one means by 'method' a *rational* method, then there is no method. But in any case there is a 'way,'" writes Stevenson. This includes, in a disagreement between A and B, "build[ing] up, by the contagion of his [A's] feelings, an influence which will modify B's temperament. . . . This is often the only way to obtain ethical agreement, if there is any way at all. It is persuasive, not empirical or rational; but that is no reason for neglecting it." Charles L. Stevenson, "The Emotive Meaning of Ethical Terms," *Mind* 46, no. 181 (1937): 14–31, at 29.

47. See Mackie, *Ethics*; R. M. Hare, *Moral Thinking* (Oxford: Clarendon Press, 1981). For the philosophical debate on noncognitivism in ethics, see Philippa Foot, *Virtues and Vices* (Berkeley: University of California Press, 1978); David Wiggins, "Truth, Invention, and the Meaning of Life," in *Needs, Values, Truth: Essays in the Philosophy of Value*, 3rd ed. (New York: Oxford University Press, 1998), 87–138; McDowell, "Non-Cognitivism and Rule-Following"; Hilary Putnam, "The Entanglement of Fact and Value," in *Collapse of Fact/Value Dichotomy*, 28–45.

48. McDowell, "Non-Cognitivism and Rule-Following," 201. McDowell's critique applies as well to the "plausible idea that evaluative classifications are supervenient on non-evaluative classifications." His point, directed here against R. M. Hare's remarks on the thesis of universalizability, is that even at the so-called descriptive level, where Hare would locate any justification to an alteration in moral judgment, we would need to grasp that certain things belong together and that this "may essentially require understanding the supervening [evaluative] term" (ibid., 202).

49. Putnam, "Entanglement of Fact and Value," 28. For Putnam's detailed account of contemporary responses to thick ethical concepts as counterexamples to the idea that there exists an absolute fact/value dichotomy, see pp. 35–36.

50. Ibid., 34–35. Putnam's full description is as follows:

The sort of entanglement I have in mind becomes obvious when we study words like "cruel." The word "cruel" obviously . . . has normative and, indeed, ethical uses. If one asks me what sort of person my child's teacher is, and I say, "He is very cruel," I have both criticized him as a teacher and criticized him as a man. I do not have to add, "He is not a good teacher," or, "He is not a good man." . . . Similarly, I cannot simply say, "He is a very cruel person and a good man," and be understood. Yet "cruel" can also be used purely descriptively, as when a historian writes that a certain monarch was exceptionally cruel, or that the cruelties of the regime provoked a number of rebellions. (Ibid.)

51. Ibid., 35.

52. The concept of democracy is often expressed in terms of "thin" and "thick" definitions. According to the former, democracy is defined as popular sovereignty or majority rule. But what popularly elected officials do with the popular mandate of their authority leads into a "thicker" conception of democracy that includes notions of rights, of citizen participation, and so on.

53. For an excellent critique of the fact/value distinction from within the political theory literature on Wittgenstein, see Hanna Fenichel Pitkin, *Wittgenstein and Justice: On the Significance of Ludwig Wittgenstein for Social and Political Thought* (Berkeley: University of California Press, 1993), esp. chaps. 8 and 10. Putnam's pragmatist challenge to the fact/value dichotomy shows that evaluative thought extends to scientific judgments: "Pragmatist philosophers did not refer only to the kind of normative judgments that we call 'moral' or 'ethical'; judgments of 'coherence,' 'plausibility,' 'reasonableness,' 'simplicity' and of what Dirac famously called the beauty of a hypothesis, are all normative judgments in Charles Peirce's sense, judgments of 'what ought to be' in the case of reasoning." Putnam, "Entanglement of Fact and Value," 31. As we shall see in chapter 2 when we turn to Wittgenstein's remarks on the theory of natural selection, to say that a scientific hypothesis is coherent in its structure or that it exhibits an admirable simplicity is to give reasons for agreeing with it. "Yet *coherence* and *simplicity* and the like are *values*," Putnam contends (31). To say that there are epistemic values is not to say that there is no difference between these and, say, ethical values. It is merely to say that values permeate all aspects of judging and that we cannot speak of "value" as if it were one thing (commonly a synonym for "ethics")—namely, the opposite of "fact." The problem with the fact/value dichotomy, as Putnam argues, is that it reifies the difference that we, speaking in an ordinary idiom, may well wish to discern in any given judgment into a metaphysical binary that bears no relation to the particular case.

54. I discuss Habermas's and Rawls's approaches to values in chapters 4 and 5, respectively.

55. David Wiggins, "A Sensible Subjectivism," *Needs, Values, Truth*, 185–214, at 186.

56. Bertrand Russell, "Notes on Philosophy January 1960," *Philosophy* 35 (1960): 146–47. Quoted in Wiggins, "Sensible Subjectivism," 210.

57. Habermas rejects "noncognitivist approaches [which] seek to reduce the content of moral judgments directly to feelings, dispositions, or decisions of subjects who take certain positions. These versions of ethical subjectivism draw a sharp line between judgments of fact and judgments of value, but they can account for why normative and evaluative sentences behave differently from sentences in the first person only by appealing to an 'error theory' [i.e., Mackie]." This approach reduces the self-descriptions of participants to be engaging in normative reason-giving in any moral debate to mistakes, thereby offering a "revisionary" account of the moral language game itself. Trying to explain how a judgment that involves a feeling can still be cognitive, Habermas grants, "feelings have propositional content, which goes hand in hand with the moral evaluation of thematic behavior [and that therefore] we can take them—like perceptions—to be implicit judgments." Jürgen Habermas, *Truth and Justification*, trans. Barbara Fultner (Cambridge, MA: MIT Press, 2003), 240-41, 242 (hereafter cited as *TJ*).

58. Wiggins, "Sensible Subjectivism," 210.

59. McDowell, "Non-Cognitivism and Rule-Following," 200.

60. Wiggins, "Sensible Subjectivism," 186.

61. Thomas Nagel, "Subjective and Objective," in *Mortal Questions* (1979; repr., New York: Cambridge University Press, 2012), 196–214, at 211.

62. Stanley Cavell, "Aesthetic Problems of Modern Philosophy," in *Must We Mean What We Say?* (Cambridge: Cambridge University Press, 1976), 73–96, at 88.

63. Ibid.

64. Ibid., 89.

65. Kant continues, "And yet, if we then call the object beautiful, we believe we have a universal voice, and lay claim to the agreement of everyone, whereas any private sensation would decide solely for the observer himself and his liking." Immanuel Kant, *Critique of Judgment*, trans. Werner S. Pluhar (Indianapolis: Hackett, 1987), §8, pp. 59–60 (hereafter cited as *CJ*).

66. Cavell, "Aesthetic Problems of Modern Philosophy," 94.

67. Ibid., 93.

68. Stephen Mulhall, *Stanley Cavell: Philosophy's Recounting of the Ordinary* (Oxford: Oxford University Press, 1998), 26. For another parsing of Cavell on rationality, see Pitkin, *Wittgenstein and Justice*, 153–57.

69. I discuss these passages in detail in chapter 8.

70. Attacking the objectivism of the rationalist approaches taken to be the main target of Wittgenstein's philosophical investigations, Anthony Giddens, Roy Bhaskar, Charles Taylor, Pierre Bourdieu, and Jürgen Habermas, among other social theorists, have argued for an agent-centered approach to rules and rule following, which also avoids subjectivism by

putting "tacit knowledge" of rules or practical competence at the heart of judging and acting. Rather than portray subjects as engaging the objective tracks of rules as a kind of mechanical ability to intuit propositional content and meaning prior to the actual action of following a rule, these theorists emphasize the skillful ability of judging and acting subjects to correctly apply rules without necessarily being able to formulate an explicit discursive account of what they are able to do. The ontological idea of tacit knowledge of rules can appear to be a genuine alternative to what Habermas calls "the philosophy of consciousness" shared by both rationalist and empiricist philosophers. It appears to refuse the intellectualist position and to argue for the difference between theoretical ("knowing that") and practical, or tacit, knowledge ("knowing how"). Tacit knowledge is generally taken to constitute the "fundamental background knowledge [of the life-world] that must tacitly supplement" propositional knowledge, as Habermas puts it. Quoted in Nigel Pleasants, *Wittgenstein and the Idea of a Critical Social Theory: A Critique of Giddens, Habermas and Bhaskar* (New York: Routledge, 1999), 58. Anthony Giddens, *Profiles and Critiques in Social Theory* (London: Macmillan, 1982), 57. For a good critique of the ascription of tacit rule following to Wittgenstein, see Pleasants, *Wittgenstein and Critical Theory*, chap. 4. As we shall see in chapter 7, Habermas will in this way ground democratic ideals of justice, rationality, and autonomy in the rule-governed structure of ordinary language use and the "rule-consciousness" of individuals as competent speakers.

71. Pleasants, *Wittgenstein*, 63.

72. Ibid. See also *PI*, §92.

73. Furthermore, comments Steven Affeldt, "insinuating a rule that we must be following beneath the surface description of our activity invites the idea that we do—must—possess more than these examples and explanations, and it also invites the idea that in learning concepts through the examples and explanations provided by others we must make a leap from what they offer to the rule that they are unable to offer." Steven Affeldt, "The Normativity of the Natural," in *Varieties of Skepticism: Essays after Kant, Wittgenstein, and Cavell*, ed. James Conant and Andrea Kern, 311–61 (Boston: Walter de Gruyter, 2014), 335.

74. Quoted in Pleasants, *Wittgenstein*, 66.

75. Even in ball games, which we normally think of as wholly rule-governed, our normative assessment does not always require rules. As Affeldt explains:

> It [our play] may be assessed as strategically shortsighted ("He should have tried to bunt the runner to second base"), as sloppy ("She isn't giving enough attention to her defensive position"), as mean-spirited ("They had the game well in hand and could have/should have played substitutes for the last several minutes. There was no need to humiliate

the opponents"), as selfish ("He is hogging the ball"), etc. ("Normativity of the Natural," 328–29)

76. Ibid., 340.

77. Pitkin, *Wittgenstein and Justice*, 3. Carefully attuned as she is to the crucial importance played by context in Wittgenstein's critique of metaphysical and idealist accounts of meaning, it is hard to make sense of this reading of grammar as a kind of Kantian a priori (ibid., 93). See also Pitkin's brilliant reading of the debate over justice between Socrates and Thrasymachus (also in *Wittgenstein and Justice*, chap. 8). As I argue shortly, this view of grammar appeals to what we think must be the case for there to be meaning at all.

78. Ibid., 120. Just this interpretation is put into question by Pitkin herself, when in the final pages of the book she writes, "If language defines our world, then for that world to retain any kind of stability language *must* be a system of fixed, exhaustive, systematic rules. . . . That, I think, is the spirit of the *Tractatus*." The author of *Philosophical Investigations*, by contrast, sought "a release from the rigid and frantic commitment to unambiguous order. Instead of retreating to a last island of certainty, Wittgenstein's later philosophy examines the craving for certainty itself, and concludes that we are, after all, able to live on the sea" (ibid., 336–37).

79. Pitkin, *Wittgenstein and Justice*, 120.

80. Ibid., 121.

81. Mulhall, *Stanley Cavell*, 152, 18. For an excellent critique of Mulhall on this point, see Steven Affeldt, "The Ground of Mutuality: Criteria, Judgment, and Intelligibility in Stephen Mulhall and Stanley Cavell," *European Journal of Philosophy* 6, no. 1 (1998): 1–31, at 5. According to Affeldt, Mulhall's *Stanley Cavell: Philosophy's Recounting of the Ordinary*, though also a deeply appreciative and clarifying reading of Cavell's Wittgenstein, shares the same tendency I am describing in relation to Pitkin to see language as a grammatical framework of rules that sets limits in a quasi-transcendental way on what can be meaningfully said or done. See also Affeldt, "Normativity of the Natural." In this context it is worth noting that Pitkin worked with Cavell's dissertation "The Claim to Rationality," which was later revised and published as *The Claim to Reason*. This might explain some of the discrepancies in our interpretations of Cavell.

82. Affeldt, "Normativity of the Natural," 320.

83. Stanley Cavell, "The Availability of Wittgenstein's Later Philosophy," in *Must We Mean What We Say?* (Cambridge: Cambridge University Press, 1976), 44–72, at 52. See also Affeldt, "Normativity of the Natural," 336.

84. Affeldt, "Normativity of the Natural," 337.

85. Ibid., 337. What haunts the demand for a standard of correctness is skepticism. As Affeldt explains:

Challenging the idea that there are things that function as explanations or justifications apart from specific confusions and the like must
be a central target of Wittgenstein's. For the idea that there just *are*
things that function as explanations is the twin of the idea that there
just *are* questions about what we do and say, that there just *are* things
that need to be explained or justified—that there just *are* "gap[s] in the
foundations" (PI §87). But if we allow that it will seem, and rightly,
"that secure understanding is only possible if we first doubt everything
that *can* be doubted, and then remove all these doubts" (PI §87). And
here we are pushed toward a full-blown standard of correctness—
something that must remove all possible misunderstandings and cover
all possible cases of a word's applications. (Affeldt, "Normativity of the
Natural," 337)

86. For Affeldt's criticism of Mulhall on this point, see Affeldt, "Normativity
of the Natural," 350–52.
87. Cavell, "Wittgenstein's Later Philosophy," 52.
88. McDowell, "Non-Cognitivism and Rule-Following," 207.
89. Ibid.
90. Wittgenstein quoted in Cavell, "Wittgenstein's Later Philosophy," 52.
And here too, on the importance of form of life to understanding Wittgenstein's Copernican revolution, both Pitkin's and Mulhall's writings
are beautifully attuned. To my mind, as I aim to show in chapter 8, the
demand that something *must* guarantee normativity leads to a conception of form of life as ethnographically static, rather than as dynamic and
potentially world-opening.
91. Affeldt, "Normativity of the Natural," 344.
92. Ibid., 347.
93. See also Affeldt, "Ground of Mutuality," 16–17.
94. Quoted in ibid., 17.
95. Affeldt, "Normativity of the Natural," 354.
96. See ibid., 354–55.
97. For a good discussion of this problem in language generally, see ibid.,
355–56.
98. Hannah Arendt, *The Life of the Mind*, vol. 1, *Thinking* (New York: Harcourt
Brace, 1978), 22, 23, 22 (hereafter cited as *LMT*). This edition presents
both volumes of *The Life of the Mind* in a single book but preserves the
original pagination of each volume, thus the differentiation: *LMT* for
Thinking and *LMW* for *Willing*. Arendt adds, "Seeming—the it-seems-
to-me, *dokei moi*—is the mode, perhaps the only possible one, in which an
appearing world is acknowledged and perceived" (*LMT*, 21).
99. Ibid. Arendt cites here Maurice Merleau-Ponty's work on perception.
100. For a powerful critique of political theory's continued dependence on
philosophy as an authorizing metadiscourse, see the work of John G.
Gunnell, esp. *The Orders of Discourse: Philosophy, Social Science, and Politics*

(Boston: Rowman and Littlefield, 1998); *The Descent of Political Theory: The Genealogy of an American Vocation* (Chicago: University of Chicago Press, 1993). Gunnell's most recent book on Wittgenstein also offers an excellent discussion of how philosophy continues to animate the penchant for the order of rules in social science and political theory. John G. Gunnell, *Social Inquiry after Wittgenstein and Kuhn: Leaving Everything as It Is* (New York: Columbia University Press, 2014).

101. Hannah Arendt, *The Human Condition* (Chicago: University of Chicago Press, 1989), 254 (hereafter cited as *HC*). On "world alienation," see also Hannah Arendt, "The Concept of History," in *Between Past and Future*, 41–90, at 53 (hereafter cited as "CH" in text and notes).

102. For the distinction between theories and events as the origin of Cartesian doubt, see *HC*, 254, and chap. 5, esp. 259.

103. The new modern god of Science, Arendt argues, which has in any case deposed philosophy as the master discourse, cannot restore our confidence in the truth-revealing capacity of the senses, for it is precisely the task of science to call such confidence into question. Within its own realm, of course, such scientific questioning is justified. But when the scientific attitude overtakes all aspects of human existence, when the entire idea of truth and objectivity is claimed by science and its method, then the loss of common sense can only result in extreme subjectivism and the flight into an abstract ideal of the external standpoint that "Droysen rightly denounced as 'eunuchic objectivity'" ("CH," 49).

104. Linda M. G. Zerilli, *Feminism and the Abyss of Freedom* (Chicago: University of Chicago Press, 2005).

105. She continues, "Impartiality, and with it all true historiography, came into the world when Homer decided to sing the deeds of the Trojans no less than those of the Achaeans, and to praise the glory of Hector no less than the greatness of Achilles" ("CH," 51). On Homeric impartiality, see also "IP," 166–67. For a reading of Arendt's conception of judgment as based on Homeric impartiality, see Lisa Disch, "More Truth than Fact: Storytelling as Critical Understanding in the Writings of Hannah Arendt," *Political Theory* 21, no. 4 (November 1993): 665–94.

106. Readings of Arendt that emphasize the importance of a refigured conception of objectivity to her political thought include Liisi Keedus, *The Crisis of German Historicism: The Early Political Thought of Hannah Arendt and Leo Strauss* (Cambridge: Cambridge University Press, 2015); Richard J. Bernstein, *Beyond Objectivism and Relativism: Science, Hermeneutics, and Praxis* (Philadelphia: University of Pennsylvania Press, 1983). Notwithstanding his awareness of Arendt's unique project, Bernstein sides with Habermas in arguing that Arendt fails to provide criteria according to which judgments with objective validity could be reached.

107. Arendt's idea of a common world built on plural perspectives departs from the idea of commonality as the normative ground of a shared democracy.

For an excellent critique of this idea, see Michaele L. Ferguson, *Sharing Democracy* (New York: Oxford University Press, 2012).

108. On the narrow or conventional view of objectivity, perspectival modes of thought, because they are infused with subjectivity, have an intrinsic tendency to interfere with our access to reality. And though Arendt insists on plural perspectives as the very condition of judging, she also argues that there is a certain mode of subjectivity that cuts us off from the world. This is the form of the subject enclosed within his or her mind and certain only of the capacity for radical doubt, as described by Descartes. It is the subjectivism that attends the "world-alienation" that Arendt called "the hallmark of the modern age" (*HC*, 254). Such alienation marks our sense of a boundary separating us from the world and that is rooted in "the conviction that objective truth is not given to man but that he can know only what he makes himself" (*HC*, 293). What a person can know are the conceptual categories of his or her own mind; he or she cannot know whether and how these are connected to how things stand in the world.

109. As Putnam likewise argues, "reality does *not* have an existence and character wholly independent of human practices, beliefs, and evidence for the simple reason that human practices beliefs and evidence are a very large part of the reality we talk about, and reality would be quite different were they different." Hilary Putnam, "Pragmatism and Nonscientific Knowledge," in *Hilary Putnam: Pragmatism and Realism*, ed. James Conant and Urszula M. Żegleń (New York: Routledge, 2002), 14–24, at 18.

110. Arendt writes:

> The destruction of the common world . . . is usually preceded by the destruction of the many aspects in which it presents itself to human plurality. This can happen under conditions of radical isolation, where nobody can any longer agree with anybody else, as is usually the case in tyrannies. But it may also happen under conditions of mass society or mass hysteria, where we see all people suddenly behave as though they were members of one family, each multiplying and prolonging the perspective of his neighbor. In both instances, men have become entirely private, that is, they have been deprived of seeing and hearing others, of being seen and being heard by them. They are all imprisoned in the subjectivity of their own singular experience, which does not cease to be singular if the same experience is multiplied innumerable times. (*HC*, 58)

111. Hannah Arendt, "What Remains? The Language Remains: An Interview with Gunther Gauss," in Hannah Arendt, *Essays in Understanding, 1930–1954*, ed. Jerome Kohn (New York: Harcourt and Brace, 1994), 1–23, at 20.

112. Conant, "Perspectivism, I," 32.

113. Ibid., 33.

114. Quoted in ibid., 35.

115. On this point see ibid., 34.

116. For a brilliant defense of Nietzsche against this reading of perspectivism as relativism, see Conant, "Perspectivism, I," and James Conant, "Dialectic of Perspectivism, II," *Sats: Nordic Journal of Philosophy* 7, no. 1 (2006): 6–57. Throughout this discussion I am once again deeply indebted to Conant's recovery of the ordinary concept of perspective.

117. For a summary of this ordinary understanding of perspective that I am ascribing to Arendt, see Conant, "Perspectivism, I," 15.

118. Quoted in Conant, "Perspectivism, II," 45n57.

119. Ibid., 45.

120. Michael Rosen, *On Voluntary Servitude: False Consciousness and the Theory of Ideology* (Cambridge, MA: Harvard University Press, 1996), 78.

CHAPTER 2

1. *CJ*, §8, pp. 59–60/101. I have drawn (in some cases) on the Pluhar edition of Kant's *Critique of Judgment* (see chap. 1, n. 65) and (in most cases) on the Paul Guyer and Eric Matthews translation. Immanuel Kant, *Critique of the Power of Judgment* (2000; repr., New York: Cambridge University Press, 2006). Page numbers refer, respectively, to these two translations.

2. Kant writes:

   This problem can also be represented thus: How is a judgment possible which, merely from *one's own* feeling of pleasure in an object, independent of its concept, judges this pleasure as attached to the representation of the same object in every other subject, *a priori*, i.e., without having to wait for the assent of others? (*CJ*, §36, p. 153/168–69)

3. For a sympathetic and astute reading of Arendt's turn to Kant and the value of aesthetic judgment for democratic politics, see Tracy B. Strong, *Politics without Vision: Thinking without a Bannister in the Twentieth Century* (Chicago: University of Chicago Press, 2012).

4. The phrase is from Mary Mothersill, *Beauty Restored* (Oxford: Oxford University Press, 1984), 187. I mentioned this problem in the preface and discuss it further in this chapter.

5. David Hume, "Of the Standard of Taste" [1757], in *Essays: Moral, Political, and Literary* (Indianapolis: Liberty Fund, 1994), 226–49, at 230 (hereafter cited as "ST.")

6. For a similar account of the relative nature of taste and the need for tolerance, see David Hume, "The Sceptic," in *Essays*, 159–80, at 163.

7. David Hume, *An Enquiry Concerning the Principles of Morals*, in *Enquiries Concerning Human Understanding and Concerning the Principles of Morals*, ed. L. A. Selby-Bigge, rev. P. H. Nidditch (Oxford: Oxford University Press, 1975), 294.

8. Hume writes:

> Reason is the discovery of truth or falsehood. Truth or falsehood consists in an agreement or disagreement either to the *real* relations of ideas, or to *real* existence and matter of fact. Whatever, therefore, is not susceptible of this agreement or disagreement, is incapable of being true or false, and can never be an object of our reason. Now 'tis evident our passions, volitions, and actions, are not susceptible of any such agreement or disagreement; being original facts and realities, compleat in themselves, and implying no reference to other passions, volitions, and actions. 'Tis impossible, therefore, they can be pronounced either true or false, and be either contrary or conformable to reason.

  David Hume, *A Treatise of Human Nature*, 2nd ed., ed. L. A. Selby-Bigge, rev. P. H. Nidditch (New York: Oxford University Press, 1978), 458.

9. In general, the secondary literature on Hume's essay has produced an account that "by insulating Hume's aesthetics from his scepticism . . . leaves us with a schizophrenic 'two-Humes' reading." Susan Hahn, "How Can a Sceptic Have a Standard of Taste?" *British Journal of Aesthetics* 53, no. 4 (October 2013): 379–92, at 380. Although Hahn's interpretation, virtually singular in the now voluminous literature on Hume's text, avoids the problem of the "two Humes" reading, according to which *Hume's* practical norms come to outweigh his skepticism, it does so by accepting the skeptical problematic that creates problems for Hume and at the expense of eliminating any tension in Hume's thought on the subject at all.

10. Ibid.

11. Ibid., 387.

12. Ibid., 388.

13. Ibid., 386.

14. Ibid., 384, 389.

15. Paul Guyer admires the naturalistic character of Hume's standard, which he characterizes as "an empirically discoverable fact that there is agreement about the validity of some preferences and absurdity of others." By contrast with Hahn, Guyer downplays Hume's skepticism and is willing to declare what that standard is for Hume. Paul Guyer, "The Standard of Taste and the 'Most Ardent Desire of Society,'" in *Values of Beauty: Historical Essays in Aesthetics* (New York: Cambridge University Press, 2005), 37–74, at 39.

16. In the view of Guyer, Hume's search for a "standard of taste, or canon of agreed upon objects of taste, plays not just a regulative role in the individual pursuit of pleasure . . . but also a constitutive role in both aesthetic response and aesthetic judgment; that is, agreement in taste actually turns out to be a crucial factor in both our pleasurable experience of beautiful objects and our meaningful discourse about them." Guyer, "Standard of Taste," 45.

17. Kant writes:

> By a principle of taste would be understood a fundamental proposition
> under the condition of which one could subsume the concept of an
> object and then by means of an inference conclude that it is beautiful.
> But that is absolutely impossible. For I must be sensitive of the pleasure
> immediately in the representation of it, and I cannot be talked into it
> by means of any proofs. Thus although critics, as Hume says, can rea-
> son more plausibly than cooks, they still suffer the same fate as them.
> They cannot expect a determining ground for their judgment from
> proofs, but only from the reflection of the subject on his own state
> (of pleasure or displeasure), rejecting all precepts and rules. (*CJ*, §34,
> p. 149/166)

Kant is referring here to an "objective principle of taste," which is what
Hume seeks, not an (a priori) "subjective principle of taste," which
governs the reflection of the judging subject on his or her own state and
which Kant's transcendental critique will defend (*CJ*, §34, p. 149, 150/166).
For a good account of the literature on whether Hume's essay on taste
influenced Kant, see Timothy M. Costelloe, "Hume, Kant, and the Antinomy of Taste," *Journal of the History of Philosophy* 41, no. 2 (April 2003):
165–85.

18. For an account of arguments in this vein see Timothy M. Costelloe,
"Hume's Aesthetics: The Literature and Directions for Research," *Hume
Studies* 30, no. 1 (April 2004): 87–126, at 100. See also Mothersill, *Beauty
Restored*, 69.

19. See Costelloe, "Hume's Aesthetics," 103.

20. McDowell, "Non-Cognitivism and Rule-Following," 217 (see chap. 1,
n. 37).

21. As discussed in chapter 1, the absolute conception distinguishes the world
as it is independent of our experience from the world as it seems to us.
The former requires response independent concepts (i.e., concepts of science, mathematics, etc.), the latter requires response dependent concepts
(e.g., color concepts, secondary features, aesthetic, moral, and other evaluative features). See Williams, *Descartes*.

22. Hume, "Sceptic," 164; quoted also in Peter Kivy, "Hume's Standard of
Taste: Breaking the Circle," *British Journal of Aesthetics* 7, no. 1 (1967): 57–
66, at 59. It is important to see, as Hilary Putnam writes, that

> Hume's criterion for "matters of fact" presupposed what might be
> called a "pictorial semantics." Concepts, in Hume's theory of the mind,
> are a kind of "idea," and "ideas" are themselves pictorial: the only way
> they can represent any "matter of fact" is by *resembling* it (not neces-
> sarily visually, however—ideas can also be tactile, olfactory and so on).
> Ideas have, however, nonpictorial properties as well; they can involve
> or be associated with *sentiments*, in other words, emotions. Hume

does not just tell us that one cannot infer an "ought" from an "is"; he claims, more broadly, that there is no "matter of fact" about *right* and no matter of fact about *virtue*. The reason is that if there *were* matters of fact about virtue and vice, then it would have to be the case (if we assume "pictorial semantics") that the property of virtue would be *picturable* in the way that the property of being an apple is picturable. Hume was quite correct, *given his semantical views*, to conclude that there are no such matters of fact. Furthermore, *given that "passions" or "sentiments" were the only remaining properties of "ideas," Hume thought he had at his disposal to explain why it so much as seems to us that there are such matters of fact*, it was quite reasonable for him to conclude that the components of our "ideas" that correspond to judgments of and vice are nothing more than "sentiments" aroused in us by the "contemplation" of the relevant actions owing to "the particular structure and fabric" of our minds.

Hillary Putnam, "The Empiricist Background," in *Collapse of Fact/Value*, 7–27, at 15.

23. Hume, "Sceptic," 164–65. Hume continues, "Now, it is evident, that this sentiment must depend upon the particular fabric or structure of the mind, which enables such particular forms to operate in such a particular manner, and produces a sympathy or conformity between the mind and its objects. Vary the structure of the mind or inward organs, the sentiment no longer follows, though the form remains the same" (ibid.). On this point, see Kivy, "Hume's Standard of Taste," at 59.

24. Kivy, "Hume's Standard of Taste," 59.

25. Barry Stroud, "'Gilding or Staining' the World with 'Sentiments' and 'Phantasms,'" *Hume Studies* 19, no. 2 (November 1993): 253–72; Barry Stroud, *Hume* (New York: Routledge, 2000); Mackie, *Ethics* (see chap. 1, n. 33). Stroud is deeply critical of Hume's noncognitivism, whereas Mackie redescribes it as an "error theory" and endorses it as the proper way to speak of evaluative judgments. As Maximilian de Gaynesford summarizes:

> In Mackie's view, our evaluative thinking presents our awareness of value like experience presents our awareness of primary qualities. . . . If what it is like for us to be presented with value is what it is like for us to be presented with primary properties, then the phenomenology can be assessed by a simple empirical test. Are there, in fact, items in the world which both count as values and have the properties of primary qualities—perceptibility; causal efficacy; intelligibility independent of human sensibility? There are not [Mackie claims]. . . . Hence our evaluative thinking is empirically false; our phenomenology is in error.

Maximilian de Gaynesford, *John McDowell* (Malden, MA: Polity Press, 2004), 171–72.

26. Distinguishing between the two faculties of "reason" and "taste," Hume writes:

> The former conveys the knowledge of truth and falsehood: the latter gives the sentiment of beauty and deformity, vice and virtue. The one discovers objects as they really stand in nature, without addition or diminution: the other has a productive faculty. . . . From circumstances and relations, known or supposed, the former leads us to the discovery of the concealed and unknown: after all circumstances and relations are laid before us, the latter makes us feel from the whole a new sentiment of blame or approbation.

Hume, *Enquiry Concerning Morals*, 294. Hume describes feeling or sentiment (e.g., virtue, vice, beauty, deformity) as that which "lies in yourself, not in the object." Hume, *Treatise of Human Nature*, 469.

27. Stroud, "'Gilding or Staining' the World," 254.

28. Hume clearly associates the modern philosophy with the idea of projection as error, but it is this same philosophy that "cuts off all hopes of success [in an effort to attain] . . . any standard of taste" ("ST," 229).

29. Blackburn, *Spreading the Word* (see chap. 1, n. 35). R. M. Sainsbury usefully parses the difference between Mackie and Blackburn thus:

> There are at least two species of projectivist. Some, like J. L. Mackie, hold that the projection involves error: we are deceived into thinking that the apparent ascription of properties is really what it seems, which, according to the projectivist, it cannot be. Others, like Blackburn himself, see no need to convict us of error. Rather, this species of projectivist, the "quasi-realist," seeks to explain how the apparently property-ascribing activities are quite natural, even given projectivism, and how, properly understood, they involve no error.

R. M. Sainsbury, review of *Spreading the Word: Groundings in the Philosophy of Language*, by Simon Blackburn, *British Journal for the Philosophy of Science* 36, no. 2 (June 1985): 211–15, at 213. The projectivist as quasi-realist (Blackburn's Hume), then, is not telling us that we have made a mistake but is trying to call our attention to the ordinary character of our speaking about values. Though I agree that this is much closer to what Hume is doing, especially in "Of a Standard of Taste," Blackburn's commitment to projectivism in ordinary evaluative judgments is hard to square with our ordinary sense, recognized by Kant, of their claim to validity. See Sainsbury review, 214. The problem is how to square this claim with a conception of objectivity that takes account of our affective response and is not beholden to the absolute conception of the world.

30. In the view of Mary Mothersill, Hume's point about agreement in masterpieces points to a subtext that counters his official doctrine. It is not, as Hume seems to claim, the judgments of ideal critics (discussed sub-

sequently) or rules of composition that form the standard. Rather, it is the body of works that have stood the test of time, exemplars of human aesthetic excellence, which indicate what real beauty is. Mary Mothersill, "Hume and the Paradox of Taste," in *Aesthetics: A Critical Anthology,* ed. George Dickie, Richard Sclafani, and Ronald Roblin, 2nd ed. (New York: St. Martin's Press, 1989), 269–86. See also Mothersill, *Beauty Restored,* chap. 7. I would agree with Jerrold Levinson, however, when he observes that masterpieces alone "cannot serve directly as yardsticks of artistic worth, since relevant similarity, say, between a given work and some masterwork would, in the first place, itself require judgment to estimate." Jerrold Levinson, "Hume's Standard of Taste: The Real Problem," *Journal of Aesthetics and Art Criticism* 60, no. 3 (Summer 2002): 227–38, at 232.

31. Hahn, "Sceptic Standard of Taste?" 389. This notion of cause is a non-explanatory sense of causality allowed by Hume's Pyrrhonism, argues Hahn. Generally speaking, the description of Hume's theory as causal, argues Peter Jones, is based on "the view that certain objects cause normal percipients under normal conditions to have an aesthetic sentiment, which itself causes them to utter an aesthetic verdict or judgement." Peter Jones, "Hume's Aesthetics Reassessed," *Philosophical Quarterly* 26, no. 102 (January 1976): 48–62, at 58. For a vigorous debate about the causal basis of aesthetic judgments in Hume's thought, see Roger A. Shiner, "Hume and the Causal Theory of Taste," *Journal of Aesthetics and Art Criticism* 54, no. 3 (Summer 1996): 237–49. With Hume as his example, Shiner attacks the causal theory and defends the criterial theory of taste. For critical responses to Shiner's essay, see Mary Mothersill, "In Defense of Hume and the Causal Theory of Taste," *Journal of Aesthetics and Art Criticism* 55, no. 3 (Summer 1997): 312–17; John W. Bender and Richard N. Manning, "On Shiner's 'Hume and the Causal Theory of Taste,'" *Journal of Aesthetics and Art Criticism* 55, no. 3 (Summer 1997): 317–20.

32. David Wiggins, "Sensible Subjectivism," 194 (see chap. 1, n. 55).

33. As Brent Kalar observes, "Hume clearly believes that, in the bulk of cases, disagreement is fully explained in terms of defects or abnormalities in individual subjects. This belief is rational only to the extent that he has grounds for assuming that there is a universal beauty-sensibility." Brent Kalar, *The Demands of Taste in Kant's Aesthetics* (New York: Continuum, 2006), 15. Kalar goes on to describe Hume's reasoning that if the great works have endured, that speaks to the existence of a universal beauty-sensibility, which will eventually produce agreement in taste. And Hume does seem to assume such a thing. He continues, "But when these obstructions are removed, the beauties, which are naturally fitted to excite agreeable sentiments, immediately display their energy; and while the world endures, they maintain their authority over the minds of men" ("ST," 233); quoted in Kalar, *Demands of Taste,* 15. Kalar argues that Hume's case for the existence of a universal beauty-sensibility, which is

built on a broader "factual claim about what sentiment would occur in an idealized set of circumstances, namely, those embodied in the actual judgements of the true judges," fails (*Demands of Taste*, 18–19). I discuss the factual basis of Hume's argument for ideal judges as the standard subsequently. Though Kalar is right to emphasize the extent to which Hume seems to assume that, were it not for defects of one sort or another, we would agree in our judgments of taste, it is also the case that Hume, toward the end of the essay, lists a wide range of contingent circumstances (e.g., age, past experiences, location in time and space) that cannot properly be described as internal or psychological "defects" yet nonetheless influence such judgments. He points in effect to something in the world rather than the subject that impairs taste, and, as I argue in the concluding chapter, this is important for any theory of judgment, especially a democratic one. This is the point in the essay where it seems as if no standard could ever possibly be found. In a sense, then, one could agree with Kalar that Hume's argument depends on the existence of a universal beauty-sensibility, with the caveat that it is Hume himself who puts that sensibility, and thus the existence of a standard, in question.

34. For a good discussion of this point, see Gary Hatfield, "Kant and Helmholtz on Primary and Secondary Qualities," in *Primary and Secondary Qualities: The Historical and Ongoing Debate*, ed. Lawrence Nolan (New York: Cambridge University Press, 2011), 304–38; A. E. Pitson, "Hume on Primary and Secondary Qualities," *Hume Studies* 8, no. 2 (November 1982): 125–38.

35. McDowell, "Non-Cognitivism and Rule-Following," 199.

36. Ibid., 200–201, 201.

37. Ibid., 201.

38. Reaching a different conclusion than the one offered here, Simon Blackburn argues that Hume did not subscribe to Locke's distinction between the primary and secondary qualities. Simon Blackburn, "Hume on the Mezzanine Level," *Hume Studies* 19, no. 2 (November 1993): 273–88. Kenneth P. Winkler, arguing against Blackburn, holds that in Hume's Pyrrhonnian skepticism, "a distinction between primary and secondary qualities does survive, . . . [and] permit[s], at the level of common life, a distinction between what is 'really there' in things, taken by themselves, and what is there only in relation to us." (The former maps onto primary qualities and the latter onto secondary qualities in Hume's account.) Winkler recognizes that this is a "crude distinction" but holds that it is an important contribution of Hume's to the critique of rationalist theories of aesthetics and morals, which exclude the subjective element. Kenneth P. Winkler, "Hutcheson and Hume on the Color of Virtue," *Hume Studies* 22, no. 1 (April 1996): 3–22; quotation at 16.

39. Hume, *Treatise of Human Nature*, 228.

40. According to Winkler, "a distinction between primary qualities can, in

Hume's view, survive the excessive doubts of *T[reatise]* I iv 4 and [the] *E[nquiry Concerning Human Nature]* XII i." Winkler, "Hutcheson and Hume on Color," 15.

41. Hume, *Treatise of Human Nature*, 227–28.

42. Pitson, "Hume on Primary and Secondary Qualities," 132, emphasis in original.

43. Conant, "Perspectivism, I" (see chap. 1, n. 11).

44. Commentators who read Hume as downplaying the modern philosophy's skeptical account of qualities include Jones, "Hume's Aesthetics Reassessed"; Peter Kivy, "Hume's Neighbour's Wife: An Essay on the Evolution of Hume's Aesthetics," *British Journal of Aesthetics* 23, no. 3 (Summer 1983): 195–208; Theodore A. Gracyk, "Rethinking Hume's Standard of Taste," *Journal of Aesthetics and Art Criticism* 52, no. 2 (1994): 169–82; Mothersill, *Beauty Restored*. On these accounts, Hume's theory should be understood as causal: there are qualities in objects that give rise to the sentiment of beauty (or deformity), but these arise in us only when there is a "fit" or match "between the object and a subject who is capable of being affected in a certain manner" (Costelloe, "Hume's Aesthetics," 91).

45. This ideal critic definition has led some critics to argue that Hume is involved in what Peter Kivy calls "a vicious circle whereby good art is defined in terms of the good critic and the good critic in terms of good art" ("Hume's Standard of Taste," 60). The criticism, originally made by S. G. Brown, "Observations on Hume's Theory of Taste," *English Studies* 20 (1938): 93–98, has been debated in the readings of Kivy, "Hume's Standard of Taste"; James Noxon, "Hume's Opinion of Critics," *Journal of Aesthetics and Art Criticism* 20, no. 2 (1961): 157–62; Carolyn W. Korsmeyer, "Hume and the Foundations of Taste," *Journal of Aesthetics and Art Criticism* 35, no. 2 (1976): 201–15; Nick Zangwill, "Hume, Taste, and Teleology," *Philosophical Papers* 23, no. 1 (1994): 1–18. For a good summary of these arguments, see Costelloe, "Hume's Aesthetics," 99–100.

46. Peter Kivy, "Recent Scholarship and the British Tradition: A Logic of Taste—The First Fifty Years," in *Aesthetics: A Critical Anthology* (New York: St. Martin's Press, 1977), 626–687, at 638.

47. Wiggins, "Sensible Subjectivism," 193.

48. According to Kivy, Hume's attempt to reduce sentiment to matters of fact involves him in an "infinite regress" ("Hume's Standard of Taste," 63). See also Harold Osborne, "Hume's Standard and the Diversity of Aesthetic Taste," *British Journal of Aesthetics* 7, no. 1 (1967): 50–66; Korsmeyer, "Hume and Foundations of Taste," esp. 205–6.

49. Levinson, "Hume's Standard of Taste," 229. Levinson argues that Hume provides some rational reasons to care about what ideal critics think, but only if "you are not in fundamental respects cognitively or affectively different from such critics" (235). According to Guyer, Hume is interested not in finding a set of rules for the training of individual taste as such but in

the modeling of taste in the work of ideal critics. Thus, his project is one of "establishing the standard of taste as conditions for identifying a body of actual critics whose preferences would then determine the standard of taste." Guyer, "Standard of Taste," 71. Though I fully agree that Hume is really developing a theory of exemplarity rather than a standard based on rules, his projectivist metaphysic cannot shake the idea that there must be something beyond the actual practices of aesthetic judgment that secures them as correct.

50. Levinson, "Hume's Standard of Taste," 230.

51. Anthony Savile, *Kantian Aesthetics Pursued* (Edinburgh, UK: Edinburgh University Press, 1993), 78. Savile would have us read *Of the Standard of Taste* as "minimiz[ing] the sort of full-bloodedly internalist account of the valuational properties that he [Hume] proposes elsewhere"—in a word, projectivism (*Kantian Aesthetics*, 78). Accordingly, Hume's search for a standard reflects not only his debt to neoclassical aesthetic theory but, more important, his philosophical hesitations about the relational character of evaluative judgments. "Conflating a liability to produce feelings on the part of some object with something 'belonging entirely to the sentiment,' and, still looking for something in the object to call forth the sentiments, [Hume] feels obliged to talk of rules and principles to supply the need," comments Savile (*Kantian Aesthetics*, 79). The problem is especially evident in Hume's account of Sancho Panza's kinsmen (from *Don Quixote*), a story told to underscore the importance to the true judge of having delicacy of taste, "where the organs are so fine, as to allow nothing to escape them; and at the same time so exact as to perceive every ingredient in the composition" ("ST," 235). In this case, what the organs of the kinsmen perceive is the taste of leather and iron in the wine, which turns out, when the hogshead is later emptied, to originate in a key and leather thong that were at the bottom. As Hume tells the story, "finding the key with the leathern thong" is like discovering "general rules [of taste]" ("ST," 235). Savile would "advise Hume not to say . . . that it is the key and the leather that the tastevins taste. Rather, it is the taste of leather and iron that has infiltrated the wine that their expertise makes them sensitive to" (*Kantian Aesthetics*, 78). I agree that this is what Hume *should* say, but I question whether it is something he *could* say given his view of evaluative thought within the larger absolute conception of the world. As argued earlier, there is a tension in Hume's thought, which can also be seen in his relation to the radical idealism of Berkeley and the dissolution of the distinction between primary and secondary properties.

52. Kalar, *Demands of Taste*, 18.

53. "Taste makes claim merely to autonomy. To make the judgments of others into the determining ground of one's own would be heteronomy" (*CJ*, §32, p. 146/163).

54. Hume points in this direction when he describes how we might try to get

"the bad critic" to see "an avowed principle of art" by showing him "ex-amples, whose operation, from his own particular taste, he acknowledges to be conformable to the principle" ("ST," 236). As Savile observes, "The evidence of the good judge is, properly speaking, indicative, not induc-tive" (*Kantian Aesthetics*, 82).

55. McDowell, "Non-Cognitivism and Rule-Following," 200.

56. Wiggins, "Sensible Subjectivism," 194.

57. Paul Guyer, *Kant and the Claims of Taste*, 2nd ed. (Cambridge: Cambridge University Press, 1997).

58. Kalar, *Demands of Taste*, 21.

59. Guyer, *Kant and Taste*, 130. Guyer is emphatic: "We [must] think of taste's imputation of agreement as a qualified prediction of aesthetic response under ideal circumstances" (288); "an attribution of pleasure to others . . . is, after all, a prediction, but an ideal prediction—a prediction which pre-supposes ideal knowledge of one's own responses and ideal circumstances of response for others" (129–30). For a good summary of the Humean construction of "Kant's deduction of taste . . . as an argument designed to warrant the prediction of a uniform response to certain objects, at least in ideal circumstances," see Kalar, *Demands of Taste*, 21.

60. Guyer, *Kant and Taste*, 242.

61. Ibid., 348.

62. According to Guyer, Kant's deduction in the third *Critique* must show that we are justified in attributing specific feelings to particular individuals in particular circumstances. Kant, he claims, bases his argument about our shared aesthetic response on an argument about our shared cognitive ca-pacity—namely the capacity to unify a manifold of intuition. Guyer then proceeds to show that Kant's argument for this analogy does not hold up, mostly because unifying a manifold under a concept is what characterizes cognition but unifying without a concept is what characterizes aesthetic response. We cannot, therefore, assume that just because everyone has the ability to unify in the first case, they can in the second. Even if we were warranted to universally ascribe a general capacity for aesthetic response, it doesn't follow that we are justified in attributing specific feelings to particular individuals in particular circumstances. There is more than one way to unify a manifold, in the cognitive as in the aesthetic case. Two people could unify in two different ways. The two cases might produce different "proportions of the faculties" (i.e., understanding and imagina-tion) or different degrees of harmony. Why should we assume that the resultant feelings of pleasure would all be the same? It seems possible that we could all share the capacity for aesthetic response, yet diverge mark-edly in our particular judgments of taste. For Guyer, it is the task of the deduction to provide a method that would show *particular* judgments of taste to be correct—that is, normatively binding. But that is just the issue that Guyer's critics dispute.

63. Critics include Henry E. Allison, *Kant's Theory of Taste: A Reading of the Critique of Aesthetic Judgment* (New York: Cambridge University Press, 2001); Henry Allison, "Dialogue: Paul Guyer and Henry Allison on Allison's *Kant's Theory of Taste*," in *Aesthetics and Cognition in Kant's Critical Philosophy*, ed. Rebecca Kukla (2006; repr., Cambridge: Cambridge University Press, 2010), 11–137; Kalar, *Demands of Taste*; Robert Pippen, "The Significance of Taste: Kant, Aesthetic and Reflective Judgment," *Journal of the History of Philosophy* 34 (1996): 549–69; Richard E. Aquila, "A New Look at Kant's Aesthetic Judgments," in *Essays in Kant's Aesthetics*, ed. Ted Cohen and Paul Guyer (Chicago: University of Chicago Press, 1982), 87–114; Hannah Ginsborg, "On the Key to Kant's Critique of Taste," *Pacific Philosophical Quarterly* 72 (1991): 290–313; Hannah Ginsborg, "Aesthetic Judging and the Intentionality of Pleasure," *Inquiry* 46, no. 2 (2003): 164–81. In response to critics, writes Kalar, "Guyer acknowledges that 'we must distinguish between grounds for defending the rational expectation that others *will* agree with our own aesthetic responses, and grounds for demanding . . . that they *ought* to agree.' He argues, however, that the latter actually *depends* upon the former—that the defense of the demand that everyone *ought* to agree hinges on the rational expectation that they *will* agree" (*Demands of Taste*, 29).

64. Kalar, *Demands of Taste*, 28.

65. There are important exceptions here. Anthony Savile, Joseph Tinguely, and Henry Allison, whose readings are discussed subsequently, describe in different but compelling terms the importance of arguing/quarreling [*streiten*] for understanding the transcendental question of how Kant justifies judgments of taste. In stark contrast to Eva Schaper (see next note), each discusses the ways in which quarreling indicates that there is a fact of the matter about which we can agree and disagree. The question of arguing/quarreling then turns on how it is that we have access, so to speak, to that fact. Although all three recognize the importance of feeling and thus of the so-called subjective pole of a judgment, Tinguely goes the furthest in arguing for the irreducible role placed by affective response in discerning the objective features of aesthetic objects, and I am indebted to his compelling interpretation.

66. Eva Schaper, "The Pleasures of Taste," in *Pleasure, Preference and Value: Studies in Philosophical Aesthetics*, ed. Eva Schaper (New York: Cambridge University Press, 2009), 39–56, at 47. Kant writes:

> With regard to the *agreeable*, everyone is content that his judgment, which he grounds on a private feeling, and in which he says of an object that it pleases him, be restricted merely to his own person. Hence, he is perfectly happy if, when he says that sparkling wine from the Canaries is agreeable, someone else should improve his expression and remind him that he should say "It is agreeable *to me*"; . . . thus with

regard to the agreeable, the principle *Everyone has his own* taste (of the senses) is valid.

   With the beautiful it is entirely different. It would be ridiculous if (the precise converse) someone who prided himself on his taste thought to justify himself thus: "This object (the building we are looking at, the clothing someone is wearing, the concert that we hear, the poem that is presented for judging) is beautiful *for me*." For he must not call it *beautiful* if it pleases merely him. Many things may have charm and agreeableness for him; no one will be bothered about that. But if he pronounces that something is beautiful, then he expects the very same satisfaction of others; he judges not merely for himself, but for everyone, and speaks of beauty as if it were a property of things. Hence he says that the *thing* is beautiful, and does not count on the agreement of others with his judgment of satisfaction because he has frequently found them to be agreeable with his own, but rather *demands* it from them. He rebukes them if they judge otherwise, and denies that they have taste, though he nevertheless requires that they ought to have it; and to this extent one cannot say "Everyone has his special taste." That would be as much as to say that there is no taste at all, i.e., no aesthetic judgment that could make a rightful claim to the assent of everyone. (*CJ*, §8, pp. 55–56/97–98)

67. Schaper, "Pleasures of Taste," 47. For a similar argument, according to which the only error about which we can speak in a judgment of taste is whether we have falsely believed ourselves to have made a judgment of taste, see Ted Cohen, "Why Beauty Is a Symbol of Morality," in T. Cohen and Guyer, *Essays in Kant's Aesthetics*, 221–36. For Allison's critique of Cohen on this point, see Allison, *Kant's Theory of Taste*, 108–9. Mary Mothersill agrees with the view that "a particular judgment of taste (sentence) cannot be, on Kant's view, simply false. . . . For Kant, there are only what pretend to be universally valid demands and what actually *are* such." Though she agrees with this reading of Kant, she disagrees with Kant: "I by contrast would say that the sentence . . . 'Op. 59, No. 1 is musically worthless,' is false" (*Beauty Restored*, 156). For Mothersill, great works of art come to serve in the place of principles of taste—that is, to serve in argument as examples to defend the genuine character of any particular judgment of taste (*Beauty Restored*, 174).

68. Schaper, "Pleasures of Taste," 48.

69. Ibid.

70. I am indebted to Joseph Tinguely for sharpening my understanding of this connection.

71. As Allison explains, "As an expression of aesthetic subjectivism or relativism, the former [commonplace: *'Everyone has his own taste'*] entails that any putative 'dispute' over taste is at bottom nothing more than a clash of personal preferences (perfectly analogous to one regarding the agreeable)

for which neither side can produce any justifying grounds. And this is tantamount to claiming that there is no disputing about taste" (*Kant's Theory of Taste*, 238).

72. To anticipate the argument that follows: The move to the supersensible can be partly understood as an attempt to show how there can indeed be a second order of correctness—that is, a fact of the matter which makes possible not only a dispute but an argument/quarrel without there being a determinate decision procedure. Let us recall that this issue is part and parcel of the larger question that arises in critiques (e.g., Habermas's) of the aesthetic turn in political thought: What could a so-called fact of the matter about which one can be right or wrong possibly amount to absent the means (i.e., concepts) for adjudicating competing points of view? One response to this question, I shall suggest, can be found by querying, as Kant himself will go on to do, the "natural understanding of what is meant by a *concept*, namely, a determinate set of marks that provides a rule or decision procedure for the recognition of what falls under it," to speak with Allison (*Kant's Theory of Taste*, 239). It is this understanding of a concept, after all, that structures the antinomy of taste and that leads Kant, in his search for a solution, to put forward another way of thinking about what a concept could be.

73. On this point, see Allison, *Kant's Theory of Taste*, 238.

74. As Allison notes, Kant expands the second commonplace ("There is no disputing about taste") into a third principle ("One can quarrel about taste [though one cannot dispute about it]") because he sees that there is "a fact of the matter, that is, a right and a wrong view," which "suffices to make the disagreement [when we quarrel] genuine, even though there may be no available means to resolve it definitively" (*Kant's Theory of Taste*, 238).

75. Stanley Cavell, "Aesthetic Problems of Modern Philosophy," 94.

76. This is the substance of Guyer's reading of the deduction as a failed effort—failed because it does not ground the right to expect, albeit under ideal conditions, agreement in particular claims of taste.

77. As Allison claims, Kant's argument for a common sense in sections 20 and 21 should be read as an epistemological argument about the necessary conditions of cognition that must be presupposed if skepticism is to be avoided. Without this attunement, in other words, cognition could not occur. Allison sees that the *sensus communis logicus* is not the *sensus communis aestheticus*, but he resists the idea that "aesthetic common sense or taste must itself be presupposed as a condition of cognition." In the aesthetic case, "the common sense at issue . . . is the effect of the *free play* of the cognitive faculties. There is simply no way in which a feeling resulting from the noncognitive condition of free play could serve as a condition of cognition." Allison, *Kant's Theory of Taste*, 153. For a critique of Allison on this point, see Tinguely, "Orientation," 130–31 (see chap. 1, n. 21). I side

here with Tinguely because his reading allows us to bring out the crucial aesthetic character of cognition that can rightly be discerned in the third *Critique*, thus bridging the text to my discussion of Wittgenstein's aesthetic remarks that follow.

78. Immanuel Kant, "First Introduction to the Critique of Judgment," in *Critique of the Power of Judgment*, trans. Paul Guyer and Allen W. Wood (New York: Cambridge University Press, 2006), 1–51, at 31. See also Joseph J. Tinguely, "Kantian Meta-Aesthetics and the Neglected Alternative," *British Journal of Aesthetics* 53, no 2 (April 2013): 211–235, at 212.

79. In chapter 1 I argued that we should think of judging politically on the model of Kantian judgments of taste so understood. To think about what is "political" in a political judgment as the *mode* of judging, rather than an *object* that is external and prior to the act of judging itself, is also to question the idea that what we call "political judgments" are propositions in which "political" is predicated of the object, or assertions that a particular object is "political."

80. Tinguely, "Orientation," 112. The interpretations at issue here are responses to Paul Guyer's claim that Kantian aesthetic judging consists of "two acts": the first act involves the encounter with an aesthetic object that gives rise to a feeling of pleasure, and the second act judges the validity of this pleasure. Guyer, *Kant and Taste*, 99. This two-act view treats pleasure not as the means by which we judge but as entirely prior to and independent of the judgment itself. What one judges is one's pleasurable reaction to an object—that is, whether one can demand that others too feel this pleasure. Furthermore, Guyer advances a causal theory of pleasure, according to which such feeling is caused by the free play of the faculties (i.e., of imagination and understanding), which suggests that there is nothing normative in the feeling itself. Tinguely explains:

> It follows on the causal theory, then, that neither the feeling of pleasure nor the harmonious play of the faculties can be considered as an accomplishment for which we can take credit—a rational mode of engaging or discerning an object for which we are responsible or for which we could criticize others—rather it is something that merely *happens* to one under the right conditions by virtue of what Robert Pippin decries as "a peculiar psychological quirk" which happens to be shared by all humans. . . . Just as it is a physical quirk that some people laugh when tickled, so too is it a psychological quirk—albeit one universally shared by all humans—that we feel pleasure when apprehension and exhibition reinforce each other in harmonious play. In neither case is there anything anyone can *do* about it, except perhaps cultivate an awareness or sensitivity in recognizing what is causing the experience of pleasure; because feelings, like sensations, are causal and thus not rational, it would be as ridiculous to praise or blame someone

for their good sense of taste as it would be to praise or blame them for
being ticklish.

Tinguely, "Orientation," 107.

81. Ginsborg argues against Guyer that pleasure is internal to judgment,
not prior and external to it. Pleasure consists in the awareness that one's
pleasure is universally valid, that is, normative. This self-referential act
of judgment makes a claim on the feelings of others, "demanding that all
perceivers of the object in question should judge as I do," writes Ginsborg.
"But this demand, being universal applies just as much to myself as to
any other perceiver of the object." Ginsborg, "Key to Kant's Critique,"
302. There is, in other words, every reason to remain in this subjective
state, leaving the judging subject in a kind of endless self-referential
circle. Ginsborg agrees with Guyer that the object of a judgment of taste
is not the aesthetic object but one's subjective mental state. As Tinguely
explains, the only difference is that "for Guyer taste is a judgment *about*
a (external) pleasure; for Ginsborg taste judges *by means* of a (internal)
pleasure" ("Orientation," 115). See Hannah Ginsborg, "Aesthetic Judging
and the Intentionality of Pleasure," *Inquiry* 46, no. 2 (2003): 164–81.

82. See especially Ginsborg, "Key to Kant's Critique."

83. Tinguely, "Orientation," 117. In the view of Vivason Soni, for example, the
self-reflexive character of aesthetic judgment leaves the object stranded.
"The retreat into self-reflexivity is the privileged strategy for evading
judgment about the object itself," he writes. Vivason Soni, "Introduction:
The Crisis of Judgment," *Eighteenth Century* 51, no. 3 (Fall 2010): 261–288,
at 278. I agree with Soni that there are real dangers associated with the
suspension of judgment and that they arise in certain interpretations of
Kant (though I would disagree that the interpretations get Kant right on
this score). In the case of Arendt, however, whom Soni finds equally susceptible to this subjectivizing move, the point is not to suspend judgment
but rather to create the space in which the objects of judgment can appear
in the first place.

84. Ralf Meerbote observes, if the judgment of beauty reflects only the purely
subjective relation of the judging subject's mental faculties and has no
relation to actual features of the judged object, then any object can in
principle be judged beautiful if taken up in the right mental state. Ralf
Meerbote, "Reflections on Beauty," in T. Cohen and Guyer, *Essays in Kant's
Aesthetics*, 55–86, esp. 81. For a good discussion of this point, see Tinguely,
"Orientation," 40. Karl Ameriks argues that Kant does not provide good
reasons for rejecting the objectivity of beauty: "How to Save Kant's Deduction of Taste as Objective," in Karl Ameriks, *Interpreting Kant's Critiques*
(Oxford: Oxford University Press, 2003), 285–306. Taking up Ameriks's
argument about the objectivism of beauty, Hannah Ginsborg argues that
Ameriks cannot explain autonomy as a crucial condition of aesthetic

judgments. The Kantian judgment of beauty, she holds, rests on the idea of beauty as self-referential awareness. Hannah Ginsborg, "Kant on the Subjectivity of Taste," in *Kant's Ästhetik/Kant's Aesthetics/L'esthétique de Kant*, ed. Herman Parret (Berlin: Walter de Gruyter, 1998), 448–65. See also Hannah Ginsborg, *The Role of Taste in Kant's Theory of Cognition* (New York: Garland Publishing, 1989), esp. 463–65. For a good discussion of this debate, see Katalin Makkai, "Kant on Recognizing Beauty," *European Journal of Philosophy* 18, no. 3 (2010): 385–413.

85. Tinguely, "Kantian Meta-Aesthetics," 215–16.

86. Ibid., 216, 217.

87. Ibid., 219. Commentators who advance a similar view of pleasure as the means through which we discriminate features of empirical objects include Richard Aquila, "New Look at Kant's Aesthetic Judgments"; Barrie Falk, "The Communicability of Feeling," in Schaper, *Pleasure, Preference, and Value*, 57–85.

88. Stanley Cavell, "Music Decomposed," in *Must We Mean What We Say?* (Cambridge: Cambridge University Press, 1976), 180–212, at 192.

89. Tinguely, "Orientation," 112.

90. Tinguely, "Kantian Meta-Aesthetics," 223.

91. Tinguely, "Orientation," 51.

92. Ibid., 25.

93. This point is compellingly made by Tinguely: ibid., 50.

94. The full quotation: "Hence he [the judging person] will speak of the beautiful as if beauty were a property of the object and the judgment logical (constituting a cognition of the object through concepts of it), although it is only aesthetic and contains merely a relation of the representation of the object to the subject, because it still has the similarity with logical judgment that its validity for everyone can be presupposed" (*CJ*, §6, 54/97).

95. Cavell, "Aesthetic Problems of Modern Philosophy," 89n8.

96. Mothersill, *Beauty Restored*, 153.

97. Ibid.

98. Cavell, "Aesthetic Problems of Modern Philosophy," 93.

99. Savile, *Kantian Aesthetics*, 13.

100. Cavell, *Claim of Reason*, 45, 51 (see chap. 1, n. 38).

101. Schaper, "Pleasures of Taste," 46.

102. Tinguely, "Orientation," 179.

103. "For if one did not assume such a point of view [that a judgment of taste relies on some concept or other], then the claim of a judgment of taste to universal validity could not be saved" (*CJ*, §57, p. 212/216).

104. Savile, *Kantian Aesthetics*, 50.

105. Allison, *Kant's Theory of Taste*, 248.

106. For a good explication of this point, see ibid., 241.

107. Savile, *Kantian Aesthetics*, 46.

108. Tinguely, "Orientation," 180. As Savile observes, Kant not only speaks of the "supersensible substratum of appearances" (*CJ*, §57, p. 213/216), he also refers to "the supersensible substratum of humanity," that which is in us (Savile, *Kantian Aesthetics Pursued*, 57). According to Allison, if we assume that "beauty, construed as the form of purposiveness, is the indeterminable concept that Kant has in mind in §57, the introduction of the supersensible is perfectly appropriate" (*Kant's Theory of Taste*, 250). Though it is far from obvious, "the concept of the beautiful qualifies as an idea of reason that leads us inevitably from something sensible to its supersensible ground or substrate" (Allison, *Kant's Theory of Taste*, 249).

109. In the view of Guyer, for example, Kant's deduction proceeds on the basis that any empiricist could accept until he gets to "The Solution to the Antinomy of Taste" in section 57 and proposes the supersensible. For Guyer, "Kant's theory of taste must survive by its epistemological analysis of aesthetic judgment if it is to survive at all," and the move to the supersensible is in no way required by Kant's theory of taste, but is merely an attempt to bring the discussion of taste within the scope of the official critical architectonic. Rather than move to the supersensible, Kant could have put forward the indeterminate concept of harmony of the faculties, which is not identical with the concept of any supersensible object, but is rather an epistemological or psychological one. Guyer, *Kant and Taste*, 309. But Guyer's critique holds only on the assumption that all that is needed to resolve the antinomy is an indeterminate concept, whereas what is needed is an indeterminate and indeterminable one. See Allison, *Kant's Theory of Taste*, 246–49.

110. Immanuel Kant, *Critique of Pure Reason*, trans. and ed. Paul Guyer and Allen W. Wood (Cambridge: Cambridge University Press, 1997), A255/B311, 350.

111. Savile, *Kantian Aesthetics Pursued*, 61. He continues:

> The capacity that presents Kant with the riddle of taste is just the capacity to make judgments which are true and yet indeterminate, and it rests in the end on our finding that we are bound in certain circumstances to respond in certain ways to certain objects, where this being bound cannot be explained discursively and without residue from inside—since to do that only provides additional factors that bear on being bound and which will themselves need explanation—yet cannot be explained from the outside either. The trouble comes when we yield to the temptation to think that Kant is suggesting a further positive explanation of the force of the necessity; but we do not have to think of him as doing that. The more generous way of taking his allusions to the supersensible is a reminder of just where our questions must stop (ibid., 62).

112. Conant, "Perspectivism, I," 30 n20. "Kant thus denies that we can assign any real sense or reference to the minimally intelligible (i.e., non-contradictory) notion of a reality which is utterly screened off from us by the conditions of knowledge" (ibid., 29n20).

113. Ibid., 31.

114. See Allison, *Kant's Theory of Taste*, 244.

115. Savile, *Kantian Aesthetics Pursued*, 55.

116. Ibid., 44.

117. Ibid.

118. Tinguely, "Orientation," 180.

119. Mothersill, *Beauty Restored*, 241.

120. Wittgenstein gave two sets of lectures on aesthetics, the first in 1930–1933, which is described by G. E. Moore, "Wittgenstein's Lectures in 1930–33," in G.E. Moore, *Philosophical Papers* (London: Allen and Unwin, 1959), 252–324; the second set of lectures was given in 1938 and transcribed from student notes and published as part of Ludwig Wittgenstein, *Lectures and Conversations on Aesthetics, Psychology, and Religious Belief*, ed. Cyril Barrett (Berkeley: University of California Press, 2007; hereafter cited as *LC*).

121. Jean-Pierre Cometti, "On Standard and Taste: Wittgenstein and Aesthetic Judgment," *Aisthesis: Revista on-line del Seminario di Estetica*, 6, no. 1 (2013): 5–15. As Cometti explains, aesthetic judgment is for Wittgenstein a normative practice, which means that

> aesthetic appreciation or evaluation, as any appreciation, depends on rules. These rules are what helps anyone to meet "claims" and expectations included in any judgment, and to say for instance: "too high or too low" (about a door), "more slowly or more sustained," "allegro, ou *allegro ma non troppo*" (about a melody), all these ways of making something better or more relevant in such or such area. . . . Wittgenstein takes examples in architecture, in clothing or music, and this seems to mean that for him the question of aesthetic judgment does not differ depending on the artefacts we are dealing with, including art. And this could mean too that we don't have any reason—unlike Kant—to make a distinction between "aesthetic judgment" and "cognitive judgment" (Cometti, "On Standard and Taste,"10–11).

For a similar argument about the importance of rules in Wittgenstein's aesthetic thought, see David Novitz, "Rule, Creativity, and Pictures," *Wittgenstein, Aesthetics, and Philosophy* ed. Peter Lewis (Burlington, VT: Ashgate Publishing, 2004), 55–72. I agree that Wittgenstein allows rules in aesthetic judgments in a way that Kant did not, but the question is what role rules really play and how far they bound an aesthetic practice. Once we see the radical indetermination of rules in aesthetics (as in other language games), the differences between Wittgenstein and Kant are radically attenuated.

122. Likewise, "One asks such a question as 'What does this remind me of?' or one says of a piece of music: 'This is like some sentence, but what sentence is it like?' Various things are suggested; one thing, as you say, clicks. What does it mean, it 'clicks'? Does it do anything you can compare to the noise of a click? . . . It is as though you needed some criterion, namely the clicking, to know the right thing has happened. . . . You might say the clicking is that I'm satisfied (*LC*, 19).

123. Hilary Putnam, "Entanglement of Fact and Value," 31 (see chap. 1, n. 47).

124. Moore, "Wittgenstein's Lectures in 1930–33," 315.

125. Cavell, *Must We Mean What We Say?* 95, 95–96.

126. Richard Shusterman, "Aesthetic Argument and Perceptual Persuasion," *Crítica: Revista Hispanoamericana de Filosofía* 15, no. 45 (December 1983): 51–74, at 60–61.

127. Ibid., 61.

128. Wiggins, "Sensible Subjectivism," 205.

129. Shusterman, "Aesthetic Argument," 70–71.

130. On this point, see Savile, *Kantian Aesthetics Pursued*, chap. 1. For Savile it is an issue not of content but grounds. I would see the shift more in terms of the mode of judging than the grounds for judging, though I fully agree that there must be something in the world that elicits our capacity to judge and our shared feeling (*sensus communis*). This is why Kant himself, notwithstanding his ambiguous stance on the place of the object, speaks of the ground [*Grund*] of an aesthetic judgment.

CHAPTER 3

1. Leo Strauss, "The Living Issues of German Postwar Philosophy," in *Leo Strauss and the Theologico-Political Problem*, ed. Heinrich Meier, trans. Marcus Brainard (Cambridge: Cambridge University Press, 2006), 115–39, at 133 (hereafter cited as "LI").

2. Shadia B. Drury, *The Political Ideas of Leo Strauss*, rev. ed. (New York: Palgrave Macmillan, 2005), xii. Neoconservatives said to be under the spell of Strauss's teaching include Allan Bloom, William Kristol, Irving Kristol, and Paul Wolfowitz. See also Stephen Holmes, *The Anatomy of Anti-Liberalism* (Cambridge, MA: Harvard University Press, 1993); Ted V. McAllister, *Revolt against Modernity: Leo Strauss, Eric Voegelin, and the Search for a Postliberal Order* (Lawrence: University Press of Kansas, 1997). For an early attempt to link Strauss to the neoconservatives, see Myles Burnyeat, "Sphinx without a Secret," *New York Review of Books*, May 30, 1985, 30–36; Jacob Weisberg, "The Cult of Leo Strauss," *Newsweek*, August 3, 1987. For a more recent critical account of Strauss's role in the policies of the neoconservatives, see Anne Norton, *Leo Strauss and the Politics of American Empire* (New Haven, CT: Yale University Press, 2004); C. Bradley Thompson, *Neoconservatism: An Obituary for an Idea*, with Yaron Brook

(Boulder, CO: Paradigm, 2010). For a defense of Strauss against critics such as Drury, see Catherine Zuckert and Michael Zuckert, *The Truth about Leo Strauss: Political Philosophy and American Democracy* (Chicago: University of Chicago Press, 2006). For a sympathetic defense of Strauss as no enemy of liberalism, see Nassar Behnegan, "The Liberal Politics of Leo Strauss," in *Political Philosophy and the Human Soul: Essays in Memory of Allan Bloom*, ed. Michael Palmer and Thomas. L. Pangle, 251–68 (Lanham, MD: Rowman and Littlefield, 1995); Robert Howse, "From Legitimacy to Dictatorship—and Back Again: Leo Strauss's Critique of the Anti-Liberalism of Carl Schmitt," in *Law as Politics: Carl Schmitt's Critique of Liberalism*, ed. David Dyzenhaus, 56–90 (Durham, NC.: Duke University Press, 1998).

3. Drury, *Political Ideas of Strauss*, xx.

4. Ibid., xxi–xxiv.

5. "One of the great services that Strauss and his disciples have performed for the Bush regime has been the provision of a philosophy of the noble lie, the conviction that lies, far from being simply a regrettable necessity of political life, are instead virtuous and noble instruments of wise policy." Earl Shorris, "Ignoble Liars: Leo Strauss, George Bush, and the Philosophy of Mass Deception," *Harper's*, June 2004, 65–71, at 68.

6. Leo Strauss, *Natural Right and History* (Chicago: University of Chicago Press, 1965), 5 (hereafter cited as *NRH*).

7. Much of the debate on the crisis of liberalism takes place around the work of John Rawls and Isaiah Berlin. The worry here is how to square the liberal commitment to value pluralism with the defense of the specific values of liberalism such as (negative) liberty. Further, there is concern about whether liberal values can be considered universally valid—that is, normatively justifiable across cultures. For a discussion of the vicissitudes of value pluralism in relation to debates about toleration, see Wendy Brown, *Regulating Aversion: Tolerance in the Age of Identity and Empire* (Princeton, NJ: Princeton University Press, 2006); Rainer Forst, *Toleranz im Konflikt: Geschichte, Gehalt, und Gegewart eines umstrittenen Begriffs* (Frankfurt am Main: Suhrkamp, 2003). For debates on liberalism, value pluralism, and the relativity of values, see George Crowder, *Liberalism and Value Pluralism* (London: Continuum, 2002); Michael Blake, "Political Liberalism Abroad" (paper presented at Global Justice Seminar, Stanford University, Stanford, CA, 2007); Charles Larmore, *The Autonomy of Morality* (Cambridge: Cambridge University Press, 2008); Martha C. Nussbaum, *Frontiers of Justice: Disability, Nationality, Species Membership* (Cambridge, MA: Harvard University Press, 2007); Jonathan Riley, "Interpreting Berlin's Liberalism," *American Political Science Review* 95, no. 2 (June 2001): 283–95; John Gray, *Isaiah Berlin* (Princeton, NJ: Princeton University Press, 1996); Amy Gutmann, "Liberty and Pluralism in Pursuit of the Non-Ideal," *Social Research* 66, no. 4 (Winter 1999): 1039–62; William Galston, "Value Pluralism and Liberal Political Theory," *American Political Science Review* 93,

no. 4 (December 1999): 769–78; William A. Galston, *Liberal Pluralism: The Implications of Value Pluralism for Political Theory and Practice* (Cambridge: Cambridge University Press, 2002); Daniel M. Weinstock, "The Graying of Berlin," *Critical Review* 11, no. 4 (Fall 1997): 481–501; Steven Lukes, "The Singular and the Plural: On the Distinctive Liberalism of Isaiah Berlin," *Social Research* 61, no. 3 (Fall 1994): 687–717; George Kateb, "Can Cultures Be Judged? Two Defenses of Cultural Pluralism in Isaiah Berlin's Work," *Social Research* 66, no. 4 (Winter 1999): 1009–38.

8.   Leo Strauss, *Spinoza's Critique of Religion*, trans. E. M. Sinclair (Chicago: University of Chicago Press, 1997), 6 (hereafter cited as *SCR*).

9.   George Kateb, "The Questionable Influence of Arendt (and Strauss)," in *Hannah Arendt and Leo Strauss: German Émigrés and American Political Thought after World War II*, ed. Peter Graf Kielmansegg, Horst Mewes, and Elisabeth Glaser-Schmidt, 29–44 (Cambridge: Cambridge University Press, 1995), 29. According to Kateb, friends of modern liberal democracy should also be suspicious of Hannah Arendt.

10. In the Spinoza book, Strauss claimed that it was "the weakness of liberal democracy in Germany," not the very existence of such a regime, that "explains why the situation of the indigenous Jews was more precarious in Germany than in any other Western country" (*SCR*, 2–3). He believed the liberal "solution of the Jewish problem" to be deeply flawed, but it was still better than, say, "the Communist 'solution'" (*SCR*, 7). And he never blamed Weimar liberalism for the rise of National Socialism: "The weakness of the Weimar Republic made certain its speedy destruction. It did not make certain the victory of National Socialism" (*SCR*, 1).

11. On this point, see Nathan Tarcov, "Philosophy and History: Tradition and Interpretation in the Work of Leo Strauss," *Polity* 16, no. 1 (Autumn 1983): 5–29. For a strong defense of Strauss as a friend of liberalism, see Steven B. Smith, *Reading Leo Strauss: Politics, Philosophy, Judaism* (Chicago: University of Chicago Press, 2006). Smith's otherwise valuable effort to show the ways in which Strauss's thought is friendly to liberalism makes Strauss into a defender of liberalism with little critique to offer.

12. Leo Strauss, "Social Science and Humanism," *The Rebirth of Classical Political Rationalism: An Introduction to the Thought of Leo Strauss*, ed. Thomas L. Pangle (Chicago: University of Chicago Press, 1989), 3–12, at 6 (hereafter cited as "SSH").

13. This was just the kind of thinking that had led "Western men" in the nineteenth century, who saw "much, if not all, sufferings as consisting of problems which as such were soluble as a matter of course," and who "in this manner, too, . . . had come to speak of the Jewish problem. . . . Prior to Hitler's rise to power most German Jews believed that their problem had been solved in principle by liberalism" (*SCR*, 4). More generally, Strauss saw the irreducible tension between reason and revelation as the vital force in the Western tradition, a tension between two codes or ways

of asking the fundamental questions that could not and should not be resolved. Thus interpretations that seek to align Strauss on one side or the other of the debate between Athens and Jerusalem are misguided when they imply that he thought that the future of Western culture hinged on making a final choice. Each individual must make a choice; but Western civilization as a whole would remain divided—and that was a good thing. See Leo Strauss, "Thucydides: The Meaning of Political History," in Pangle, *Rebirth of Classical Rationalism*, 72–102.

14. For an example of this kind of argument, see Galston, "Value Pluralism," 769.

15. Karl Mannheim, "Historicism," in *Essays on the Sociology of Knowledge*, ed. Paul Kecskemeti (London: Routledge and Kegan Paul, 1952), 84.

16. Georg G. Iggers, "Historicism: The History and Meaning of the Term," *Journal of the History of Ideas* 56, no. 1 (January 1995): 129–52, at 133.

17. As Wittgenstein explains the working of these principles of judgment:

> All testing, all confirmation and disconfirmation of a hypothesis takes place already within a system. And this system is not a more or less arbitrary and doubtful point of departure for all our arguments: no, it belongs to the essence of what we call an argument. The system is not so much the point of departure, as the element in which arguments have their life.

Ludwig Wittgenstein, *On Certainty*, ed. G. E. M. Anscombe and G. H. von Wright (New York: Harper and Row, 1972), §105; see also §124.

18. John G. Gunnell, "Strauss before Straussianism: Reason, Revelation, and Nature," *Review of Politics* 53, no. 1 (Winter 1991): 53–74, at 71.

19. See also *NRH*, 35. As Strauss puts this zetetic stance, "What Pascal said with anti-philosophic intent about the impotence of both dogmatism and skepticism, is the only possible justification of philosophy which as such is neither dogmatic nor skeptic, and still less 'decisionist,' but zetetic (or skeptic in the original sense of the term). Philosophy as such is nothing but genuine awareness of the problems, i.e., of the fundamental and comprehensive problems." Leo Strauss, *On Tyranny*, ed. Victor Gourevich and Michael S. Roth (Chicago: University of Chicago Press, 2000), 196. For a defense of Strauss as a zetetic philosopher, see Zuckert and Zuckert, *Truth about Strauss*; Daniel Tanguay, *Leo Strauss: An Intellectual Biography*, trans. Christopher Nadon (New Haven, CT: Yale University Press, 2007), esp. 201. For a critique of Strauss's account of the fundamental problems as a refigured Platonism, see Thompson, *Neoconservatism*, chap. 5.

20. Smith, in *Reading Leo Strauss*, also reads Strauss as a thinker who resists attempts to resolve fundamental contradictions. But in Smith's view, this spirit should be read as a defense of liberalism as the society that does not aim to resolve such contradictions. I argue, by contrast, that resolving contradictions is what the crisis liberals try to do.

21. Gunnell, "Strauss before Straussianism," 54.

22. That the other great thinker of the crisis of judgment in the wake of totalitarianism is Hannah Arendt is significant for my argument. As argued subsequently, Arendt too was deeply critical of historicism. What Arendt shares with Strauss on the problem of historicism will become visible only when we see Strauss's approach as therapeutic. As the few existing critical commentaries on Strauss and Arendt reveal, it is easier to read Arendt (theorist of freedom) against Strauss (theorist of virtue) than to find some common ground on which we could deepen our understanding of the problems raised for politics and judgments by historicism. See, for example, Ronald Beiner, "Hannah Arendt and Leo Strauss: The Uncommenced Dialogue," *Political Theory* 18, no. 2 (May 1990): 238–54. According to Beiner, it is Arendt's commitment to Kantian egalitarianism that most starkly distinguishes her antihistoricism from that of Strauss.

23. I discuss these diverse accounts later in the chapter. By *historicism*, I do not mean Karl Popper's use of the term, where it designates "an approach to the social sciences which assumes that historical prediction is their principle aim" and which attempts to discover "patterns" or "laws" of historical evolution. Karl R. Popper, *The Poverty of Historicism* (London: Routledge, 1957), 3. For a good overview of the historicist problematic, see Annette Wittkau, *Historismus: Zur Geschichte des Begriffs und des Problems* (Göttingen: Vandenhoeck und Ruprecht, 1994); Georg Iggers, *The German Conception of History: The National Tradition of Historical Thought from Herder to the Present* (Middletown, CT: Wesleyan University Press, 1968); Georg Iggers, "Historicism"; Jeffrey Andrew Barash, *Martin Heidegger and the Problem of Historical Meaning* (New York: Fordham, 2003); Charles R. Bambach, *Heidegger, Dilthey, and the Crisis of Historicism* (Ithaca, NY: Cornell University Press, 1995).

24. As a rule, the secondary literature focuses on Weber and Heidegger, but these two intellectual giants, though obvious targets of Strauss's critique of historicism, were themselves reacting to the larger debate in the German context. It is not possible to assess Strauss's critique of historicism if one does not have some grasp of what all the fuss was about.

25. Georg Iggers ("Historicism") observes that the whole debate on historicism has been construed as one in mostly German nineteenth-century philosophy, whereas, in fact, it encompassed Italian, French, and other sources. Strauss locates the origins of historicism in the beginning of the modern period, in the sixteenth century, and his account is for the most part influenced by and focused on German thinkers. I will therefore center my discussion on the issues as they arose in the German context.

26. Friedrich Meinecke, *Historism: The Rise of a New Historical Outlook*, trans. J. E. Anderson (1936; repr., New York: Herder and Herder, 1972). For Meinecke, historicism combines two key ideas: the importance of the indi-

vidual and the notion of development. Each individual is seen as unique, though such uniqueness is to be grasped in the larger context of the particular culture to which he (or she) belongs. To appreciate this uniqueness, it was necessary to practice a form of empathetic understanding, which involved trying to put oneself in the place of the person whom one wishes to understand. Judgments about individuals had to take into account particular historical circumstances and the larger context in which humans act. The idea of the individual, central not only to Meinecke's account of historicism but also to those of Wilhelm von Humboldt, Eduard Spranger, and Ernest Troeltsch, was centered on creative individuals such as scientists and artists. In the case of historicists such as Leopold von Ranke, Heinrich von Treitschke, and Georg von Below, the state was the most important form of individuality. With the exception of the early Humboldt, the former group of thinkers was not worried about the threat of the state to the individual's development. These men simply took for granted, as Colin Loader writes, "the basic harmony between the 'objective *Geist*' of that realm and the 'subjective *Geist*,' the soul of the individual." They were in this way "very different from the individualism of Western liberal thinkers, who emphasized the potential threat of the state to the individual." Colin Loader, "German Historicism and Its Crisis," *Journal of Modern History* 48, no. 3 (September 1976): 85–119, at 98.

27. Meinecke, *Historism*, lvi.
28. Barash, *Heidegger and Meaning*, 6.
29. Ibid.
30. Ibid., 11.
31. Bambach, *Heidegger, Dilthey, and Historicism*, 171.
32. Paul Ricoeur, foreword to Barash, *Heidegger and Meaning*, xi.
33. It was this core assumption of historical coherence that Heidegger's ontological investigation of *Dasein* would soundly reject. See Barash, *Heidegger and Meaning*, 174.
34. Allan Megill, "Why Was There a Crisis of Historicism? Review of *Heidegger, Dilthey, and the Crisis of Historicism* by Charles Bambach," *History and Theory* 36, no. 3 (October 1997): 416–29, at 419. "The term *Krisis des Historismus*," writes Megill, "acquired currency only toward the end of the period 1880–1927, thanks largely to the [liberal] theologian Ernst Troeltsch" (418). See Ernst Troeltsch, *Der Historismus und seine Probleme* (Tübingen: Mohr, 1922); *Der Historismus und seine Überwindung* (Berlin: Heise, 1924); "Die Krisis des Historismus," *Die Neue Rundschau 33* (June 1922): 572–90. See also Karl Heussi, *Die Krisis des Historismus* (Tübingen: Mohr, 1932). Megill points out that "The 'crisis of historicism' was so named only late in the game, and even if it had been generally named and recognized earlier the historian is not compelled to accept contemporaries' definitions. In short, the relatively late naming of the crisis of historicism, and its lack of any well-defined material or institutional embodiment, give a

lot of freedom to the historian in reconstructing—or, perhaps better, in constructing—the thing. Consequently, one must judge the historian's account less by attempting to compare it with something 'out there' . . . than by seeing what problems it raises or resolves and what insights it generates" (Megill, "Why Crisis of Historicism?" 418–19). On the difference between earlier (Rankean) historicism and the crisis historicists, see Herman J. Paul, "A Collapse of Trust: Reconceptualizing the Crisis of Historicism," *Journal of the Philosophy of History* 2 (2008): 63–82; Friedrich Jaeger, "Theorietypen der Krise des Historismus," in *Die Historismusdebatte in der Weimarer Republik*, ed. Wolfgang Bialas and Gérard Raulet (Frankfurt am Main: Peter Lang, 1996).

35. Megill, "Why Crisis of Historicism?" 419.
36. Ibid., 420.
37. Ibid., 420–21.
38. Critical works, such as Martin Kaehler's essay *"Der soggenannte historische Jesus und der geschichtliche, biblische Christus"* ("The So-Called Historical Jesus and the Historical, Biblical Christ"; 1892), were subsequently published, which argued that no sources exist for the life of Jesus of Nazareth that can possibly satisfy the standards of historical scholarship and that what matters anyway is the Christ of faith. They attempted to draw a line in the sand between the "historical" Jesus and the "historic" Christ. Albert Schweitzer's *Geschichte der Leben-Jesu-Forschung* (*History of the Life of Jesus*; 1906) finally brought to an end what had become a whole "life of Jesus" movement, declaring that the effort had been a failure and theology would have to use weapons other than history.
39. A similar debate arose in the first decades of the twentieth century among liberal theologians such as Ernst Troeltsch (as well as Adolf von Harnack, Wilhelm Bousset, Johannes Weiss, and Wilhelm Wrede), who argued for a historically based faith and the study of Christianity as a historical movement. Insofar as these theologians—even the most radical of them, including Troeltsch—never declared that the absoluteness of the Christian essence could be historically verified, as Heidegger would later point out, the question arises as to what the purpose of a historical understanding in theology could possibly be. Recognizing the liberal theologians' tendency to impose secular criteria on theological phenomena, Heidegger agreed with orthodox critics who argued that historical knowledge of Jesus Christ threatens to deprive theology of its very topic—namely, belief in Revelation.
40. Loader, "German Historicism," 87.
41. Ibid., 87–88.
42. Ibid., 90.
43. Ibid., 98.
44. Quoted in ibid., 98–99.
45. Ibid., 101.

46. Ibid., 102.
47. Ibid., 103.
48. Quoted in ibid., 103–4.
49. Ibid., 111.
50. John Gunnell has argued that Strauss's account of Weber is questionable insofar as Weber's argument about the impossibility of rationally adjudicating ultimate value orientations is more a statement about the standing of social science at that point in time than a general comment about the limits of rationality. See John Gunnell, "The Paradox of Social Science: Weber, Winch, and Wittgenstein," in *Max Weber's "Objectivity" Reconsidered*, ed. Laurence McFalls (Toronto: University of Toronto Press, 2007). For a defense of Weber against Strauss's charges of relativism and historicism, see Alan Mittleman, "Leo Strauss and Relativism: The Critique of Max Weber," *Religion* 29 (1999): 15–27.
51. The strongest proponent of this view is Heinrich Meier, *Carl Schmitt, Leo Strauss und der Begriff des Politischen: Zu einem Dialog unter Abwesenden* (Stuttgart: J. B. Metzler, 1998).
52. Already in the Spinoza book, Strauss recognized the limits of modern reason for confronting Jewish orthodoxy. In his view, Spinoza's rationalist effort to defeat orthodoxy had failed: it was not possible to refute the existence of God on the basis of proofs, for belief in God never depended on evidence. Strauss concluded that orthodoxy had won due to the "self-destruction of rational philosophy" (*SCR*, 30). This conclusion led him to see, observes John Gunnell, that "[modern] reason ultimately rested on irrational decisions. Reason and revelation were rooted in irreducible commitments" (Gunnell, "Strauss before Straussianism," 62).
53. The problem is how to find a place from which it would be possible to judge. As Strauss writes, "But when *studying* the genesis of historical consciousness, we *judge* it, we look at it with critical eyes: we are in the first steps and the imperfect beginnings of something wonderful, but the first step away from the right approach: for we know from experience the ultimate result to which that first step led. I.e., when studying the genesis of historical consciousness, we look at it with the eyes of pre-modern philosophy—we stand on the other side of the fence. Only by doing this, shall we be enabled to find the *right* name of that which *we* call history (*Geschichte ≠ Historie*)" ("LI," 134).
54. Strauss, "Political Philosophy and History," in *What Is Political Philosophy?* (Chicago: University of Chicago Press, 1988), 56–77, at 67.
55. Ibid.
56. This dependence of insight on fate differs from the understanding of insight that belongs to natural right. "All natural right doctrines claim that the fundamentals of justice are, in principle, accessible to man as man. They presuppose, therefore, that a most important truth can, in principle, be accessible to man as man" (*NRH*, 28).

57. Strauss, "Thucydides," 75.

58. Nikolas Kompridis, *Critique and Disclosure: Critical Theory between Past and Future* (Cambridge, MA: MIT Press, 2006), 75.

59. Ibid.

60. Ibid.

61. Strauss, "Political Philosophy and History," 68.

62. It is instructive here to consider Strauss's critique of Hans-Georg Gadamer, who was likewise critical of historicist approaches to understanding the past. In Gadamer's hermeneutical approach, interpretation entails a fusion of horizons, those of the present and the past. For Strauss, such a fusion forecloses the possibility of radical self-questioning and undermines Gadamer's recognition that past texts must be understood in terms of their claim to truth. "Meeting" the other, writes Strauss, entails not only openness to what strikes us as familiar but also to what is radically strange: it "means that I can, nay, must accept it [what the text says] as true or reject it as untrue . . . or recognize my inability to decide and therefore the necessity to think or learn more." In Strauss's view, Gadamer's own account of historical openness as the superior way of relating to the past closes down the very possibility of understanding the past in terms of the claim to truth that his hermeneutical approach is said to endorse. There is no room for the possibility that this historically minded openness could be radically questioned. See Leo Strauss and Hans-Georg Gadamer, "Correspondence Concerning *Wahrheit und Methode*," *Independent Journal of Philosophy* 2 (1978): 5–12 at 6. As Catherine Zuckert summarizes the main issue between them:

> According to Strauss, Gadamer's own hermeneutics required him to posit something like an absolute moment in which it became clear, as it had not been clear to earlier thinkers, that all thought is essentially historical and that philosophers can never, therefore, attain the truth in the traditional sense. Thinkers informed by the historical insight would obviously no longer continue to seek truth, that is, to philosophize, as before.

Catherine H. Zuckert, *Postmodern Platos: Nietzsche, Heidegger, Gadamer, Strauss, Derrida* (Chicago: University of Chicago Press, 1996), 104.

63. Although the timeless quality of Weber's notion of ultimate values represents a departure from the historical school, the subjectivizing logic by which values lose any relation to an objectively given reality and to the powers of human judgment is characteristic of the problems that Strauss associates with historicism. Thus, while Weber "parted company with the historical school," argues Strauss, his work on the fact/value distinction reflects some of the deepest problems associated with it. For Weber, the historical school should have rejected the idea of natural

right but instead historicized it, while also preserving the idea of human history as "a meaningful process or a process ruled by intelligible necessity" (*NRH*, 37). Rejecting this idea as "metaphysical, i.e., as based on the dogmatic premise that reality is rational," Weber insisted that "there is no 'meaning' of history apart from the 'subjective' meaning or the intentions which animate the historical actors" (*NRH*, 37), though "these intentions are of such limited power that the actual outcome is in most cases wholly unintended" (*NRH*, 37–38). Furthermore, whatever meaning or value one claims to find in a historical process is always suspect. The heterogeneity of facts and values prohibits such value judgments, at least on the part of social scientists.

64. As I show in chapter 4, Arendt makes a similar point in her reading of Socratic dialectics.

65. According to Strauss, the search for truth itself is "made possible or necessary by the fact that opinions about what things are . . . contradict one another. Recognizing the contradiction, one is forced to go beyond opinions toward the consistent view of the nature of the thing concerned. That consistent view makes visible the relative truth of the contradictory opinions; the consistent view proves to be the comprehensive or total view" (*NRH*, 124). If "philosophy consists . . . in the ascent from opinions to knowledge or to the truth, in an ascent that may be said to be guided by opinions" (*NRH*, 124), there is "no guaranty that the quest for adequate articulation will ever lead beyond an understanding of the fundamental alternatives or that philosophy will ever legitimately go beyond the stage of discussion or disputation and will ever reach the stage of decision" (*NRH*, 125).

66. Strauss distinguishes two types of historicism: conventionalism, whose origins he locates in the ancient debates, and a radical type, which he associates with modernity. Conventionalism claims that there can be no natural, immanent standard of right because there are in fact a wide variety of values and practices. Strauss claims that, far from defeating the quest for natural right, this awareness of an open-ended pluralism is the basic condition, the incentive, for the quest (*NRH*, 10–11). As Alan Mittleman explains:

> Conventionalism, which is after all, the classical, sophistic position, is distinguished from modern historicism in that conventionalism, like its ancient opponent, Platonism, assumes that, in the face of diversity, the fundamental distinction is still that of *nomos* and *physis*. It holds that *physis* continues to have a higher dignity than human custom but that right cannot be located there. Right belongs only to custom: justice is a matter of sheer human agreements, with no natural, meta-conventional basis. Modern historicism, by contrast, rejects both Platonism's and conventionalism's ascription of normativity to nature. The distinction between nature and custom loses its fundamental

status or, at least, its fundamental point: nature is not the source of norms. Human creativity, based on freedom, is itself the source of norms. But insofar as this free, creative, 'world-constructing' activity takes place within history, it can never rise to a vantage point beyond history; it can never leave the Platonic cave. Philosophy, as the attempt to rise above opinion and ascertain truth, is not possible. . . . There are no eternal things to be grasped, or, minimally, there is no way of grasping them. ("Leo Strauss and Relativism," 16)

67. "Greek thought recognized eternal first things beyond the gods and that limited the gods' power. This is why in Platonic theology the ideas hence-forth took the place of the traditional gods. The gods submit to a necessity that both goes beyond and governs them" (Tanguay, *Strauss Intellectual Biography*, 176).

68. Ibid.; Zuckert, *Postmodern Platos*.

69. Leo Strauss, "Progress or Return?" in Leo Strauss, *Jewish Philosophy and the Crisis of Modernity: Essays and Lectures in Modern Jewish Thought*, ed. Kenneth Hart Green (Albany, NY: State University Press, 1997), 87–136, at 114. On this point, see Tanguay, *Strauss Intellectual Biography*, 176–77.

70. For a good example of this critique, see Stephen Holmes, "Strauss: Truths for Philosophers Alone," in *The Anatomy of Antiliberalism* (Cambridge, MA: Harvard University Press, 1993), 61–87.

71. Tracy B. Strong, "Exile and the Demos: Leo Strauss in America," *European Legacy: Toward New Paradigms* 18, no. 6 (2013): 715–26, at 720.

72. For Arendt's clear formulation of what she practices as "political theory" and not "political philosophy," see Arendt, "What Remains?" 2 (see chap. 1, n. 111).

73. The central difference between Arendt and Strauss is that, for her, any public claim to truth, which will always be expressed as opinion (it-seems-to-me), must be understood in terms of the larger raison d'être of politics, which is freedom. Accordingly, though she too is deeply critical of historicism (in all its German guises, from Hegel's philosophy of history to Heidegger's notion of historicity), the central problem historicism raises is not, as Strauss holds, that it denies the very possibility of philosophy, the quest for truth, but that it occludes from our view "the very center of politics—man as an acting being." Hannah Arendt, "Concern with Politics in Recent European Philosophical Thought," in *Essays in Understanding, 1930–1954*, ed. Jerome Kohn (New York: Schocken, 1994), 428–47, at 433.

74. Conant, "Perspectivism, I," 25 (see chap. 1, n. 11).

75. Ibid., 26.

76. Ibid.

77. There were no easy "recipes for today's use" to be found in classical philosophy. Leo Strauss, *The City and Man* (Chicago: University of Chicago Press, 1964), 11.

78. Liisi Keedus, "Omitted Encounters: The Early Political Thought of Hannah Arendt and Leo Strauss" (PhD diss., European University Institute, 2010), 203. For an excellent comparison of Strauss and Arendt on the question of politics and history, see Keedus, *Crisis of German Historicism* (see chap. 1, n. 106).

79. Keedus observes that for

> Arendt, in contrast [to Strauss], the irreversible break in tradition had made the recovery of the "trans-historical" (to use Strauss's formulation) impossible, and in this sense all quests along these lines were self-deceptive. She opposed not the claims of historicity in the understanding of human life and thought, but only a particular kind of universalistic historicism: one that embraced the teleological view of history as a process. Hence the aim of Arendt's critique was not to overcome thinking that had history as its guiding horizon, but to rethink the meaning of history, first, as the realm of the singular, unpredictable and memorable, and second as the realm of *past* that had remembered the singular and thus endowed it with a meaning from a purely human perspective. ("Omitted Encounters," 203)

80. Arendt contends that

> what is really undermining the whole modern notion that meaning is contained in the process as a whole, from which the particular occurrence derives its intelligibility, is that . . . we can take almost any hypothesis and *act* upon it, with a sequence of results in reality which not only make sense but *work*. This means quite literally that everything is possible not only in the realm of ideas but in the field of reality itself. . . . The totalitarian systems tend to demonstrate that action can be based on any hypothesis and that, in the course of consistently guided action, the particular hypothesis will become true, will become actual, factual reality. The assumption which underlies consistent action can be as mad as it pleases; it will always end in producing facts which are then "objectively" true. ("CH," 87).

As I argue in the next chapter, this is the kind of fantastic "fact creation" that Arendt relates to the manipulation of facts for the purposes of political expediency.

81. Here, Arendt observes, the attempt to escape the "haphazard character of the particular . . . [meets] the answer from all sides: Any order, any necessity, any meaning you wish to impose will do. This is the clearest possible demonstration that under these conditions there is neither necessity nor meaning" ("CH," 88–89).

1. Quoted in Peter Novick, *That Noble Dream: The "Objectivity Question" and the American Historical Profession* (Cambridge: Cambridge University Press, 1988), 290.
2. The critique of cognitive relativism and that of moral relativism were conceptually distinct and in important ways at odds with each other. As Peter Novick observes, "For critics of moral relativism . . . it was the 'neuter' qualities of objectivity and detachment which had morally disarmed the West for the battle against totalitarianism. For critics of cognitive relativism, objectivity and detachment were the distinctive values of Western life and thought which distinguished the democracies from the totalitarian regimes." Ibid., 288.
3. Ibid., 283.
4. Quoted in ibid., 285.
5. Zerilli, "'We Feel Our Freedom'" (see chap. 1, n. 2).
6. Hans-Georg Gadamer, *Truth and Method*, trans. Joel Weinsheimer and Donald G. Marshall (New York: Continuum, 1994), 41 (hereafter cited as *TM*).
7. Mark Danner, "Reply" to "The Secret Way to War: An Exchange," *New York Review of Books*, July 14, 2005 (hereafter cited as "Reply"). I discuss Danner's argument later in the chapter.
8. Hannah Arendt, "Philosophy and Politics," *Social Research* 57, no. 1 (1990): 73–103 (hereafter cited as "PP").
9. This would be something like the quest for that which is generalizable in an otherwise "impenetrable pluralism of ultimate value orientations" that governs the work of validity thinkers such as Habermas. On this point, see Zerilli, "'We Feel Our Freedom.'" Although there is a plausible interpretation of the dialogic character of Socratic dialectic that would accord with the communicative model proposed by Habermas, this is not the interpretation Arendt offers.
10. Strauss, "What is Political Philosophy?," in *What Is Political Philosophy?* (Chicago: University of Chicago Press, 1988), 9–55, at 12.
11. Ibid., 11.
12. In his reading of Strauss contra Arendt on the teaching of Socrates, Dana Villa criticizes Strauss's insistence on the need for yardsticks or absolute standards and argues that Strauss's "definition of political philosophy assimilates the Socratic position to Plato's, and it is motivated by the demand that there be *some* way of rationally adjudicating the fundamental questions and controversies of political life." Dana Villa, "The Philosopher versus the Citizen: Arendt, Strauss, and Socrates," in *Politics, Philosophy, Terror: Essays on the Thought of Hannah Arendt* (Princeton, NJ: Princeton University Press, 1999), 155–79, at 168. However that may be, Strauss's challenge is not so easily dismissed. It raises in acute form the question

of the relation between opinion and truth as the fundamental problem of judgment that arises once we deny the existence and/or desirability of yardsticks or absolute standards.

13. Hannah Arendt, "Thinking and Moral Considerations," in *Responsibility and Judgment*, ed. Jerome Kohn (New York: Schocken, 2003), 159–89, at 170 (hereafter cited as "TMC").

14. Ernesto Grassi, *Vom Vorrang des Logos: Das Problem der Antike in der Auseinandersetzung zwischen italienischer und deutscher Philosophie* (Munich: C. H. Beck, 1939), 38 (hereafter cited as *VL*). All translations are my own.

15. That the world presents itself or appears (*sich zeigen*) is central to Heidegger's phenomenology of being-in-the-world. Heidegger contests the notion that human beings are subjects standing over and against a world of objects, which they then try to "know." "Self and world belong together in the single entity, the *Dasein*. Self and world are not two beings, like subject and object. . . . [Instead] self and world are the basic determination of the *Dasein* itself in the unity of the structure of being-in-the-world." Martin Heidegger, *The Basic Problems of Phenomenology*, trans. Albert Hofstadter (Bloomington: Indiana University Press, 1982), 297. Rather, as Charles Guignon explains, "entities in general—the tools in a workshop, the unknown chemical in the chemist's beaker, even the precise kinds of sensation and emotion we can have—these can show up *as* what they *are* (i.e., in their *being* such and such) only against the background of the interpretive practices of a particular historical culture." Charles B. Guignon, introduction to *The Cambridge Companion to Heidegger*, 1–41 (Cambridge: Cambridge University Press, 1993), 13.

16. The ancient conception of truth as *alètheia*, writes Heidegger, means to "take beings that are being talked *about* in *legein* as *apophainesthai* out of their concealment; to let them be seen as something unconcealed (*alēthes*); to *discover* them." This unconcealment happens through speech or *logos*—not *logos* understood in the modern sense as "reason, judgment, concept, definition, ground, relation," but as that which lets something be seen (*phainesthai*)." Martin Heidegger, *Being and Time*, trans. Joan Stambaugh (Albany: State University of New York Press, 1996), 29, 28.

17. According to Grassi, Heidegger overcomes the objectivist conception of truth, calling our attention instead to the act or process through which things show up for us. But Heidegger leaves unanswered the question of the various forms of appearance (*sich-zeigen*) and *légein*.

18. In *Kunst und Mythos*, for example, Grassi differentiates among a "hermeneutical *légein*," an "empirical *légein*," and a "*téchne-légein*." For the purposes of this chapter, however, I will concentrate on the philosophical, aesthetic, and political forms of *légein* discussed subsequently. Ernesto Grassi, *Kunst und Mythos* (Hamburg: Rowohlt, 1957). In Grassi's later work the notion of *légein* is developed as that of *metaphérein*. See especially

Ernesto Grassi, *Macht des Bildes: Ohnmacht der rationalen Sprache* (Cologne: DuMont Schauberg, 1970).

19. Comparing Socrates again to Kant, Arendt writes:

> What Socrates actually did when he brought philosophy from the heavens down to earth and began to examine opinions about what went on between men was that he extracted from every statement its hidden or latent implications; that is what his midwifery actually amounted to. . . . This examination, in turn, presupposes that everyone is willing and able to render an account of what he thinks and says. (*LKPP*, 41)

20. Villa, "Philosopher versus Citizen," 165.

21. Hans-Georg Gadamer, "The Problem of Historical Consciousness," in *Interpretive Social Science: A Reader*, ed. Paul Rabinow and William M. Sullivan (Berkeley: University of California Press, 1979), 103–60, at 54 (hereafter cited as "PHC").

22. Gadamer writes, "Those views of the world are not relative in the sense that one could oppose them to the 'world in itself,' as if the right view from some possible position outside the human, linguistic world could discover it in its being-in-itself. No one doubts that the world can exist without man and perhaps will do so. This is part of the meaning in which every human, linguistically constituted view of the world lives. In every worldview the existence of the world-in-itself is intended. It is the whole to which linguistically schematized experience refers. The multiplicity of these worldviews does not involve any relativization of the 'world.' Rather, what the world is is not different from the views in which it presents itself" (*TM*, 447). The knowledge of the world that Gadamer has in mind, then, does not presuppose that there is some absolute conception of the world that captures the way the world (already) is, in and of itself, independent of our particular conceptions of it. The philosophical idea of knowing the whole truth in some absolute way is premised on the possibility of attaining the presuppositionless standpoint. By contrast with the Archimedean ideal that has governed the idea of philosophical truth as well as the application of scientific method in the *Geisteswissenschaften*, Gadamer holds that no opinion can be declared absolutely true—or, for that matter, false—because every opinion expresses a view of the world that is both conditioned and limited by one's linguistic or historical perspective. For a good discussion of these issues, see Brice Wachterhauser, "Gadamer's Realism: The 'Belongingness' of Word and Reality," in *Hermeneutics and Truth*, ed. Brice Wachterhauser (Evanston, IL: Northwestern University Press, 1994), 148–71.

23. We are, as Heidegger famously says, in "a circle of understanding," a hermeneutical circle. To see this circle as a limitation, he writes, to see it as *"vitiosus,"* or *"even to 'feel' that it is an inevitable imperfection* [of human

knowing], *is to misunderstand understanding from the ground up* . . . . What is decisive is not to get out of the circle, but to get in it in the right way" (*Being and Time*, 143). In other words, comments Gadamer, we need to recognize that "the circle possesses an ontologically positive significance" (*TM*, 266), which, far from excluding the possibility of genuine knowledge, is the very condition of all understanding and critical thinking.

24. Prejudices can count on the agreement of others without any rational argumentation or recourse to evidence, argues Arendt. "In this respect, prejudice differs from judgment," though we should not think of judgment itself as presuppositionless. "Upon closer examination, we realize that a genuine prejudice always conceals some previously formed judgment which originally had its own appropriate and legitimate experiential basis, and which evolved into a prejudice only because it was dragged through time without its ever being reexamined or revised" ("IP," 100, 101).

25. What can it mean to unearth the truth of the judgment that is buried in prejudice? In "Thinking and Moral Considerations," another essay that deals with the Socratic search for truth, Arendt talks about this process as that of "unfreez[ing]" a concept or a "frozen thought" ("TMC," 173, 172). This concept can be as everyday as the word *house* or as abstract as the words *happiness, justice,* and *courage*. If we think of this concept as the rule under which particular cases are subsumed in a rule-governed judgment, we can perhaps begin to see what is at stake in the Socratic effort to recover the "particular cases as they [originally] *appear* to us (we *see* a happy man, *perceive* the courageous deed or the just decision)" ("TMC, 171"). This appearance is not the substance that the concept ("what Plato . . . called ideas perceivable only by the eyes of the mind" ["TMC," 171]) indicates but a process, a becoming that we grasp in the course of our activity (seeing, perceiving, etc.). What we want to recover in the judgment, then, is the particular. More precisely, we want to recover that which is no object (as captured by a concept, e.g., courage) but is instead what originally shows up for us, what appears (*sich zeigen*) through the originary act of *légein* in the course of our daily activity.

26. According to Habermas, Gadamer has no adequate answer to the all-important question of validity: "Gadamer's prejudice for the rights of prejudices certified by tradition denies the power of reflection. The latter proves itself, however, in being able to reject the claim of tradition." Jürgen Habermas, "A Review of Gadamer's *Truth and Method*," in *Understanding and Social Inquiry*, ed. Fred R. Dallmayr and Thomas McCarthy (Notre Dame, IN: Notre Dame University Press, 1977), 335–363, at 358. Although Habermas grants the *Vorurteilstruktur* of understanding, he rejects (what in his view is) Gadamer's rehabilitation of prejudices and authority, for it undermines critical reflection. Even if we were to grant Gadamer his claim about the historicity of understanding, says Habermas, we would still

be left with the epistemological question of how to establish a universal normative basis to distinguish rational and irrational aspects of tradition, legitimate from illegitimate prejudices. Gadamer does not accept the charge and maintains that Habermas overestimates the power of reason. For the related critique of Arendt, see "ACCP."

27. Rightness (justice) is a wholly procedural concept, a metanorm that structures the discourses by which first-order norms and judgments are generated. Rightness has no trace of the Good that characterizes ethical evaluative judgments that are rooted in the lifeworld. Stripped of any value connotation, "rightness" is an empty rule of argumentation to which we ought to adhere when making claims from a moral point of view.

28. Steven Levine, "Truth and Moral Validity: On Habermas' Domesticated Pragmatism," *Constellations* 18, no. 2 (2011): 244–59, at 255.

29. For an excellent critique of Habermas on this point, see ibid.

30. Quoted in Novick, *Noble Dream*, 290.

31. Hannah Arendt, "Lying in Politics," in Hannah Arendt, *Crises of the Republic* (New York: Harcourt Brace, 1972), 1–48, at 6 (hereafter cited as "LP").

32. Habermas would argue that where the ideal conditions of speech are respected, we could never reach conclusions that deny brute facts; that is, facts whose existence does not depend on our attitude toward them (or, if such facts were denied in any particular instance—we do make mistakes—our judgment could be corrected by following the same procedural norms). Given ideal conditions of speech, the best argument will be the one that will survive throughout the deliberative process. Strictly speaking, such a brute fact could be the existence of Mount Everest, but it could also be a factual truth such as "on the night of August 4, 1914, German troops crossed the frontier of Belgium," as Arendt put it. In the case of Mount Everest, it would seem that we have the objective world as a reference in the course of communicative action, though a pragmatist such as Hilary Putnam would say that even here our validity claims about a brute fact are shot through with values pertaining to what counts as scientific evidence. The question that concerns us here, however, is whether, in the midst of a political quarrel about, say, the responsibilities borne by the Germans for World War II in the matter of postwar reparations, we can "redeem" competing validity claims in a deliberative manner that would not require us to recognize the radical entanglement of fact, value, and norm, an entanglement that necessarily points precisely toward a justification-transcendent point of reference—namely, "the objective world."

33. Factual truths are clearly relevant to politics, in Arendt's view, for without them we would not be able to form opinions. The mutual entanglement of opinion and truth makes it "relatively easy to discredit factual truth as just another opinion. Factual evidence, moreover, is established through

testimony by eyewitnesses—notoriously unreliable—and by records, documents, and monuments, all of which can be suspected as forgeries. In the event of a dispute, only other witnesses but no third and higher instance can be invoked, and settlement is usually arrived at by way of a majority; that is, in the same way as the settlement of opinion disputes—a wholly unsatisfactory procedure, since there is nothing to prevent a majority of witnesses from being false witnesses" ("TP," 243). Arendt clearly recognizes the fragility of factual truth; however, the putative antidote to such fragility (e.g., setting up a higher instance that would not be subject to error or lies by which to judge) is not only impossible (it would be, after all, yet another opinion) but also dangerous. It would be an escape into the solidity of order that transforms action into rule and divides those who know but do not act from those who act (i.e., execute orders) but do not know.

34. Mark Danner, "The Secret Way to War," *New York Review of Books.* June 9, 2005 (hereafter cited as "SWW").

35. As Jack Straw, former British foreign secretary, observed, there was little legal basis for going to war with Iraq (the desire for regime change was not legal grounds). Danner explains, "In order to secure such a legal base, the British officials agree, the allies must contrive to win the approval of the United Nations Security Council, and the Foreign Secretary puts forward a way to do that: 'We should work up a plan for an ultimatum to Saddam to allow back in the UN weapons inspectors'" ("Reply"). Danner remarks, "Thus, the idea of UN inspectors was introduced not as a means to avoid war, as President Bush repeatedly assured Americans, but as a means to make war possible" ("Reply"). The Bush administration, especially such hard-liners as Vice President Dick Cheney, were opposed to the United Nations route from the start, but the British refused to join the US-led attack on Iraq without the "fig leaf" of UN approval. Pressured by the British, Bush gambled that Hussein would not let the inspectors in, but even when he did and they found nothing, the politically constructed reality of "weapons of mass destruction" that had already been sold to the American public proved impervious to empirical evidence to the contrary. For example, Cheney, speaking on August 26 (three weeks before Bush came before the UN Security Council to secure the resolution to demand inspections), declared that the United States already had all the information it needed and publicly denounced the UN route: "Simply stated, there is no doubt that Saddam Hussein now has weapons of mass destruction [and] there is no doubt that he is amassing them to use against our friends, against our allies, and against us." The UN route, said Cheney, would produce the dangerous illusion or "false comfort that Saddam was somehow 'back in the box'" (quoted in Danner, "SWW").

36. The memo describes a secret meeting on July 23, 2002, between Tony

Blair and top British defense and intelligence figures to discuss the possible war with Iraq. It was published by the London *Sunday Times* on May 1, 2005. This account led to a huge uproar in Britain and nearly cost Blair the election. In the United States, by contrast, the memo was ignored, save for a few exceptions, including a signed letter dated May 5, 2005, from some US senators to President George W. Bush asking for an explanation of the memo. For a copy of the memo, see *The Downing Street Memo(s)*, May 13, 2005, http://www.downingstreetmemo.com. According to Bob Woodward, the war was planned as early as November 21, 2001, when President Bush ordered Secretary of Defense Donald Rumsfeld to examine "what it would take to protect America by removing Saddam Hussein if we have to." Military planning between Rumsfeld and General Tommy Franks began during the late spring of 2002. See Danner, "SWW," and especially Bob Woodward, *Plan of Attack* (New York: Simon and Schuster, 2004), chaps. 2–4.

37. "In the United States," continues Danner, "the Downing Street memorandum has attracted little attention. As I write, no American newspaper has published it and few writers have bothered to comment on it" ("SWW," 14). In a *New York Times* editorial, Paul Krugman likewise observes, "There has been notably little U.S. coverage of the Downing Street memo." Paul Krugman, "Staying What Course?" *New York Times,* May 16, 2005.

38. Mary G. Dietz, "Working in Half-Truth: Habermas, Machiavelli, and the Milieu Proper to Politics," in *Turning Operations: Feminism, Arendt, and Politics* (New York: Routledge, 2002), 141–69, at 143.

39. Stanley Cavell, "Knowing and Acknowledging," in *Must We Mean What We Say?* (Cambridge: Cambridge University Press, 1969), 238–66, at 257.

40. Ibid.

CHAPTER 5

1. Samuel Huntington, *Who Are We? The Challenges to America's National Identity* (New York: Simon and Schuster, 2004); John Rawls, *Political Liberalism* (New York: Columbia University Press, 1993), xxvi (hereafter cited as *PL*).

2. For Rawls's discussion of the burdens of judgment, see *PL*, 54–58. These burdens, as Thomas McCarthy summarizes, concern the free use of reason and the "difficulties in assessing evidence and differences in weighing it, indeterminacy of concepts and conflicts of interpretation, experiential and normative divergencies, the diversity of values and variations in selecting and ordering them." Thomas McCarthy, "Kantian Constructivism and Reconstructivism: Rawls and Habermas in Dialogue, *Ethics* 105 (October 1994): 44–63, at 58.

3. John Rawls, "Justice as Fairness: Political Not Metaphysical," in *Collected Papers*, ed. Samuel Freeman (Cambridge, MA: Harvard University Press, 1999), 388–414, at 394.

4. "When attributed to persons, the two basic elements of the conception of the reasonable are, first, a willingness to propose fair terms of social cooperation that others as free and equal also might endorse, and to act on these terms, provided others do, even contrary to one's own interest; and, second, a recognition of the burdens of judgment and accepting their consequences for one's attitude (including toleration) toward other comprehensive doctrines." John Rawls, "Political Liberalism: Reply to Habermas," *Journal of Philosophy* 92, no. 2 (March 1995): 132–80, at 134.

5. For critiques of public reason in Rawls's work, see Veit Bader, "Religious Pluralism: Secularism or Priority for Democracy?" *Political Theory* 27, no. 5 (1999): 597–633; Bryan Garsten, *Saving Persuasion: A Defense of Rhetoric and Judgment* (Cambridge, MA: Harvard University Press, 2006); Jürgen Habermas, "Reconciliation through the Public Use of Reason: Remarks on John Rawls's Political Liberalism," *Journal of Philosophy* 92, no. 3 (March 1995): 109–31; McCarthy, "Kantian Constructivism and Reconstructivism"; Michael J. Sandel, *"Political Liberalism* by John Rawls," *Harvard Law Review* 107 (May 1994): 1765–94; Jeremy Waldron, "Religious Contributions in Public Deliberation," *San Diego Law Review* 30 (1993): 817–48. For a defense of Rawls's idea of public reason against these critics, see Samuel Freeman, *Rawls* (New York: Routledge, 2007); Anthony Simon Laden, *Reasonably Radical: Deliberative Liberalism and the Politics of Identity* (Ithaca, NY: Cornell University Press, 2001); Richard Rorty, "The Priority of Democracy to Philosophy," *Objectivity, Relativism, and Truth: Philosophical Papers*, vol. 1 (Cambridge: Cambridge University Press, 1990), 175–96.

6. Rawls calls political liberalism a "method of avoidance" insofar as it does not engage in traditional philosophical controversies about the nature of the good or the true. This same method then becomes the rule for what it means to engage in public reason. See Rawls, "Justice as Fairness," 395.

7. In "The Idea of Public Reason Revisited," Rawls takes great pains to answer critics who claim that political liberalism suffers from a democratic deficit called "public reason." Here he states explicitly: "It is imperative to realize that the idea of public reason does not apply to all political discussions of fundamental questions, but only to discussions of those questions in what I refer to as the public political forum. This forum may be divided into three parts: the discourse of judges in their decisions, and especially of the judges of a supreme court; the discourse of government officials, especially chief executives and legislators; and finally, the discourse of candidates for public office and their campaign managers, especially in their public oratory, party platforms, and political statements." John Rawls, "The Idea of Public Reason Revisited," in *The Law of Peoples with "The Idea of Public Reason Revisited"* (Cambridge, MA: Harvard University Press,

1999), 131–80, at 133–34. (hereafter cited as "IPRR"). Rawls adds, "Political liberalism, then, does not try to fix public reason once and for all in the form of one favored political conception of justice" ("IPRR," 142). In this spirit, Rawls grants that there is such a thing as a "background culture" ("IPRR, 134), where the rules of public reason do not apply in any case; that nonpublic reasons made there and elsewhere can be made good in terms of public reason at a later date (the "proviso" exception [152]); that "there are many liberalisms . . . and therefore many forms of public reason" (141); that indeed "new variations [of public reason] may be proposed from time to time" (142), including ones that do not prioritize justice as fairness (141); and that this is important, "otherwise the claims of groups or interests arising from social change might be repressed and fail to gain their appropriate political voice" (142–43). In fact, by the end of the essay, it appears that the only criterion that is unassailable as far as political liberalism and public reason are concerned is "the criterion of reciprocity" ("IPRR," 141, 173). This finding leads a seemingly rather exasperated Rawls to declare at the end of the essay, "I do not know how to prove that public reason is not too restrictive, or whether its forms are properly described. I suspect it cannot be done" ("IPRR," 175).

8. Important exceptions here are Bryan Garsten, *Saving Persuasion*; and Ronald Beiner, *What's the Matter with Liberalism?* (Berkeley: University of California Press, 1995).

9. Martha C. Nussbaum, "Political Objectivity," *New Literary History* 32 (2001): 883–906, at 897.

10. Ibid., 896.

11. Wittgenstein, *On Certainty*, §10 (see chap. 3, n. 17).

12. James Conant, "Wittgenstein on Meaning and Use," *Philosophical Investigations* 21, no. 3 (July 1998): 222–50.

13. Ibid., 223.

14. Ibid., 239.

15. Ibid., 240.

16. Affeldt, "Ground of Mutuality," 18-19 (see chap. 1, n. 81).

17. Part of what Wittgenstein is questioning here is the distinction between meaning and intelligibility. This is the idea that we have, on the one hand, the meaning of a proposition and, on the other hand, the context of use in which that meaning is properly communicated and thus intelligible. On this view, propositions can be fully meaningful yet unintelligible: as sentences they have meaning, but that meaning has not found a suitable context of use. See Conant, "Wittgenstein on Meaning and Use," 228. The distinction between meaning and intelligibility is at work in Rawls's approach to comprehensive claims to truth. In his view, comprehensive claims (e.g., about God as the creator of human equality) are meaningful—his point is not to endorse skepticism about claims to truth. But when the generalized context of use is the "public political form,"

such claims are to be considered unreasonable—that is to say, unintelligible as legitimate political speech. We understand the words, but we cannot credit them as intelligible insofar as they make no political sense according to the public criterion of reasonableness. The semantic content of the assertion is in order but the context of its utterance is just wrong.

18. I discuss this point in Zerilli, *Feminism and Abyss of Freedom*, chap. 4 (see chap. 1, n. 104); and in Linda M. G. Zerilli, "This Universalism Which Is Not One," *Diacritics* 28, no. 2 (August 1998): 3–20.

19. For Rawls, the example of slaves serves to support his argument that the view of the person as free and equal is a political conception. I agree that it is. But that is all the more reason to consider how it is that one comes to be seen as the originator of claims. Married women in the United States in the mid-nineteenth century could not vote, legally own property, make a will, sign a contract, or, if employed, claim their own wages.

20. For an account of Douglass's speech that sets it in historical context and relates it to the struggle for women's rights, see James A. Colaiaco, *Frederick Douglass and the Fourth of July* (New York: Palgrave Macmillan, 2006). Douglass text quoted from Frederick Douglass, "The Meaning of July Fourth for the Negro," in *The Life and Writings of Frederick Douglass*, ed. Philip S. Foner, vol. 2 (New York: International Publishers, 1952), 181–204.

21. Douglass, "Meaning of July Fourth," 190–92.

22. George Shulman, *American Prophecy: Race and Redemption in American Political Culture* (Minneapolis: University of Minnesota Press, 2008), 19.

23. George Shulman, "Thinking Authority Democratically: Prophetic Practices, White Supremacy, and Democratic Politics," *Political Theory* 36, no. 5 (October 2008): 708–34, at 721.

24. Douglas, "Meaning of July Fourth," 182, emphasis added. On this point see Colaiaco, *Frederick Douglass and Fourth of July*, 33–34.

25. Douglass, "Meaning of July Fourth," 192.

26. Jason Frank, *Constituent Moments: Enacting the People in Postrevolutionary America* (Durham, NC: Duke University Press, 2010), 224.

27. Ernesto Grassi, *Rhetoric as Philosophy: The Humanist Tradition* (Carbondale: Southern Illinois University Press), 20. I discuss Grassi's view of rhetoric more extensively in Zerilli, "'We Feel Our Freedom,'" esp. 166–68 (see chap. 1, n. 2).

28. Rawls, "Justice as Fairness," 394.

29. Frank, *Constituent Moments*, 218.

30. Ibid.

31. Zerilli, *Feminism and Abyss of Freedom*, 171. Frank describes what I am calling the predicative moment of politics as a "constituent moment." See ibid., 8.

32. Colaiaco, *Frederick Douglass and Fourth of July*, 92.

33. Ibid. As Colaiaco explains, "Douglass put his pragmatism into practice. For national elections, he did everything in his power to advance the

cause of freedom by supporting the platform of the Liberty Party, later known as the Radical Abolitionist Party, calling for the immediate abolition of slavery everywhere in the United States. But once the election drew near, recognizing that an abolitionist victory was unlikely, he prudently switched his support to those political parties, such as the Free Soil Party [which sought merely to contain rather than abolish slavery], and subsequently to the Republican Party, which had better chances of success" (ibid., 94). Likewise, Douglass transferred his support of the abolitionist Gerrit Smith to the Republican Abraham Lincoln in the 1860 presidential election, even though Lincoln's party advanced a strategy of containment rather than abolition (ibid., 94).

34. Quoted in ibid., 92. See Michael Sandel's reading of the role played by morality in the 1858 debates over abolition between Abraham Lincoln and Stephen Douglass. "The debate between Lincoln and Douglass was not primarily about the morality of slavery, but about whether to bracket a moral controversy for the sake of political agreement." Sandel, *"Political Liberalism by John Rawls,"* 1780. For Rawls's response to this critique, see "IPRR," 174.

35. See Hannah Arendt, *On Revolution* (New York: Viking, 1965), chap. 5; Zerilli, *Feminism and Abyss of Freedom*, chap. 4.

36. I discuss this point in Zerilli, *Feminism and Abyss of Freedom*, chap. 4.

37. At the 1833 American Anti-Slavery Convention, Garrison argued, "All those laws which are now in force, admitting the right of slavery, are therefore before God utterly null and void." Quoted in Colaiaco, *Frederick Douglass and Fourth of July*, 84. Like Douglass, Garrison drew on the natural law tradition to contest the validity of positive law; unlike Douglass, he used that tradition to denounce the Constitution as a proslavery document that, thanks to natural law, ought to be rejected as null and void.

38. As Rawls sees it, "given the fact of reasonable pluralism . . . liberal principles meet the urgent political requirement to fix, once and for all, the content of certain basic political rights and liberties, and to assign them special priority. Doing this takes those guarantees off the political agenda and puts them beyond the calculus of social interests, thereby establishing clearly and firmly the rules of political contest" (*PL*, 161).

39. On this point, see Garsten, *Saving Persuasion*, 182–83.

40. "What Remains?" 20 (see chap. 1, n. 111).

41. Bader, "Religious Pluralism," 618.

42. Although "the idea of public reason" applies only to "the public political forum" (discussed earlier), Rawls also describes "the *ideal* of public reason" as something that should be aspired to and can be "realized by citizens who are not government officials." In accordance with this ideal, "citizens are to think of themselves *as if* they were legislators and ask themselves what statutes, supported by what reasons satisfying the criterion of reciprocity, they would think it most reasonable to enact." Thinking and acting in ways that are consistent with public reason is a "moral duty" of

all citizens. This distinction between the idea and the ideal of public reason clearly expands the normative claim of such reason way beyond the boundaries of the official public sphere ("IPRR," 135) and into the everyday political lives of citizens and the background culture of a democratic society.

CHAPTER 6

1. Susan Moller Okin, "Is Multiculturalism Bad for Women?" in *Is Multiculturalism Bad for Women?* by Susan Moller Okin with respondents, ed. Joshua Cohen, Matthew Howard, and Martha C. Nussbaum (Princeton, NJ: Princeton University Press, 1999), 10–11 (hereafter cited as "IMBW").

2. For critiques of Okin, see Azizah Y. al-Hibri, "Is Western Patriarchal Feminism Good for Third-World Minority Women?" in Okin et al., *Is Multiculturalism Bad for Women?* 41–46; Homi K. Bhabha, "Liberalism's Sacred Cow," in Okin et al., *Is Multiculturalism Bad for Women?* 79–84; Sander Gilman, "'Barbaric' Rituals?" in Okin et al., *Is Multiculturalism Bad for Women?* 53–58; Bonnie Honig, "'My Culture Made Me Do It,'" in Okin et al., *Is Multiculturalism Bad for Women?* 35–40; Martha Nussbaum, "A Plea for Difficulty," in Okin et al., *Is Multiculturalism Bad for Women?* 105–14.

3. Al-Hibri, "Western Patriarchal Feminism," 41.

4. Ibid.

5. Uma Narayan, *Dislocating Cultures: Identities, Traditions, and Third-World Feminism* (New York: Routledge, 1997), 150 (hereafter cited as *DC*).

6. Ernesto Laclau, *Emancipation(s)* (London: Verso, 1996), 24. For a detailed reading of Laclau, see Zerilli, "Universalism Not One" (see chap. 5, n. 18).

7. Laclau, *Emancipation(s)*.

8. For Laclau, a new universalism would be based not on the presumed neutrality of reason but on the creation of political chains of equivalence among otherwise diverse and competing particular claims. See Zerilli, "Universalism Not One."

9. "Objectivism," as Richard Bernstein explains, is "the basic conviction that there is or must be some permanent, ahistorical matrix or framework to which we can ultimately appeal in determining the nature of rationality, knowledge, truth, reality, goodness, or rightness." Richard J. Bernstein, *Beyond Objectivism and Relativism: Science, Hermeneutics, and Praxis* (Philadelphia: University of Pennsylvania Press, 1983), 8.

10. Martha Nussbaum, *Women and Human Development: The Capabilities Approach* (New York: Cambridge University Press, 2000), 34 (hereafter cited as *WHD*).

11. Drawing on the work of both Rawls and Amartya Sen, Nussbaum proposes to construct a universal framework with which to assess the lives of women in developing countries, arguing that certain universal values "are

important for each and every citizen, in each and every nation" (*WHD*, 6) and that they should therefore be adopted by every national government.

12. Seyla Benhabib, *The Claims of Culture: Equality and Diversity in the Global Era* (Princeton, NJ: Princeton University Press, 2002), 25 (hereafter cited as *CC*).

13. As Nikolas Kompridis argues, Benhabib's "antiessentialist" view of culture so "exaggerates the fluidity, permeability, and renegotiability of culture" that it is hard to understand how anyone could or would make claims in the name of culture. Nikolas Kompridis, "Normativizing Hybridity/Neutralizing Culture," *Political Theory* 33, no. 3 (2005): 318–43, at 319. Benhabib minimizes cultural attachments, he argues, to advance her strong universalism as being compatible with sensitivity to cultural differences.

14. I owe this point to Angela Maione.

15. Judith Butler, "Competing Universalities," in *Contingency, Hegemony, Universality: Contemporary Dialogues on the Left*, by Judith Butler, Ernesto Laclau, and Slavoj Zizek (London: Verso, 2000), 163.

16. Ibid., 35.

17. John G. Gunnell, "Relativism: The Return of the Repressed," *Political Theory* 21, no. 4 (1993): 563–84, at 565–66.

18. Ibid., 563.

19. Ibid., 566.

20. Nancy Hartsock, "The Feminist Standpoint: Toward a Specifically Feminist Historical Materialism," in *Money, Sex, and Power: Toward a Feminist Historical Materialism* (Boston: Northeastern University Press, 1985), 231–51.

21. Sandra Harding, "Other 'Others' and Fractured Identities: Issues for Epistemologists," in *The Science Question in Feminism* (Ithaca, NY: Cornell University Press, 1986), 163–96. On this point, see Zerilli, *Feminism and Abyss of Freedom*, chap. 4 (see chap. 1, n. 12).

22. Donna Haraway, "Situated Knowledges: The Science Question in Feminism and the Privilege of Partial Perspective," in *Simians, Cyborgs, and Women: The Reinvention of Nature* (New York: Routledge, 1991), 191. As Gunnell explains, "The actual locus of relativism is philosophy. It is a philosophical dilemma that has no real practical counterpart. It is the logical mirror image of rationalism, and outside the context of rationalism and philosophical foundationalism the problem has no meaning" ("Relativism," 565).

23. Haraway, "Situated Knowledges," 191. However appealing this response to the relativist charge may be, it is not easy to see why an argument "for politics and epistemologies of location, positioning, and situating, where partiality and not universality is the condition of being heard to make rational knowledge claims" (195) would constitute an adequate response to the impossible choice between relativism and objectivism.

24. Ibid., 190.

25. For an example of these rebuttals, see Sandra Harding, "From Feminist Empiricism to Feminist Standpoint Epistemologies," in *Science Question in Feminism*, 136–62. Notwithstanding many attempts to respond, standpoint theorists find themselves continually accused of relativism. Although this criticism may well be the result of a misreading, it may also reflect standpoint theory's own entanglement in the entire philosophical/epistemological framework (as a way of thinking about political questions of judgment) in which relativism and rationalism have their life.

26. Gunnell, "Relativism," 576.

27. Hannah Arendt, "Preface: The Gap between Past and Future," in *Between Past and Future*, 15.

28. As argued in chapters 1 and 2, the faculty of reflective judgment was extensively treated by Kant and became the basis for Arendt's late work on political judgment (*LKPP*). Kant states, "Judgment in general is the ability to think the particular as contained under the universal. If the universal (the rule, principle, law) is given, then judgment, which subsumes the particular under it, is *determinative* . . . . But if only the particular is given and judgment has to find the universal for it, then this power is merely *reflective*" (*CJ*, 18–19/66–67).

29. Haraway, "Situated Knowledges," 191.

30. Ibid., 190.

31. Cornelius Castoriadis, *The Imaginary Institution of Society*, trans. Kathleen Blamey (Cambridge, MA: MIT Press, 1987), 34.

32. Ibid., 163.

33. Mikhail Bakhtin, "Response to a Question from the *Novy Mir* Editorial Staff," in *Speech Genres and Other Late Essays*, trans. Vern W. McGee, 1–9 (Austin: University of Texas Press, 1986), 6.

34. Ibid., 6–7.

35. Castoriadis, *Imaginary Institution of Society*, 163.

36. Gunnell, "Relativism," 567.

37. Hannah Arendt, "Understanding and Politics," in *Essays in Understanding, 1930–1954* (New York: Harcourt Brace, 1994), 307–27, at 325n8.

CHAPTER 7

1. Hannah Arendt, *On Violence* (1969; repr., New York: Harcourt Brace, 1970; hereafter as *OV*).

2. Most of these critiques agree with Habermas that Arendt's view of violence reflects not only her narrow view of politics but also her refusal to define a set of moral standards according to which violent action can be judged. Arendtian action stands accused of having what Martin Jay calls "a special affinity for violence" by virtue of its glorification of novelty absent any moral constraints. Martin Jay, "Hannah Arendt: Opposing Views," *Partisan Review* 45 (1978): 348–68, 363. See Martin Jay, "The Political Existential-

ism of Hannah Arendt," in *Permanent Exiles* (New York: Columbia University Press, 1985), 237–56; George Kateb, "Political Action: Its Nature and Advantages," in *The Cambridge Companion to Hannah Arendt*, ed. Dana Villa (Cambridge: Cambridge University Press, 2000), 130–50; John McGowan, "Must Politics Be Violent?: Arendt's Utopian Vision," in *Hannah Arendt and the Meaning of Politics*, ed. Craig Calhoun and John McGowan (Minneapolis: University of Minnesota Press, 1997), 263–96. McGowan thinks that *On Violence* represents a departure from Arendt's earlier and "idealized and utopian" view of politics that saw violence as nonpolitical ("Must Politics Be Violent?" 293). For an effort to apply Arendt's thoughts on violence to issues in international relations such as terrorism, see Patricia Owen, *Between War and Politics: International Relations and the Thought of Hannah Arendt* (New York: Oxford University Press, 2007).

3. Such institutionalized forms of strategic action include "the admission of an opposition, . . . the competition of parties and associations, . . . [and] the legalization of labor struggles, etc." ("ACCP," 221).

4. Arendt's view of the Black Panthers is an important exception to her otherwise sympathetic if also critical account of the new movements that emerged in the sixties. In her provocative view,

> Serious violence entered the [American] scene [of student protests] only with the appearance of the Black Power movement on the campuses. Negro students, the majority of them admitted without academic qualification, regarded and organized themselves as an interest group, the representatives of the black community. Their interest was to lower academic standards. . . . [Additionally,] there stands a large minority of the Negro community behind the verbal or actual violence of the black students. Black violence can indeed be understood in analogy to the labor violence in America a generation ago. . . . It seems that the academic establishment, in its curious tendency to yield more to Negro demands, even if they are clearly silly and outrageous, than to the disinterested and usually highly moral claims of the white rebels, also thinks in these terms and feels more comfortable when confronted with interests plus violence than when it is a matter of nonviolent 'participatory democracy.' (*OV*, 18–19)

Arendt's remarks on black violence are stunningly naive, politically offensive, and difficult to read but also hard to square with her own insights into the history of the radical political exclusion of African Americans and the original racial violence that lay at the heart of the American founding, which she did not think could be easily remedied. She could have brought but sadly did not bring that insight to bear on the eruption of violence—which, after all, she defines as an absence or loss of power (*OV*, 54)—within the Black Power movement.

5. Arendt refused to interpret protest actions such as the student occupation

of People's Park as a form of lawlessness that was crushed—and rightfully so, in the view of many Americans of her generation—with tremendous police brutality. And, once again unlike many members of her generation, she refused to draw a line in the sand between so-called illegitimate uses of violence (as, say, the violence exercised by participants in the movements) and so-called legitimate exercises of violence (as, say, the violence employed by the democratic state in response to those movements).

6. For the Kant lectures, see *LKPP*. I discuss Arendt's account of Kant in Zerilli, "'We Feel Our Freedom'" (see chap. 1, n. 2).

7. Arendt linked this idea of change through violence to the modern notion of progress, which, as we saw in chapter 3, she associated most closely with the historicist illusions of liberalism. "If we look on history in terms of a continuous chronological process, whose progress, moreover, is inevitable, violence in the shape of war and revolution may appear to constitute the only possible interruption. If this were true, if only the practice of violence would make it possible to interrupt automatic processes in the realm of human affairs, the preachers of violence would have won an important point. (Theoretically, as far as I know, the point was never made, but it seems to me incontestable that the disruptive student activities in the last few years are actually based on this conviction)" (*OV*, 30). Arendt did not deny that violence surely played a role in a whole string of reforms (especially at the university), but she denied precisely that these were revolutionary (*OV*, 79–80).

8. The problem with all these ways of talking about violence, according to Arendt, is that they lend to violence a sense of necessity: "So long as we talk in non-political, biological terms, the glorifiers of violence can appeal to the undeniable fact that in the household of nature destruction and creation are but two sides of the natural process, so that collective violent action . . . may appear as natural a prerequisite for the collective life of mankind as the struggle for survival and violent death for continuing life in the animal kingdom" (*OV*, 75). Once you define violence as irrational, beastly behavior, you don't have to think about it in relation to politics: the former George W. Bush administration's position on U.S. state-sanctioned torture of suspected (Islamic) terrorists is a case in point. For Arendt, "violence, being instrumental by nature, is rational to the extent that it is effective in reaching the end that must justify it" (*OV*, 79). Her point is not to defend violence as rational against those who see it as irrational; rather, it is to break the logic of mean-ends political thinking and the tenacious understanding of politics as rule in which this way of thinking about violence has its life.

9. Habermas attributes this failure to "specify a critical standard and to distinguish between illusionary and nonillusionary convictions" to Arendt's attachment to "an antiquated [classical] concept of theoretical knowledge that is based on ultimate insights and certainties" ("ACCP," 225). In her

wish to protect the public realm of opinion from the supposedly compulsory demands of rational truth, he explains, Arendt "sees a yawning abyss between knowledge and opinion that cannot be closed with arguments" ("ACCP," 225).

10. In a discussion of Arendt and decisionism, Andreas Kalyvas argues that there are, schematically speaking, two camps of Arendt interpretation. The first camp, which includes critics such as George Kateb and Richard Wolin, faults Arendt for "expel[ling] rationality and morality from the public realm of appearances." This leaves a "normative deficit" in Arendt's thought, which results in her inability, among other things, "to distinguish between legitimate and illegitimate forms of action." The second camp, which includes Jürgen Habermas, Seyla Benhabib, and Margaret Canovan, argues Kalyvas, faults her critics for neglecting the role of reflective judgment and her refutation of the will in the political realm. In their view, Arendt exhibits a "principled opposition to decisionism." Andreas Kalyvas, "From the Act to the Decision: Hannah Arendt and the Question of Decisionism," *Political Theory* 32, no. 3 (June 2004): 320–46, at 321. I agree with Kalyvas that critics such as Habermas and Benhabib are concerned to distinguish Arendt's thought from the decisionism of a Carl Schmitt. But they also think that Arendt's work suffers under a normative deficit and that by expelling claims to truth from the political realm, she has, finally, no way to determine what is legitimate and what is not. Thus Arendt, in their view, falls into the decisionism she would reject. For this reason, her work must be supplemented by a detranscendentalized, discourse-based conception of reason and truth.

11. Arendt's failure to specify criteria of judgment, argues Habermas, leads her to place "more trust in the venerable figure of the contract than in her own concept of a praxis, which is grounded in the rationality of practical judgment" ("ACCP," 225). I have discussed Arendt's supposed failure to specify rational criteria of judgment in Zerilli, "'We Feel Our Freedom.'"

12. For Habermas's views on the student movement in Germany, see Jürgen Habermas, "Die Scheinrevolution und ihre Kinder: Sechs Thesen über Taktik, Ziele und Situationsanalysen der oppositionellen Jugend," in *Die Linke Antwort*, ed. Jürgen Habermas (Frankfurt am Main: Europäische Verlagsanstalt, 1968), 5–15; Jürgen Habermas, *Protestbewegung und Hochschulreform* (Frankfurt am Main: Suhrkamp, 1969); Jürgen Habermas, *Autonomy and Solidarity: Interviews with Jürgen Habermas*, ed. Peter Dews (London: Verso, 1986). Like Arendt, Habermas is sympathetic to the participatory demand in the students' protests. He is also, like Arendt, highly critical of the students' grandiose and Marxist inspired claims to be an extension of either the Third World struggle or the workers' struggle in advanced capitalist countries such as Germany. For him, the student movement tried but ultimately failed to bring about "serious democratic will-formation in all social realms" ("Die Scheinrevolution und ihre Kinder," 14).

13. Jürgen Habermas, *Between Facts and Norms: Contributions to a Discourse Theory of Democracy*, trans. William Rehg (Cambridge, MA: MIT Press, 1998), 484 (hereafter cited as *BFN*).

14. Hannah Arendt, "What Is Freedom?" in *Between Past and Future*, 143–72, at 152.

15. Philosophies of the will—which I shall refer to as belonging more generally to the philosophy of the will, though this should not be understood as composing a unified body of thought—do not emerge until the rise of Christianity, says Arendt, as "the faculty of the Will was unknown to Greek antiquity" (*LMW*, 3). Whatever their differences, most philosophers of the will—the first being Augustine in Arendt's view—were entangled in denying that the will was free. Showing how the philosophers denied such freedom, Arendt can easily be taken to be defending the freedom of the will. In fact, her whole point is to contest this view, for freedom of the will is associated with sovereignty and politics as rule.

16. Hannah Arendt, "What Is Freedom?" 145.

17. Ibid., 162.

18. At the center of Habermas's effort to refigure will-formation as rational will-formation is a conception of the self-reflexive subject as a speaking being characterized by (albeit mostly tacit) rule consciousness and embedded in a rule-governed practice of language; a rule-governed subject capable of submitting its will to the exercise of reason and thus competing validity claims to critique in the manner outlined in the theories of communicative action and discourse ethics.

19. My argument here is not that Arendt entirely abandons the language of the will, for the concept of the will is, as Wittgenstein might say, built into our grammar of the subject. What she breaks with is the tendency to foreground the will as the power of freedom and thus as the central political faculty. Andreas Kalyvas has called this break injudicious—after all, the will can be subjected to reason and, besides, how else would we talk about democratic agency (e.g. "the will of the people")? He sees Arendt's "hasty" break with the will as symptomatic of the extent to which she remained hostage to the sovereign idea of the will that she found and criticized in Rousseau. In his view, the will is the faculty of beginning; the later Arendt began to see this view when she wrote volume 2 of *The Life of the Mind*; and, further, any beginning that can claim political legitimacy must entail rational will-formation. Kalyvas's claim that, in her later work (*The Life of the Mind*) Arendt "suddenly, against all expectations, proposed a different, more positive reading, linking the will with the power to make new beginnings," mistakes Arendt's attempt to lay bare the presuppositions of the philosophy of the will with her own preferences. Kalyvas, "From Act to Decision," 322.

20. Although Arendt often invokes the Kantian notion of spontaneity, understood as the ability to begin a new series in time, in her account of

freedom, she did not think that the idea of an absolute beginning, which is what the Kantian notion posits, was possible. Perhaps most important, as argued in chapter 1, the Kantian idea of spontaneity was not political. She may have been led to invoke Kant's idea of spontaneity as an alternative to the other idea of freedom as *liberum arbitrium* (the choice between two or more existing objects), which Arendt found to be the preferred idea in the philosophy of the will (which mostly denied freedom). By contrast with Kantian spontaneity, political freedom consists for Arendt in the exchange of word and deed and requires the presence of others—that is, plurality. Freedom understood in the political sense does not produce anything (as does the spontaneity of the artist) and it is not a property of the subject (as it is in the philosophy of the will). See "IP," esp. 127–28.

21. As argued in the preface and chapter 1, Arendt was not troubled by the specter of decisionism any more than she, the great defender of plurality and multiple points of view, was troubled by relativism. Was she blind to the consequences of her own disinterest in the problem of legitimation that dominates the thought of Habermas and other deliberative democrats? Was she naive about the consequences of her apparent unwillingness to redeem the will as the central political faculty by subjecting it to the claim of (communicative) reason? Until we recognize the specific character of Arendt's break with the philosophy of the will, and how it differs from that of Habermas, we shall be tempted to agree with his verdict that her view of politics is inapplicable to modern conditions, her reflections on violence naive, and her unfinished work on judgment deeply puzzling.

22. Bonnie Honig, "Between Decision and Deliberation: Political Paradox in Democratic Theory," *American Political Science Review* 101, no. 1 (February 2007): 1–17, at 12.

23. Ibid., 12. On the fraught place of affect in Habermas's constitutional patriotism, see Patchen Markell, "Making Affect Safe for Democracy? On 'Constitutional Patriotism,'" *Political Theory* 28 (February 2000): 38–63.

24. Ibid., 12.

25. This potential, in turn, quickly gives way in Habermas's interpretation to a full-blown agreement, whose rationality is secured by engaging in the universalizing practice of judgment. He continues:

> She [Arendt] opposes "power" (*Macht*) to "violence" (*Gewalt*); that is, she opposes the consensus-achieving force of a communication aimed at reaching understanding to the capacity for instrumentalizing another's will for one's own purposes: "Power corresponds to the human ability not just to act but to act in concert." A communicative power of this kind can develop only in undeformed public spheres; it can issue only from structures of undamaged intersubjectivity found in non-distorted communication. It arises where opinion- and will-formation instantiate the productive force of the "enlarged mentality" given with

the unhindered communicative freedom each one has "to make public use of one's reason at every point." This enlargement is accomplished by "comparing our judgment with the possible rather than the actual judgments of others, and by putting ourselves in the place of any other man." (*BFN*, 148)

26. The constitutional assemblies at Philadelphia and Paris, for example, are described by Habermas, writes Honig, "as an 'entirely new beginning'" and constitutional democracy is cast as "'a tradition-building project with a clearly marked beginning in time.'" (Honig, "Between Decision and Deliberation," 14). The problem with this way of thinking about political events, she rightly suggests, is that it sets up an impossible choice between the capacity of democratic citizens to create political arrangements of their own choosing and the need for democratic societies to have a measure of stability and durability over time: "With their focus on conflicting principles . . . or incommensurable 'logics' . . . , democratic theorists drive us into binary paradoxes that shuttle us back and forth between decision and deliberation" (14).

27. Ibid., 14.

28. Richard J. Bernstein, "The Retrieval of the Democratic Ethos," in *Habermas on Law and Democracy: Critical Exchanges*, ed. Michael Rosenfeld and Andrew Arato, 287–305 (Berkeley: University of California Press, 1998), 291.

29. See Hilary Putnam, "Values and Norms," in *The Collapse of the Fact/Value Dichotomy and Other Essays* (Cambridge, MA: Harvard University Press, 2002), 111–34.

30. Bernstein, "Democratic Ethos," 296.

31. Honig, "Between Decision and Deliberation," 14.

32. Habermas's enterprise as a critical theorist, observes Nigel Pleasants, can be understood as an attempt at "rationally reconstructing the presuppositions and conditions of communicative action"—that is, rendering the individual's implicit knowledge and abstract social structures and mechanisms into explicit propositional form. It is Habermas's wager that when people become aware of the implicit normativity of their communicative action they will seek to institute "reflexive discourses" as the only legitimate procedure for "collective will formation." This supposedly gives what is an otherwise highly philosophical and academic account of such action its political relevance. Pleasants, *Wittgenstein and Critical Theory*, 156 (see chap. 1, n. 70).

33. Ibid., 170.

34. Jürgen Habermas, *Moral Consciousness and Communicative Action* (Cambridge: Polity Press, 1990), 130. Located at the ontological level where things just are as they are, observes Pleasants, Habermas can be read as "professing to embrace *epistemological fallibility*, but at the same time insisting upon *ontological infallibility*," with consequences for the practices

of public debate and judgment that are so crucial to his discourse ethics. Pleasants, *Wittgenstein and Critical Theory*, 163. Pleasants explains,

> To do this, Habermas argues that the principle of universalisation (the "priority of the right over the good") is not as such a *moral or political principle at all*; rather, he attempts to pass it off as a necessarily unavoidable "rule of argumentation," which [Habermas writes] is "part of the logic of practical discourses." Thus the "rules of discourse are not mere *conventions*; rather, they are inescapable presuppositions" [as Habermas puts it]. Yet if anything involves a "performative contradiction" it is surely this: a fundamental moral principle which is not actually a moral principle at all (it is somehow "deeper" than a moral principle). (Ibid., 170)

35. Bernstein, "Democratic Ethos," 304, 296.
36. Bonnie Honig, *Democracy and the Foreigner* (Princeton, NJ: Princeton University Press, 2001), 20.
37. Kant, *Critique of Pure Reason*, 484–85 (see chap. 2, n. 110).
38. Kant's third antinomy in the first *Critique* suggests how rule and beginning come to be set apart. In the "thesis," which claims that "causality in accordance with the laws of nature is not the only one from which all the appearances of the world can be derived" (A444/B472), Kant posits the possibility of "an *absolute* causal *spontaneity* beginning *from itself*" (A446/B474). This spontaneity is the source of some "embarrassment," as Arendt reads Kant. If we look more closely at Kant's own description of the problem raised in the thesis, however, a somewhat more interesting problem emerges. The "proof" Kant offers for the "antithesis" ("There is no freedom, but everything in the world happens solely in accordance with laws of nature") (A445/B473) states:

> Thus we have nothing but *nature* in which we must seek the connection and order of occurrences in the world. Freedom (independence) from the laws of nature is indeed *liberation* from *coercion*, but also from the *guidance* of all rules. . . . Thus nature and transcendental freedom are as different as lawfulness and lawlessness; the former burdens the understanding with the difficulty of seeking the ancestry of occurrences ever higher in the series of causes, because the causality in them is at every time conditioned, but it promises in compensation a thoroughgoing and lawful unity of experience, while the mirage of freedom, on the contrary, though of course offering rest to the inquiring understanding in the chain of causes by leading it to an unconditioned causality that begins to act from itself, since it is itself blind, breaks away from the guidance of those rules by which alone a thoroughly connected experience is possible. (A447/B475)

The problem Kant describes concerns the question of whether the positing of "a power of spontaneously beginning a series of successive things or states" amounts to "a mirage of freedom." Freedom is illusory because if our actions really are radically unconditioned then they will lack coherent connection with anything else—either "inside" or "outside" the individual, and hence will be totally capricious: freedom not only from the laws of nature but "also from the guidance of all rules." From the perspective of Kant's theory of knowledge, this would leave us unable to constitute a coherent experience and make sense of our free actions or the world around us. What fails here is our capacity to make judgments. This failure takes for granted that rule following wholly defines the capacity to judge for Kant in the first, though not the third, *Critique*.

39. Nadia Urbinati, *Representative Democracy: Principles and Genealogy* (Chicago: University of Chicago Press, 2005), 97.

40. Ibid., 97.

41. Ibid., 10.

42. Patchen Markell, "The Rule of the People: Arendt, Archê, and Democracy," *American Political Science Review* 100, no. 1 (February 2006): 1–14, at 2 (hereafter cited as "RP").

43. To understand why it may be in the register of the will that beginning and rule are wrenched apart, let us return to Arendt's account of how *archein* came to mean "to rule" rather than "to begin." She observes, "Here it seems as though each action were divided into two parts, the beginning made by a single person and the achievement in which many join by 'bearing' and 'finishing' the enterprise, by seeing it through" (*HC*, 189). Furthermore, "the role of the beginner and leader . . . changed into that of a ruler; the original interdependence of action, the dependence of the beginner and leader upon others for help and the dependence of his followers upon him for an occasion to act themselves split into two altogether different functions: the function of giving commands, which became the prerogative of the ruler, and the function of executing them, which became the duty of his subjects" (*HC*, 189). We can recognize in Arendt's prose Nietzsche's point about the will as a relationship of command and obedience. But it is more than that. For the relationship at issue here is played out not so much in the realm of the inner but through the constitution of an inner (willing) and an outer (acting), two discrete registers and faculties which are then projected onto two different agents: the one who begins and the one who achieves.

44. Markell's intervention answers to the "maddeningly difficult" ("RP," 4) task of deciding which activities will count as examples of action and thus beginning in Arendt's view. He rightly observes that, taken as such a subset, genuine action in the Arendtian sense "can seem vanishingly rare" ("RP," 4). If providing an alternative definition of beginning were Markell's objective, we would find ourselves engaged in another "mad-

deningly difficult" task, for it is hard to see why a seemingly all-inclusive account of beginning would be any less elusive than a deeply exclusive one. His point is not to provide a "correct" definition of beginning but rather to move the discussion from the abstract register of word definitions to a contextualized understanding of what it means for something to count as an instance of something. Accordingly, whether something will count as an instance of beginning is not unlike whether something will count as the intelligible use of a word. It depends on who is acting/speaking (to whom and) in what context.

45. "Recall that what makes a beginning a beginning for Arendt, what lends it its eruptiveness, is not its degree of departure from what preceded it, but rather our attunement to its character as an irrevocable event, which also means: as an occasion for response" ("RP," 10).

46. Friedrich Nietzsche, *Also Sprach Zarathustra*, bk. 2, "Von der Erlösung," in *Sämtliche Werke, Kritische Studien-ausgabe*, ed. Giorgio Colli and Mazzino Montinari, 15 vols. (Berlin: de Gruyter, 1999), 4:179.

47. It is precisely this affirmation of contingency that Arendt cites as one of the greatest challenges to thinking about occurrences as events and events as beginnings. Seen from the perspective of consciousness, Arendt writes, what is appears as "absolutely necessary."

> A thing may have happened quite at random, but, once it has come into existence and assumed reality, it loses its aspect of contingency and presents itself to us in the guise of necessity. And even if the event is of our own making, or at least we are one of its contributing causes—as in contracting marriage or committing a crime—the simple existential fact that it now is as it has become (for whatever reasons) is likely to withstand all reflections on its original randomness. Once the contingent has happened, we can no longer unravel the strands that entangled it until it became an *event*—as though it could still be or not be. (*LMW*, 138)

The power that enables us to affirm an event as at once irrevocable and contingent, an occasion for beginning, is the power of judgment.

48. Efforts to revisit the consensus about 1968 are especially visible in the scholarship on the civil rights movement and its connections to the Black Power movement. See, for example, Peniel E. Joseph, ed., *The Black Power Movement: Rethinking the Civil Rights-Black Power Era* (New York: Routledge, 2006); Kimberly Springer, *Living for the Revolution: Black Feminist Organizations, 1968–1980* (Durham, NC: Duke University Press, 2005).

49. Lucy Cane, "Hannah Arendt on the Principles of Political Action," *European Journal of Political Theory* (Online First), February 24, 2014, 1–20, at 3, doi: 10.1177/1474885114523939.

50. As Max Elbaum describes this spirit:

In 1968 more college students (20 percent) identified with Latin American revolutionary Che Guevara than with any of the candidates for the U.S. presidency. A 1971 *New York Times* survey indicated that four out of ten students—nearly 3 million people—thought that a revolution was needed in the United States.

Max Elbaum, "What Legacy from the Radical Internationalism of 1968?" *Radical History Review* 82 (Winter 2002): 37–64, at 37.

51. Ibid., 38. See, for example, Todd Gitlin's narrative of demise, *The Sixties: Years of Hope, Days of Rage* (New York: Bantam, 1987). In his view, the real failure of radical politics emerges with identity politics in the 1970s and 1980s, both of which represent a turn away from the universalism that inspired the best of the sixties. See Todd Gitlin, *The Twilight of Common Dreams: Why America Is Wracked by Culture Wars* (New York: Metropolitan, 1995).

52. Arendt, "What Is Freedom?" 152. Modifying Montesquieu's account to accommodate the rich plurality of ways in which human beings can share the world in common, writes Cane, Arendt

> identifies the principles of "fame," and Athenian form of "freedom," "justice," "the belief in the innate worth of every human being," "solidarity," "public or political freedom," "public or political happiness," "the interconnected principle of mutual promise and common deliberation," "consent and the right to dissent," "rage," "charity," "distrust," and "hatred." Furthermore, unlike Montesquieu, Arendt implies that a political community is not necessarily bound by a single central principle and may be animated by several principles at once. Finally, Arendt places less emphasis on attaching principles to particular forms of government and relates principles to the political realm in the broader, less state-centric sense of a public space in which individuals interact and perform.

Cane, "Arendt on Political Action," 8.

53. Cane, "Arendt on Political Action," 8.
54. Ibid., 7.
55. Ibid., 5.
56. Seyla Benhabib, "Judgment and the Moral Foundations of Politics in Arendt's Thought," *Political Theory* 16, no. 1 (February 1988): 29–51. I return to Benhabib's argument about the universal morality of judgment in the concluding chapter.
57. Ibid., 42.
58. Ibid.
59. Cane, "Arendt on Political Action," 14. See Arendt, "What Is Freedom?" 152.
60. Arendt, "What Is Freedom?" 152.
61. Ibid.

CHAPTER 8

1. Nussbaum, "Political Objectivity," 884 (see chap. 5, n. 9).
2. Donald Davidson, "On the Very Idea of a Conceptual Scheme," *Proceedings and Addresses of the American Philosophical Association* 47 (1973–1974): 5–20, at 5.
3. Davidson condenses this point into the principle of "charity" that guides radical interpretation—our attempt to interpret a completely unknown language. Making sense of someone means treating him or her as a rational agent. We try to optimize agreement between ourselves and those whom we try to interpret by taking for granted that they hold true beliefs. Ibid., 19.
4. Ibid., 12.
5. Hilary Putnam, "The Face of Cognition," in *The Threefold Cord: Mind, Body, and World* (New York: Columbia University Press, 1999), 43–70, at 43.
6. John McDowell too challenges the scheme-content dualism attacked by Davidson and what Putnam called the interface-like relationship between mind and world. The Kantian slogan "Thoughts without content are empty, intuitions without concepts are blind," McDowell holds, has been misinterpreted as breaking empirical content down into two separable elements: a conceptual structure and a nonconceptual experience, or scheme and content. Experience, as McDowell rereads Kant, is always already conceptual. See John McDowell, *Mind and World* (Cambridge, MA: Harvard University Press, 1996), esp. "Lecture 1: Concepts and Intuitions," 3–23; see also chap. 9, n. 35.
7. Davidson, "Conceptual Scheme," 20.
8. Charles Taylor, "Foundationalism and the Inner-Outer Distinction," in *Reading McDowell On Mind and World*, ed. Nicholas H. Smith (New York: Routledge, 2002), 106–19, at 117.
9. Ibid., 116.
10. Donald K. Barry, *Forms of Life and Following Rules: A Wittgensteinian Defence of Relativism* (New York: E. J. Brill, 1996), 88.
11. Quoted in ibid., 88, n. 1.
12. Bernard Williams, "Wittgenstein and Idealism," in *Moral Luck* (New York: Cambridge University Press, 1981), 144–63, at 160.
13. Ibid., 150.
14. Jonathan Lear, "Leaving the World Alone," *Journal of Philosophy* 79, no. 7 (1982): 382–403, at 385. For a similar argument, see Jonathan Lear, "The Disappearing We I," supplement, *Proceedings of the Aristotelian Society*, 58 (1984): 219–42.
15. Lear, "Leaving the World Alone," 386. For an excellent comparative reading of Lear and Williams on this point, see Barry, *Forms of Life*, 109–14.
16. Yet other critics, argues Barry, find commonality in "a *foundational* common behavior [of humankind]" that they claim to find in Wittgenstein's

later work (*Forms of Life*, 115). As Barry rightly observes, however, both the idea of a unified subjectivity or mindedness and a common behavior posit a single form of life, the "Human Form," and amount to the same thing: the shared ground on which the undeniable empirical cultural plurality of language games and their corresponding principles of reality do not invite relativism but can meet and be rationally judged (113–14). For another excellent critique of the transcendentalist reading of Wittgenstein, see Kathy Emmett Bohstedt, "Convention and Necessity," *Essays in Philosophy* 1, no. 2 (2000): article 6 [does not have page numbers].

17. Alice Crary, "Wittgenstein's Philosophy in Relation to Political Thought," in *The New Wittgenstein*, ed. Alice Crary and Rupert Read (New York: Routledge, 2000): 118–45, at 119.

18. Ibid., 120.

19. Quoted in ibid., 122.

20. Quoted in ibid.

21. Richard Rorty, "Introduction: Antirepresentationalism, Ethnocentrism, and Liberalism," in *Objectivity, Relativism, and Truth: Philosophical Papers*, vol. 1 (Cambridge: Cambridge University Press, 1991), 1–20, 15. In response to the hostility that his use of the term aroused in leftists, Rorty seeks to clarify that ethnocentrism is an epistemological position, not simply a political statement of loyalty to bourgeois democracy.

22. Wittgenstein writes:

> "How am I to obey a rule?"—if this is not a question about causes, then it is about the justification for my following the rule in the way I do.
> If I have exhausted the justifications I have reached bedrock, and my spade is turned. Then I am inclined to say: "This is simply what I do." (*PI*, §217)

23. Farid Abdel-Nour lucidly clarifies Rorty's description of "wet liberals":

> They hold the following three positions simultaneously and develop as a result a "psychological problem": they insist upon the "distinction between rational judgement and cultural bias," they have a deep commitment to liberal Enlightenment moral ideals and to human equality . . . , and they know "that most of the globe's inhabitants simply do not believe in human equality." When they find themselves shocked or horrified by practices such as Female Genital Mutilation (FGM) or other human rights abuses, wet liberals suffer from the guilt of imposing liberal standards on nonliberal contexts. They question whether their liberal commitments are not merely the outcome of cultural bias. In doing so they presume that there is a neutral alternative set of standards that is free from "contamination" by cultural particularity, and that can be had from an external point of view such as Thomas Nagel's famous "view from nowhere."

Farid Abdel-Nour, "Liberalism and Ethnocentrism," *Journal of Political Philosophy* 8, no. 2 (2000): 207–26, at 209. See also Richard Rorty, "On Ethnocentrism: A Reply to Clifford Geertz," *Michigan Quarterly Review* 25:523–34, at 531.

24. Wittgenstein, *On Certainty*, §110 (see chap. 3, n. 17).

25. Abdel-Nour, "Liberalism and Ethnocentrism," 209.

26. Hilary Putnam, "What Is a Philosopher," in *Realism with a Human Face*, ed. James Conant (Cambridge, MA: Harvard University Press, 1990), 105–19, at 118.

27. Elizabeth Anscombe, "The Question of Linguistic Idealism," in *From Parmenides to Wittgenstein* (Oxford: Blackwell, 1981), 112–33, at 125.

28. Peter Winch, "Understanding a Primitive Society," *American Philosophical Quarterly* 1, no. 4 (October 1964): 307–24 (hereafter cited as "UPS"). The source to which Winch refers is E. E. Evans-Pritchard, *Witchcraft, Oracles, and Magic among the Azande* (Oxford: Clarendon Press, 1937).

29. Cited in "UPS," 308. The source to which Winch refers is E. E. Evans-Pritchard, "Science and Sentiment," *Bulletin of the Faculty of the Arts*, University of Egypt, 1935.

30. Ludwig Wittgenstein, "Remarks on Frazer's Golden Bough," in *Philosophical Occasions, 1921–1951*, ed. James Klagge and Alfred Nordman (Indianapolis, IN: Hackett, 1993), 115–55.

31. Bernard Williams, *Ethics and the Limits of Philosophy* (London: Fontana, 1985), 138–39.

32. Jürgen Habermas, *The Theory of Communicative Action*, trans. Thomas McCarthy, vol. 1, *Reason and the Rationalization of Society* (1981; repr., Boston: Beacon, 1984), 56 (hereafter cited as *TCA*).

33. Cristina Lafont, *The Linguistic Turn in Hermeneutic Philosophy*, trans. José Medina (Cambridge, MA: MIT Press, 1999), xiii.

34. Ibid., 122. See esp. chaps. 3 and 4.

35. Ibid., 122. As argued in chapter 4, Habermas's attempt in *Truth and Justification* to answer Lafont's criticism and to avoid the contextualism that he associates with the work of Richard Rorty is to distinguish claims to truth from claims to normative rightness, whose validity lies wholly in warranted assertibility. But even in that text, Habermas merely rescues the idea of truth from contextualism by redefining it as that to which our practices of justification and argument strive, rather than to the warranted assertibility that defined truth claims in *The Theory of Communicative Action*. Normative rightness is still defined as warranted assertibility, and moral norms are still understood as radically distinguished from the ethical norms of any particular lifeworld.

36. Winch writes:

> It is important to distinguish a system of magical beliefs and practices like that of the Azande, which is one of the principal foundations of

their whole social life and, on the other hand, magical beliefs that might be . . . practiced, by persons belonging to our own culture. . . . [As Evans-Pritchard himself observes,] "When a Zande speaks of witch-craft he does not speak of it as we speak of the weird witchcraft of our own history." . . .

The difference is not merely one of the degree of familiarity. . . . Concepts of witchcraft and magic in our culture, at least since the advent of Christianity, have been parasitic on, and a perversion of other orthodox concepts, both religious and, increasingly scientific. To take an obvious example, you could not understand what was involved in conducting a Black Mass unless you were familiar with the conduct of a proper Mass and, therefore, with the whole complex of religious ideas from which the Mass draws its sense. . . . It is impossible to keep a discussion of the rationality of Black Magic or of astrology within the bounds of concepts peculiar to them; they have an essential reference to something outside themselves. ("UPS," 310)

37. Castoriadis, *Imaginary Institution of Society*, 168 (see chap. 6, n. 32).
38. According to Hanna Pitkin, Winch can at times seem to be saying "that explanations and understandings are better, deeper, more successful if framed in the actor's terms than if framed in the terms of an external, detached observer." This framing is to be distinguished from "the more moderate position Winch ultimately wants to assume: that actions can be explained in terms unintelligible to the actors, but only if those terms are translatable into the actor's own. The social scientist does not need 'to stop at the unreflective kind of understanding' which the participants in a social institution have of what they are doing; but 'any more reflective understanding must necessarily presuppose, if it is to count as genuine understanding at all, the participant's unreflective understanding.'" Pit-kin, *Wittgenstein and Justice*, 250, 251 (see chap. 1, n. 53).
39. John G. Gunnell, "Political Judgment and the Problem of 'Criticizing from the Outside'" (paper presented at American Political Science Association meeting, 2014), 23.
40. Ibid.
41. Cora Diamond, "Criticising from 'Outside,'" *Philosophical Investigations* 36, no. 2 (April 2013): 114–32 (hereafter cited as "CO").
42. Wittgenstein, *On Certainty*, §§609–12.
43. Diamond continues:

There is thus an important sort of contrast between the way the notion of real and unreal works *in the dispute* and the way that notions of real and unreal work in the two systems of thought that are at odds. There, as Winch and Dilman emphasise, in such systems of thought, there are standards that operate independently of any particular move that someone makes; but in the kind of conflict with which we are concerned, as it may be seen by Anscombe (as I am imagining her view), giving what one takes to be rational grounds for one's judgement is itself part of the articulation of the logical space here, the space of reasons in this conflict. ("CO," 119)

44. Gunnell, "Political Judgment," 24.
45. Ibid., 24.
46. Ibid., 25.
47. Grassi, *Rhetoric as Philosophy*, 26 (see chap. 5, n. 27).
48. Ibid., 19.
49. Ibid., 20.
50. Ibid., 20.
51. Ernesto Grassi, "The Priority of Common Sense and Imagination: Vico's Philosophical Relevance Today," *Social Research* 43 (1976): 553–80, at 565.
52. Grassi, *Rhetoric as Philosophy*, 8.
53. Ibid., 10.
54. Ibid.. 97.
55. Ian Hacking, "Language, Truth, and Reason" and "'Style' for Historians and Philosophers," both in *Historical Ontology*, 159–77, 178–99 (Cambridge, MA: Harvard University Press, 2002; hereafter cited as *HO*).
56. Hacking does not provide a precise definition of a style of reasoning, but he is clear about what it is not: "by reasoning I don't mean logic. I mean the very opposite, for logic is the preservation of truth, while a style of reasoning is what brings in the possibility of truth and falsehood" (*HO*, 167). From this difference between logical reasoning and styles of reasoning, Hacking sets out several theses about the latter, including: (1) a style "introduces a new type of object, individuated by means of the style, and not previously noticeable among the things that exist" (*HO*, 189); (2) a style is "self-authenticating"—that is, it sets out the criteria of validity and objectivity according to which we determine "candidates for truth or falsehood" (*HO*, 191); (3) though a style comes into existence contingently, by means of "microsocial interactions and negotiations," it can appear as "a rather timeless canon of objectivity, a standard or model of what it is to be reasonable or unreasonable about this or that types of subject matter" (*HO*, 188).
57. Gunnell "Political Judgment," 23.
58. McDowell, *Mind and World*, 35.
59. Ibid., 35–36.
60. Wittgenstein, *On Certainty*, §97. What stands fast for us, then, does so not because it is convincing but because "it is . . . held fast by what lies around it." Wittgenstein elaborates the complex relationship between what is subject to doubt and what is certain with this river metaphor:

> It might be imagined that some propositions, of the form of empirical propositions, were hardened and functioned as channels for such empirical propositions as were not hardened but fluid; and that this

relation altered with time, in that fluid propositions hardened, and hard ones became fluid.

The mythology may change back into a state of flux, the river-bed of thoughts may shift. But I distinguish between the movement of the waters on the river-bed and the shift of the bed itself; though there is not a sharp division of the one from the other.

. . .

And the bank of that river consists partly of hard rock, subject to no alteration or only to an imperceptible one, partly of sand, which now in one place now in another gets washed away, or deposited. (*On Certainty*, §§96- 97, 99)

61. Hilary Putnam, *The Many Faces of Realism* (LaSalle, IL: Open Court, 1987), 85.
62. Barry, *Forms of Life*, 119.
63. Ibid.
64. McDowell, "Non-Cognitivism and Rule-Following," 207 (see chap. 1, n. 37).
65. Ibid., 211.

CHAPTER 9

1. For accounts of affect in feminist theory, see Sara Ahmed, "Open Forum Imaginary Prohibitions: Some Preliminary Remarks on the Founding Gestures of the 'New Materialism,'" *European Journal of Women's Studies* 15, no. 1 (2008): 23–39; Patricia T. Clough, "The Affective Turn: Political Economy, Biomedia and Bodies," in *The Affect Theory Reader*, ed. Melissa Gregg and Gregory J. Seigworth (Durham, NC: Duke University Press, 2010), 206–25 (volume hereafter cited as *AT*); Lisa Blackman, "Affect, Relationality, and the 'Problem of Personality,'" *Theory, Culture and Society* 25, no. 1 (2008): 23–47; Myra J. Hird, "Feminist Matters: New Material- ist Considerations of Sexual Difference," *Feminist Theory* 5, no. 2 (2004): 223–32; Karen Barad, "Posthumanist Performativity: Toward an Under- standing of How Matter Comes to Matter," *Signs: Journal of Women in Culture and Society* 28, no. 3 (2003): 801–3; Anu Koivunen, "An Affective Turn? Reimagining the Subject of Feminist Theory," in *Working with Affect in Feminist Readings: Disturbing Differences*, ed. Marianne Liljeström and Susanna Paasonen (New York: Routledge, 2010), 8–28.
2. As noted in chapter 1, recent work on affect in political theory includes Connolly, *Neuropolitics* (see chap. 1, n. 8); Bennett, *Vibrant Matter* (see chap. 1, n. 8); Panagia, *Political Life of Sensation* (see chap. 1, n. 8); Thiele, *Heart of Judgment* (cee chap. 1, n. 4); Nedelsky, "Receptivity and Judgment" (see chap. 1, n. 8); Livingston, "Avoiding Deliberative Democracy?" (see chap. 1, n. 8); Protevi, *Political Affect* (see chap. 1, n. 8). For an excellent critique of the turn to cognitive neuroscience and affect in political

theory, see Gunnell, "Unpacking Emotional Baggage" (see chap. 1, n. 8); Gunnell, "Are We Losing Our Minds?" (see chap. 1, n. 8). There is debate about the extent to which the work of affect theorists such as Brian Massumi can be linked up with affective neuroscientists such as Antonio Damasio. Whereas Massumi is heavily influenced by Gilles Deleuze, who stresses the irreducible difference between a register of affective embodied intensity from a register of symbolic mediation, Damasio relies on the 1960s research of Silvan S. Tomkins and Paul Ekman, for whom the basic emotions such as fear, anger, disgust, joy, sadness, and surprise are rapid, phylogenetically old, automatic responses of the organism that have evolved for survival purposes. I would agree with Ruth Leys, however, that there is a striking compatibility between Spinozist-Deleuzian-inspired affect theorists and affective neuroscientists at the level of their shared anti-intentionalism—hence Connolly can appeal to both Massumi and Damasio. See Brian Massumi, *Parables for the Virtual: Movement, Affect, Sensation* (Durham, NC: Duke University Press, 2002); Antonio Damasio, *Descartes' Error: Emotion, Reason, and the Human Brain* (1994; repr., New York: Penguin, 2005); Ruth Leys, "The Turn to Affect: A Critique," *Critical Inquiry* 37, no. 3 (2011): 434–72, at 437 (hereafter cited as "TA").

3. I take ordinary-language philosophy with Toril Moi "to mean the philosophical tradition after Ludwig Wittgenstein and J. L. Austin as established and extended by Stanley Cavell." For reasons explained shortly, I include aspects of Gilbert Ryle's work in this tradition. For Ryle, *Concept of Mind* (cited as *CM*), see chap. 1, n.15.

4. Hubert L. Dreyfus, "The Myth of the Pervasiveness of the Mental," in *Mind, Reason, and Being-in-the-World: The McDowell-Dreyfus Debate*, ed. Joseph K. Schear (New York: Routledge, 2013), 15–40, at 15.

5. William E. Connolly, "Experience and Experiment," *Daedalus* 135, no. 3 (2006): 67–75, at 73.

6. Hubert L. Dreyfus, "Overcoming the Myth of the Mental," *Topoi* 25 (2006): 43–49, at 43.

7. Ibid., 43.

8. Jason Stanley, *Know How* (Oxford: Oxford University Press, 2013), 13, 14. Stanley offers a brilliant critique of nonconceptualist or nonpropositionalist accounts of know how.

9. Clive Barnett, "Political Affects in Public Space: Normative Blind Spots in Non-Representational Ontologies," in *Transactions of the Institute of British Geographers* 33, no. 2 (2008): 186–200, at 188 (hereafter cited as "PA").

10. For the distinction between "knowing how" and "knowing that," see Gilbert Ryle, "Knowing How and Knowing That: The Presidential Address," *Aristotelian Society Proceedings* 46 (1945–46): 1–16. See also chapter 2 of *CM*.

11. Zerilli, *Feminism and Abyss of Freedom* (see chap. 1, n. 104). Other works in the postfoundationalist or phenomenological tradition that examine gender as a kind of embodied know how include Judith Butler, *Gender Trouble: Feminism and the Subversion of Identity* (New York: Routledge, 1990); Iris Marion Young, *On Female Bodily Experience: Throwing Like a Girl and Other Essays* (New York: Oxford University Press, 2005); Sonia Kruks, *Retrieving Experience: Subjectivity and Recognition in Feminist Politics* (Ithaca, NY: Cornell University Press, 2001); Elizabeth Grosz, *Volatile Bodies: Toward a Corporeal Feminism* (Bloomington: Indiana University Press, 1994); Toril Moi, *What is a Woman? and Other Essays* (New York: Oxford University Press, 1999); Sandra Bartky, *Femininity and Domination: Studies in the Phenomenology of Oppression* (New York: Routledge, 1990).

12. "The nonconceptuality of social norms," writes Dreyfus, means "we are always already absorbed in a nonconceptual background understanding of our shared social world." We learn, for example, what the appropriate distance is to stand in relation to other people in certain contexts not by consciously following rules but by means of an infinite number of micropractices in which we engage fully "unaware." The same goes for other "styles of normative comportment such as gender roles and ethnic stereotypes." Dreyfus, "Pervasiveness of Mental," 23, 24.

13. See Robert Stalnaker, "Intellectualism and the Objects of Knowledge," *Philosophy and Phenomenological Research* 85, no. 3 (2012): 754–61.

14. Ibid., 756. Stalnaker offers a discussion of Ryle in the context of a review of Stanley's *Know How* (cited in note 8), arguing persuasively for more continuity in Stanley's view and Ryle's than Stanley's own defense of intellectualism would suggest. For a sympathetic reading of Ryle along the lines suggested here, see Julia Tanney, "Rethinking Ryle: A Critical Discussion of *The Concept of Mind*," in *The Concept of Mind*, 60th anniversary ed., Gilbert Ryle (New York: Routledge, 2009), ix–lvii.

15. On the alternative reading of Ryle proposed here, we would not be able to distill out a purely mental concept-guided form of knowing from an embodied nonconceptual form of doing. The idea of the mind as fully detached from the body in expressions of propositional knowledge is a Cartesian phantasm: what Ryle unforgettably coined the "dogma of the Ghost in the Machine" (*CM*, 15–16). As I argue in this chapter, certain iterations of affect theory retain this ghostly figure of the mind as a fully disembodied intellect at the very moment that they deny its autonomy.

16. The term Barnett cites here is elaborated in *CM*, 10.

17. Eve Kosofsky Sedgwick and Adam Frank, "Shame in the Cybernetic Fold: Reading Silvan Tompkins," in *Shame and Its Sisters: A Silvan Tomkins Reader*, ed. Sedgwick and Frank, 1–28 (Durham, NC: Duke University Press, 1995). Leys folds Sedgwick into the layer-cake affect theorists that Barnett describes subsequently. But that characterization seems less useful when

trying to account for the original and important work done by Sedgwick in the area of queer studies.

18. Lauren Berlant, *Cruel Optimism* (Durham, NC: Duke University Press, 2011).

19. Within the political theory literature, see Krause, *Civil Passions* (see chap. 1, n. 10); Susan Bickford, "Emotion Talk and Political Judgment," (see chap. 1, n. 10); Hall, "Passion in Deliberation" (see chap. 1, n. 10); Sanders, "Against Deliberation" (see chap. 1, n. 10).

20. For a similar argument, cited by Clough, see Rei Terada, *Feeling in Theory: Emotion after the "Death of the Subject"* (Cambridge, MA: Harvard University Press, 2001).

21. See Massumi, *Parables for Virtual*; Nigel Thrift, "Summoning Life," in *Envisioning Human Geographies*, ed. Paul Cloke, Philip Crang, and Mark Goodwin (London: Routledge, 2004), 90; Nigel Thrift, *Non-Representational Theory: Space, Politics, Affect* (London: Routledge, 2007); Protevi, *Political Affect*; Connolly, *Neuropolitics*; Elizabeth Grosz, *The Nick of Time: Politics, Evolution and the Untimely* (Durham, NC: Duke University Press, 2004); and Elizabeth A. Wilson, *Psychosomatic: Feminism and the Neurological Body* (Durham, NC: Duke University Press, 2004).

22. The Robert Brandom quote is from *Tales of the Mighty Dead: Historical Essays in the Metaphysics of Intentionality* (Cambridge, MA: Harvard University Press, 2002), 332. More broadly, layer-cake theories in philosophy posit a particular relationship between our sentient and rational cognitive faculties, according to which one could operate without the other and give us cognition of objects. According to the two most well-known variants, empiricism and rationalism, we could have cognition based, respectively, on sense experience or on our intellectual powers alone. Although affect theory aims to undercut our powers of cognition, it remains entangled in the basic presupposition that our cognitive faculties operate fully separately. As we shall see later in this chapter, affect and cognitions are two different systems, utterly distinct.

23. As Eric Shouse explains, "affect is not a personal feeling. Feelings are *personal* and *biographical*, emotions are *social*, and affects are *pre-personal* . . . . An affect is a non-conscious experience of intensity; it is a moment of unformed and unstructured potential. . . . Affect cannot be fully realised in language . . . because affect is always prior to and/or outside consciousness. . . . The body has a grammar of its own that cannot be fully captured in language." Eric Shouse, "Feeling, Emotion, Affect," *M/C Journal* 8, no. 6 (2005): journal.mediaculture.org.au/0512/03-shouse.php, par. 1, 5. Quoted in "TA," 442. On a similar point, see Massumi, *Parables for Virtual*, 27.

24. Nathanson continues, "There is nothing about sobbing that tells us anything about the steady-state stimulus that has triggered it; sobbing itself has nothing to do with hunger or cold or loneliness. Only the fact that we grow up with an increasing experience of sobbing lets us form some ideas

about its meaning." Donald Nathanson, *Shame and Pride: Affect, Sex, and the Birth of the Self* (New York: Norton, 1992), 66. Quoted in "TA," 438.

25. Connolly, *Neuropolitics*, 90.

26. Thrift, *Non-Representational Theory*, 26.

27. Ibid., 192. Connolly also focuses on the delay, arguing that neuroscientific experiments offer evidence that a "lot of thinking and interpretation" goes on during the "'half-second delay' between the reception of sensory material and conscious interpretation of it" (quoted in "TA," 983).

28. Feminism has a stake in questioning norms of rational political deliberation that advance the image of a sovereign judging subject. As Susan Bickford writes, these norms are "not neutral, but tend to reflect the communicative style of already powerful groups." Bickford, "Emotion Talk and Political Judgment," 1025. See also Iris Marion Young, "Communication and the Other: Beyond Deliberative Democracy," in *Democracy and Difference*, ed. Seyla Benhabib (Princeton, NJ: Princeton University Press, 1996), 120–35.

29. Leys asserts, "The affects are only contingently related to objects in the world; our basic emotions operate blindly because they have no inherent knowledge of, or relation to, the objects or situations that trigger them" ("TA," 437). Leys is referring specifically to the writings of Tomkins and his follower Ekman, whose work has had tremendous influence in affect theory.

30. Connolly, *Neuropolitics*, 81, 84.

31. Leys, "Affect and Intention: A Reply to William E. Connolly," *Critical Inquiry* 37 (2011): 799–805, at 802; Connolly, "The Complexity of Intention," *Critical Inquiry* 37 (2011): 791–98.

32. Charles Altieri, "Affect, Intentionality, and Cognition: A Response to Ruth Leys," *Critical Inquiry* 39 (2002): 878–79, at 878, 879.

33. Wondering in the last sentence of her essay "why anti-intentionalism exerts such a fascination" over contemporary cultural critics, Leys suggests that the relevant text here would be Walter Benn Michaels, *The Shape of the Signifier*, which explores the basic shift in cultural and literary theory to a discourse of identity over ideology and belief. See "TA," 472.

34. Wilfrid Sellars, *Science, Perception, and Reality* (London: Routledge and Kegan Paul, 1963), 176.

35. Sellars, *Empiricism and Philosophy of Mind*, 87 (see chap. 1, n. 14). Sellars's Kantian argument that experience is always already conceptual is developed a decade later by John McDowell, who insists that all receptivity is always already rational and normative. There can be no "experiential intake" (what Kant calls intuition) without the use of concepts: "The relevant conceptual capacities are drawn on *in* receptivity. . . . It is not that they are exercised *on* an extra-conceptual deliverance of receptivity," contends McDowell (*Mind and World*, 9; see chap. 8, n. 6). I am sympathetic to McDowell, but more work is required to explain why his conceptualist

account of intentionality as a critique of empirical naturalism does not exclude any significant role for affect in cognition.

36. "Once one brings the background to the foreground and distances it from the thinker it is radically transformed." Dreyfus, "Pervasiveness of Mental," 27. The spatial metaphor has changed (background/foreground versus upstairs/downstairs), but the idea is the same.

37. Joseph K. Shear, introduction to *Mind, Reason, and Being-in-the-World: The McDowell-Dreyfus Debate* (New York: Routledge, 2013), 1–12, at 3.

38. Lisa Blackman, *Immaterial Bodies: Affect, Embodiment, Mediation* (Thousand Oaks, CA: Sage, 2012), xi.

39. Stephen Mulhall, *On Being in the World: Wittgenstein and Heidegger on Seeing Aspects* (New York: Routledge, 1990), 21.

40. Ibid., 79. Wittgenstein's treatment of aspect perception, to which Mulhall refers here, can be found in *PI*, 212d.

41. Wittgenstein's reflections on aspect perception resonate strongly with those of Heidegger, who is typically drawn upon by critics such as Dreyfus to make the case for a nonconceptual embodied coping. See Mulhall, *On Being in the World*; Peter Dennis, "Was Heidegger a Nonconceptualist?" *Ratio* 25, no. 1 (2012): 1–7.

42. Wittgenstein, *Remarks on the Foundations of Mathematics*, vol. 1, ed. G. H. von Wright, R. Rhees, and G. E. M. Anscombe (Cambridge, MA: MIT Press, 1996), §115.

43. Barry Stroud, "Wittgenstein and Logical Necessity," *Philosophical Review* 74, no. 4 (1965): 504–18, at 507.

44. Cavell, "Wittgenstein's Later Philosophy," 52 (see chap. 1, n. 83).

45. Quoted in McDowell, "What Myth?" *Inquiry* 50, no. 4 (2007): 338–51, at 339.

46. McDowell, "Non-Cognitivism and Rule-Following," 41–42. For an excellent discussion of this point in moral theory, see Alice Crary, *Beyond Moral Judgment* (Cambridge, MA: Harvard University Press, 2009).

47. Cavell, "Music Discomposed," in *Must We Mean What We Say?* 192 (see chap. 2, n. 88).

48. For a creative attempt to deal with the world-giving character of affect, see Tinguely, "Orientation," 99 (see chap. 1, n. 21).

49. McDowell, *Mind and World*, 57.

50. Ibid.

51. For Freud, "emotions are embodied, intentional states governed by our beliefs, cognitions, and desires," observes Leys ("TA," 437).

52. For an excellent summary of these sources, see Stanley, *Know How*, esp. chaps. 5–6.

53. Conant, "Perspectivism, I." (see chap. 1, n. 11). I discussed Conant's account of perspectivism in chapter 1.

54. Claire Hemmings, "Invoking Affect: Cultural Theory and the Ontological Turn," *Cultural Studies* 19, no. 5 (September 2005): 548–67, at 564.

CONCLUSION

1. Martha Nussbaum, "Veiled Threats," *New York Times*, July 11, 2010.
2. Ibid.
3. Ibid.
4. Nussbaum, "Political Objectivity," 901 (see chap. 5, n. 9). "What we have on our hands here," writes Nussbaum, "is the entire debate between political and comprehensive liberalism" (901). This debate comes down to whether or not you think you "owe respect" to a view with which you are in complete disagreement. As we saw in chapter 6, Susan Moller Okin ("IMBW") clearly does not. Although she too holds to the universal principle of human autonomy and equality of persons, for Okin it is not a matter of according respect to views with which she utterly disagrees but of exposing them in public as bad for women and refusing them any political support.
5. Ibid.
6. Ibid., 902.
7. For a discussion of this point, see *PL*, 147.
8. Nussbaum, "Veiled Threats."
9. I discuss Nussbaum's endorsement of Rawls's political liberalism in Linda M. G. Zerilli, "Against Civility: A Feminist Perspective," in *Civility, Legality, and Justice in America*, ed. Austin Sarat (Cambridge, MA: Cambridge University Press, 2014).
10. Ideal theory starts with the notion that we have first to get our political and ethical principles in place and, once this is done, we shall know how to judge and ultimately to act. It is merely a matter of the correct application of the correct principles. Raymond Geuss calls this the "ethics-first" approach to politics, and I agree with most of what he says about the tendency (especially among Kantians such as Rawls and Habermas) to idealize political life. These theorists, argues Geuss, imagine that citizens not only have a coherent and clearly delineated set of beliefs and values but also act in ways that are consistent with whatever ones they hold. This ethics-first view of politics leads to a highly distorted understanding of political judgment, wherein judgment is understood as an idealized form of deliberation, and deliberation is construed as a discussion, basically Socratic in spirit, though also fully armed with all sorts of rules. This rule-governed mode of deliberation takes for granted that judgments are individual opinions that can and should be adjudicated publicly to test their validity, whether understood in epistemic terms with Habermas or in terms of their reasonableness with Rawls. Against this idealized model of judgment Geuss proposes that we think about a judgment as always embedded in a context of action and as part of a larger pattern of judgments, which can be seen as consistent with aspects of Wittgenstein's account. Raymond Geuss, *Philosophy and Real Politics* (Princeton, NJ: Princeton University Press, 2008), 1.

11. As of January 2016, European national bans on full-face veils existed in Belgium and France, and local bans on various forms of face-, head-, or body-coverings (burqas, niqabs, burqinis (modest swimsuits worn by religious Muslim women) and head scarves existed in Spain, Italy, Russia, and Switzerland.

12. Arendt, "What Remains?" 20 (see chap. 1, n. 111).

13. Habermas, *Legitimation Crisis*, 108 (see chap. 1, n. 6).

14. Max Weber, "The Vocation of Science," in *The Essential Weber*, ed. Sam Whimster (New York: Routledge, 2004), 270–87, at 284.

15. Ibid., 277.

16. Thomas McCarthy, "Kantian Constructivism and Reconstructivism: Rawls and Habermas in Dialogue," *Ethics* 105, no. 1 (October 1994): 44–63, at 47.

17. Quoted in Conant "Perspectivism, I," 35 (see chap. 1, n. 11), 35.

18. For an excellent discussion of these passages, see James Conant, introduction to Putnam, *Realism with a Human Face*, esp. lxvii–lxix (see chap. 8, n. 26).

19. Saul Kripke, *Wittgenstein on Rules and Private Language* (Cambridge, MA: Harvard University Press, 1982), 146, n. 87.

20. Peter Winch, *Ethics and Action* (London: Routledge and Kegan Paul, 1972), 3.

21. Affeldt, "Normativity of the Natural," 347 (see chap. 1, n. 73).

22. Lisa Wedeen, "Conceptualizing Culture: Possibilities for Political Science," *American Political Science Review* 96, no. 4 (December 1996): 713–28, at 720.

23. *Merriam-Webster's Collegiate Dictionary*, 11th ed., s.v. "form."

24. Wiggins, "Sensible Subjectivism," 207 (see chap. 1, n. 55).

25. Conant, "Perspectivism, II," 51 (see chap. 1, n. 116).

26. Affeldt, "Normativity of the Natural," 344.

27. Pitkin, *Wittgenstein and Justice*, 237 (see chap. 1, n. 53).

28. Ibid.

29. Ibid.

30. Wiggins, "Sensible Subjectivism," 210.

31. According to Beiner, after 1971 Arendt considers judgment from the point of view not of the common world and the *vita activa*, but the *vita contemplativa*, the life of the mind. More specifically, he writes, the contemplative stance is focused on "judgment . . . as the 'opening' or 'solution' of an 'impasse'": how to affirm human freedom. Ronald Beiner, "Hannah Arendt on Judging," in *Hannah Arendt, Lectures on Kant's Political Philosophy*, ed. Ronald Beiner, (Chicago: University of Chicago Press, 1992), 89–156, at 93.

32. See "IP," 130–36 (see chap. 1, n. 1). "The free space of the Academy was intended as a fully valid substitute for the marketplace, the agora, the central space for freedom in the polis," writes Arendt, and "liberation from politics was a prerequisite for the freedom of the academic" ("IP," 131, 132).

33. "Withdrawal from the 'beastliness of the multitude' into the company of the 'very few' but also into the absolute solitude of the One has been the most outstanding feature of the philosopher's life ever since Parmenides and Plato discovered that for those 'very few,' the *sophoi*, the 'life of thinking' that knows neither joy nor grief is the most divine of all, and *nous*, thought itself, 'is 'the king of heaven and earth'" (*LMT*, 47; see also 81–89 for an account of Plato, the Thracian peasant girl, and the philosopher's war on common sense). Interestingly, it is Kant whom Arendt cites as "unique among the philosophers in being sovereign enough to join in the laughter of the common man" ("IP," 83).

34. *LMT*, 92. The same point holds in Arendt's refiguration of the philosophical tradition's conception of "thinking," which rejects the philosopher's retreat from the world of appearances and advances instead thinking as a worldly practice. This is the kind of practice in which Eichmann failed to engage, a practice that, as we saw in chapter 4, is a necessary prelude to judging.

35. Benhabib, "Judgment and the Moral Foundations," 31 (see chap. 7, n. 55).

36. Ibid.

37. Hannah Arendt, "Thinking and Moral Considerations: A Lecture," 5th anniversary issue, *Social Research* (Spring/Summer 1984): 8. Quoted in Benhabib, 30. Benhabib takes this passage as further evidence of Arendt's concern with judging as a moral faculty, ignoring Arendt's point that judging is not only the ability "to tell right from wrong, [but also] beautiful from ugly." In other words, Benhabib conflates judging with morality, whereas Arendt would have us focus on the ability to tell differences, be they moral, aesthetic, or political.

38. Benhabib, "Judgment and Moral Foundations," 39.

39. Ibid., 38, 43.

40. Ibid., 43.

41. Ibid.

42. Ibid., 41.

43. Ella Myers, *Worldly Ethics: Democratic Politics and Care for the World* (Durham, NC: Duke University Press, 2013). Myers provides an excellent account of how ethical thinking understood as "care for the world" fits with an Arendtian approach to politics. For an attempt to bring together the Habermasian concern with reason with the Foucauldian concern with ethos in political life, see Amanda Anderson, *The Way We Argue Now: A Study in the Cultures of Theory* (Princeton, NJ: Princeton University Press, 2006).

44. As we saw in chapter 2, even Hume was pushed to admit that it is not just our flawed nature, defects in our character, that impair taste and our ability to see the things of this world aright. Rather, it is a complex mix of what is given in the world and our place in relation to it.

45. Zerilli, *Feminism and Abyss of Freedom*, esp. 9–16 (see chap. 1, n. 104).

46. Geuss, *Philosophy and Real Politics*, 1.

47. Margaret Canovan, "Politics as Culture: Hannah Arendt and the Public Ream," *History of Political Thought* 6, no. 3 (1985): 617–42, at 634.

48. Jürgen Habermas, *Justification and Application: Remarks on Discourse Ethics*, trans. Cioran Cronin (Cambridge, MA: MIT Press, 1994), 176.

49. Cornelius Castoriadis, "Logic, Imagination, Reflection," in *World in Fragments: Writings on Politics, Society, Psychoanalysis, and the Imagination*, ed. and trans. David Ames Curtis (Stanford, CA: Stanford University Press, 1997), 246–72, at 271.

Index

Made in the USA
Lexington, KY
21 April 2019